PROBABILITY CHARTS FOR DECISION MAKING

PROBABILITY CHARTS FOR DECISION MAKING

James R. King

INDUSTRIAL PRESS INC.

200 Madison Avenue, New York, N. Y. 10016

Contents

— Mixed Weibull Effects — Some Important Cautions in the
Analysis and Interpretation of Life Test Data — Design Considerations Arising from the Weibull Distribution — Exercises

List of Tables

Preface

This book is the outgrowth and expansion of an earlier manual, *Graphical Data with Probability Papers,* which was published in 1965. That manual was written to assist customers of *Technical and Engineering Aids for Management* in the application of probability papers to the solution of problems in statistical analysis and it was well received. Many users suggested including additional topics relating to probability plotting which required the expansion of existing material and the development of new material. One recurring common concern was for improved criteria to determine the correct choice of a probability paper. More correctly, this concern should be with the choice of appropriate procedures for determining a probability distribution for optimum representation and analysis of observed data.

The solution to the problem of a proper distribution choice was derived from mathematical rather than statistical considerations. Furthermore, a family of solutions was derived which constitutes the underlying structure and motif of this book. The solutions are summarized in Table 23-1 which is based on set-theoretic notions of sets of familiar mathematical operations which are ordered by steps of increasing operational complexity. One important result of ordering by operational complexity was the recognition of classes of processes associated with specific mathematical operational forms. This gives an additional set of criteria for choosing distributions which can be used in conjunction with known mathematical operations, or used independently when the correct underlying mathematics are unknown. This combination of mathematical and process identification obviously greatly facilitates the choice of a properly descriptive statistical distribution.

Probability charts, or graphs, are a highly efficient method of testing distribution assumptions. This results primarily because one is plotting the cumulative distribution function which appears as a straight line on that probability graph which correctly represents the data. Failure to obtain a straight line can result from:

1. An incorrect choice of the expected distribution form
2. Nonlinearities caused by nonrandom sampling
3. Nonlinearities caused by truncation resulting from inspection, selection, or other kinds of screening of data
4. "Wild" points usually indicating errors in obtaining or recording of data.

Each of the preceding categories results in rather consistent patterns on probability plots. Visual examination of a probability plot, therefore, is an easy test for consistency of sample data and of the underlying statistical assumptions about representative sampling and validity of observed data. These are important preconditions for successful data analysis including the correct determination of statistical parameters.

When used in accordance with detailed instructions given in this book, probability charts are additionally valuable since many powerful statistical tests can be applied by persons with little or no statistical training. This is a significant extension of the utility of applied statistics and should appeal to a wide range of physical and social scientists who desperately need to analyze and interpret data without having to resort to more complex and difficult methods of mathematical and analytical statistics.

The pressure for improved methods of analysis in probability and statistics is being caused by the demands of our continuing need for technical, social, and economic progress. Progress, competition, and sheer need are combining to require ever earlier decisions in the research, development, and implementation cycle. This, of course, means that fewer experiments and less data are available to make important decisions which must be right, or nearly optimum, the first time. As a direct consequence, improved methods of analysis and evaluation are required. Probability theory and statistical methods have become important tools in the decision-making processes, emphasizing the increasing interest in probability papers as analytical tools.

My interest in probability plotting was first aroused by work on the logarithmic-normal distribution by Dr. Enoch B. Ferrell, then of the Bell Telephone Laboratories. This interest was further stimulated by the late Dr. Emil J. Gumbel of Columbia University, with his work on the extreme value distributions; by Dr. John H. K. Kao of New York University and Dr. J. N. Berretoni of Western Reserve University, with the Weibull distribution; as well as by Dr. Paul S. Olmstead, another Bell Labs retiree; and Dr. Franklin E. Satterthwaite of the Statistical Engineering Institute, with his applications of the binomial distribution.

I would like to acknowledge a great debt to those who taught me the subject of statistics and statistical methods in an exciting and provocative way: the late Professor H. J. Ball of Lowell Technological Institute; Mr. Robert Kennedy of the U. S. Army Quartermaster Laboratory; Mr. Leonard A. Seder of L. A. Seder Associates; Mr. Dorian Shainin, Vice-President of Rath and Strong, Consultants; and Mr. Warren Purcell of Raytheon Company.

Further, writing this book would not have been possible without the encouragement, criticism, and stimulation of a long series of outstanding associates and colleagues. These include Dr. Raphael Miller, Consultant; Mr. A. J. Borofsky of Borofsky Associates; Mr. Michael Leppanen and Mr. John C. Shannon of the Autonetics Division of North American Rockwell Corporation; Mr. Richard F. Powell of Viatron Corporation; and Mr. Michael J. Malanga of Sprague Electric Company. Generous assistance in solving technical writing problems was given by Mr. William J. Gallagher of Arthur D. Little, Consultants.

I wish also to thank the following individuals for significant topical contributions to portions of this book which have not previously been treated in published statistical texts: Mr. Gerald J. Bradley for his development of Bradley binomial plotting papers used in Chapter 21; Dr. Wayne S. Nelson of the General Electric Research and Development Laboratories for his brilliant development of hazard plotting which is the basis for Chapter 19; again, Dr. P. S. Olmstead and his work in stochastic analysis of binomial data for reliability analysis and sales forecasting used in Chapter 22; and to Mr. D. W. Whaley of the Dupont Development Laboratory, Circleville, Ohio, for material on particle sizing and the Rosin-Rammler distribution used in Chapter 13.

I must also comment on the extent to which this book was a family project. My wife, Marguerite, contributed many hours of typing and copy services; my daughter, Mrs. Celine M. Clark, conducted many experiments and prepared the resulting data; my son, James, was responsible for excellent artwork and critical editing; and my son, Michael, contributed the concepts and the data for the sports examples in Chapters 20 and 22. They also contributed other peripheral help as well as encouragement and an atmosphere most conducive to creative endeavour.

Last, but not at all least, I wish to acknowledge the patient and understanding work of those persons most responsible for turning a manuscript into a book. First, there was the great insight and expertise of my technical editor, Dr. Norbert L. Enrick of Kent State University; and second, the general editorial and organizational skills of Mr. Holbrook L. Horton and Mrs. Clara F. Zwiebel of the Editorial Department of Industrial Press.

Finally, the author assumes all responsibility for any shortcomings of this book. However, since much of the material is relatively new, and certainly subject to further development, all users of this book are requested and encouraged to criticize, to comment, and to suggest corrections, improvements, and/or practical examples of notable success or failure in applications of this material.

Pads of probability graph paper in sets of 80 sheets can be obtained from Technical and Engineering Aids for Management, RFD Tamworth, New Hampshire 03886 at $4.95 per set.

CHAPTER 1

Introduction

The Role of Decision-Making

Many people do not like to make decisions. The common reason for this distaste seems to be that people do not like to risk the criticism or ridicule which might follow a wrong decision. They feel that if an impending decision can be deferred, the need for making the decision will vanish. Also, if a decision can be delayed long enough, many feel, the appropriate information to make a foolproof decision will ultimately materialize. But these attitudes are unproductive.

The modern work environment is fast-paced and high-pressured. The rate of technological discovery and innovation, the political and economic pressures for continued business growth, and rising economic and social aspirations have all combined to require earlier decisions at each step of the research, development, and production cycle. This faster pace results in less available time, and so research is accelerated, fewer experiments are conducted, and fewer preproduction models are built. These measures, in turn, yield less information and data from which to derive decisions.

Due to the large, overall environmental pressure, decisions must be correct, or nearly so, as soon as possible. This stringent goal requires effective, fast, and practical methods of information and data analysis and correlated methods of feedback of the resulting conclusions and decisions. The methods of graphical analysis, based on probability plots, which are presented in this book meet these requirements. The relationship of probability analysis to research, development, and production is shown in the flow chart of Fig. 1-1. Data often contain errors which may be detected by direct observation of probability plots. Detection of erroneous data should result in a decision to review procedures in order to determine the causes

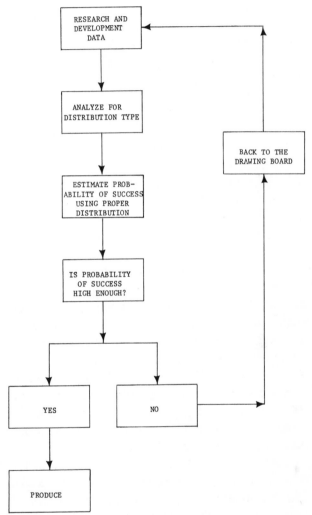

Fig. 1-1. Graphic analysis for determination of underlying distribution for research and development decisions.

of error and to eliminate them, as shown in Fig. 1-2.

The Probabilistic View of Data Analysis

When we make observations of some situation in order to obtain values which are representative

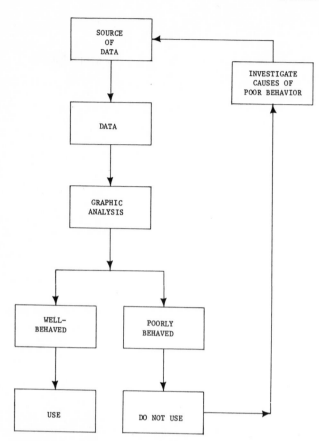

Fig. 1-2.   Graphic analysis for error determination.

of that situation, the resulting values are called *data*. A set of data usually includes a number of different values which represent different results occurring under apparently similar conditions. The data cover some interval of the scale of measurement used to obtain the representative values. The data do not fall haphazardly but tend to assume patterns which are called *probability distributions* or, simply, *distributions*.

Table 1-1 gives the results of observations of the time required to assemble a simple postage scale. The 24 observed times are given in the order of observation; the data are uninformative in this kind of tabulation. Table 1-2 presents the same data rounded off to the nearest second of assembly time. The number of times observed is also given. It is immediately obvious that most of the values occur at 14 or 15 seconds and that the number of values observed decreases as we move away from 14 or 15 in either direction. These results are shown

Table 1-1. Times Required to Assemble a Postage Scale

Assembly Time, Seconds	
14.4	15.2
11.9	13.0
16.3	13.2
13.7	14.3
14.8	14.0
13.8	15.1
15.0	15.3
13.8	15.8
16.2	15.0
15.4	14.3
13.7	14.6
16.8	15.1

graphically in Fig. 1-3. The number of observations for each time is shown as a dot. The general outline of the data is shown by a smooth curve, known as a *frequency* or *distribution curve*. This curve has an appearance rather like a head and shoulders, with a peak near the center and tails running out to the higher and lower values. The

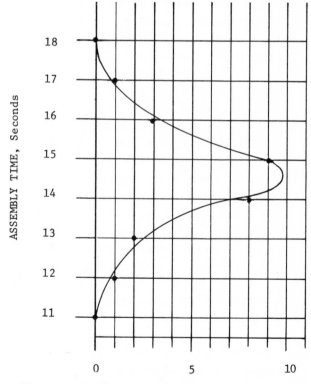

Fig. 1-3.   Graph of assembly time versus frequency of occurrence.

peak represents a concentration of values and the tails represent a scarcity of values.

The *actual* number of times that a particular observation, known as the *frequency of occurrence,* was obtained, is shown in Fig. 1-3. To generalize the findings of a particular set of data, it is convenient to express the results in proportional, or relative, terms, called the *probability of occurrence.* The probability of occurrence for each time of observation in Table 1-2 is obtained by dividing the observed frequency of occurrence by the total number of observations increased by one, that is, by $(n + 1)$. For example, at 12 seconds there is one occurrence. Then, $1/(24 + 1) =$ 0.04. At 13 seconds, there are two occurrences; thus, $2/(24 + 1) = 0.08$.

In Fig. 1-4, the assembly times are plotted against probability of occurrence as given in Table

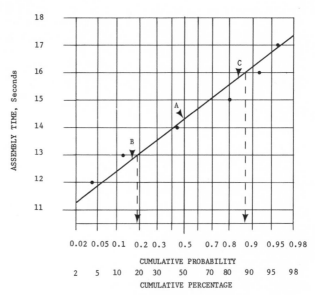

Fig. 1-5. Graph of assembly time versus cumulative probability and cumulative percentage.

1-2. A smooth curve is drawn as before. The probability value for any point on the curve is obtained by projection down to the bottom probability scale and is called the *probability density.* The curve is therefore called a *probability density curve,* which is a graphical approximation of the characteristic of a probability distribution called a *probability density function.*

There is still another way in which we can arrange the data. We can add the number of observed occurrences successively starting with the smallest observed value and proceeding up to the largest value. The successive totals so obtained are called *cumulative totals.* For example, at 12 seconds there is one occurrence and the cumulative total is 1. At 13 seconds there are two occurrences giving a cumulative total of $1 + 2 = 3$. At 14 seconds there are eight occurrences giving $3 + 8 = 11$. When the cumulative totals are divided by $(n + 1)$, we now obtain *cumulative probabilities* as shown in Table 1-2. When the cumulative probabilities are plotted against a suitable probability scale, we obtain a straight-line graph which is an approximation to the *cumulative distribution function* of a probability distribution. Figure 1-5 is the cumulative probability plot for the cumulative data of Table 1-2.

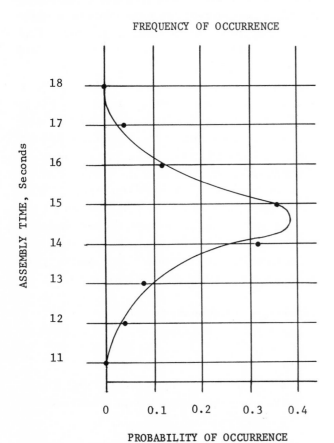

Fig. 1-4. Graph of assembly time versus probability of occurrence.

Table 1-2. Table of Assembly Times Showing Frequency Cumulation
and Probability Calculations

Assembly Time, Seconds	Observed Frequency of Occurrence	Probability of Occurrence	Cumulative Frequency	Cumulative Probability
11	0	0	0	0
12	1	0.04	1	0.04
13	2	0.08	3	0.12
14	8	0.32	11	0.44
15	9	0.36	20	0.80
16	3	0.12	23	0.92
17	1	0.04	24	0.96

Probability Plots

Figure 1-5 is called a *probability plot,* a *probability graph,* or a *probability chart.* Probability plots are what this book is all about. The basic methods of data arrangement, data preparation, and data presentation in the form of probability plots will be discussed. Then common patterns which occur in probability plots and assist in interpreting the meaning of the plotted data will be dealt with. Each of the major probability distributions will be considered in detail for the special characteristics and meaning which can be assigned to each kind of distribution. Important special cases of specific distributions will be presented, as will some new and advanced applications of probability plots to the solutions of contemporary engineering and management problems.

Plotting of the cumulative probability and the observed value of the variable against a suitable probability scale which results in linearization of the data is illustrated in Fig. 1-5. The linearization is emphasized by the addition of a "best-fit" straight line through the plotted points. The plot may now be used directly to obtain estimates of key distribution characteristics, also known as *distribution parameters* or as *statistical parameters.*

The first parameter of interest is the *average,* or *mean,* which is the measure of central tendency in the data. The mean is obtained at the intersection of the best-fit line and the vertical line from the 0.5 probability point, or 50 percent point. This is indicated by arrow A and is 14.3. The second parameter of interest is the *standard deviation,* which is a measure of the amount of dispersion existing in the data; that is, how much it is spread out around the mean. The standard deviation is determined by obtaining the values at the intersection of the best-fit line with the 84 and 16 percent lines. The difference between the two values is divided by 2 to obtain the standard deviation. In Fig. 1-4, the required points are at arrows B and C, giving 12.8 and 15.8. The difference is 3.0. The standard deviation is therefore 1.5.

Another question of interest might be, "What percentage of assembly times is 13 seconds or less?" This question is answered simply by projecting the intersection of the best-fit line and the line for 13 seconds down to the percentage scale. The value obtained is 19 percent. This is known as a *percentile estimate.* A related question is, "What percentage of assembly times falls between 13 and 16 seconds?" This is answered by obtaining the percentile for 13 seconds and subtracting it from the percentile for 16 seconds. The resulting value is 87 percent — 19 percent, or 68 percent.

Advantages of Probability Plotting

Probability plotting as a graphical method for data analysis is: (1) simple, (2) fast, and (3) flexible.

These methods are simple because they require only a few easy operations that are readily learned. The operations are:

a. Ordering, or arranging, the data into a sequence of values

b. Grouping into logical and manageable increments

c. Computing the plotting points

d. Selecting an appropriate probability paper

e. Plotting the points

f. Fitting a best line to the data.

These methods are fast because:

a. The right choice of a probability paper results in a straight-line fit of the plotted points.

b. The wrong choice is immediately obvious.

c. Erroneous data are identified by specific shape patterns in the plots.

d. On linear plots, the values of distribution characteristics, the *distribution* or *statistical parameters,* are obtained by visual observation and/or by simple calculations.

The methods are flexible because:

a. One picture is worth ten thousand words

b. The probability points, or *percentiles,* corresponding to many values of the variable of interest, may be determined visually.

When a set of data is displayed as a probability plot, the entire set is considered in relationship to its parts. A probability plot shows clearly that data has high, low, and intermediate values, as well as an average. If some high or low values are undesirable, an estimate of the probability of occurrence may be made directly from the plot. Furthermore, if one wishes to obtain the probabilities associated with several alternative definitions of high or low, such probabilities are also obtained directly from probability plots.

There is always a need for practical, quick, dependable, and inexpensive analytical results in any field. Besides the necessity to arrive at clear and correct final decisions, one must cope with a large number of intermediate decisions or conclusions. Therefore, the immediate benefit of much testing

and experimentation is to develop a "direction vector" indicating the direction most likely to yield further useful results. Such "action" answers are readily obtained from probability plots.

Probability plots present the significant characteristics of data distributions and facilitate numerical estimates of distribution by simple manual methods. Manual data analysis is necessary and desirable in spite of the wide availability of electronic computers. Some typical situations for which manual data analysis is ideal are:

1. Where the quantity of data is small; for example, where there are less than 1000 observations

2. Where the underlying distribution is unknown, as with a new product

3. To obtain estimates of distribution parameters

4. To check data for abnormal behavior such as test bias or measurement error

5. For a quick glance at test results

6. For intelligent and effective preparation of more extensive analytical work, with or without the aid of computer programming and processing, once the general trends and relationships among the data and the variables are established graphically.[1]

Plan and Purpose of This Book

Chapters 2 through 8 contain the general basic materials for probability plotting, including applications to the normal distribution. This portion of the book can be used as a statistics laboratory course in conjunction with a conventional Statistics I or II course.

Chapters 9, 11, 13, 14, 16, 17, 18, and 20 may serve as a laboratory course at the Advanced Statistics level.

Chapters 10, 12, 15, 19, 21, 22, and 23, in addition to all of the earlier chapters, may be used as a complete reliability engineering course or as corollary reading for such a course.

[1] *Note:* A folder of all probability papers required to work the Exercises is available from Technical and Engineering Aids for Management, Tamworth, N.H. 03886.

There are a number of derivations and special tables presented herein which have never been published before. Some new and important topics which are published in detail for the first time are:

1. Hazard plotting for failure data with different causes

2. Applications of Bradley binomial plotting papers

3. Applications of binomial plotting papers to the analysis of sales, sports records, and stock market performance.

CHAPTER 2

The Nature of a Distribution

In the natural order of things, no two events ever occur in quite the same way. There is always some difference, and whether or not we can effectively determine the difference depends on our powers of observation, which are often limited, and on our methods of measurement. Let us refer to these naturally occurring differences as *variation*. Variation of natural events occurs because the factors which cause such events are numerous and vary from time to time. Such causative factors are referred to as *variables*.

The relationship of causative input variables and the resultant output variation is illustrated dia-grammatically in Fig. 2-1. The inputs represent different sources of input variations, such as materials, the machine, and the operator. They also represent differences in kind of variation within each source, such as hard or soft, sharp or dull, etc. The effects of these variables combine within the operation to give a finished dimension for each part made. However, different combinations of the inputs will give different output dimensions. Over a certain period of time, there will be a number of different values of the output dimension, and therefore there will also be variation in the observed output dimension.

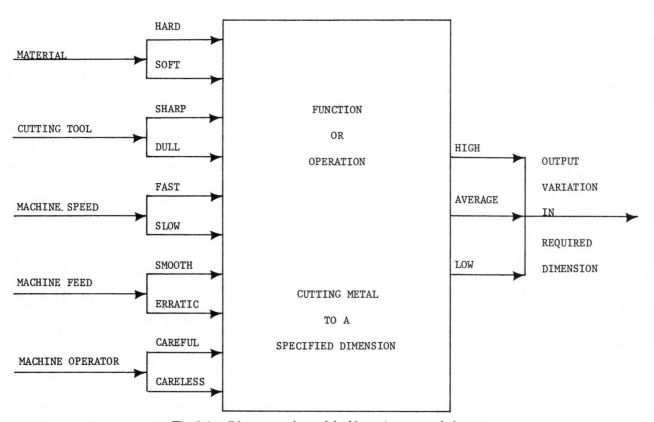

Fig. 2-1.   Diagrammatic model of input/output variation.

The classification of inputs is on a relative basis. For example, a material used in processing may be harder or softer, depending on which side of the allowable tolerance it comes from. A tool may be sharper or duller, depending on whether it is in the early or late part of its dressing cycle. This relative classification operates as though there were two possible states or conditions for a variable. This is not always true, however, because many variables can occur anywhere within a range of permissible values. But two-state systems are useful for illustrating the generation of distributions with variational patterns which is discussed below.

If one observes the results of a number of output events and applies some kind of measurement to one or more of the characteristics of the output, such as dimensions or other parameters, then many individually different values will be observed. When such data are arranged into a suitable format, the collective results are referred to as a *distribution plot*. Different statistical distributions result in different-looking distribution plots.

There are many different kinds of statistical distributions. Some of these have simple origins and others have more complex origins. However, within a reasonable approximation, the more complex distributions are mathematically definable combinations of the simple distributions. Therefore, it is useful and instructive to consider some of the properties of simple distributions; to see where they come from and how they behave.

Binary (Dichotomous) Distribution

The *binary distribution*, shown in Fig. 2-2, is the simplest of all distributions. It is called a *dichotomous* distribution by statisticians. It is

descriptive of a two-state or two-condition situation which may be variously described as:

1. Yes or No — a characteristic (signal) is *present* or it is *not present*
2. On or Off — as with switches or controls
3. Go or Not-Go — an item meets a specific requirement or it does not
4. High or Low — the relative value of a characteristic or control variable
5. A or B — one of two possible states of a variable
6. 0 or 1 — as in digital logic states.

The physical significance of a two-state system is that if one state is present at some point in time, then the other state cannot be present. A simple example of a binary system is given by a coin, which we assume to be honest and unbiased. The following results, which hold generally for all binary systems, occur:

1. The outcome of either one of two events (heads or tails for a coin) is *equally likely*. Over a large number of occurrences (tosses, trials), we would expect each state (head or tail) to occur approximately an equal number of times.
2. As a result of (1), we say that the probability of either one of the two occurrences is 50 percent.
3. The result of any occurrence has no influence on any subsequent occurrence. In other words, since a coin has "neither a memory nor a conscience," it is in fact not affected by any individual outcome of a toss, and so no one event has any relation to a subsequent event.

Assumptions 1 and 2 are the conditions which result in what is called *random behavior*, and Assumption 3 is the condition which is called *statistical independence*. In formal statistical texts, randomness and independence are defined as rigorous mathematical notions as first steps in the development of the theorems of probability theory. However, for our purposes it is sufficient to retain

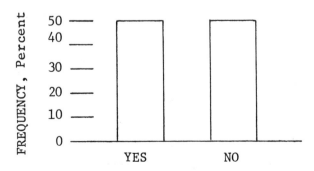

Fig. 2-2. Ideal binary distribution.

a simple conceptual and intuitive idea of what these terms represent.

Since it is our ultimate objective to understand the origins of different distributions along with some of their useful mathematical and engineering properties, let us simulate a real life situation and observe the consequences. Once the underlying behavior of simple models is understood, it is possible to develop the behavior of more complex models in terms of rearrangements of the simple models. This is done by the use of rules which are simple and straightforward.

As a simple model, again consider a coin. The two sides, head and tails, represent an ideal two-state system. When a coin is tossed freely and allowed to fall, it will come to rest as either a head or a tail. (Although it is also possible for it to rest on edge, this state is so rare that we will ignore it.) A coin meets the requirements of the three assumptions basic to a two-state system. That is, heads or tails each occur approximately half the time. One toss has no influence on any other toss. Consequently, a group of coins will simulate a binary system effectively. Each coin in the group represents the influence of a different input variable. By shaking a group of coins simultaneously and allowing them to fall together, one creates a function generator which produces a set of completely random results for each shake. If one then applies a method of measurement to the results of each shake, it is possible to define a *random output variable* quantitatively. This is best accomplished by *counting* the number of occurrences of one of the possible states; that is, either the number of heads or tails.

To develop specific data for further study, let us consider a group of 10 coins. After each toss, the results are counted for one of the states — for example, heads. This number becomes the *value* of the *output variable,* also called the *event.* Table 2-1 gives the results of a classroom experiment during which 9 students each tossed a separate group of ten coins and recorded the number of heads occurring for each of ten different tosses. This is similar to an operation with ten different binary input characteristics. The ten coins in each group represent 10 possibilities for random variation of the inputs, such as in Fig. 2-1. The nine students represent possible process variations such as mold cavities, oven positions, tool locations, or production shifts. The aggregate results simulate the occurrence of 90 events during a sequence of ten repeat operations, or *trials.*

In Fig. 2-3, a gross look at results of this experiment shows that values from 1 to 10 have occurred. The theoretical possibilities from using 10 two-sided coins would obviously be a range from 0, or no heads at all, to 10, or all heads occurring. But what actually happened?

First of all, what is Fig. 2-3? It is a simple and useful display form for data. This kind of figure is obtained by listing all of the values which can

Table 2-1. Number of Heads Recorded by Nine Students from Ten Tosses of Ten Coins

Trial	Student									
	I	II	III	IV	V	VI	VII	VIII	IX	
	Number of Heads Recorded									
1	4	6	5	5	5	3	6	4	7	
2	7	6	7	6	3	7	7	8	6	
3	6	5	5	3	4	3	5	3	5	
4	8	6	4	10	3	4	6	6	3	
5	6	8	7	7	3	5	5	6	6	
6	4	4	6	3	7	5	7	5	5	
7	5	6	3	6	4	6	3	4	4	
8	6	2	5	4	6	4	4	1	5	
9	7	4	3	6	4	5	4	4	6	
10	4	3	7	5	5	5	3	6	4	
Sub-Totals	57	50	52	55	44	47	50	47	51	453 Total

possibly occur, in this case, 0 to 10. Then, a tally is made of the actual number of occurrences of each value. The number of occurrences is called the *frequency of occurrence*. The combination of terms gives this kind of display its name of *frequency tally*.

A common variant of the frequency tally is called a *histogram*. Figure 2-4 shows the same data as Fig. 2-3 except that bars are used to represent frequency; and so it is also called a *bar chart*. A collection of other useful methods of data presentation are given in (13).[1]

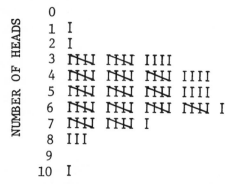

FREQUENCY OF OCCURRENCE

Fig. 2-3. Frequency tally of number of heads.

Such displays give a ready visual representation of the form and appearance of a distribution of values. Remember that these values are the result of the combination of a number of variables operating completely at random. A set of output values from such a random system has been simulated. The theoretical set, 0 to 10, is absolutely required by the conditions of the experiment. The graphical appearance results from the manner of combination of random variables. In this example, the variables were combined by *simple addition*. Consequently, the distribution display in Fig. 2-3 of these results has some obvious and important features, such as:

1. *Central tendency,* or concentration near the middle value, in this case 5, with very few values near the extremes

[1] Bibliography references throughout the text are given in parentheses.

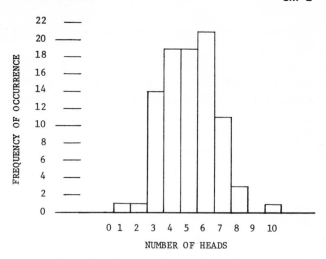

Fig. 2-4. Histogram of number of heads.

2. *Symmetry,* or the appearance of being reasonably balanced around the middle value.

Such results are surprising when presented to the uninitiated for the first time. Moreover, the level of surprise rises to disbelief when the following statement is added: "If similar experiments are conducted many times, the results will continue to be quite similar, although almost never identical. This is experimental evidence that an arbitrary number of random variables, operating *simultaneously* but *independently*, will give an output of *consistent* and, as will be shown, *predictable results*." Such ideas are quickly rejected by those who hold to the nonstatistical concept that the operation of a large number of simultaneous independent random variables can result only in chaos. The entire discussion may break down completely

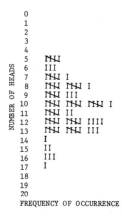

Fig. 2-5. Frequency tally of number of heads.

Table 2-2. Number of Heads Recorded by Nine Students from Ten Tosses
of Twenty Coins

Trial	Student								
	I	II	III	IV	V	VI	VII	VIII	IX
	Number of Heads Recorded								
1	10	16	15	13	8	5	11	9	8
2	10	5	15	7	11	5	10	10	17
3	13	12	12	7	13	12	13	13	11
4	8	10	9	9	8	13	10	10	12
5	12	13	5	8	12	9	10	10	10
6	11	9	11	7	13	12	10	6	7
7	6	13	16	8	10	8	12	7	12
8	13	12	13	8	12	8	14	13	10
9	12	9	12	8	9	10	9	10	11
10	12	8	16	6	11	5	10	13	7
Sub-Totals	107	107	124	81	107	87	109	101	105	928 Total

when an additional assertion is made, "If more variables are added, the results will become relatively more consistent and predictable."

However, experience demonstrates that the preceding statements are not incredible. Table 2-2 and Fig. 2-5 show some additional results, using

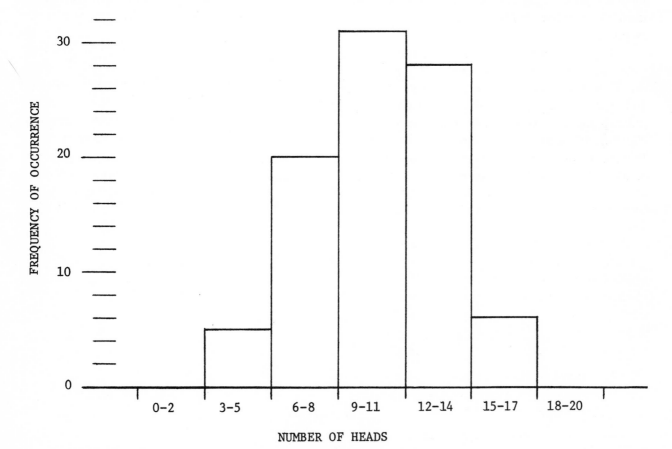

Fig. 2-6.   Histogram of number of heads.

20 coins which were tossed 10 times by the same class. Although the results of Fig. 2-5 appear rather ragged, this is due to their being tabulated against 21 possible value categories as compared to 11 categories for Fig. 2-3. However, it is still apparent that we have central tendency, no values near the extremes, and a reasonable degree of symmetry.

Sturges' Rule

In many data displays, the use of too many categories obscures the form of the distribution characteristics. To achieve optimum data grouping in data displays for better visual presentation of distribution data, a simple method called *Sturges' Rule* can be used. This rule will be discussed in detail in the next chapter.

The data of Fig. 2-5 are now replotted in Fig. 2-6, using Sturges' Rule. The features of centrality and symmetry are enhanced in appearance and the lack of values at the extremes is accordingly emphasized.

In Fig. 2-3, observe that only 2 of the 11 possible categories, or approximately 18 percent of the theoretically definable values, did not appear. In Fig. 2-5, 8 of 21 categories, or about 40 percent, did not appear. This is twice the percentage for Fig. 2-3, and is an example of the earlier statement that the use of more variables gives more consistent results. It is of additional interest to note that the values which did not occur were those furthest away from the middle values.

The foregoing behavior can be explained formally and rigorously by the theorems of probability theory. However, for an understanding of what causes distribution behavior, such formality is unnecessary at this point. It is far more important to acquire the knowledge and ungrudging belief that this kind of behavior does, in fact, occur. This can best be verified on an experimental and, therefore, experiential basis. It is highly instructive to conduct personal experiments similar to those above, to record the results, and to study them.

Exercises

Note: Record all data in a bound notebook and retain for further use.

2-1. Using 5 coins, make 400 tosses and record the result of each toss, counting either heads or tails.

2-2. Make a frequency tally of all 400 tosses against the possible values 0 through 5.

2-3. Combine the results of each two successive tosses to obtain 200 results of 10 each.

2-4. Make a frequency tally of Exercise 2-3 against the values 0 through 10.

2-5. Combine the results of each 4 successive tosses to obtain 100 results of 20 each.

2-6. Make a frequency tally of Exercise 2-5 against the values 0 through 20.

CHAPTER 3

Simple Data Presentation

Introduction

The previous chapter considered the representation of a distribution of values by means of graphical devices such as frequency tallies and histograms. The examples chosen lent themselves to straightforward and apparently simple plotted displays. However, when using data covering a wide range of the values of the variable of interest, there arises a problem of arranging, or *grouping,* the data into meaningful increments. This is an important detail which is often assumed to be obvious in the general literature of statistics and data analysis. Therefore, many persons new to such efforts encounter serious difficulties in preparing data for subsequent presentation and analysis. There are some useful methods to ease this task which will be developed below.

Sturges' Rule

The effect of grouping one specific set of data by Sturges' Rule (17), was illustrated in Figs. 2-5 and 2-6. Sturges' Rule is a method of determining the optimum number of groups, or *cells,* for arranging data into a graphical summary. This rule states that the optimum number of cells is found by solving the simple equation:

$$\text{Number of cells} = 1 + 3.3 \log N$$

where log N is the common logarithm of the number of items of data in the sample; and N is the *sample size.*

In order to eliminate the need to recalculate the number of cells for each sample size used, a graph giving direct solutions of Sturges' Rule is included as Fig. 3-1. This graph is used as follows:

1. Enter the graph from the left scale at the value corresponding to the sample size, for example, $n = 100$.

2. Proceed to the right to the diagonal line and then drop vertically to the bottom scale.

3. Read the value on the bottom scale. For $n = 100$, the number of cells required is between 7 and 8 at 7.7.

4. Since a whole number of cells is required and 7.7 is nearer to 8 than to 7, use 8 cells for the first trial.

Example 3-1

From the data of Table 2-2, we find: $1 + 3.3 \log 90 = 1 + 3.3 \times 1.954 = 1 + 6.45 = 7.45$, indicating either 7 or 8 cells. In this particular case, there are a total of 21 possible values for the expected outputs; therefore, the use of 7 cells will result in assigning 3 values to each cell. This result is illustrated in Fig. 2-6.

Determining Cell Sizes

The *range* of the data is calculated next. This is the arithmetical difference between the largest and smallest values of the variable of interest obtained in the sample data. When values have both positive and negative signs, proper regard for the signs must be observed to obtain the correct range.

The range is next divided by the number of cells obtained by Sturges' Rule. This gives the number of measurement units to be assigned to each cell, that is:

$$\text{Number of units per cell} = \frac{\text{Range in units}}{\text{Number of cells required}}$$

Example 3-2

Given: The 25 observations of Table 3-1 with a maximum reading of 8.8 and a minimum of 5.7. How many units per cell should be used?

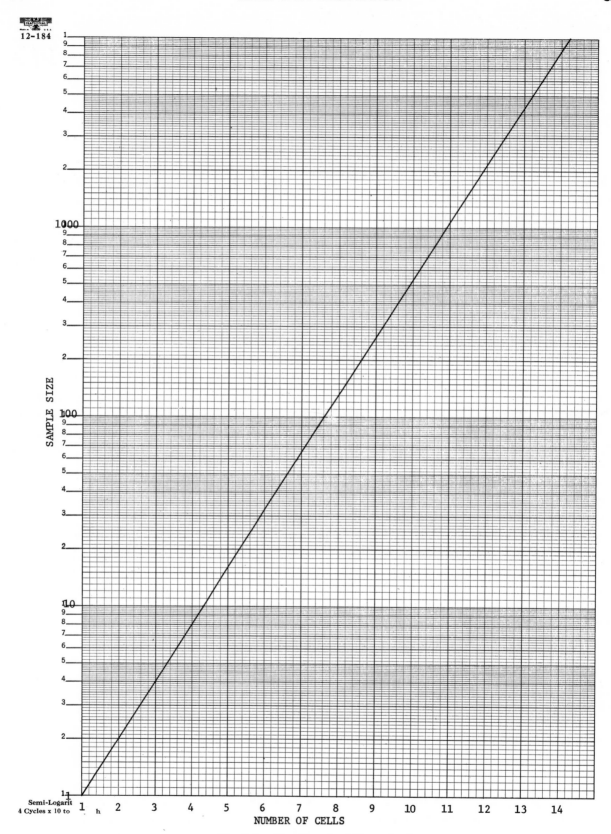

Fig. 3-1. Nomograph of Sturges' rule.

From Fig. 3-1, a sample of 25 falls between 5 and 6 cells.

$$\text{Range} = 8.8 - 5.7 = 3.1$$

Since we are interested in units, observe that the data of Table 3-1 are given to the nearest 0.1 unit.

Table 3-1. Salt Atmosphere Test Data

Test Specimen Number	Before	After
	Contact Resistance, Milliohms	
1	7.8	8.7
2	6.7	7.2
3	7.3	8.8
4	7.4	8.9
5	6.9	7.8
6	5.7	6.3
7	6.4	7.1
8	8.1	8.7
9	8.8	10.4
10	5.9	6.2
11	7.4	8.1
12	6.2	7.4
13	7.0	7.1
14	7.8	8.6
15	6.2	6.4
16	5.9	6.5
17	6.4	7.0
18	7.0	7.7
19	6.7	7.5
20	6.8	7.3
21	7.0	6.9
22	7.6	7.8
23	7.4	7.9
24	6.7	7.7
25	7.3	7.2

Therefore, we ignore the decimal point and obtain the range as: $88 - 57 = 31$ units.

$$\text{Using 5 cells, number of units} = \frac{31}{5} = 6.2$$

$$\text{Using 6 cells, number of units} = \frac{31}{6} = 5.02$$

Use only the nearest unit value to calculate the number of units per cell, i.e., 6 or 5. From rounding off, we will actually obtain either 6 or 7 cells, that is: $\frac{3.1}{6} = 5^+$, or 6 cells and $\frac{3.1}{5} = 6^+$, or 7 cells. Either number of units per cell may be used.

Example 3-3

Given: A statement that 49 observations have a maximum reading of 11.3 and a minimum of 6.2. How many units per cell should be used?

From Fig. 3-1, the number of cells to be used for a sample size of 49 falls between 6 and 7.

$$\text{Number of units} = \frac{113 - 62}{6} = \frac{51}{6} = 8.5, \text{ use } 8$$

or,

$$\text{Number of units} = \frac{113 - 62}{7} = \frac{51}{7} = 7.3, \text{ use } 7$$

After rounding off, recalculate the number of cells as $\frac{51}{8} = 6^+$ or $\frac{51}{7} = 7^+$.

Balancing Cell Endpoints

Cell boundaries are determined after the number of cells and measurement units per cell have been found. This step is rarely given the attention which it deserves and, as a result, often leads to odd-looking, confusing, or ambiguous data displays.

Example 3-4

Given: Data of Table 3-1 and Example 3-2, determine the cell boundaries.

One frequently used method is to start with the minimum value and simply add the number of units per cell until a cell is defined which includes the maximum reading. From Example 3-2, using 7 cells:

Minimum cell values = 5.7, 6.2, 6.7, 7.2, 7.7, 8.2, and 8.7.

Maximum cell values = 6.1, 6.6, 7.1, 7.6, 8.1, 8.6, and 9.1.

The last cell therefore contains the maximum observed value of 8.8. However, using this choice of cell endpoints, the first cell will contain five of the observed values but the last cell would only have two: 8.7 and 8.8. Similar results can occur from careless rounding-off to whole numbers or rational fractions simply because they look nice and easy to use.

A better arrangement of cell values is as follows:

Minimum cell values = 5.5, 6.0, 6.5, 7.0,
7.5, 8.0, and 8.5.

Maximum cell values = 5.9, 6.4, 6.9, 7.4,
7.9, 8.4, and 8.9.

In this case there are two unused unit values in the first cell and one unused in the last cell. The spread of all observed values is now approximately balanced in the two end cells.

Example 3-5
Given: Data of Example 3-3, 49 observations falling between 6.2 and 11.3, determine the cell boundaries.

Ignoring the 0.1 measurement units, between the values of 62 and 113, there are: $(113 - 62) + 1 = 51 + 1 = 52$ units. From Example 3-3, if we require 8 cells; therefore, $52 \div 8 = 6^+$, say 7, units per cell. Using 7 units per cell, 8 cells would contain a total of 56 units. Then: $56 - 52 = 4$ extra units. If these extra units are then split between the two end cells, the first cell starts at a value 2 units smaller than the minimum observed value, and the last cell ends 2 units larger than the maximum observed value, giving good balance. Cell endpoints would be as follows:

Minimum cell values = 6.0, 6.7, 7.4, 8.1, 8.8,
9.5, 10.2, 10.9.

Maximum cell values = 6.6, 7.3, 8.0, 8.7, 9.4,
10.1, 10.8, 11.5.

Defining Cell Endpoints Correctly

The cell endpoints must be defined so as to prevent having two choices for which cell an item of data is to be assigned. One common error is to define cell endpoints such as 6.5–7.0, 7.0–7.5, etc. At each cell boundary, this results in an apparent choice of two cells in which to place the boundary value. This causes confusion and errors in subsequent analysis.

Example 3-6
Given: Data of Table 3-1 and Example 3-2, define the cell endpoints.

Since the reported units in this case are given to the nearest 0.1 units, the cell boundaries should be stated as in Example 3-4; that is, 5.5–5.9, 6.0–6.4, 6.5–6.9, etc., and this will automatically eliminate any possible confusion.

If these data were reported in 0.01 units, then the boundaries would be 5.50–5.99, 6.00–6.49, 6.50–6.99, etc. Such division of the value scale covers all possible values of the reported variable without permitting overlap between cells and thus eliminates all ambiguity.

Simple Data Summarization

After determining the number of cells, the number of measurement units per cell, and balancing and defining the cell endpoints, the data are ready for numerical analysis or for plotting into displays such as Frequency Tallies, Histograms, or Bar Charts.

Some Useful Variations

The methods given above apply typically to one data set at a time. However, one common requirement is to compare two or more sets of data simultaneously. Such situations occur as before-and-after readings, Method A as compared to Method B, comparisons between several samples from one lot, or samples from different lots of the same item. Direct comparisons among samples is difficult if each of several comparable data sets is treated in strict accordance with these methods. Each data set could have a different number of cells, units per cell, and cell endpoints due to variations in sample sizes and different amounts of spread in the range of the observed data.

From Fig. 3-1, we see that the number of cells changes slowly with sample size: 6 for a sample of 32; 7 for a sample of 64; and 8 for a sample of 130. Thus the number of cells used is not a major criterion. One can compromise and use the number of cells appropriate for the average, or most typical, sample size.

On the other hand, the range may vary quite widely so that if several data sets are to be compared simultaneously, two possible approaches may be used. The first is to use the combined range of all of the data. However, if comparison is of the before-and-after variety, it is preferable to use the results of the "before" sample to define cells in order to emphasize any differences which occur from the cause of the before-and-after conditions. The above methods may then be applied as though only one data set was being used. This results in common cell sizes and endpoints for all samples being compared and makes direct comparisons easy. The one minor disadvantage is that an occasional data set for "after" values may look peculiar due to accidental imbalance caused by its particular arrangement of values.

Example 3-7

Table 3-1 contains data for the before-and-after readings for contact resistance on the same sample taken to determine the effects of a Salt Atmosphere Test on the contacts.

The procedure for obtaining a before-and-after Frequency Tally is as follows:

Step 1. Range of "before" readings = 8.8 − 5.7 = 3.1.

Step 2. Number of cells = 6, from Fig. 3-1.

Step 3. Cell size = $\frac{3.1}{6}$ = 0.517, use 0.5 because data is in 0.1 units.

Step 4. Balance the cell endpoints:

Ignoring the decimal point, 31 + 1 = 32 units spread.

At 5 units per cell, 7 cells cover a 35 units spread.

Start the first cell 2 units below 5.7, the minimum observed value, and end 1 unit above 8.8, the maximum value.

Step 5. Define cell endpoints and include enough cells to accommodate the "after" readings:

Minimum: 5.5, 6.0, 6.5, 7.0, 7.5, 8.0, 8.5, 9.0, 9.5, 10.0.

Maximum: 5.9, 6.4, 6.9, 7.4, 7.9, 8.4, 8.9, 9.4, 9.9, 10.4.

Step 6. Construct the Frequency Tally.

The Frequency Tally in Fig. 3-2 illustrates the comparison of the before-and-after readings on the sample of parts which were tested. In this case, the cells were laid out using the "before" readings in order to accentuate any systematic changes due to the test conditions. As a result, it is easy to see that the "after" values have shifted to typically

CONTACT RESISTANCE, Milliohms

Range	BEFORE	AFTER
5.5– 5.9	III	
6.0– 6.4	IIII	III
6.5– 6.9	ʃHJ	II
7.0– 7.4	ʃHJ III	ʃHJ II
7.5– 7.9	III	ʃHJ I
8.0– 8.4	I	I
8.5– 8.9	I	ʃHJ
9.0– 9.4		
9.5– 9.9		
10.0–10.4		I

FREQUENCY OF OCCURRENCE

Fig. 3-2. Frequency tally for Table 3-1.

higher values and that the resultant distribution is less smooth than the initial one, due to corrosion products on the contacts.

Example 3-8

Table 3-2 contains data for the results of weight loss due to solvent evaporation in an oven test be-

Table 3-2. Oven Test Data

Test Specimen Number	Lot #1	Lot #2
	Weight Loss, Milligrams	
1	18.7	20.7
2	17.2	18.4
3	18.8	20.1
4	18.9	19.6
5	17.8	19.8
6	16.3	18.8
7	17.1	20.8
8	18.7	19.8
9	20.4	19.2
10	16.2	20.8
11	18.1	18.6
12	17.4	18.8
13	17.1	20.9
14	18.6	20.0
15	16.4	18.5
16	16.5	20.9
17	17.0	20.9
18	17.7	20.0
19	17.5	20.6
20	17.3	20.4
21	16.9	21.3
22	17.8	18.4
23	17.9	19.4
24	17.7	19.0
25	17.2	

tween samples from two different manufacturing runs of the same product. Since no difference in results was anticipated, all data were combined to define the cell requirements.

The procedure for obtaining the Comparison Frequency Tally is:

Step 1. Range of $25 + 24 = 49$ readings is $21.3 - 16.2 = 5.1$.

Step 2. Number of cells = 7.

Step 3. Cell size = $\frac{51}{7} = 7.3$; use 7.

Step 4. Balance the cell endpoints:
$51 + 1 = 52$ units spread
At 7 units per cell, 8 cells give 56 units spread
Start the first cell 2 units below 16.2 and end 2 units above 21.3.

Step 5. Define the cell endpoints:
Minimum: 16.0, 16.7, 17.4, 18.1, 18.8, 19.5, 20.2, 20.9.
Maximum: 16.6, 17.3, 18.0, 18.7, 19.4, 20.1, 20.8, 21.5.

Step 6. Construct the Frequency Tally.

The Comparison Frequency Tally is shown in Fig. 3-3. In spite of an anticipated similarity of results, there is a distinct difference in solvent loss of the samples tested. The peaks of the two sample distributions are nearly 20 percent different. This is an excessive amount which was due to improper formulation of the batch with the higher loss. No additional analysis was necessary for these data.

WEIGHT LOSS, Milligrams

Range	LOT A	LOT B
16.0–16.6	IIII	
16.7–17.3	NHI II	
17.4–18.0	NHI II	
18.1–18.7	IIII	IIII
18.8–19.4	II	NHI
19.5–20.1		NHI I
20.2–20.8	I	NHI
20.9–21.5		IIII

FREQUENCY OF OCCURRENCE

Fig. 3-3.   Frequency tally for Table 3-2.

Exercises

3-1. Table 3-3 contains data for results of dissipation factor measurements on two independent

Table 3-3. Data for Exercise 3-1

Lot #1	Lot #2
Percent Dissipation	
8.3	6.9
7.5	6.4
8.9	6.6
7.9	7.6
9.2	6.2
7.8	6.8
6.0	6.6
7.1	7.0
6.8	7.3
6.4	6.0
6.0	7.0
6.1	5.9
7.0	9.0
6.7	8.6
6.4	8.5
7.6	6.4
7.3	6.3
6.1	6.3
6.4	8.1
6.8	11.1
7.4	9.0
7.6	10.0
6.6	9.4
6.8	6.7

(handwritten: min 6.0, max 9.2 next to Lot #1; min 5.9, max 11.1 next to Lot #2)

samples from the same batch of liquid electrolyte, porous anode tantalum capacitors.

a. Expecting equivalent results, obtain the *average* range. (handwritten: 3.2, 5.2 r_{av} 4.7)

b. Using Fig. 3-1 and item a, determine the appropriate cell size.

c. Balance the cell endpoints.

d. Define the cell endpoints.

e. Construct the two sample Frequency Tallies.

f. Discuss the appearance of the results.

3-2. Samples of material were obtained from two different sources of supply. These samples were tensile tested and the amount of elongation at rupture was recorded for each specimen. Percent elongation for each specimen is given in Table 3-4.

Table 3-4. Data for Exercise 3-2

Source A		Source B	
Percent Elongation			
2.6	2.1	1.4	0.9
1.4	2.4	1.3	1.0
1.8	2.1	1.8	1.2
2.3	2.7	1.6	1.5
1.3	2.3	1.9	2.0
2.1	1.6	1.5	0.9
2.5	1.6	1.0	2.1
2.8	1.6	1.6	1.2
1.8	2.5	1.6	1.4
2.6	2.2	1.3	0.9
2.9	3.2	1.7	2.2
1.2	1.9	1.5	1.8
1.8	0.5	1.6	2.0
1.8	2.0	1.7	2.0
1.5	2.2	1.0	0.9
1.9	2.3	0.0	1.6
2.5	2.5	1.0	1.2
2.5	2.2	1.5	1.7
0.7	2.3	1.5	1.9
1.4	2.2	1.6	1.7
1.0	2.3	1.6	1.4
2.4	1.7	1.2	1.4
0.4	2.1	1.6	1.1
2.6	2.0	0.9	1.1
2.3		1.2	

min 0.0
max 3.2

a. Without knowing any expected results, use the *combined* range to establish the cell intervals. *3.2*

b. Determine the number of cells and the cell size. *8 Cells* *5 on 72/cell*

c. Balance the cell endpoints and define them.

d. Construct the Frequency Tallies.

e. Discuss the results.

3-3. A group of small electronic assemblies was processed through a potting and curing process. In order to determine weight gain due to potting, weights of the individual assemblies were taken before potting and again after curing.   These weights are given in Table 3-5.

Table 3-5. Data for
Exercise 3-3

Before	After
Weight, in Grams	
98	108
91	105
126	147
156	176
140	166
140	158
93	113
102	111
91	119
125	148
97	110
113	119
120	147
84	106
83	105
96	108
108	132
92	109
147	172
117	130
91	105
92	108
110	128
90	107

max 176
min 105

min 83
max 156

a. Expecting a difference in weights, use the range of the "before" sample and the number of cells for that sample size to obtain the cell size.   This will emphasize differences in before-and-after weights.

b. Balance and define the cell endpoints.

c. Construct the Frequency Tallies and discuss the results.

CHAPTER 4

Further Methods of Data Presentation

It is important to remember that a set of data represents the results obtained from a sample of a large grouping called a *population*. The values actually observed are more or less random values from the population (see Chapter 2). These *sample values* represent all the values which exist in the parent population. Sample values will not all be identical but will occur over some numerical range, as shown in Figs. 2-3 and 2-5. Distributions of sample values typically tend to bunch up near some middle value; hence, away from the middle fewer values will occur.

One method of presenting data is in tabular form, as in Table 4-1. This shows a range of vary-

Table 4-1. Table of Assembly Times

Assembly Time, Seconds	Frequency of Occurrence
12	1
13	2
14	8
15	9
16	3
17	1

ing values for time of assembly taken from Table 1-2. There are clearly more values near the middle part of the range. This same information is represented pictorially in Fig. 4-1, in the form of a histogram. Because it is easier to grasp the information content of the histogram, it is more commonly used to display data than either the table or the graphical form of Fig. 1-3.

In statistical work, the form of Table 4-2 is often used. This is called a *cumulative frequency table*. It displays all of the numbers of occurren-

Table 4-2. Cumulative Frequency Table for Assembly Times

Time, Seconds	Frequency		Cumulative Percentage
	Actual	Cumulative	
(1)	(2)	(3)	(4)
11	0	0	0
12	1	1	4.2
13	2	3	12.5
14	8	11	45.8
15	9	20	83.3
16	3	23	95.8
17	1	24	100.0
Total	24		

ces which are greater than some low value. This table contains values for the variable of interest, time, in Column 1. The number of assemblies, or *frequency of occurrence,* completed for each time interval is given in Column 2. The *cumulative frequency* is shown in Column 3. This is derived by adding the actual frequencies observed to obtain consecutive totals. For example, $0 + 1 = 1$ at 12 seconds; $1 + 2 = 3$ at 13 seconds; $3 + 8 = 11$ at 14 seconds; etc. The *cumulative percent-*

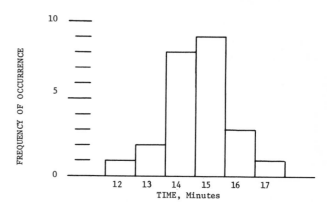

Fig. 4-1. Data from Table 4-1, presented as a histogram.

age, Column 4, is obtained by dividing the cumulative frequencies by the total of all actual frequencies observed, in this case 24, and then multiplying by 100%. For example:

$$\frac{1 \times 100\%}{24} = 4.2\% \qquad \frac{3 \times 100\%}{24} = 12.5\%$$

Thus, in Column 4, for the cumulative percentages one reads as follows: 12.5% of the observed values are equal to or less than the value 13. The plot of this data is shown in Fig. 4-2. This plot is called an ogive. It is characterized by double curvature, or double inflection.

Probability Plots

In general, technical and scientific people prefer to work with straight-line plots of data because a straight line is simple and convenient for interpolation and extrapolation. It is possible to make

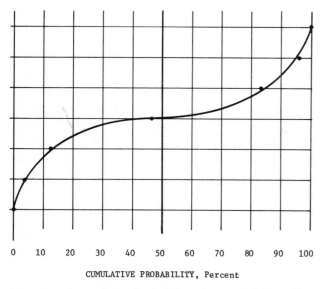

CUMULATIVE PROBABILITY, Percent

Fig. 4-2. Cumulative probability plot, commonly called an *ogive.*

cumulative frequency data appear as a straight line by plotting such data against a suitable scale. Suitably scaled graph papers for such use in distribution analysis are called *probability papers.*

There are as many basically different probability scales as there are statistical distributions. In addition, the variables of interest also have vari-

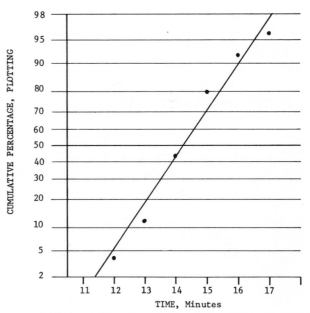

Fig. 4-3. Probability plot for data in Table 4-3.

ous mathematical forms and widely different ranges of values so that many variations in probability papers are possible.

Remember that a probability paper is a device which spaces the dimensions of a particular distribution so that plots of cumulative frequency data result in a straight line, provided that one knows the right distribution and has chosen a corresponding probability paper for plotting. Figure 4-3 illustrates a probability plot for the data of Table 4-3.

Table 4-3. Cumulative Frequency Table for Assembly Times and Adjusted Percentages

Time, Seconds	Frequency		Cumulative Percentage*
	Actual	Cumulative	
(1)	(2)	(3)	(4)
12	1	1	4
13	2	3	12
14	8	11	44
15	9	20	80
16	3	23	92
17	1	24	96
Total	24		

* Adjusted values obtained by multiplying each value in Column (3) by $100\%/(n+1) = 100\%/(24+1) = 100\%/25 = 4\%$.

A probability plot is derived similarly to an ogive with one important exception. Instead of using the observed cumulative percentage at a given value level, one uses what is known as a *cumulative percentage for plotting.*

The cumulative percentage for plotting position differs from the conventional cumulative percentage. For example, with a sample of 10 values, it appears straightforward to plot each value at 10% intervals. That is, starting with 10% for the position of the first value, continue in 10% steps until 100% is reached on the last step. However, let us suppose that the data consists of samples of 10 observations each. The value of the first observation in a given sample of ten would be expected to be in the same relationship to 0% as the tenth observation is to 100%. Thus, on the average, we expect the first and last observations to be about equidistant from 0% and 100% respectively. Gumbel (21) and Ferrell (16) resolve the problem of defining a cumulative percentage plotting position for each observation in a sample by adjusting the cumulative frequency. The adjustment is made by multiplying the cumulative frequency by 100% $(n + 1)$, where n is the sample size. Note that the denominator $(n + 1)$, is obtained simply by adding 1 to the sample size. We will refer to the adjusted value as a *cumulative percentage plotting,* to distinguish it from the conventional cumulative percentage value.

For a sample size of 10, the plotting adjustment results in points at 9.1, 18.2, . . . , 81.8, and 90.9%. The first and last observations are therefore plotted symmetrically with respect to 0, 50, and 100%. Johnson (27) and Abbott (1) recommend different adjustment methods. However, the $(n + 1)$ rule is easy to remember and to use for calculations on a slide rule. A table of cumulative percentage plotting is given in Table A-1, Appendix, for selected sample sizes from 15 to 50.

Example 4-1
The cumulative percentage plotting used in Fig. 1-5 is shown in Table 4-2. The calculations for

the 12- and 13-second entries are:

$$\frac{1 \times 100\%}{(24 + 1)} = 4\%; \qquad \frac{3 \times 100\%}{(24 + 1)} = 12\%; \text{ etc.}$$

After the points are plotted, examine them by eye or by using a transparent straightedge to see if a reasonably straight line has resulted. If so, then a line may be fitted to the data points by Ferrell's Method (16). First, make a good "eyeball fit," using the straightedge. Then place a pencil point near the smallest plotted point. Pivot the straightedge around the pencil point until the points in the *upper half* of the plot are divided into two equal parts. This is readily done by counting. Next, shift the pencil point up near the largest plotted point on the new trial line and divide the points in the *lower half* of the plot into two equal parts. Two or three such adjustments should result in a fit which divides all of the plotted points into an upper half and a lower half with respect to the straightedge. The line in Fig. 1-5 is such a line.

The line so defined is called a *median regression line* and is the practical "best fit" for most data. We have already considered that data is likely to be contaminated with some kinds of error and to contain a certain amount of imprecision. Consequently, calculation of a classical *least squares regression line,* while more proper statistically, will require considerably more time without any assurance of more correct estimates.

Exercises
4-1. Prepare cumulative frequency tables with cumulative percentage plotting for the data of Exercise 3-1. Construct each histogram.
4-2. Prepare cumulative frequency tables with cumulative percentage plotting, for the data in Exercise 3-2. Construct each histogram.
4-3. Prepare cumulative frequency tables with cumulative percentage plotting, for the data in Exercise 3-3. Construct each histogram.

CHAPTER 5

Simple Interpretation of Probability Plots

If one has sufficient information beforehand and a reasonable choice of probability paper is made, an acceptable straight-line fit to a set of sampling data will be achieved after plotting on the selected probability paper. It is then possible to estimate the statistical parameters of the observed distribution directly, without the need for tedious calculations. Such estimates will be adequate for most purposes. Specific methods for particular distributions will be discussed in subsequent chapters.

When data is plotted on a suitable probability paper, it often happens that the plot is not a straight line. There are two common reasons for this. The first is due to the influence of specifications and the second is due to mixing of outputs having different sources of variation.

Influence of Specifications

Up to this point, we have considered only the complete distribution of an output from a random process. However, most processes are required to operate to a specification. A specification represents an ideal value or a target for a process. The bulls-eye on this target is the ideal value. However, one cannot expect to score bulls-eyes 100% of the time. Therefore, specifications include a *tolerance*. The tolerance represents the amount by which a process output may be allowed to miss the bulls-eye.

There are two general types of specifications. One type is called two-sided. This occurs when the specification calls for some ideal value plus or minus a tolerance value, such as: The length shall be $1.00'' \pm 0.10''$. This is interpreted to mean that any item whose measured value is between $0.90''$ and $1.10''$ will be considered as acceptable. Conversely, items smaller than $0.90''$ and larger than $1.10''$ will not be acceptable.

The second kind of specification is called "one-sided." This calls only for an item which is neither too small nor too large. For example, the length of a slot may be specified as: not to be less than $0.50''$; or the thickness of a piece of sheet metal may be specified as: not to exceed $0.010''$.

Two simple facts need to be clearly understood. First, many processes do *not* produce output which meets specification 100 percent of the time. Second, many specifications are established without *knowledge or understanding* of the process which produces the item of interest.

The first situation occurs because, as Fig. 2-1 shows, there are inherent variations in materials, machine settings, methods of operation, and human behavior. If the process is well understood, these sources of variation may be carefully controlled to the point where a specification can be met with almost any preassigned percentage of success. In spite of this, a recent nationally based conference of representatives of all major industries found in a poll that shipments of manufactured goods checked at receiving failed to meet specifications, for one or more reasons, on an average of 40% of the time. This is truly deplorable.

The second situation occurs because many specifications are based on a "user" requirement which has no connection with the processes of the "producer." Furthermore, the user frequently plays safe by introducing a safety factor. This normally has the effect of reducing the tolerance allowed to the producer. This partially explains why the 40% failure to meet specifications does not bring our economy to a grinding halt. Most such shipments are accepted and used as long as they do not exceed the ideal value plus the tolerance *plus the safety factor*. Burr (6), (7), and (8), has treated the ramifications of this problem in depth. Enrick

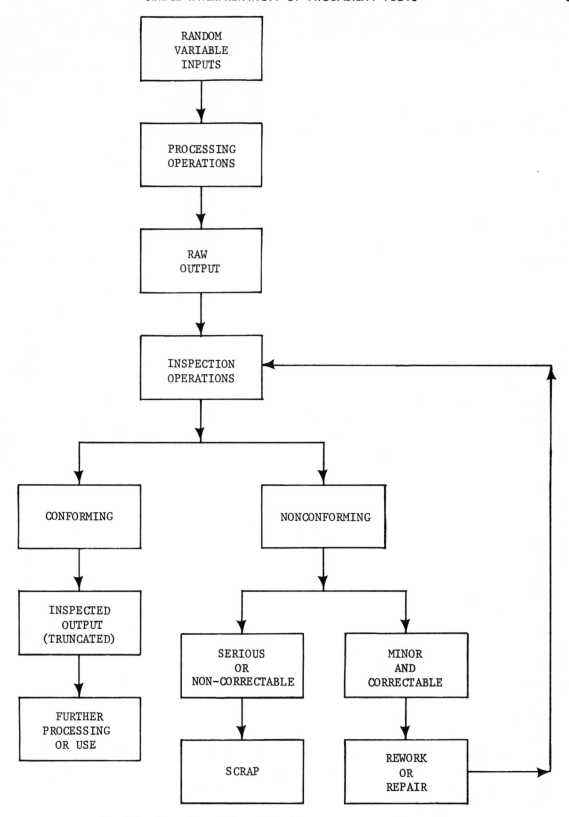

Fig. 5-1.   Flow chart of the relationship of processing and inspection.

(12) presents practical methods of specification engineering.

Two-sided Specifications

As a result of recognizing that processes do produce results which are outside of specification limits (*nonconforming*), many process outputs are subjected to an inspection operation wherein 100 percent of the product is measured, or otherwise examined, for one or more specified output characteristics.

Ideally, inspection should identify and remove all nonconforming items from each batch which is inspected. The nonconforming items may then be scrapped if the failure to meet specification is gross or noncorrectable. If the failure to meet specification is minor and/or correctable, such items may be reworked or reprocessed to achieve acceptable conformity. Such items may then be routed through inspection a second time. The relationship between processing and inspection is shown in the flow chart of Fig. 5-1.

The net result is that the raw output of the process becomes *truncated* by the inspection op-

erations which separate the process output into conforming and nonconforming categories. However, the selected output has different distribution characteristics than the raw output. Figure 5-2 is a histogram of the distribution of an actual dimension as produced by a machining operation. Histograms in this and subsequent chapters are shown using the variable of interest on the horizontal scale because this is the conventional method of plotting histograms. Dimensional data is given in Table 5-1, for one sample. The specification for this dimension is 1.000″ ± 0.030″, or 0.970″ to 1.030″. If 100 percent inspection discovers all out-of-specification items, then 15 out of 99 items are removed, representing an approximate rejection of 15.2 percent.

For this example, the number of cells was obtained as in Chapter 3. The cell sizes and cell endpoints were adjusted to coincide with the tolerance interval to illustrate the impact of a specification clearly.

A probability plot for the raw output of this dimension is shown in Fig. 5-3. The histogram and the probability plot for the truncated output

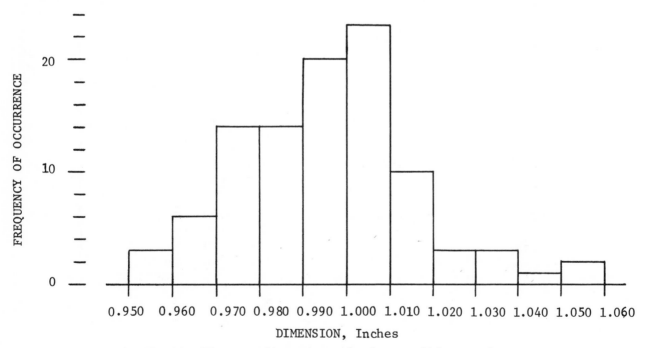

Fig. 5-2.   Histogram of inspection results after a machining operation.

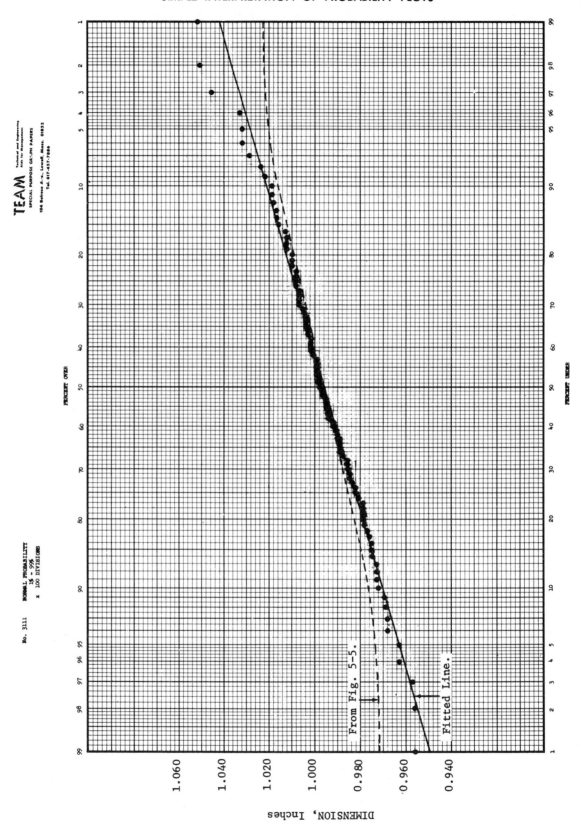

Fig. 5-3.   Probability plot of inspection results after a machining operation.

Table 5-1. 99 Consecutive Measurements from Machine A *

1.010	1.004	1.007	0.979	1.019	0.969	1.013	0.982	1.019	0.984
1.018	1.024	0.978	0.989	0.973	0.989	0.995	0.972	1.010	0.994
1.017	0.998	1.002	0.982	1.033	0.985	0.997	1.010	0.979	1.046
1.012	0.994	0.999	1.006	1.002	0.997	1.002	0.968	1.008	0.995
1.008	1.022	0.975	1.012	0.999	0.992	1.007	1.003	1.032	0.963
0.973	0.999	1.004	1.012	1.007	0.998	0.991	1.004	1.029	1.008
1.003	0.956	0.995	0.986	1.032	1.007	0.999	1.016	0.986	1.001
0.973	0.978	0.963	0.975	0.989	1.017	0.992	0.976	0.975	0.989
0.968	0.956	0.969	0.990	0.978	0.981	0.999	1.005	1.052	0.985
0.998	1.051	0.988	1.008	0.986	0.994	0.957	1.002	0.977	

* In inches.

due to inspection are shown below, in Figs. 5-4 and 5-5.

The histogram of Fig. 5-4 is notable for its lack of distribution tails. It has, instead, a squared-off appearance which is characteristic of a truncated distribution. In the probability plot of Fig. 5-5, there are two lines fitted to the data. The dashed line is a "best estimate" of a linear fit while the solid line is distinctly a nonlinear fit. This solid-line fit is also shown superimposed on Fig. 5-3 as a dashed line.

In Fig. 5-3, there is little practical difference in either line between the 20% and 80% points. The departure between the raw distribution and the truncated distribution increases as the distance from the middle of either distribution increases.

As a user, whether of purchased goods or of goods moving between different departments of the same company, probability plots such as Fig. 5-5 are a clue that the raw distribution has been modified. This is indicated by the flattened appearance at both the low and the high ends of the plot.

A conservative estimate of the actual operating results of the process or operations which produced these items may be obtained from such a probability plot. By noting the points at which flattening starts to occur, one may estimate the amount of scrap, rework, or waste which is generated at the producing point. In purchases inspection, estimates of nonconforming product percentages can be used directly as an input to vendor rating systems and to cost/value studies of various sources of supply. The start of flattening is illustrated by the arrows in Fig. 5-5. The lower point is at about 9% and the upper point is at 7% for a total of 16%, as compared to the known removal of 15.2% under ideal circumstances.

A simple test may be applied, after a "best-fit" line is established by dividing the points into equal parts following the instructions in Chapter 4. If the sum of points above the line at the low end and below the line at the high end is 11 or more, there is significant evidence of truncation. See (48).

One-sided Specifications

If the requirement for the dimension given in Table 5-1 were such that it should not exceed some value, such as 1.020″, a different situation would occur. Inspection would remove only items which exceed 1.020″. The result would be as shown in

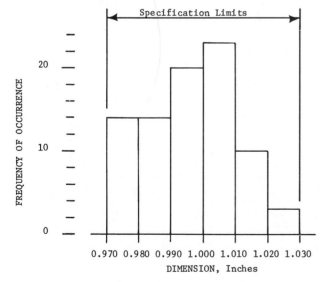

Fig. 5-4.   Histogram of truncated output after inspection operations.

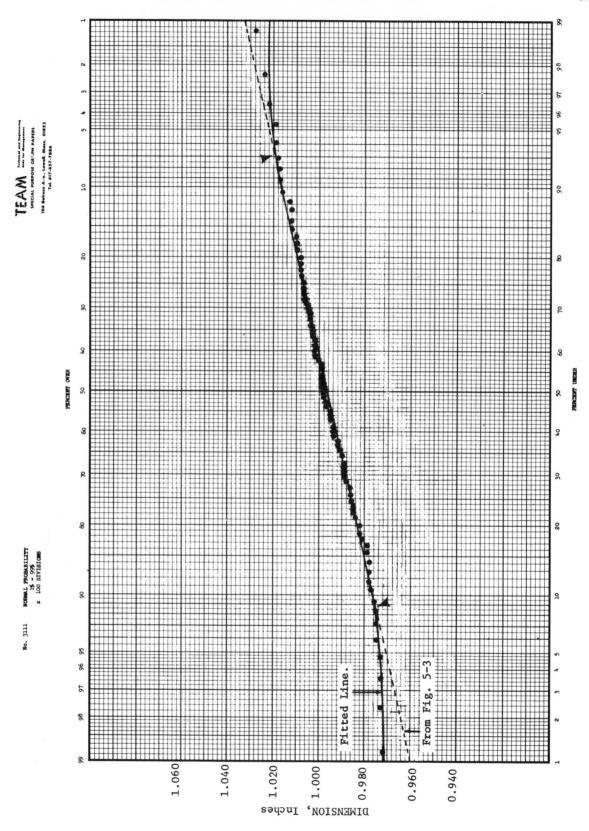

Fig. 5-5. Probability plot of truncated output after inspection operations.

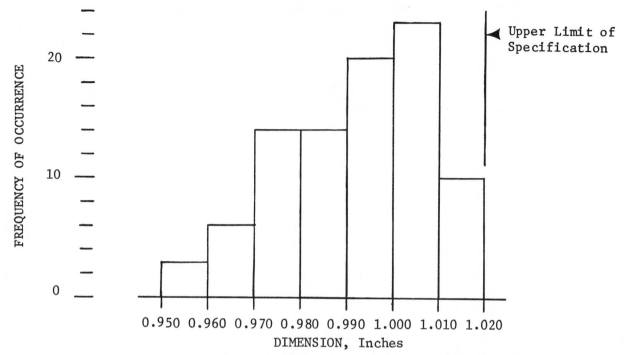

Fig. 5-6. Histogram of truncated output after upper-limit inspection.

the histogram, Fig. 5-6, and the probability plot, Fig. 5-7.

Here the plot is flattened at the high end. Once again, losses in the originating process can be estimated from the probability plot. This is accomplished by using one-half of the value at the point where the flattening starts to occur. In Fig. 5-7, this occurs at about 20%. Half of this value is 10%. From the actual data, we know that 9 items, or about 9.1%, were removed from a sample of 99. A count of 11 or more points below the high end of the *best* straight line is again a clue to truncation. In this case, the truncation is at the high end of the plot.

If the requirement for a dimension is such that it should not be less than some value, then a probability plot would be obtained with flattening at the low end. Once again, the losses at the producing point can be estimated in a manner similar to estimating losses at the high end by observing the start. Again, a count of 11 points above the fitted best line is a significant clue.

There is another significant cause for this kind of pattern at the low end. This occurs in measurements of surface roughness, leakage currents of electronic components, and bridge/null-balance detection. The particular equipment used may not have the capability to resolve measurements below some absolute value of the variable of interest. Consequently, all low values will be of nearly the same magnitude. This will cause flattening of the low end of the plot. The point where flattening starts is usually representative of an inherent lower measurement limit resulting from the combined effects of design limitations, manufacturing, or purchased parts tolerances, inadequate operator training, and/or the particular conditions of equipment usage. This kind of information represents a simple and useful way of determining the lower bound of measurement capability for a specific piece of equipment. Measurement limitation is discussed further in connection with Fig. 9-9, in Chapter 9.

Mixed Outputs

Figure 5-8 illustrates another nonlinear probability plot. This figure is characterized by two relatively straight portions which are connected by a jog, or lazy S-shaped connection. The histogram for the inspection measurements which resulted in

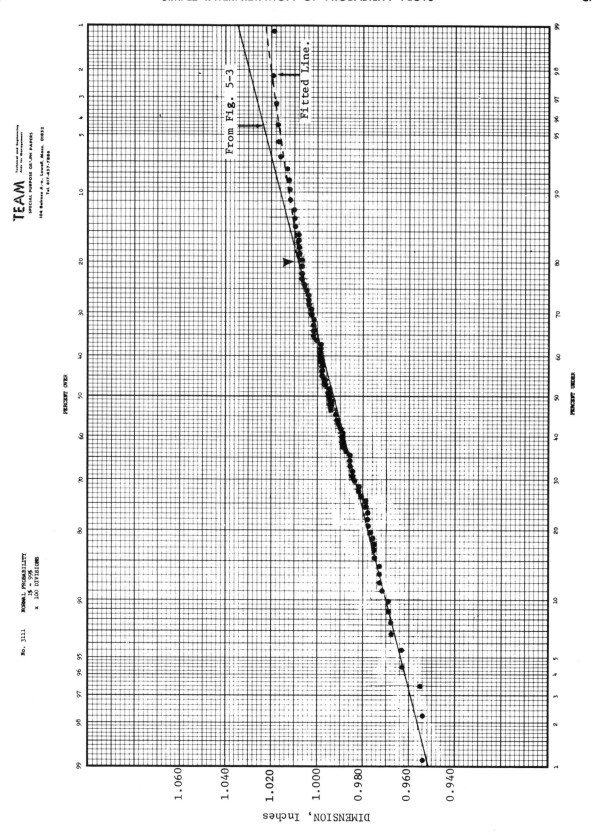

Fig. 5-7. Probability plot of truncated output after upper-limit inspection.

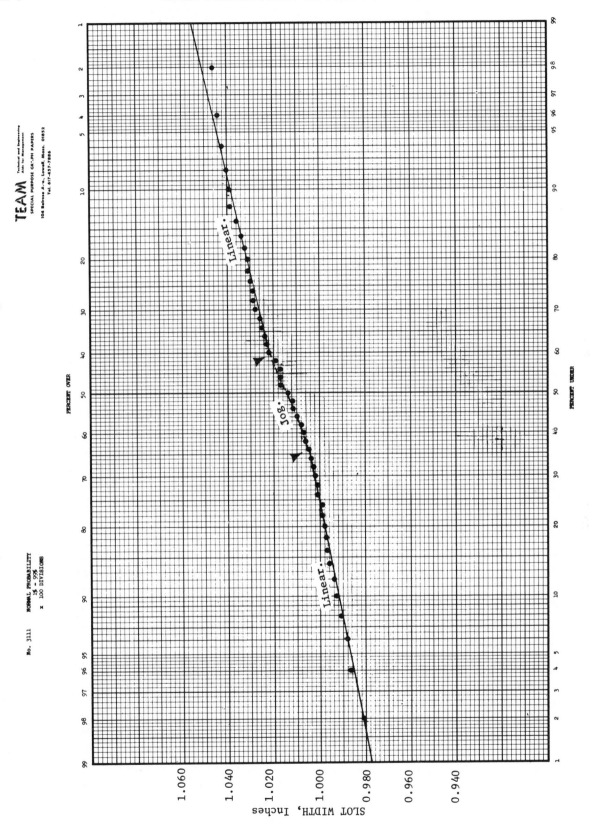

Fig. 5-8.   Probability plot of mixed output from two milling machines.

Table 5-2. 49 Measurements of Groove Width from Milling Machines *

0.981	1.044	1.003	1.074	0.999	1.001	0.987
1.040	0.997	0.996	1.001	1.039	1.025	1.014
0.988	1.044	1.031	1.023	0.994	1.008	1.029
0.042	1.017	1.033	0.991	1.007	1.046	1.017
1.010	1.012	1.019	1.030	1.029	0.993	0.997
1.026	1.039	1.028	0.998	1.036	1.002	1.004
1.005	0.999	1.017	1.031	1.022	1.006	1.012

* In inches.

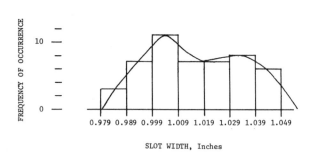

Fig. 5-9.   Histogram of mixed output from two
milling machines.

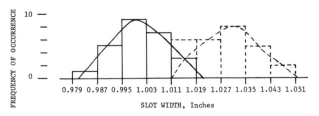

Fig. 5-10.   Joint histogram of outputs from two
milling machines.

this plot is shown in Fig. 5-9. Investigations of the origins of this data indicated that the output from two milling machines had been mixed. The original data is given in Table 5-2.

The data were separated into two groups, each representing one of the milling machines. This data is given in Table 5-3, by machine. A joint histogram of these data, now using cells and cell sizes based on separate sample sizes of about 25, is shown in Fig. 5-10. The results for milling machine #1 are shown as a solid line and the results for milling machine #2 are shown as a dashed line.

The most notable feature of this figure is the existence of two separate peaks. This is emphasized by also drawing a rough curve of each individual distribution. The appearance of two peaks was also observed in Fig. 5-9, but to a lesser degree.

This kind of appearance is called *bimodal* to describe the existence of two different peak values. Bimodal results occur from the mixing of the outputs from two different sources of variation in a single sample. The sources of variation may be two different levels of values for input materials; two different production machines, operators, or shifts; or, differences in the operating settings of a process due to poor control standards or inadequate instructions.

In such situations, it is more important to find the cause(s) of such nonuniform behavior than to worry about the difficulty of obtaining good parameter estimates from such data. The symptoms indicated are usually quite serious, from a practical standpoint, and require basic and fundamental improvements. Although it is possible to utilize sophisticated corrections for such data to derive corrected sample estimates, such estimates are unimportant compared to the clear signal of assignable causes of process variation which will require correction and which are often quite easily correctable.

Table 5-3. Groove Width by Milling Machine *

Milling Machine #1			Milling Machine #2		
0.981	1.017	1.008	1.040	1.033	1.029
0.988	1.001	0.993	1.042	1.019	1.036
1.010	0.991	1.002	1.026	1.028	1.022
1.005	0.998	1.006	1.034	1.024	1.025
0.997	0.999	0.987	1.044	1.023	1.046
1.012	0.994	0.997	1.017	1.030	1.014
0.999	1.007	1.004	1.039	1.031	1.029
1.003	1.001	1.012	1.031	1.039	1.017
0.996					

* In inches.

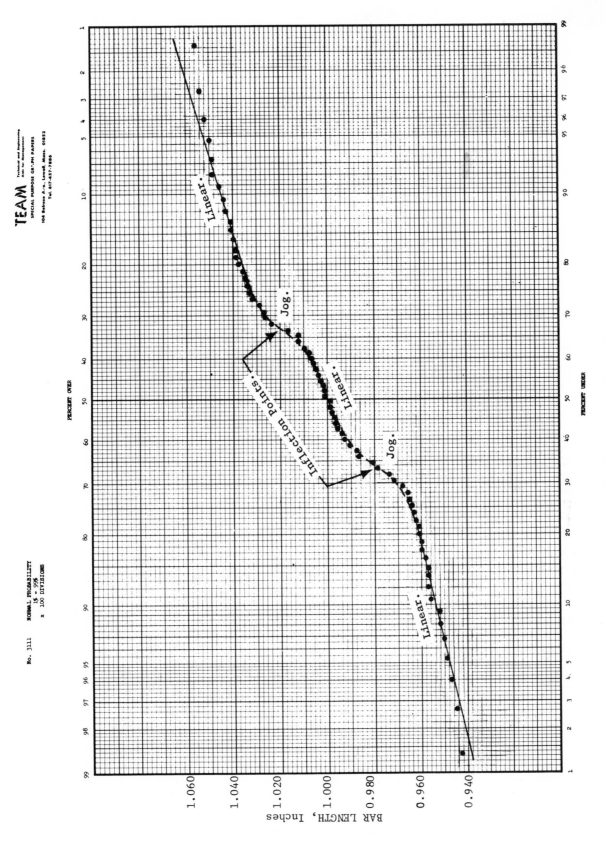

Fig. 5-11.   Probability plot of mixed output from three saws.

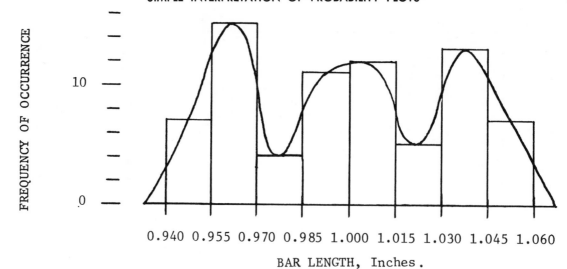

Fig. 5-12.   Histogram of mixed output from three saws.

One type of variation of this pattern is shown in Figs. 5-11 and 5-12 which are obtained from the data in Table 5-4, for saw data.   The stepwise

Table 5-4. 74 Measurements of Bar Length from Saws *

0.981	1.036	0.998	0.961	0.943
0.988	0.974	1.029	1.008	1.035
1.010	1.044	1.038	0.993	0.957
0.979	1.054	0.958	0.952	0.956
1.050	1.027	0.999	1.041	1.004
0.965	1.003	0.994	0.949	1.012
0.950	0.996	1.034	0.960	1.056
1.005	1.049	1.007	1.002	1.024
0.997	0.952	0.959	1.006	0.962
1.052	1.017	0.963	0.987	0.968
0.945	0.966	0.964	1.049	0.961
1.012	1.041	0.972	1.039	1.039
0.974	1.001	1.033	1.046	1.027
0.999	0.991	1.001	1.032	...
0.960	1.043	1.040	0.997	0.957

* In inches.

effect in Fig. 5-11 is a consequence of the multi-modal pattern shown in Figs. 5-12 and 5-13.   Figure 5-12 is obtained by treating all of the data in Table 5-4 as a single sample.   Figure 5-13 is obtained by once again investigating the cause of such behavior.   In this case, it was determined that the output from three different machines was mixed together into one inspection batch.   Table 5-5, gives the results by individual machines.   From this data, the individual machine histograms are prepared and plotted as a joint histogram.

The joint histogram emphasizes the several separate sources of peakedness more than the combined histogram of Fig. 5-12.

If many significantly different sources are combined, there will be approximately one step for each different source of variation in probability plots such as Fig. 5-11.   These sources of variation are similar to those discussed above for the bimodal case.

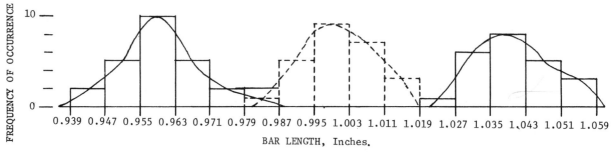

Fig. 5-13.   Joint histogram of outputs from three saws.

Table 5-5. Bar Lengths by Individual Saws *

Saw #1			Saw #2			Saw #3		
1.012	1.007	1.003	0.957	0.952	0.952	1.027	1.049	1.041
1.004	0.994	0.999	0.961	0.961	0.947	1.039	1.041	1.049
0.997	0.999	1.012	0.968	0.972	0.960	1.024	1.040	1.027
0.987	0.998	0.997	0.962	0.964	0.974	1.056	1.033	1.054
1.006	0.991	1.005	0.956	0.963	0.945	1.035	1.034	1.044
1.002	1.001	1.010	0.957	0.959	0.950	1.032	1.038	1.036
0.993	1.017	0.988	0.943	0.958	0.965	1.046	1.029	1.052
1.008	0.996	0.981	0.960	0.966	0.979	1.039	1.043	1.050
1.001	. . .	. . .	0.949	. . .	. . .	. . .	. . .	. . .

* In inches.

When probability plots are obtained with multiple steps, one has a rough estimate of the number of individual sources of variation which are operating. In addition, by observing where the jogs occur, one can also approximate the percentage mix from the several sources of variation which exist in the observed sample. The point of inflection in the jog, or the crossover point, estimates the percentage present. For example, in Fig. 5-11 the inflection points occur at about 33% and 67%. We know that this sample was composed of three practically equal parts from each of three saws, so this result checks. If, for instance, in a group of five machines, three were running close to the same output level and two were running close together at some other level, the inflection would occur at about the 60% point.

Utilization of Nonlinear Plots

When one has reliable knowledge that a process should have a specific distribution behavior, nonlinear plots lead to the following useful information:

1. Reasonable estimates of the actual spread of the producing process

2. Estimates of percentage rejection or losses at the producing point

3. Indication of measurement equipment limitations and/or thresholds of measurement sensitivity

4. Evidence of mixed results in samples indicates that there are determinable causes of nonuniform behavior which should be investigated.

5. Estimates of the number of significantly different sources of variation which are operating simultaneously.

It is well worth repeating that the detection of nonlinear patterns is an important indication of the need for investigation to determine the significant sources of such variation. Usually these sources are permanently removable after their identification. Such corrective action will materially alter subsequent data from the same source. As a result, later estimates of any statistical parameters will also be different, and more representative of the process capability.

Curved Plots

As opposed to the nonlinear patterns which are explainable deviations from a known underlying distribution, we also find patterns which indicate that the observed data *do not* follow the distribution represented by the particular kind of probability paper chosen for plotting. Figures 5-14 and 5-16 illustrate two basic kinds of departure from a normal distribution.

The plot in Fig. 5-14 is convex. This occurs because the data from which the plot was made has a long tail to the left, or is *negatively skewed*. The histogram corresponding to Fig. 5-14 is shown in Fig. 5-15 for the breaking strengths of samples of yarn broken in tension. The data for 24 tests are given in Table 5-6. These data show a bunched-up peak near the high-valued end and a long, thin tail toward the lower values at the left. The negatively skewed type of distribution is a characteristic of most breaking-strength data.

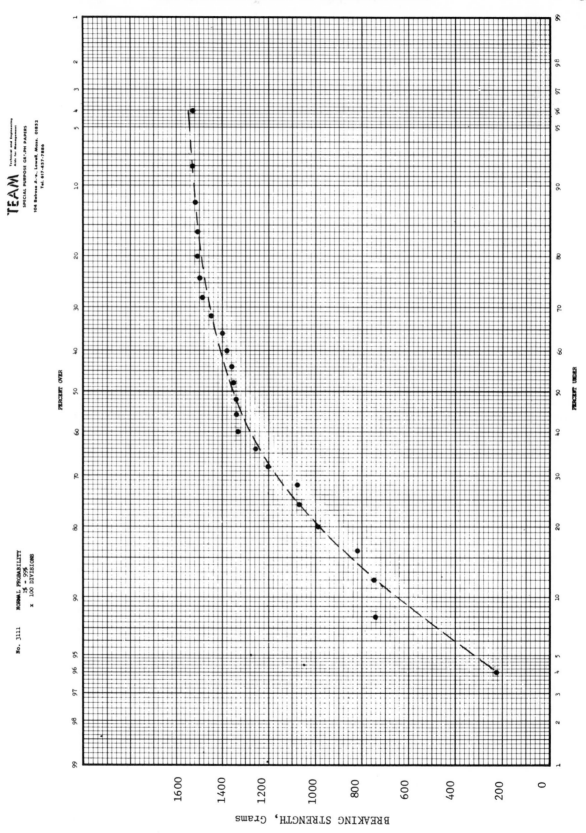

Fig. 5-14.   Probability plot of a breaking strength distribution with negative skew.

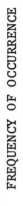

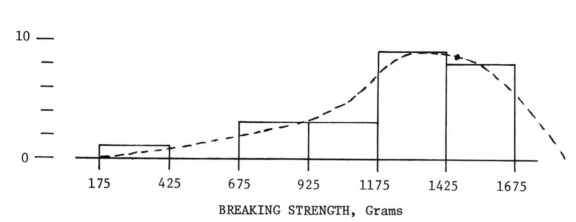

Fig. 5-15.   Histogram of tensile test breaking strengths.

Table 5-6. Tensile Test
Results

Breaking Strength, Grams	
1404	1385
996	1492
1525	744
1335	1351
1359	1529
1066	1507
1077	1331
1509	1341
749	1498
1517	1202
1448	821
1256	225

The concave shape of Fig. 5-16 is caused by data which tail off to the right, or have *positive skew*. Figure 5-17 is the histogram for percent

Table 5-7. Tensile Test
Results

Percent	Elongation
6.5	3.6
11.8	12.6
11.1	0.9
1.8	4.2
7.2	3.5
11.6	5.9
5.7	12.5
1.4	8.8
7.2	3.4
5.3	17.5
2.1	11.2
17.9	3.9

elongation of samples of yarn tested in tension. The data for 24 tests are given in Table 5.7. Positively skewed distributions are often found in yield and creep data in materials testing.

When curved patterns are found, one is not using the correct probability paper for the distribution of the observed data. If the distribution corresponding to the paper used was expected, then this is a significant indication that such a distribution behavior did not occur. If there was no prior knowledge, then this is a clue to try some other distribution paper for a better, more linear, fit.

Choosing a Probability Paper

The choice of the right probability paper for presenting data is highly dependent on the kind and amount of information available. There are three basic cases which can occur. The underlying distribution is:

Case 1 — Known for sound technical reasons.
Case 2 — Assumed to be known for some reason(s).
Case 3 — Unknown.

In cases 1 and 2, use the probability paper representing the known or assumed distribution. The results will be:

1. A straight line if the basic information is correct and both the sampling procedures and measurements are uncontaminated.

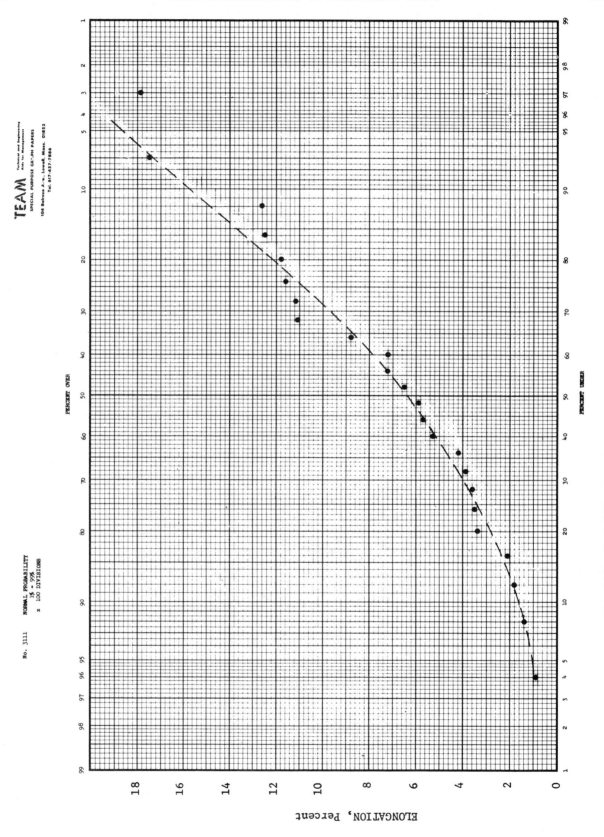

Fig. 5-16.   Probability plot of an elongation distribution with positive skew.

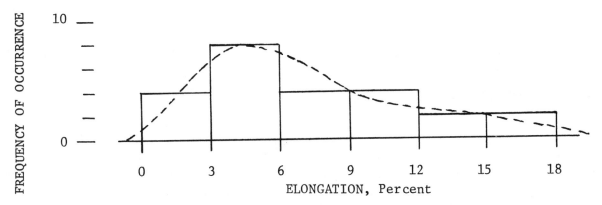

Fig. 5-17.   Histogram of tensile test elongation results.

2. A nonlinear plot for one of the reasons discussed above.

3. A curved plot which indicates that the known or assumed information is faulty or has changed.

In case 3, one important objective of the data analysis is to identify a distribution which will describe the data and/or the originating process in a useful way.

The intrinsic nature, the operating characteristics, or the mathematical equations of a process often provide a reasonable basis for assuming that some particular distribution behavior will occur. Briefly, one may assume that simple processes such as machining, extrusion, molding, or mechanical assembly will have characteristics well represented by the Normal Distribution. Processes which are rate dependent or exponential in nature, such as: chemical reactions, thermosetting, etching, and simple diffusion, will be better described by the Logarithmic Normal Distribution. Processes described by polynomials are best described by extreme value distributions. Processes which have exponential terms, such as: electro-chemical reactions, thermodynamic processes, and complex diffusions are best represented by logarithmic extreme value distributions. Processes involving boundary conditions often yield Weibull Distributions.

If one has no dependable information, it is usually worth plotting unknown data on normal probability paper as a first test because the Normal Distribution is the most common one occurring.

Then this plot is examined for linearity, nonlinearity, or curvature. The results will either be satisfactory or indicate the need for a further choice of another probability paper. Such search techniques are empirical. Some useful rules of thumb are given in the discussions of the specific kinds of probability papers which are discussed in later chapters.

Exercises

5-1. Show how the cell sizes and cell endpoints were derived for Fig. 5-2 using the data of Table 5-1.

5-2. Show how the cell sizes and cell endpoints were derived for Fig. 5-6 using the data of Table 5-1.

5-3. Again, using the data of Table 5-1, construct a histogram for the distribution remaining after inspection to only a lower specification limit of $1.000'' - 0.025''$.

5-4. Show how the cell sizes and cell endpoints were derived for Fig. 5-9 using the data of Table 5-2.

5-5. Show how the cell sizes and cell endpoints were derived for Fig. 5-12 using the data of Table 5-4.

5-6. Show how the cell sizes and cell endpoints were derived for Fig. 5-15 using the data of Table 5-6.

5-7. Show how the cell sizes and cell endpoints were derived for Fig. 5-17 using the data of Table 5-7.

CHAPTER 6

The Uniform Distribution

In Chapter 2 we discussed the binary distribution behavior resulting from coin-tossing experiments. We will now consider the behavior of the uniform distribution as a direct extension of the binary distribution. The uniform distribution is representative of variables which are more complex than the two-state variable of the binary distribution.

Figure 6-1 illustrates the uniform distribution of inputs by another diagram. Here 4 input variables are shown with the additional complication of several possible levels for each variable. This is equivalent to variable inputs representing any value between two specification limits.

Assumptions for Uniform Distributions

Again we have the same important underlying assumptions as for the binary distribution. These are:

1. Each state, or level, occurs equally over a large number of occurrences.
2. Any individual state of a given variable occurs at a rate of $1/n \times 100\%$ where n is the number of practically identifiable states.
3. The results in any one case have no influence on subsequent cases.

To develop experimental models for the uniform distribution, we can use dice, random digit generators, and random number tables. Results with dice are particularly useful because:

1. Very simple arithmetic operations are possible.
2. The six faces of a die have an interesting relationship to the partitioning of a tolerance interval which will be discussed further under the normal distribution.

3. The six die faces can also be related conveniently to typical cell numbers given by Sturges' Rule.

Four dice were used to show the effects of having several levels of variation for each input variable. Each die represents a different input variable. Each face on a die represents a different level or *quality characteristic* of the input variable on a scale from 1 to 6.

Generating a Uniform Distribution, Using Dice

Table 6-1, for 4 dice, gives detailed results for 100 throws of the dice with the number of spots showing on the face of each die. Table 6-2 summarizes this data for the six value levels by showing the total number of occurrences of each value, 1 through 6.

Figure 6-2 is a histogram of the summary of results of 100 throws of 4 dice given in Table 6-2. If the data were perfectly uniform, then there would have been 66 or 67 occurrences per value. However, Fig. 6-2 is another demonstration that there is always some departure from the perfect result. This figure shows that the six possible values have occurred *nearly* the same number of times, but not exactly the 66 or 67 predicted occurrences. Notice the squared-off appearance of the histogram in Fig. 6-2 and compare it to Fig. 4-1. Note the lack of peakedness and tails.

Figure 6-3 is a cumulative frequency plot of the data in Table 6-2. This plot is made on *rectangular coordinate paper*. No probability scale adjustments are necessary because each expected increment on the percentage scale is the same amount. Compare this plot to the curvature of the ogive in Fig. 4-2.

The uniform distribution is not very useful in distribution analysis because it represents a collec-

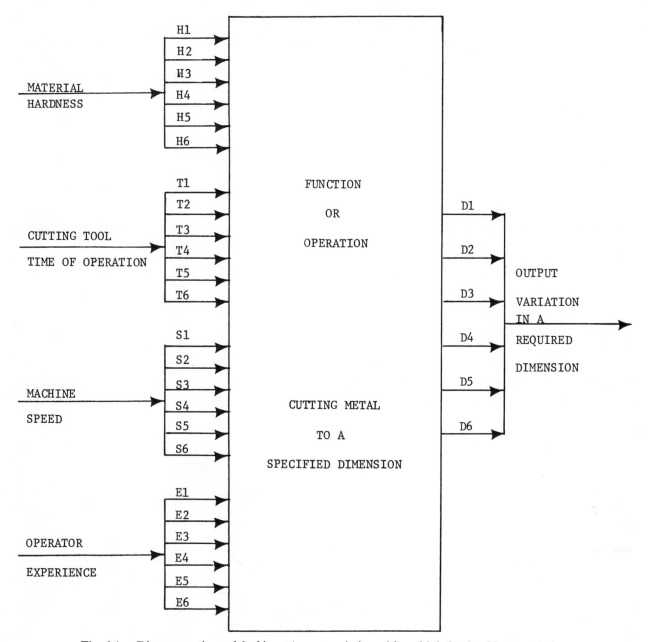

Fig. 6-1. Diagrammatic model of input/ouput variation with multiple levels of input variation.

tion of counts of occurrences which are, in advance, expected to be similar. This appearance of a uniform distribution will sometimes occur as a result of inspection to tight tolerances or from normal inspection results of materials manufactured under poor conditions of control. See Fig. 5-9 for an example.

Of particular interest is that the *simple sum* of a number of random values from uniform distribu-

tions tends to become a normal distribution, as will be shown in the next chapter.

Table 6-1 also shows values for the *sums* of the combined values occurring for each throw of four dice. Figure 6-4 displays these same data. Compare this figure with Fig. 2-5. Can you see any similarities?

Once again, we observe a central tendency and thin ends for this distribution. In fact, this dis-

Table 6-1. Values from Tosses of Dice

Value				Sum	Value				Sum	Value				Sum	Value				Sum	Value				Sum
3	2	6	3	14	3	5	1	3	12	6	3	6	4	19	3	3	1	4	11	3	2	1	3	9
5	5	4	2	16	5	4	6	6	21	1	2	3	4	10	1	4	6	4	15	4	1	4	4	13
4	6	4	4	18	5	2	6	1	14	3	2	6	1	12	6	4	5	3	17	6	2	5	2	15
6	1	3	3	14	5	3	4	6	18	5	4	3	6	18	2	2	2	5	11	1	4	4	2	11
5	1	3	6	15	5	3	2	4	14	6	3	1	6	16	5	3	2	3	13	5	6	4	6	21
5	5	4	6	20	2	5	3	2	12	6	6	4	4	20	5	1	5	5	16	5	5	4	2	18
1	3	6	4	14	4	3	6	3	16	3	5	5	3	16	4	4	4	3	15	2	3	3	1	9
4	6	1	4	15	6	2	6	3	17	3	5	5	5	18	1	4	6	2	13	2	6	2	6	16
2	3	4	5	14	6	2	1	4	13	4	2	5	1	12	1	3	6	2	12	4	6	2	2	14
3	5	5	1	14	2	5	3	2	12	1	1	2	2	6	2	3	5	1	11	6	5	1	1	13
5	5	3	5	18	6	2	6	2	16	5	2	5	3	15	2	6	4	2	14	5	1	3	6	15
6	5	5	2	18	4	2	2	1	9	2	6	3	2	13	1	1	5	1	8	1	1	4	3	9
4	6	6	4	20	1	2	6	3	12	4	6	4	5	19	1	4	2	1	7	2	2	4	1	9
4	1	4	3	12	2	1	1	3	7	3	5	5	4	17	6	2	5	5	18	3	6	1	3	13
2	2	6	2	12	5	2	5	2	14	4	1	1	5	11	5	4	6	5	20	5	5	2	1	13
2	6	5	4	17	2	4	2	2	10	6	6	5	3	20	5	3	4	2	14	2	4	6	5	17
2	3	1	1	7	4	6	4	5	19	6	3	4	4	17	2	1	3	4	10	4	5	4	4	17
3	6	4	3	16	3	1	4	2	10	5	2	6	1	14	6	2	5	1	14	4	6	4	2	16
1	4	5	1	11	2	4	2	5	13	2	6	4	3	15	1	3	3	6	13	1	5	4	2	12
1	3	6	2	12	1	5	4	3	12	2	1	6	2	11	4	1	4	5	14	4	6	5	4	19

tribution is quite similar to Fig. 1-2, but the actual method of obtaining this data is different.

In the case of the coins, we expected heads about half the time. Thus, in a sample of 20 coins, we

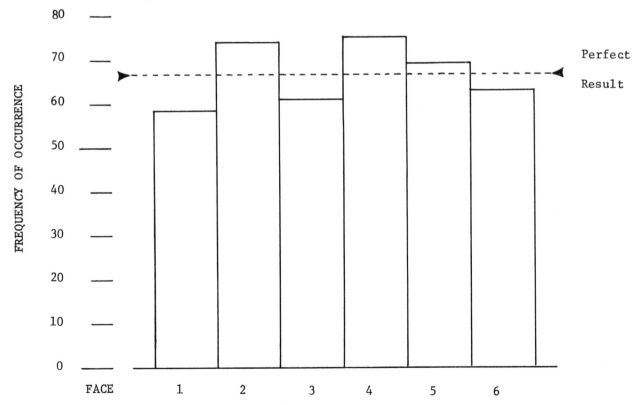

Fig. 6-2. Histogram of the face counts of 100 throws of 4 dice.

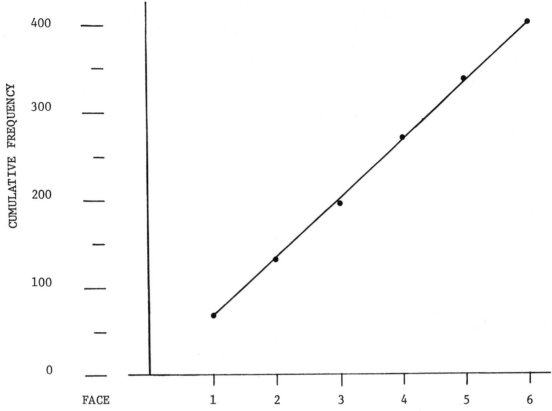

Fig. 6-3.   Cumulative frequency plot of face counts of 100 throws of 4 dice.

Table 6-2. Summary of the Number of Occurrences of Each Face in 100 Throws of Four Dice

Face	Frequency	Cumulative Frequency
1	58	58
2	74	132
3	61	193
4	75	268
5	69	337
6	63	400

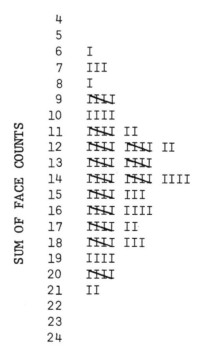

SUM OF FACE COUNTS	
4	
5	
6	I
7	III
8	I
9	卌
10	IIII
11	卌 II
12	卌 卌 II
13	卌 卌
14	卌 卌 IIII
15	卌 III
16	卌 IIII
17	卌 II
18	卌 III
19	IIII
20	卌
21	II
22	
23	
24	

FREQUENCY OF OCCURRENCE

Fig. 6-4.   Frequency tally of sums of face counts from 100 throws of 4 dice.

would expect an average occurrence of 10 heads per sample.   As a matter of observation, the most frequent result was a count of 10 in Fig. 2-5.

For the dice data, each die had the possibility of giving an average reading of $\frac{6+1}{2} = 3.5$.   This is, of course, an impossible result.   However, when the results of 4 dice thrown at one time are added together, the expected average then becomes $3.5 \times 4 = 14$.   In Fig. 6-4, the most frequent result is found to be 14, which agrees with expectations. With four 1-spots, the smallest output value possible is 4.   The largest output would be four 6-spots for a value of 24.   The maximum range of variation is therefore $24 - 4 = 20$.   This is the same as for the data of Fig. 2-15.

The only real difference between the data of Figs. 2-5 and 6-4 is the value of the average result to be expected.   In the first case it is 10 and in the second it is 14.   Otherwise, the form and behavior of the variation of these two sampling distributions are identical.   This is because we are observing the effects of *many random variables occurring simultaneously in an additive manner*. This is the practical origin of the most common statistical distribution, which is known as the normal distribution.

CHAPTER 7

The Normal Distribution Background

The characteristics of the distributions of counts from coin tossing and sums from dice throwing are also the characteristics of the distribution known as the *Gaussian* or *Normal Distribution*. It is first called Gaussian after the German mathematician Gauss, who developed the mathematics of this distribution in order to handle errors which occurred in astronomical observations. The term "normal" was applied later when it was found that this distribution form was widely occurring in natural phenomena and thus came to be considered as the underlying, and therefore *normal,* distribution for variations to be observed in nature. Historically, other early work with this distribution was on such characteristics as height and weight of humans, size and weight of animals, crop yields for different soils and localities, and examination scores of students. Later, applications of statistics to industry and manufacturing showed that many dimensions from machining operations, yields from simple chemical processes, and the behavior of some kinds of product characteristics were also normally distributed. There are many excellent texts which treat the detailed properties and applications of the Normal Distribution. References (11), (12), (15), (17), (19), (23), (35), (36), and (51) list texts which present the normal distribution at varying levels of intensity and from differing points of view.

Today, it is believed that 80 percent of all variables data can be at least approximately represented by the normal distribution function. It is important to remember the conditions under which this distribution will occur: four or more input variables which operate randomly and independently and whose effects combine additively to give an output. These conditions are sometimes referred to as *linear additive processes.*

Description of the Normal Distribution

In Chapter 1, we stated that a probability plot is an approximation of a cumulative distribution function and that a graph of a variable *versus* frequency of occurrence was an approximation of a probability density function. Each type of probability distribution has a specific statement for both the cdf and the pdf. In the case of the Normal Distribution, we have:

Cumulative distribution function

$$F(x) = \frac{1}{(2\pi)^{1/2}} \int_{-\infty}^{z} e^{-\frac{1}{2}v^2}\,dy \qquad (7\text{-}1)$$

Probability density function

$$f(x) = \frac{1}{(2\pi)^{1/2}} e^{-\frac{1}{2}z^2} \qquad (7\text{-}2)$$

where:

$$z = \frac{x - \mu}{\sigma} \qquad (7\text{-}3)$$

x = the observed value of a random variable
μ = the value of the mean
σ = the standard deviation

Mathematical statistics has produced elegant mathematical embellishments for the normal cdf and pdf, but the observations of true importance in relating the results of our earlier experiments to the cdf and pdf are quite simple:

1. The curve for the cdf is shown in Fig. 7-1. This is the ogive which was discussed in Chapter 4 as unattractive to work with.
2. The curve for the pdf is given in Fig. 7-2. This curve is usually called the normal distribution curve. It is bell shaped because more values occur near the middle of the distribution and fewer values occur as one gets further away from the middle.

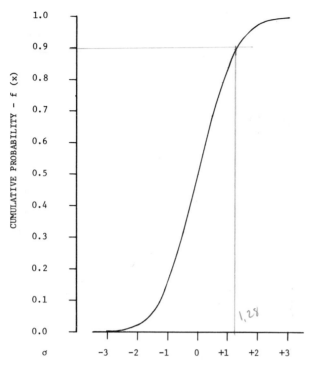

Fig. 7-1.   Normal cumulative distribution curve.

3. The normal density function is symmetrical; that is, it is balanced around its central axis.

4. The central tendency is best quantified by the simple arithmetic average, or *mean,* of

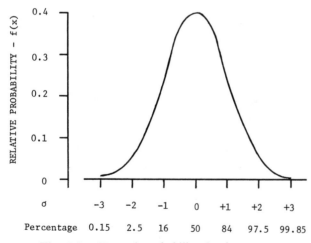

Fig. 7-2.   Normal probability density curve.

the observed values.   In mathematical notation, μ is used to represent an idealized mean.   When we have data from a sample, we conventionally use $\bar{x}$, called *x-bar,* to denote an *estimate* of the mean of the population from which the sample was taken.

5. The spreading out of the pdf, or its *dispersion,* is described numerically by the *variance* which is the simple arithmetic average of the *squared values* of the *deviations,* or differences, of the individual values from the mean.   This value is also called the *mean-square.*   It is symbolized by σ^2, called *sigma-squared.*

6. The dispersion is also often represented by the *standard deviation* which is the *square root of the variance.*   The standard deviation is also called the *root-mean-square* because of its derivation.

7. The standard deviation, symbolized by the Greek letter sigma, σ, is a useful yardstick in summarizing variational behavior of an observed set of data.   That is, if we lay out the value scale of the pdf using standard deviation units, then the area under the curve in Fig. 7-2 between the mean, x, and $\pm 1\sigma$ includes about 68% of all of the observations; $x \pm 2\sigma$ includes 95.5% and $x \pm 3\sigma$ includes 99.73%, or practically all of the values expected to be observed. With sample data, the standard deviation is symbolized by s to represent an estimate.[1]

8. The dummy variable of integration, z, from Equation 7-1 is defined in Equation 7-3; z is also called the *normalized unit variable* because dividing each deviation by the standard deviation is called *normalization* of the data.   This is an example of the statement in (7) that the standard deviation is used as a yardstick.   The util-

[1] *Note:* Due to the behavior of the $\pm 3\sigma$ points, wherein a 6σ span includes virtually all of a distribution, the 6 faces of a die are quite suited for generating random normal functions.   Each face can represent a 1σ interval, using 1 to 6 in sequence.   The sums of face counts of 4 or more dice thrown simultaneously are excellent random normal variables. In addition, the theoretical range of the sums from dice throwing break up nicely according to Sturges' Rule to give good cell endpoint balance.

ity of normalization and the normalized unit variable are discussed in the next section.

Probability Statements Based on the Normal Distribution

The quantity z, defined above, is used as a mathematical convention in integration. The symbol k is more frequently used as a textual symbol in probability and statistics.

From Equation 7-3, k is the number of multiples of the standard deviation by which an observed value departs from the mean; k also represents an area under the curve of the normal density function which is related to some probability of occurrence of some set of values. This is illustrated in the examples below.

Theoretically, k can have any value from $-\infty$ to $+\infty$. As stated in (7), above, most of the values in a Normal Distribution will occur between $\pm 3\sigma$, or in the range: $k = -3$ to $+3$. The subtraction of the mean from values of observed data does not change any of the *statistical properties* of the observed data. Division of the deviations by the standard deviation does not change the statistical properties either, but only serves to *normalize* or *standardize* the data. Consequently, only one standard table of the Normal Distribution is necessary for reference purposes.

Uses of the k Factor

Most texts on statistics include a table of the unit normal variable. This is often called the Table of Areas of the Normal Curve (Distribution) or the Table of the Normal Variable. In addition, many texts and tables use z or x/σ as the symbol, instead of k. Normal tables are usually tabulated as shown in Table 7-1 and used as follows:

Example 7-1
Given: The interval of $x \pm 1.5\sigma$. What is the probability of a value falling within this interval?

Since the normal distribution is symmetrical, we need only to work from the mean to $+1.5$ to obtain half of the answer. Then, if we double this, we have the final answer.

$$\bar{x} = 0.00 \text{ in Table 7-1}$$

For $k = +1.5$, the tabular value is 0.4332 for the area between $\bar{x} = 0.00$ and $k = +1.5$. The probability of occurrence in the interval between 0 and 1.5 is 0.4332. There is also the same area between $\bar{x}$ and $k = -1.5$. Therefore, $0.4332 \times 2 = 0.8664$, which is the cumulative probability between $\pm 1.5\sigma$. This may also be stated in terms of the cumulative percentage as: 86.64% of the expected values will fall between $\bar{x}$ and $\pm 1.5\sigma$ units.

Example 7-2
Given: The interval of $\bar{x} - 3.0\sigma$ to $+0.5\sigma$. What is the probability of a value falling in this interval?

Here, we will solve for a probability where the interval of interest is not symmetrical about the mean.

From $\bar{x} = 0.00$ to $k = -3.0$, we have an area of 0.4986.

From $\bar{x} = 0.00$ to $k = +0.5$, we have an area of 0.1915.

The cumulative probability in this case is $0.4986 + 0.1915 = 0.6901$.

That is, about 69% of the expected values will fall between -3σ and $+0.5\sigma$ around the mean.

Example 7-3
Given: An observed distribution with a mean of 70.5 and a standard deviation of 3.6. Under the conditions of Example 7-2, what values occur between -3.0 and $+0.5$?

Table 7-1. Partial Table of the Unit Normal Variable

k	0.00	0.01	0.02	0.03		
0.0	0.0000	0.0040	0.0080	0.0120	....	
0.5	0.1915	0.1950	0.1985	0.2019	....	
1.0	0.3413	0.3438	0.3461	0.3485	....	
1.5	0.4332	0.4345	0.4357	0.4370	....	
2.0	0.4773	0.4778	0.4783	0.4788	....	
2.5	0.4938	0.4940	0.4941	0.4943	....	
3.0	0.4986	0.4987	0.4987	0.4988	....	0.5000

Step 1. Substitute the observed mean for 0.00.

Step 2. Substitute k times the observed standard deviation.

That is: $(-3.0)(3.6)$ and $(+0.5)(3.6)$, giving -10.8 and $+1.8$ respectively.

Step 3. Add and subtract the k intervals from the mean:

$$70.5 - 10.8 = 59.7$$
$$70.5 + 1.8 = 72.3$$

Step 4. Express as a statement, such as:

The probability of observing values between 59.7 and 72.3 is 0.6901, or,

Observed values will occur between 59.7 and 72.3 about 69% of the time.

One of the direct advantages of using probability papers is that questions such as those in the preceding examples may be answered directly from probability plots. The majority of probability papers have either the cumulative probability or the cumulative percentage points enumerated along the horizontal probability axis. In addition, some papers have the complementary scale, which is the observed cumulative percentage subtracted from 100% along the top horizontal scale. There are also probability papers which have the cumulative probability scale along the bottom horizontal axis and the scale for normal deviates along the top horizontal scale.

The solution of problems such as those in Examples 7-1 through 7-3, by means of probability plots, will be illustrated in Chapter 8.

Simple Calculations for the Normal Distribution

To illustrate some important aspects of the behavior of the normal distribution, it is necessary to employ some simple mathematics.

Example 7-4
Given: The data of Table 2-1, find the mean, variance, and standard deviation for this data.

Figure 7-3 and Table 7-2 show the relationship between a histogram and the calculational procedures for obtaining values of the mean, variance and standard deviation of the normal distribution, from Reference (13).

The value of the observed variable, the sum of heads tossed, is called x. This is entered in Line (a). The number of times that a specific value for heads occurs is the frequency of occurrence, which is called f. This is entered in Line (b).

Next, the product of f and x is obtained for each cell. The fx products are entered in Line (c). The totals for Lines (b) and (c) are obtained. This operation is indicated by use of the symbol, Σ, meaning "the sum of" all of the values pertaining to the variable whose symbol follows. For example, Σf is the sum of all f values; Σfx is the sum of all products of f times x.

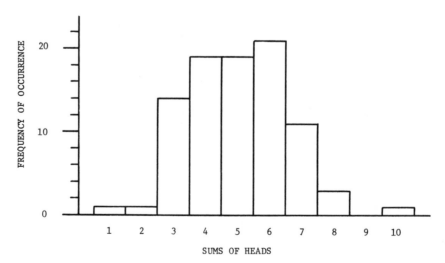

Fig. 7-3. Histogram of sums of heads.

Table 7-2. Calculations for Mean and Standard Deviation. Data from Table 2-1

Line	Entry	Symbol											Total	Symbol
a.	Sum of Heads	x	1	2	3	4	5	6	7	8	9	10		
b.	Frequency of Each Sum	f	1	1	14	19	19	21	11	3	0	1	90	Σf
c.	(a) × (b)	fx	1	2	42	76	95	126	77	24	0	10	453	Σfx
d.	Cell Deviation	d	−4	−3	−2	−1	0	+1	+2	+3	+4	+5		
e.	Squared Deviation	d^2	16	9	4	1	0	1	4	9	16	25		
f.	(b) × (e)	fd^2	16	9	56	19	0	21	44	27	0	25	217	Σfd^2

1. Mean $= \bar{X} = \dfrac{(c)}{(d)} = \dfrac{\Sigma fx}{\Sigma f} = \dfrac{453}{90} = 5.03$; round off to 5

2. Variance $= \sigma^2 = \dfrac{(e)}{(b)} = \dfrac{\Sigma fd^2}{\Sigma f - 1} = \dfrac{217}{90 - 1} = 2.4382$

3. Standard Deviation $= \sigma = \sqrt{\text{Variance}} = \sqrt{2.4382} = 1.56$

Table 7-3. Calculations for Mean and Standard Deviation. Data from Table 2-2

Line	Entry	Symbol														Total	Symbol
a.	Sum	x	5	6	7	8	9	10	11	12	13	14	15	16	17		
b.	Frequency	f	5	3	6	11	8	16	7	14	13	1	2	3	1	90	Σf
c.	(a) × (b)	fx	25	18	42	88	72	160	77	168	169	14	30	48	17	928	Σfx
d.	Deviation	d	−5.3	−4.3	−3.3	−2.3	−1.3	−0.3	+0.7	+1.7	+2.7	+3.7	+4.7	+5.7	+6.7		
e.	d Squared	d^2	28.09	18.49	10.89	5.29	1.69	0.09	0.47	2.89	7.29	13.69	22.09	32.49	44.89		
f.	(b) × (e)	fd^2	140.45	55.47	65.34	58.19	13.52	1.44	3.43	40.46	94.77	13.69	44.18	97.47	44.89	673.30	Σfd^2

1. Mean $= \bar{X} = \dfrac{\Sigma fx}{\Sigma f} = \dfrac{928}{90} = 10.31$; use 10.3

2. Variance $= \sigma^2 = \dfrac{\Sigma fd^2}{\Sigma f - 1} = \dfrac{673.30}{90 - 1} = 7.5652$

3. Standard Deviation $= \sigma = \sqrt{7.5652} = 2.75$

Table 7-4. Calculations for Mean and Standard Deviation. Data from Table 6-1

Symbol																	Total	Symbol
x	6	7	8	9	10	11	12	13	14	15	16	17	18	19	20	21		
f	1	3	1	5	4	7	12	10	14	8	9	7	8	4	5	2	100	Σf
fx	6	21	8	45	40	77	144	130	196	120	144	119	144	76	100	42	1412	Σfx
d	−8.1	−7.1	−6.1	−5.1	−4.1	−3.1	−2.1	−1.1	−0.1	+0.9	+1.9	+2.9	+3.9	+4.9	+5.9	+6.9		
d^2	65.61	50.41	37.21	26.01	16.81	9.61	4.41	1.21	0.01	0.81	3.61	8.41	15.21	24.01	34.81	47.61		
fd^2	65.61	151.23	37.21	130.05	67.24	67.27	52.92	12.10	0.14	6.48	32.49	58.87	121.68	96.04	174.05	95.22	1168.60	Σfd^2

1. Mean $= \bar{X} = \dfrac{\Sigma fx}{\Sigma f} = \dfrac{1412}{100} = 14.12$; use 14.1

2. Variance $= \sigma^2 = \dfrac{\Sigma fd^2}{\Sigma f - 1} = \dfrac{1168.60}{100 - 1} = 11.8041$

3. Standard Deviation $= \sigma = \sqrt{11.8041} = 3.44$

Next, the product of f and x is obtained for each cell. These products are given in Line (c).

The mean $\bar{x}$, is now calculated by dividing Σfx by Σf. This is equivalent to adding all of the individual values and dividing by the number of values. In this example, the mean is 5.03 which may be rounded off to 5. If we now refer to 5 as the zero cell, we count to the left and to the right from zero and obtain the cell deviation, or the number of cell steps away from zero for each remaining cell. Cells with x values less than the mean receive a minus designation and those greater than the mean, a plus designation.

After the deviations, d, are obtained as shown in Line (d), they are then squared as shown in Line (e) to obtain the squared deviations, d^2, from the mean. Then the product of f and d^2 is obtained as shown in Line (f). The sum of these products, Σfd^2 is then determined.

The variance, σ^2, is now calculated by dividing Σfd^2 by $\Sigma f - 1$. This gives the mean-squared-deviation. The value, 1, which is subtracted from Σf, is called the correction for degrees of freedom. Basically, it is a correction for estimating error due to sample size and is increasingly important as sample sizes become smaller. The value of the variance obtained is 2.4382. The standard deviation, σ, is the square root of the variance. For this example, $\sigma = 1.56$.

Using 10 coins, the expected average would be 5. Our data gave a result of 5.03, which is within 1 percent of expectation.

An approximate estimate for the standard deviation would be the maximum expected range $\div$ 6, or $10 - 0 \div 6 = 1.67$. The data of this example give a result of 1.56, which is within 8 percent of this approximation.

Example 7-5
Given: Data of Table 2-2; find the mean, variance, and standard deviation. Table 7-3 shows the procedure and calculations for this example. The one difference is in the determination of cell deviation. The mean was 10.31. To round down to 10 would introduce a 4 percent error in the calculation of the variance. Therefore, the mean is rounded to 10.3 and the cell deviations are taken from this value.

The calculations yield results which are within about 3 percent for the mean and about 17 percent for the standard deviation.

Example 7-6
Given: Data of Table 6-1; find the mean, variance, and standard deviation. Table 7-4 shows the calculations for this example. Here, the mean is within 0.8% of expectation and the standard deviation is within 3%.

In all three examples, we find estimates which agree well with theory. Absolute agreement with theory or between any two samples is not to be expected. Good consistent estimates are the real objective.

The numerical methods used to obtain estimates from these sample distributions demonstrate the behavior of estimates of the mean, variance, and standard deviation of normal distributions. These descriptive statistics are known as *statistical parameters* of the normal distribution. They involve repetitious calculations. Some shortcut methods are given in texts by Grant (19), Monroney (36), and Wallis and Roberts (51). Since this book is not directed to the development of conventional statistical methodology, the reader is referred to the cited texts for proper study of the pertinent statistical theory and methods.

Exercises

7-1. a. Using Table 7-1, what is the probability of a value falling between $\bar{x} \pm 2\sigma$?

b. Express as a statement using cumulative probability.

c. Express as a statement using cumulative percentage.

7-2. a. Using Table 7-1, what is the probability of a value falling between -2.53 and $+1.52$?

b. Express as a statement using cumulative probability.

c. Express as a statement using cumulative percentage.

7-3. a. Using the results of Exercise 7-2, what are the limits for an observed distribution with a mean of 50.2 and a standard deviation of 1.8?

b. Express as a statement using cumulative probability.

c. Express as a statement using cumulative percentage.

7-4. a. Using your own data from Exercise 2-5, compute the mean, variance, and standard deviation for this data.

b. As a class exercise, tabulate on the blackboard the results from each student for the mean, variance, and standard deviation. Compare the results and discuss the origin and meaning of the differences.

7-5. a. Using data from Table 3-1, compute the mean, variance, and standard deviation for each sample.

b. Discuss the difference in results between samples.

7-6. a. Using your own data from Exercise 6-2b, compute the mean, variance, and standard deviation for this data.

b. Compare and discuss these results to theoretical expectations.

c. As a class exercise, tabulate on the blackboard, the results from each student for each parameter. Compare the results and discuss the origin and meaning of the differences.

$$K = \frac{X - \mu}{\sigma}$$

CHAPTER 8

Normal Probability Papers

Data Preparation and Plotting

The requirements for preparing data for further use and for determining the plotting positions for a given set of data are discussed in Chapters 2 through 5. If we now suppose that there is no special reason to prefer any one distribution assumption over another, the first probability paper that we would use to attempt to obtain a straight line fit to a set of data would be the normal probability paper.

Figure 8-1 represents the layout of a normal probability scale as typically used on normal probability papers. The graduations of the cumulative probability or cumulative percentage scale are not uniform. In scanning from left to right, the percentage points are relatively spread out at first, but then they tend to bunch up around the 50% point. Proceeding to the right, the percentage points tend to open up again as the higher percentage values are reached.

The spacing of the lines on normal probability paper is made to correspond to the shape of the normal distribution curve, as shown in Fig. 7-2, where the bulk of the values is found near the center, or mean, of the distribution. Fewer values occur as one moves further away from the mean. The incremental spacing between the percentage lines on normal probability paper is determined by the relative frequency or *density* of the values which would be expected to occur in an ideal normal distribution — see (10). As a consequence of this

spacing, when data from a normal distribution are plotted on normal probability paper, after observing the procedures given in Chapters 2 to 5, the data will fall more or less along a straight line as in Fig. 8-2 and 8-3. These were plotted from the data of Figs. 2-3 and 2-4. Each probability plot is analogous, respectively, to the frequency tally and the histogram. That is, in Fig. 8-2, all of the individual values are plotted as they are tallied in Fig. 2-3. In Fig. 8-3, the values are represented as bars, or ranges of values, in a manner similar to that of Fig. 2-4.

The straight line in each figure has been fitted by eye. In Fig. 8-2, the individual points are essentially divided into an upper and a lower half. In Fig. 8-3, a simpler approach was used. Here the bars were divided in half by use of a ruler, and a mark was made in the middle. The midpoints were then connected by the best-fitting straight line. The first figure was a direct application of Ferrell's method, of (16). The second figure represents a modified, much simpler application of this method. Consider that in the first case it was necessary to calculate 100 plotting positions and to plot 100 points. In the second case, it was necessary to calculate only 15 plotting positions and to plot 15 points plus connecting points of the same value with short straight lines. In determining the position of the straight line for the data, the first case required dividing up 100 points with an associated amount of counting. In the

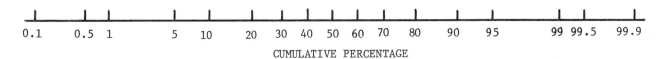

Fig. 8-1. Normal probability scale.

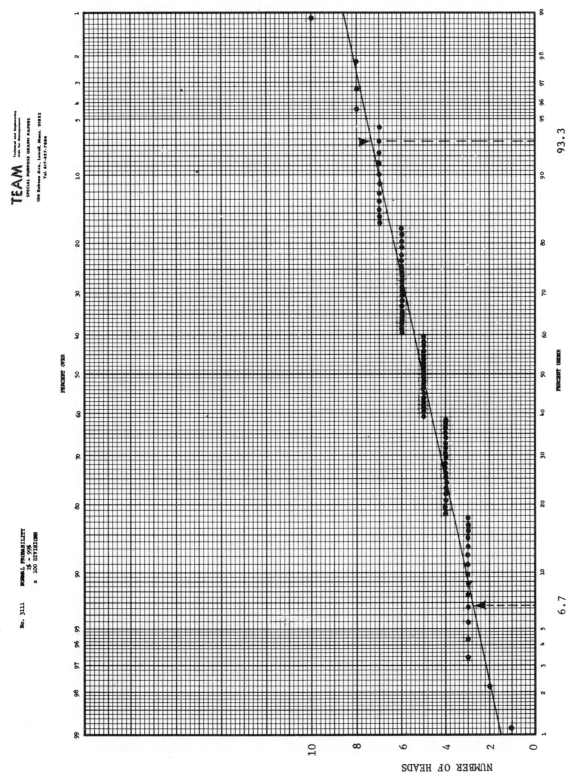

Fig. 8-2.   Probability plot showing individual values of the distribution of heads from 90 tosses of 10 coins.

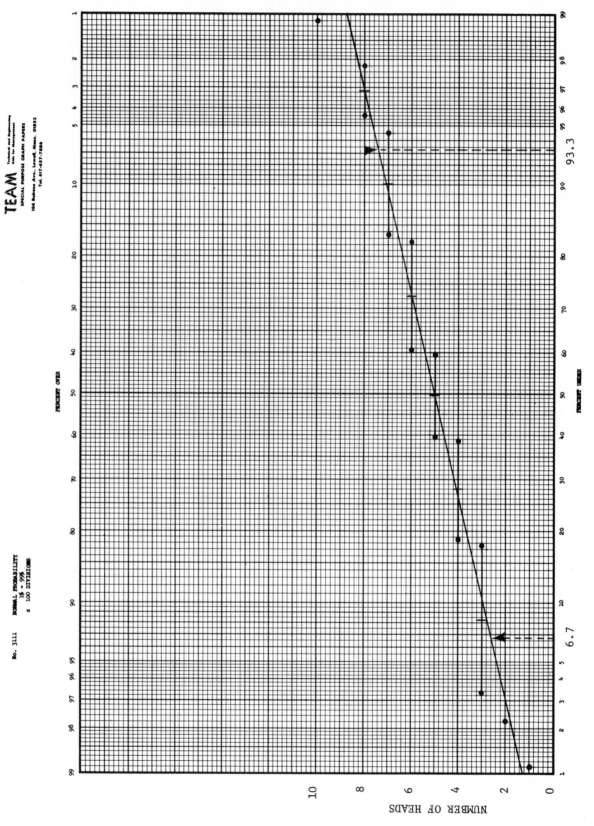

Fig. 8-3. Probability plot showing cell groups of the distribution of heads from 90 tosses of 10 coins.

second case, the straight line had to be fitted only to 9 points. This is a large — approximately 90% — saving in effort.

When one is planning to take data which will be used for probability plots, the choice of certain sample sizes will simplify the calculation of the cumulative percentage plotting and the actual plotting on probability paper. Using the $(n_i \times 100\%) / (n + 1)$ rule, a sample of 9 gives nice, neat, 10 percent increments; 19 gives 5 percent; 24 gives 4 percent; etc.

When a set of data is received with some other value which does not lead to neat plotting units, it is frequently convenient to discard a few readings to obtain the convenience of round number plotting. This may be done by a random selection process for choosing the items to be discarded.

Parameter Estimation from Linear Plots

When the results of plotting a set of data give an acceptable straight line fit, as in Figs. 8-2 and 8-3, it may be assumed that the choice of the normal distribution probability paper for plotting the data was reasonable. The statistical parameters of the distribution may be estimated directly from the probability plot without the need for calculations.

The mean is estimated by taking the value at which the fitted straight line crosses the 50% probability line. In Fig. 8-2, this is at a value of 5.05. In Fig. 8-3, it is at 5.0. The calculated value from Example 7-4 is 5.03, and the theoretical value is known to be 5.0. Over many samplings from this distribution, we would expect our estimates of the mean to vary as much as ±10% for samples of 100. Both of the graphical estimates are within 1.5% of the calculated value. This is small compared with possible sampling variation. It is of particular interest to note that the plotting method used for Fig. 8-3 gave an estimate which is equal to the theoretical expected value.

The standard deviation is estimated by obtaining the values where the fitted straight line intersects the 93.3% and 6.7% probability lines. The smaller value is subtracted from the larger one and this result is divided by 3.

From Fig. 8-2: $\sigma = \dfrac{7.30 - 2.75}{3} = \dfrac{4.55}{3} = 1.52$

From Fig. 8-3: $\sigma = \dfrac{7.40 - 2.60}{3} = \dfrac{4.80}{3} = 1.60$

Here again, the results are interesting. The estimate from Fig. 8-2 is near that obtained by calculation and the result from Fig. 8-3 is nearer that expected on theoretical grounds. The pair of results is less than 5 percent different. The amount of variation to be expected due to sampling error is about 22 percent, so that once again our results are better.

Let us further examine the result that the estimates from Fig. 8-3 are closer to the theoretical values, while results from Fig. 8-2 are closer to the calculated values. This may be explained by the fact that in the calculations and plotting of Fig. 8-2, there is equal weight given to each individual value due to the process of dividing the points into two equal groups. If a few values are somewhat out of line due to sampling variation, this will be reflected in both the calculations and the estimates based on plots of individual values. On the other hand, Fig. 8-3 uses the midpoints of the percentage intervals for each value and so there is little or no influence from a few stray values. As a result, the characteristics of the underlying distribution are more likely to be determined. This is analogous to the method of centroids used to determine the center of gravity of complex shapes in physics.

The methods employed in Fig. 8-3 overcome much of the concern expressed by many authors about the accuracy and validity of graphical estimates of statistical parameters. Reference (2) contains a discussion of experiments conducted on graphical versus calculated estimates of distribution parameters. The referenced results appear to show graphical methods as inferior. However, the experiments cited in Reference (2) may be faulted for a lack of good consistent procedures for preparing data, making probability plots, and fitting straight lines.

The use of Sturges' Rule for grouping data tends to standardize and to simplify the preparation and use of probability plots even further. Figures 8-4

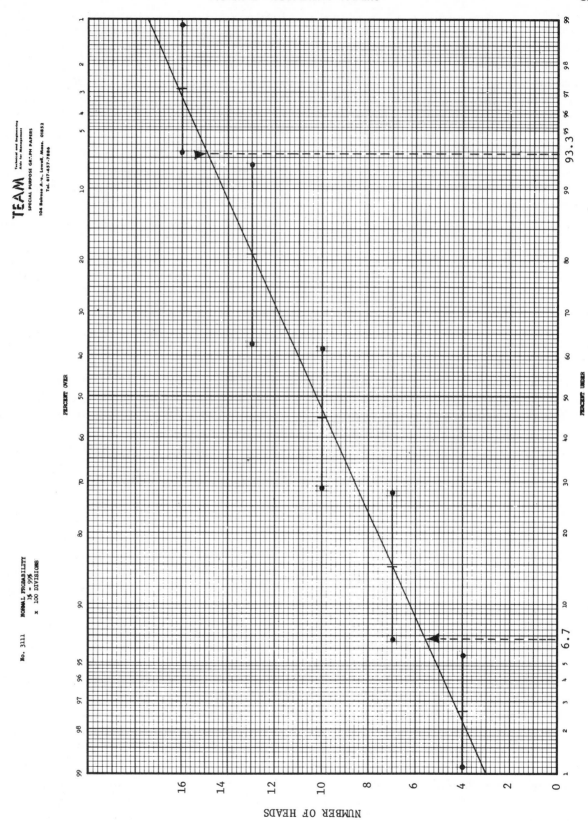

Fig. 8-4.   Probability plot showing cell groups of the distribution of heads from 90 tosses of 20 coins.

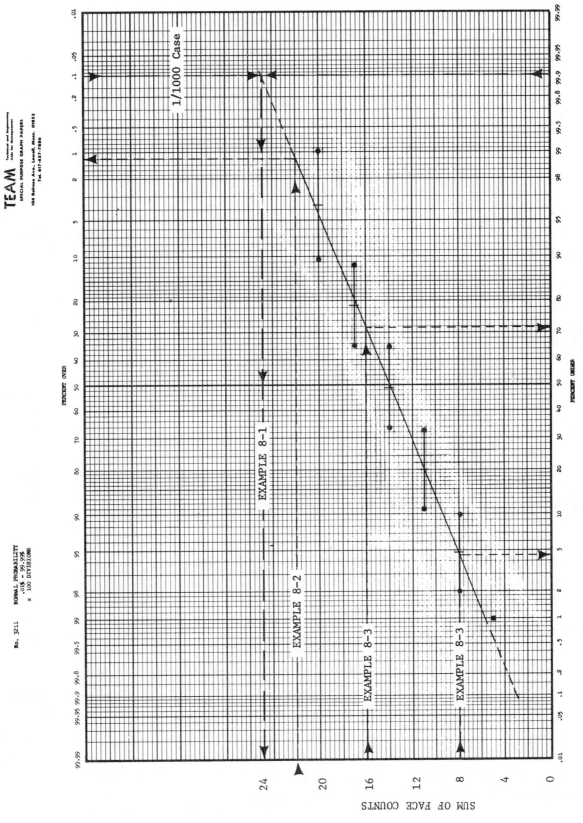

Fig. 8-5.   Probability plot showing cell groups of the distribution of the sums of face counts from 100 throws of 4 dice.

and 8-5 are taken directly from Figs. 2-6 and 6-4. The estimates obtained are compared to the results of Examples 7-2 and 7-3 and to the theoretical expected results.

From Fig. 8-4:

Mean = 10.25, compared to 10.31 and 10.0
σ = 3.10, compared to 2.75 and 3.33

From Fig. 8-5:

Mean = 14.0, compared to 14.12 and 14.0
σ = 3.10, compared to 3.44 and 3.33

The graphical estimates turn out to be closer to the theoretical values than are the calculated estimates in 5 out of 6 cases. In order to obtain maximum benefits from using the procedures such as in Figs. 8-4 and 8-5 to obtain good graphical parameter estimates, the plotting and line-fitting should be done carefully and neatly with sharp pencils or fine pens.

Further Uses of Linear Plots

On the basis of a sample size of 100 items, the fitted line is often considered to be valid only over the range of 1% to 99% of the underlying distribution. However, a frequent problem which arises is to derive estimates of the likely behavior of the variable of interest *outside* the range of observed data. This is done by extrapolation of the observed data into areas which have not been directly observed.

Example 8-1

Based on the plot of Fig. 8-5, what is the largest value which might be expected, or exceeded, on the average, in a batch of 1000 items? This is the 1 in 1000 chance. On the bottom horizontal probability scale of most probability papers, this is the 99.9 percentile. Some probability papers also have the complementary scale across the top of the grid. In such cases, the complement of the 99.9 percentile would be 100.0 − 99.9, or the 0.1 percentile. This is the percentage representation of the 1/1000 case. In Fig. 8-5, this value is obtained by projecting down from the top scale to the fitted line and then left to the scale of the observed variable. The value so obtained is 24.45.

Example 8-2

The alternative question is: What percentage of the distribution, over the long haul, will exceed some specific value? For instance, what is the likelihood of exceeding 22? This is determined by projecting from 22 on the value scale to the fitted line and then projecting vertically to the complementary scale. This indicates that 22 will be exceeded only 1.2% of the time.

In Chapter 7, Examples 7-1 through 7-3, we were concerned with the problem of determining the probability of the occurrence of some value between two limiting values. To obtain the answers, we were required to use *k,* the normal unit variate, and to perform calculations involving the observed standard deviation and tables of the unit variate. In the case where we have probability plots these questions can be answered very directly and rapidly.

Example 8-3

Again referring to Fig. 8-5, what is the probability of obtaining a value between 8 and 16? The answer is determined by projecting to the right from 8 and 16 to the fitted line and then projecting downward to the bottom scale. This yields percentile values of 4.5% and 71.5%. Subtracting the smaller from the larger gives the answer. 71.5% − 4.5% = 67%; that is, 67% of the expected values will fall between 8 and 16.

Sources of Variation in Data

Proper evaluation of data using any statistical method requires careful consideration of the sources of the variation which can occur in observed data. The principal sources of variation are two. The first source is called *random variation, random error, sampling error,* or *statistical variation.* This is the "natural" variation which occurs in data from a common source. Figures 2-3, 2-5, 4-1, 6-4, and 7-3 are all examples of data containing random variation. The amount of random variation in data influences the precision with which estimates of the distribution parameters can be made. The more variation that there is in data, the less precise are the estimates. Random variation as it affects parameter estimation has well-defined methods of analytical treatment. See (11), (12), (15), (17), (19), (23), (36), and (51).

The second principal variety of variation is called *nonrandom error, nonsampling error, error,* or *statistical noise.* This is "unnatural" variation and occurs for a variety of causes. Nonrandom error can be classified into two broad categories: (1) *Systematic* or *structured error,* and (2) *Nonsystematic, intermittent,* or *nonstructured error.*

Systematic error was illustrated in Figs. 5-8 and 5-11 for the mixed output of two or more machines producing the same nominal output. Similar results are obtained from poor calibration practices for measurement equipment and instrumentation, poor test methods and procedures, or bias of measurements or machine settings. Systematic error is an unplanned for difference between things which are easily assumed to be the same: personnel, machines, instruments, etc. Systematic error is relatively easy to detect, to identify, and to correct.

Nonsystematic error has more variety than systematic error. Figures 5-5 and 5-7 illustrate the change in an initial distribution due to inspection. The amount of change would differ from one batch to the next. Figure 9-9 shows how a limitation in measurement sensitivity affected one set of data. Figures 9-10 and 9-11 show a difference in measured results due to differences in ambient conditions at two different times of measurement. Example 3-8, however, shows the effect of a human blunder.

Nonrandom error will affect estimates of statistical parameters in an indeterminate way. Analytical methods to cope with nonsampling error have not received definitive treatment in the statistical literature. This is unfortunate because the extent and impact of nonsampling error is far greater than most people suspect. Investigation by the author indicates that 30 percent or more of industrial data contain errors large enough to lead to incorrect decisions.

Dr. J. W. Tukey of Princeton University, one of the foremost mathematical statisticians living today, has also expressed concern regarding the lack of concern and techniques for treating non-random variation (50). He predicted the emergence of

simple step-wise data analysis techniques which can be assembled into progressively more complex analytical systems. The step-wise techniques would emphasize graphical data presentation to obtain maximum insight with minimum effort through the visual impact of graphs.

A useful by-product of probability graphs results from the recognizable patterns, as discussed above, which represent specific kinds of nonrandom error. When such error exists, the detection of the error is more important than numerical statistical analysis because valid estimates of statistical parameters can only be made when no more than random variation is present. Therefore, graphical analysis is a valuable first step in a sensibly organized analytical program, as is illustrated in the flow chart of Fig. 1-2.

The Use of Confidence Intervals

The terminology of "Confidence Intervals" is misleading to the nonstatistically oriented for semantic reasons. The statistician talks about "confidence" of an estimate based on specific observed data. However, the statistician too often assumes that the data are completely valid; that is, that they do not contain any nonsampling errors, only random sampling errors. However, due to the frequency of real nonsampling errors which occur in much observed data, the technical interpretation more often is that a confidence interval is really a measure of the *factor of ignorance* in the determination of distribution behavior through the analysis of observed data. A confidence interval is more correctly the degree of uncertainty which exists about any statistical estimate. One of the truly beautiful aspects of the objective use of statistics is that one can calculate such an existing uncertainty rather well, subject to only minimal constraints, provided that only random error is present in the data.

The topic of confidence intervals for the numerical estimates of specific parameters is extensively covered in (11), (17), (19), (35), (36), and (51). The topic of confidence intervals around a regression line is less extensively covered in (14), (23), and (35). The use of confidence intervals for probability plots for the normal distribution is not well developed and so will be developed below.

The confidence interval for a line fitted to a set of data should be visualized as a region within which the "true" line may really lie. Alternatively, a confidence interval may be considered as the region within which some specified percentage of additional samples from the same stable source will result in fitted lines falling within the boundaries of this region.

From this standpoint, we can then conceive of a *distribution of lines* which is analogous to the distributions of points which we have been considering heretofore. In Chapter 7, we considered the interval $\bar{x} \pm k\sigma$ within which some percentage of observed values was expected to fall. The confidence interval for a fitted line may readily be considered as an area around a fitted line within which some percentage of future lines are expected to fall. This may be symbolized as:

$$y = \bar{L} \pm k_1 s_y \qquad (8\text{-}1)$$

where $\bar{L}$ is the mean position of the fitted line at some selected percentage point. In the case of a single fitted line, $\bar{L}$ will be the observed value of the line at that point.

The multiplier k_1 is similar to k except that it is dependent on sample size. Values for k_1 are given in Appendix, Table A-2, which is based on a confidence interval of 95 percent.

The standard error of estimate of the line is s_y, which is directly analogous to σ for a single sample or distribution. It may also be considered as the amount of vertical error or uncertainty above and below the fitted line at a specified percentage point, because over a number of samples there will be a sampling distribution of estimates of the value of $\bar{L}$ at the specified percentile. An estimate of the dispersion of that estimate at that point will be $k_1 s_y$.

To derive s_y from the standard deviation of the observed distribution, proceed as follows — (This development is based on paragraph 17.3.3 of Reference [51]):

$$s_y = s_{y \cdot x} \sqrt{\frac{1}{n} + \frac{k^2}{n-1}} \qquad (8\text{-}2)$$

where $s_{y \cdot x}$ is the estimated standard deviation from the plotted data and the fitted line as obtained by methods given in a previous section.

n is the sample size of the observed data.

k is the k factor discussed in Chapter 7 for some specified percentage or probability point.

Determination of the confidence interval may be simplified by standardizing certain numerical requirements. Due to variations between samples, $s_{y \cdot x}$ and n will always be different. However, the chosen values of k, corresponding to pre-selected percentiles, may be used repeatedly for all samples. Recommended values of k and the associated values of k^2 are given in the Appendix, Table A-3.

Additional simplification is achieved by use of Appendix Table A-4, which tabulates the solution of $k_1 \sqrt{\dfrac{1}{n} + \dfrac{k^2}{n-1}}$ for a wide variety of sample sizes and the recommended values for k. Values for sample sizes not tabulated may be obtained by linear interpolation between the given values.

The procedure for determining confidence intervals, using Appendix Table A-4, is as follows:

Step 1. Obtain the estimate for the sample standard deviation, $s_{y \cdot x}$, from the fitted line as shown in a previous section.

Step 2. Multiply $s_{y \cdot x}$ by the factors from Appendix, Table A-4, for the selected percentage points. This will result in a set of values which may be used as offsets above and below the fitted line at the selected percentiles. Connecting the offset points will establish the region within which subsequent lines are expected to fall.

The offsets about the fitted line are similar to the $k\sigma$ intervals about the mean which were discussed in Chapter 7.

Step 3. From the fitted line, estimate the intercept of the line with the pre-selected percentile.

Step 4. Add and subtract the offset values obtained in Step 2 from the values obtained in Step 3.

Step 5. Plot the values from Step 4 as points on the probability plot at the proper percentile points.

Step 6. Connect the points from Step 5, using a French curve to obtain a smooth-fitting line.

Step 7. Since Appendix Table A-4 is based on 95% confidence, the confidence interval derived in Steps 1–7 should enclose 95% of the plotted points. If 95 percent or more of plotted points lie within the confidence interval, the choice of normal probability paper for such a plot may be assumed to be reasonable. It may also be expected that 95 percent of subsequent lines from samples representing the same underlying source of variation will also fall within this interval.

Example 8-4
Given: The data of Fig. 6-4 for sums of tosses of 4 dice. This data is shown for specific observed totals without use of Sturges' Rule in Fig. 8-6.

Step 1. The fitted line gives an estimate for $s_{y \cdot x}$ of $(19.25 - 8.8)/3 = 10.45/3 = 3.48$.

Step 2. Since the sample size is 100, use preselected percentiles of 50%, 30 and 70%, 10 and 90%, 5 and 95%, and 1 and 99%. From Appendix Table A-4, obtain the multipliers for $s_{y \cdot x}$ by linear interpolation and complete the indicated multiplication:

50	$0.196 \times 3.48 = 0.682$, use 0.7
30-70	$0.221 \times 3.48 = 0.769$, use 0.8
10-90	$0.319 \times 3.48 = 1.110$, use 1.1
5-95	$0.378 \times 3.48 = 1.315$, use 1.3
1-99	$0.498 \times 3.48 = 1.733$, use 1.7

Step 3 and Step 4. From Fig. 8-6, the intercepts of the preselected percentiles, the offsets and intervals are:

1	$6.1 \pm 1.7 =$	4.4 to 7.8
5	$8.4 \pm 1.3 =$	7.1 to 9.7
10	$9.7 \pm 1.1 =$	8.6 to 10.8
30	$12.2 \pm 0.8 =$	11.4 to 13.0
50	$14.1 \pm 0.7 =$	13.4 to 14.8
70	$15.9 \pm 0.8 =$	15.1 to 16.7
90	$18.5 \pm 1.1 =$	17.4 to 19.6
95	$19.7 \pm 1.3 =$	18.4 to 21.0
99	$22.1 \pm 1.7 =$	20.4 to 23.8

Step 5 and Step 6. The resultant offset points and a smooth curve through the points are shown in Fig. 8-6.

Step 7. All of the individual points fall within the confidence interval. If no more than 5% of 100 points, or 5 points, were outside the interval, we accept the fitted line and the confidence interval as valid because the interval is based on 95% confidence. The confidence interval must be modified when Sturges' Rule is used to group data and to prepare probability plots. The modification is required to allow for the bunching up at the value of the central point of a cell when we plot the bar representing that cell. The effect of such grouping is easily compensated for by multiplying the offset values as obtained in Step 2 above by the square root of the number of units per cell actually used to group the data.

Example 8-5
Given: The data of Fig. 6-4, grouped by Sturges' Rule into 7 cells of 3 units each. Determine the confidence interval.

Step 1. $s_{y \cdot x} = 3.67$

Step 2. Use the values from Table A-4 as in Example 8-4.

50	$0.196 \times \sqrt{3} \times 3.67 = 1.2$
30-70	$0.221 \times \sqrt{3} \times 3.67 = 1.4$
10-90	$0.319 \times \sqrt{3} \times 3.67 = 2.0$
5-95	$0.378 \times \sqrt{3} \times 3.67 = 2.4$
1-99	$0.498 \times \sqrt{3} \times 3.67 = 3.2$

Step 3 and Step 4.

1	$5.6 \pm 3.2 =$	2.4 to 8.8
5	$8.1 \pm 2.4 =$	5.7 to 10.5
10	$9.4 \pm 2.0 =$	7.4 to 11.4
30	$12.1 \pm 1.4 =$	10.7 to 13.5
50	$14.1 \pm 1.2 =$	12.9 to 15.3
70	$15.9 \pm 1.4 =$	14.5 to 17.3
90	$18.7 \pm 2.0 =$	16.7 to 20.7
95	$20.1 \pm 2.4 =$	17.7 to 22.5
99	$22.6 \pm 3.2 =$	19.4 or 25.8

Step 5 and Step 6. The offsets and smooth curve are shown in Fig. 8-7.

Step 7. Three or four points at the ends of two bars fall outside the confidence interval, therefore we will accept the fitted line and the grouping at the 95% confidence level.

An interesting class of questions can be answered easily with probability plots and confidence

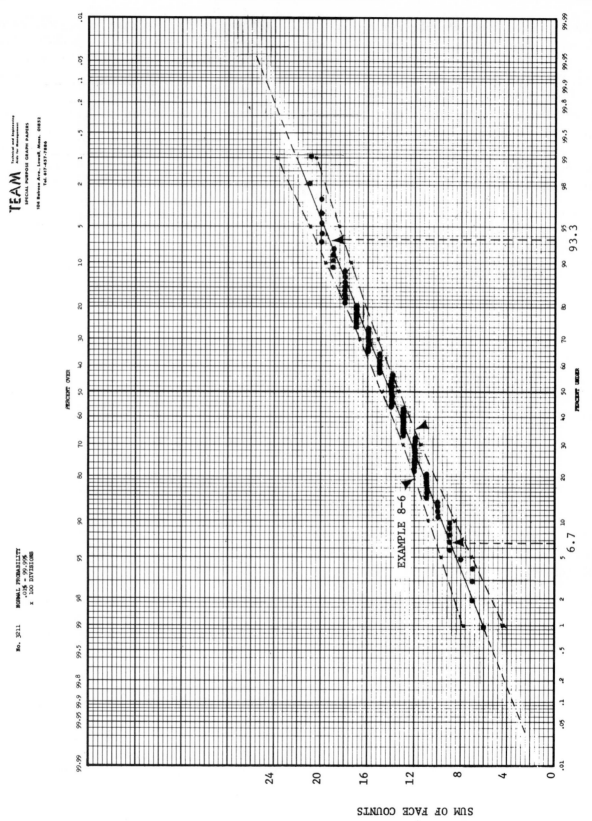

Fig. 8-6.   Probability plot showing individual values of the distribution of sums of face counts from 100 throws of 4 dice.

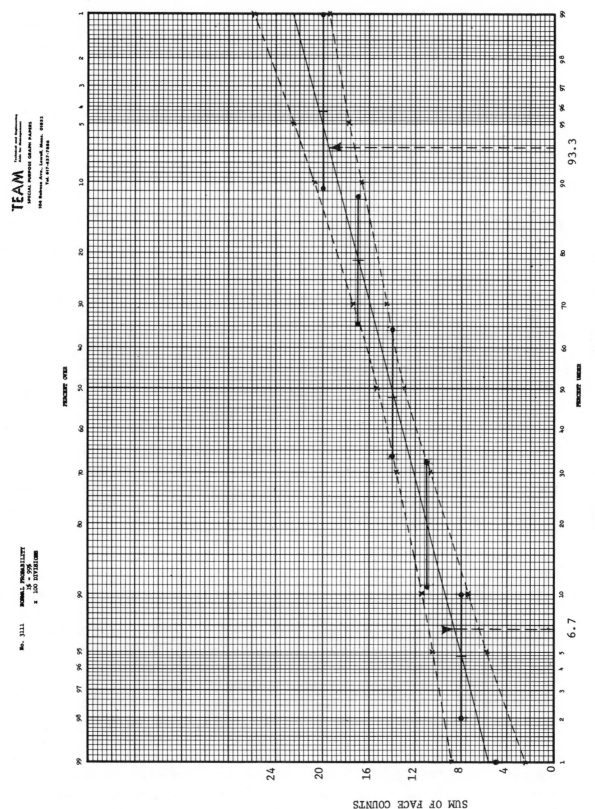

Fig. 8-7. Probability plot showing cell groups for the distribution of sums of face counts from 100 throws of 4 dice.

intervals. These are questions as to what frequency, or how often, is some particular value likely to be observed? To answer this, project horizontally from the value of interest across the confidence interval at that point and take the difference of the probability or percentage values at either side of the horizontal section of the interval.

Example 8-6
Given: The plot of Fig. 8-6. Over what percentage range of a sample is the value of 12 likely to occur?

Projecting from 12 on the left scale, we obtain intercepts at the confidence interval of 19.3% and 33.7%. 33.7 − 19.3 = 14.4%. Therefore, about 95% of the time, the value 12 will not exceed 14.4% of the sample values.

The advantage of probability plots with confidence intervals is that questions such as in Example 8-6 may be answered in almost infinite variety from a single probability plot without recourse to any additional calculations or reference to any tables.

Summary

Probability plots are obtained in the following steps:

1. Arrange the data in ascending order from the smallest value to the largest value.
2. When data are to be grouped, use Sturges' Rule to determine the number of cells to be used.
3. Determine the cell endpoints. Do not allow any overlap.
4. Obtain the values of the cumulative percentage-plotting using $(n_i \times 100\%) / (n + 1)$. Use Appendix Table A-1, where applicable.
5. Plot the individual points when all the data is used.
6. Plot the cell endpoints when grouped data is used and connect the pairs of endpoints by a straight line. Make a mark in the middle of the lines connecting the endpoints.

7. Divide the individual points into an upper half and a lower half using Ferrell's Method.
8. Divide the midpoints of the lines connecting the cell endpoints into an upper and a lower half using Ferrell's Method.
9. Draw in the best-fit line.

Evaluate the probability plot on the following points:

10. Is the best-fit line a reasonable fit to all of the data?
11. Do the plotted points indicate non-linearity or curvature?

Based on the results of (10) and (11), proceed as follows:

12. If (10), use the plot to obtain any desired statistical parameters.
13. If nonlinearity exists, review the source of the data to discover the causes of nonlinearity and eliminate the causes, if possible.
14. If curvature exists, review the assumptions underlying the process generating the data. Use of the normal distribution may not be correct and another distribution may be necessary to represent the data.

Exercises

8-1. Using the data from the frequency tally of Exercise 2-4, make probability plots similar to Figs. 8-2 and 8-3. Delete the last value to simplify the determination of cumulative percentage-plotting and the probability plot.

8-2. Estimate the mean and standard deviation from each plot made for Exercise 8-1.

8-3. Using the data from the frequency tally of Exercise 2-6, make probability plots similar to Figs. 8-2 and 8-3. Delete the last value of these data in order to simplify subsequent procedures.

8-4. Estimate the mean and standard deviation from each plot made for Exercise 8-3.

8-5. Compare the estimates of parameters for Exercises 8-2 and 8-4 to each other and to the theoretical values for each situation.

8-6. Using your data for Exercise 2-4, prepare a probability plot.

    a. Estimate the mean and standard deviation from the plot.

    b. Determine the confidence interval for the fitted line.

    c. Extrapolate and estimate the probable value of the 1/1000 occurrence.

    d. State the range of values within which the 1/1000 value could occur with 95% confidence based on these data.

8-7. As a class exercise, compare the estimates for the mean, standard deviation, 1/1000 value, and the 95% Confidence Interval. Discuss the meaning of differences which occur.

8-8. Using your data for Exercise 2-6, prepare a probability plot and do (a), (b), (c), and (d) as in Exercise 8-6.

8-9. Using the results of Exercise 8-8, compare the estimates as in Exercise 8-7 as a class exercise.

CHAPTER 9

The Logarithmic Normal Distribution

Introduction

The logarithmic normal distribution has had a confusing existence because of the varied nomenclature used to refer to it in statistical literature. It has been called the Galton-McAlister, Kapteyn, and Gibrat Distributions. Work on development of this distribution has been sporadic and scattered. Hald gives an excellent development in (23). However, Aitchison and Brown (2) make the first serious attempt to organize and to correlate existing knowledge of this distribution into a comprehensive structure. This reference is highly recommended for serious workers in modern data analysis because it covers an extremely wide range of applications.

Description of the Log-Normal Distribution

The cumulative distribution function and the probability density function for the log-normal distribution are derived in a manner similar to the corresponding functions of the normal distribution.

Cumulative distribution function:

$$P(x) = \frac{1}{(2\pi)^{1/2}} \int_{-\infty}^{f(u)} e^{-\frac{1}{2}u^2} du \qquad (9\text{-}1)$$

Probability density function:

$$p(x) = \frac{1}{(2\pi)^{1/2}} e^{-\frac{1}{2}[f(u)]^2} \qquad (9\text{-}2)$$

where:

$$f(u) = \frac{\log x - \mu_l}{\sigma_l} \qquad (9\text{-}3)$$

x = the value of the random variable.
μ_l = the mean of the *logarithms* of the variable x.
σ_l = the standard deviation of the *logarithms* of x.

The log-normal cdf looks the same as Fig. 7-1 when $f(u)$ is substituted for z, and so does the pdf. The pdf emphasizes that the logarithms of the variable x are normally distributed. Converting all of the values for x into logarithms is laborious. Ferrell (16) developed some useful relationships for the log-normal distribution which simplify its applications and facilitate the interpretation and analysis of log-normal probability plots.

Let $\tilde{x}$ = the 50th percentile, *median*, of the distribution of $\tilde{x}$.

Then $\log \tilde{x}$ is a valid estimate for μ_l, the mean of the logarithms of the x's.

Then g = the *geometric dispersion*, the antilogarithm of σ_l.

Now $f(u)$ is the normalized variate for the log-normal distribution in logarithmic terms and is numerically equal to k for the normal distribution.

Substituting $\log \tilde{x}$ for μ_l and $\log g$ for σ_l, we obtain:

$$k = \frac{\log x - \log \tilde{x}}{\log g} \qquad (9\text{-}4)$$

Transposing and taking antilogarithms, we obtain:

$$x = \tilde{x} \cdot g^k \qquad (9\text{-}5)$$

Equation 9-4 states that the variable, x, equals the median multiplied by the geometric dispersion raised to a power representing the probability of occurrence. The equivalent statement for the normal distribution is $x = \tilde{x} \pm k\sigma$. The operation of addition, represented by $+$, is replaced by multiplication ($\cdot$). The multiplication of σ by k is replaced by using k as an exponent for g; that is, raising to a power. The implications of these changes in relationships is developed in the next section.

Comparison of the Log-Normal Distribution to the Normal Distribution

In Chapter 6, we derived the normal distribution by adding random variables taken from a uniform distribution. If we now *multiply* random variables

Table 9-1. Products of Face Counts from Tosses of Four Dice (Raw Data Given in Table 6-1)

108	45	432	36	18	375	144	150	96	90
200	240	24	96	64	300	16	72	5	12
384	60	36	360	120	576	48	480	8	8
54	360	360	40	32	48	6	300	300	54
90	120	108	75	720	48	100	20	600	50
600	60	576	125	200	240	24	540	120	240
72	216	225	192	18	6	480	288	24	320
96	216	375	48	144	216	24	60	60	192
120	48	40	36	96	20	80	144	54	40
75	60	4	30	30	36	60	24	80	480

instead of *adding* them, the results are completely different.   Table 9-1 lists the products of the values of the dice throws which are given in Table 6-1.   The products are shown as a conventional histogram in Fig. 9-1.

Figure 9-1 is bunched up around the low values and has a long, thin tail out towards the high values.   It is possible to rearrange this data to allow for the operation of multiplication which was used to generate it.   When we determined cells for the additive processes, we divided the range into equal cell intervals to cover the range of the observed data.   In order to allow for the multiplication which we have performed, we now divide the range of the data into cells which have equal *ratios*.

Figure 9-2 is obtained by setting intervals on the basis of the ratio of the largest and smallest observed values, $720/4 = 180$.   This is directly comparable to taking the range as in Chapter 3.   Since we desire 8 cells, this is accomplished directly by taking the eighth root of 180.   This is easily done by dividing the logarithm of 180 by 8 and taking the antilogarithm to obtain the *cell ratio*.

Example 9-1

Largest value = 720, smallest value = 4.   Obtain 8 cells.

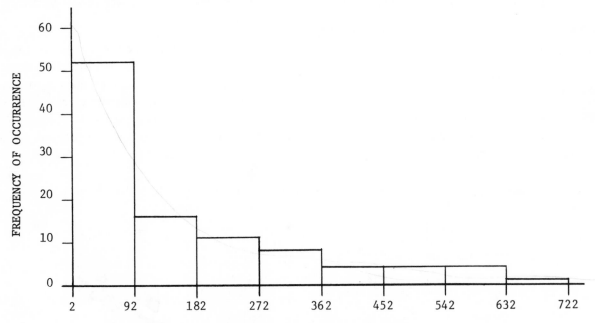

Fig. 9-1.   Value of products of random variables.

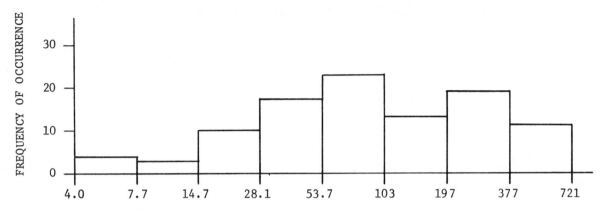

Fig. 9-2. Grouping of products using the range of observed data.

$$\frac{720}{4} = 180$$

Logarithm of 180 = 2.255273

2.255273 ÷ 8 = 0.281909

Antilogarithm = 1.9138 = Cell Ratio.

Smallest value = 4 = low end of first cell.

$$4 \times 1.9138 = 7.6552$$

Use 7.6 for end of first cell and 7.7 for start of second cell.

Then, 7.6552 × 1.9138 = 14.6512

Use 14.6 for end of second cell and 14.7 for start of third cell.

This results in cell intervals of 4.0-7.6; 7.7-14.6; 14.7-28.0; 28.1-53.6; 53.7-102; 103-196; 197-376; 377-720.

The face-count data of Table 9-1 are now classified according to the cell ratios and the results are shown in the histogram of Fig. 9-2.

Example 9-2

An alternative method is to work directly in logarithms.

Logarithm 720 − Logarithm 4 = Logarithmic Range

2.857332 − 0.602060 = 2.255272

2.255272 ÷ 8 = 0.281909 = Cell Ratio.

The value 0.281909 is the same as obtained in Example 9-1. In this case, starting with the value of Logarithm 4 and adding 0.281909 successively, the cell boundaries are obtained in logarithms. Taking antilogarithms gives the results in the original number scale.

The advantage of this method is that it is similar to the method used for the Normal Distribution except for the necessary conversions into logarithms and back again. Sample calculations are shown in Table 9-2. The values of antilogarithms rounded slightly up or down correspond to the values obtained in Example 9-1 by multiplication.

Table 9-2. Calculations to Obtain Cell Boundaries Using Logarithms (Log [Cell Lower Bound] + Log [Cell Ratio] = Log [Cell Upper Bound])

Log Lower Bound		Log Cell Ratio		Log Upper Bound	Antilogarithm
0.602060	+	0.281909	=	0.883969	7.655
0.883969	+	0.281909	=	1.165878	14.65
1.165878	+	0.281909	=	1.447787	28.04
1.447787	+	0.281909	=	1.729696	53.66
1.729696	+	0.281909	=	2.011605	102.7
2.011605	+	0.281909	=	2.293514	196.6
2.293514	+	0.281909	=	2.575423	376.2
2.575423	+	0.281909	=	2.857332	720.0

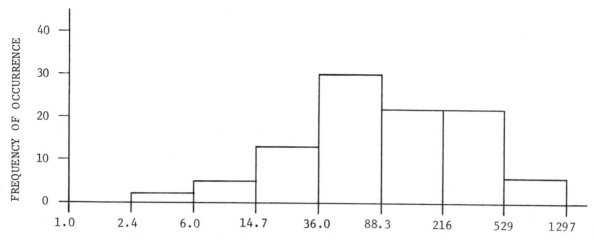

Fig. 9-3.　Grouping of products using the range of theoretical data.

Figure 9-3 is obtained by setting the cell ratios on the basis of the largest and smallest *theoretical* values which could occur.　The product of four 6's is 1296 and four 1's is 1.　This is similar to the choice of cell intervals used for Fig. 2-6.

The histograms of Figs. 9-2 and 9-3 now have similarity to those in Chapter 2.　In contrast to Fig. 9-1, there is now some central tendency and symmetry.　The difference between Figs. 9-2 and 9-3 is similar to distortions caused by improper balancing of cell endpoints as discussed in Chapter 3.　However, this distortion is due to statistical fluctuations caused by the much larger range of the number scale for the products of the random variables.　The number scale range for products is more than 60 times greater than the range for sums of random variables.

Consider another example.　The values from tosses of dice, in Table 6-1, are taken in order. The first is *divided* by the second and the third

is *divided* by the fourth, or $X_1/X_2 = R_1$ and $X_3/X_4 = R_2$.　Then, R_1 is *divided* by R_2.　These results are given in Table 9-3.

Figure 9-4 is another conventional histogram. These results appear to be even more bunched up at the low end than those of Fig. 9-1.　Again we use ratios or logarithms to obtain cell intervals which lead to Figs. 9-5 and 9-6 for the observed and theoretical ranges.　Here the features of central tendency and symmetry are more obvious than in Figs. 9-2 and 9-3.

These examples demonstrate that multiplication and division of random variables create a new kind of distribution behavior.　Remember that division is only the mathematical inverse of multiplication. Then, the relationship of multiplication and division processes for the log-normal distribution to the additive processes which lead to the normal distribution is simple.　Multiplication and division substitute directly for addition and subtraction.

Table 9-3. Quotients of Face Counts from Tosses of Four Dice　(Raw Data Given in Table 6-1)

.75	1.8	1.33	4.00	.45	1.67	1.00	1.50	.12	10.00
.50	1.2	.67	.17	4.00	.48	1.00	.22	.20	.75
.67	.42	.25	.90	1.20	.44	.25	.83	.12	.25
6.00	2.50	2.40	2.50	.12	3.00	6.00	.48	3.00	1.50
10.00	3.33	12.00	2.50	1.24	.33	1.00	20.00	1.04	.50
1.50	.28	1.00	5.00	.50	.27	.50	.60	.83	.42
.22	.67	.36	.75	.22	.67	.83	2.00	2.67	.80
2.68	1.50	.60	.08	1.00	.38	1.50	.42	.60	.33
.84	12.00	.40	.11	.67	.05	1.25	.25	.67	.10
.12	.28	1.00	.13	1.20	.11	.15	.67	5.00	.56

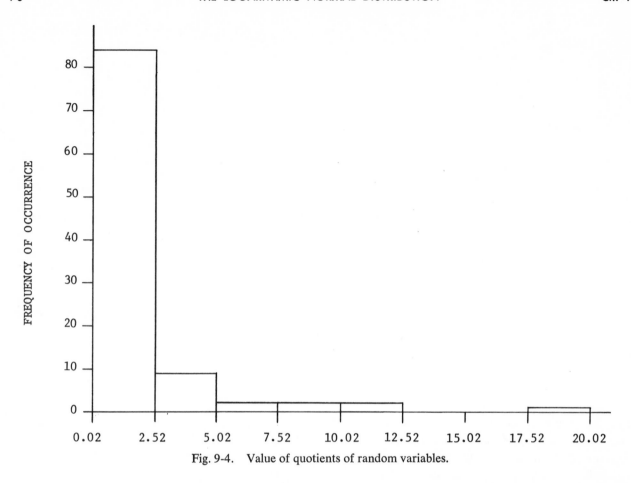

Fig. 9-4.   Value of quotients of random variables.

Example 9-2 illustrates that with the substitution of logarithms, all of the operations for preparing data for graphical presentation can be carried out as for the normal distribution.   As a result, this kind of distribution is called the logarithmic normal, or log-normal, distribution.

The more conventional method of describing the log-normal distribution is by stating that the logarithms of the observed variables are normally distributed.   Consequently, the conventional method of handling such data is to convert all of the data into logarithms prior to performing any other op-

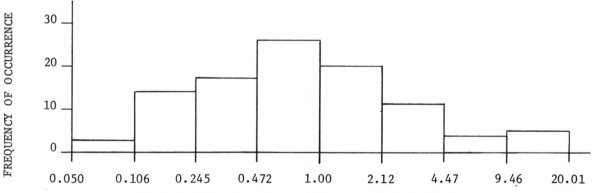

Fig. 9-5.   Value of quotients using the range of observed data.

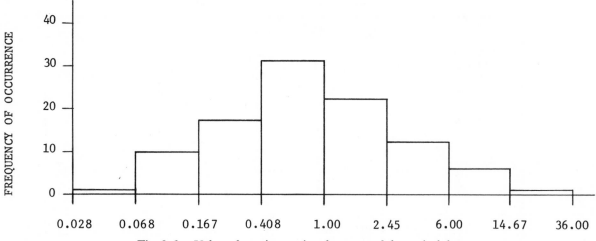

Fig. 9-6. Value of quotients using the range of theoretical data.

erations. However, the procedures given above lead directly to useful histograms without such extensive data conversion. Procedures given below lead to good estimates of the parameters of the log-normal distribution from probability plots without any further data manipulation.

Data Presentation

Sturges' Rule may be used directly as in Chapter 3. The determination of cell sizes is derived from the *ratio* of maximum to minimum values instead of the range. A convenient term for this ratio is the *geometric range* since the use of ratios implies a geometric progression rather than an arithmetic progression. Since we require the partitioning of a ratio into equivalent parts, this is done by taking the 8th root of the geometric range. As shown in Examples 9-1 and 9-2, this is readily accomplished by dividing 8 into the logarithm of the geometric range. The antilogarithm of this quotient is the value of the *cell ratio*. The formula of Chapter 3 may therefore be restated as:

$$\text{Cell Ratio} = \sqrt[c]{\text{Geometric Range}} = \frac{\text{Log } G}{c} \quad (9\text{-}5)$$

where:

c = the number of cells required by Sturges' Rule.

Balancing cell endpoints is done as in Examples 3-4 through 3-6 *except* that the logarithms of the cell endpoints are used in achieving balance of the cell endpoints. Cell endpoint definition has the same requirements as for the additive process — no overlap between cells. See Examples 9-1 and 9-2.

Probability Plots

The layout and design features of log-normal probability paper compare directly to those of normal probability paper. The probability scale is the same as in Fig. 8-1. A logarithmic scale is used in place of a linear scale to plot the values of the variable of interest. This simplifies analysis of the log-normal distribution considerably. Individual values or cell midpoints may be plotted directly in the units of observation, thus eliminating any need to take logarithms of any of the data except to determine cell endpoints.

Example 9-3

Figure 9-7 is a probability plot of the data of Table 9-1 and is derived directly from Fig. 9-3. Cell midpoints are approximated by averaging the cell endpoints. The cumulative percentage plotting for the ends of the bars is determined as shown in Table 9-4.

When a set of plotted data such as Fig. 9-7 gives an acceptable straight line fit, it may be assumed that the choice of the log-normal probability paper for plotting was reasonable. The distribution parameters may then be estimated easily as they were for the normal distribution.

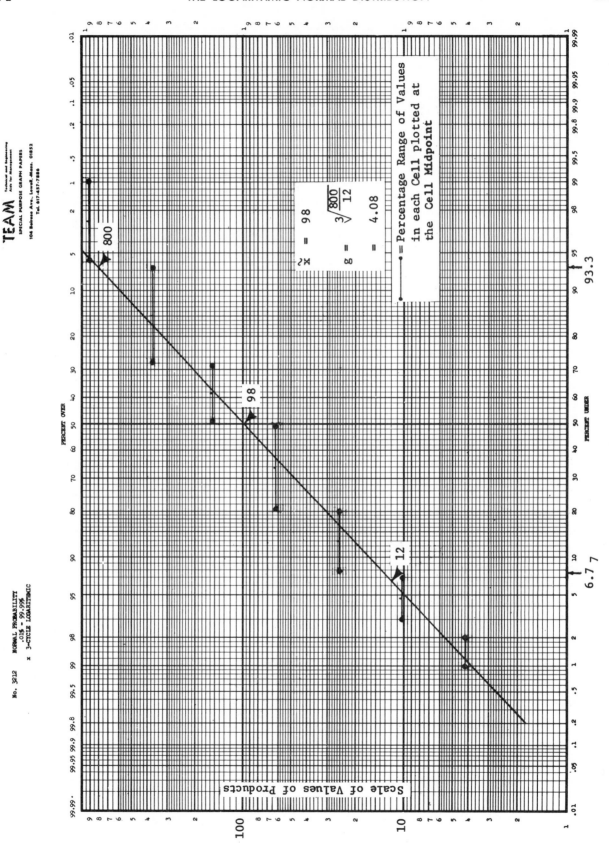

Fig. 9-7. Probability plot of products of random variables using the data of Table 9-1.

Table 9-4. Data Arrangement to Obtain Cell Midpoints and the
Cumulative Percentage Plotting for Example 9-3

Cell Interval		Mid-Point	Cumulative Occurrences	Cumulative Percentage Plotting
1.0 to	2.3	1.6	0	
2.4 to	5.9	4.2	1 to 2	0.99% to 1.98%
6.0 to	14.6	10.3	3 to 7	2.97 to 6.93
14.7 to	35.9	25.3	8 to 20	7.92 to 19.8
36.0 to	88.2	62.1	21 to 50	20.8 to 49.5
88.3 to	215	152	51 to 72	50.5 to 71.3
216 to	−528	372	73 to 94	72.3 to 93.1
529 to	1296	912	95 to 100	94.1 to 99.01

Example 9-4

Figure 9-8 is a probability plot of the data of Table 9-2 and is derived from Fig. 9-6. Cell midpoints and cumulative percentage plotting are shown in Table 9-5.

Parameter Estimation for the Log-Normal Distribution

With the normal distribution, because of its symmetry, the distribution characteristics are often given as $\bar{x} \pm k\sigma$. With this short notation, we have a useful amount of information about the data. For the log-normal distribution, the logarithms of the data have symmetry. An easy method of characterizing this distribution is given by Ferrell (15). The *median*, or *50% point*, is a good estimate of the mean of the logarithms. This value is also called the *geometric mean, $\tilde{x}$,* and can be read directly from the intersection of the fitted straight line and the 50% probability line.

The standard deviation of the logarithms is estimated from the *geometric dispersion, g*. This value is obtained by dividing the value at the 93.3% point by the value at the 6.7% point and taking the cube root of the result.

$$g = \sqrt[3]{\frac{X_{93.3}}{X_{6.7}}} \qquad (9\text{-}6)$$

Now g is used similarly to σ for the normal distribution with the substitution of multiplication and division for addition and subtraction. The summarizing expression for the log-normal distribution is now

$$x = \tilde{x} \cdot g^{\pm k} \qquad (9\text{-}7)$$

This represents the geometric mean *multiplied* by the geometric dispersion raised to a power representing the percentage of the distribution spread which is included. The expression $g^{\pm 1}$ includes about two-thirds of the values, $g^{\pm 2}$ includes about 95%, and $g^{\pm 3}$ includes about 99.7%, which is in one-to-one correspondence to the $k\sigma$ intervals used with the normal distribution. See Fig. 8-1.

Example 9-5

From the fitted line in Fig. 9-7, we obtain the median directly from the 50% line. This is ap-

Table 9-5. Data Arrangement to Obtain Cell Midpoints and the
Cumulative Percentage Plotting for Example 9-4

Cell Interval		Mid-Point	Cumulative Occurrences	Cumulative Percentage Plotting
0.0278 to	0.0679	0.048	1	0.99%
0.0680 to	0.1666	0.125	2 to 11	1.98 to 10.89
0.1667 to	0.407	0.28	12 to 28	11.89 to 27.65
0.408 to	0.99	0.70	29 to 59	28.6 to 58.5
1.00 to	2.44	1.72	60 to 81	59.5 to 80.3
2.45 to	5.99	4.20	82 to 93	81.2 to 92.1
6.00 to	14.66	10.3	94 to 99	93.1 to 98.1
14.67 to	36.00	25.0	100	99.01

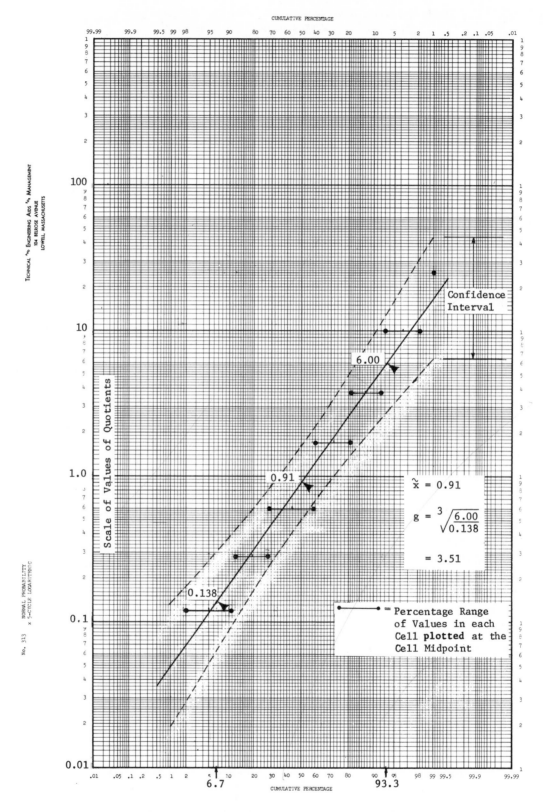

Fig. 9-8. Probability plot of quotients of random variables using the data of Table 9-2.

proximately 98. The values at $X_{93.3}$ and $X_{6.7}$ are 800 and 12 and so:

$$g = \sqrt[3]{\frac{800}{12}} = \sqrt[3]{66.8} = 4.08$$

This data may be summarized as $x = 98 \cdot 4.08^{\pm k}$.

Example 9-6

From the line in Fig. 9-8, we obtain a median of 0.91 and $X_{93.3}$ and $X_{6.7}$ of 6.00 and 0.138 respectively. This gives:

$$g = \sqrt{\frac{6.00}{0.138}} = \sqrt[3]{43.5} \quad \text{and} \quad x = 0.91 \cdot 3.51^{\pm k}$$

Comparison of Actual to Theoretical Results

Theoretically, the median for Fig. 9-7 should occur at $(3.5)^4$, or 150.06. This is the result of multiplying the expected average of 3.5 from each die by itself for 4 times, once for each die. The observed value was 98. Medians for samples of 100 from the log-normal distribution should fall within ±10% of the logarithm of the expected value; in this case, between about 91 and 248. The value 98 is within this interval, so that we have not obtained an unexpected result. The geometric dispersion should be about $\sqrt[6]{1296/1}$, or 3.3. The observed result was 4.08.

For Fig. 9-8, the median should occur at 1.0 since $(3.5 \div 3.5) \div (3.5 \div 3.5) = 1$. The observed value was 0.91 compared to a possible range of 0.79 to 1.26. The observed value for the geometric dispersion was 3.51 compared to the expected value of 3.3.

The actual results which resulted from our experimental procedures were acceptable within normal sampling error limits.

Further Uses of Linear Plots

As with the normal distribution, linear plots on log-normal paper may be extrapolated to obtain estimates outside the range of the observed variable in exactly the same way. The determination of the likely percentage greater than or less than some specific value may also be answered in the same way as for the normal distribution. The determi-

nation of the likely percentage between two values is also done the same way.

The Use of Confidence Intervals

The same general comments made about confidence intervals for the normal distribution apply to the log-normal distribution. The theoretical development of confidence intervals for log-normal cases is covered in detail only by Aitchison and Brown (2).

Remembering that the log-normal distribution is directly comparable to the normal distribution when we replace additive steps by multiplication and multiplicative steps by raising to powers, we can rewrite Equation 8-1 directly to:

$$y = \overline{L}(g_y^{\pm k_1}) \qquad (9\text{-}8)$$

where:

$\overline{L}$ is the median position of the line at a specified percentile;

g_y is the standard error of the line in terms of geometric dispersion;

k_1 is an exponent whose value is sample size dependent.

$$g_y = (g_{y \cdot x})^{\sqrt{\frac{1}{n} + \frac{k^2}{n-1}}} \qquad (9\text{-}9)$$

where:

$g_{y \cdot x}$ is the estimated geometric dispersion from the plot;

n is the sample size of the observed data;

k is the k factor as discussed in Chapters 7 and 8.

As with the normal distribution, simplification may be achieved using the recommended values of Appendix Tables A-3 and A-4.

The procedure for determining confidence intervals is now similar to that for the normal distribution except for the substitution of the operations related to the log-normal distribution.

Step 1. Obtain $g_{y \cdot x}$ from the probability plot.

Step 2. Raise $g_{y \cdot x}$ to a power using the values from Appendix Table A-4 to obtain offset ratios from the fitted line.

Step 3. Estimate the intercepts of the fitted line at the selected percentiles.

Step 4. Multiply and divide the values from Step 3 by the offset ratios from Step 2.

Step 5. Plot the values from Step 4 as points on the probability plot at the proper percentile points.

Step 6. Connect the points from Step 5 with a smooth curve.

Step 7. Determine if 95 percent of the points are enclosed by the confidence interval. If so, then accept the results at the 95% confidence level.

Example 9-7

Given: The data from Table 9-6, Sample A, and from Fig. 9-11.

Step 1. $g_{y \cdot x}$ is 1.65.

Step 2.

Percentile	$g_{y \cdot x}{}^{k1}$	Log 1.65 $\times$ Expo- nent $=$ Log Offset	Offset $=$ Antilog
50%	$(1.65)^{0.287}$	$0.21748 \times 0.287 = 0.06242$	1.112
30 + 70%	$(1.65)^{0.325}$	$0.21748 \times 0.325 = 0.07068$	1.177
10 + 90%	$(1.65)^{0.470}$	$0.21748 \times 0.470 = 0.10222$	1.265
5 + 95%	$(1.65)^{0.557}$	$0.21748 \times 0.557 = 0.12549$	1.335
1 + 99%	$(1.65)^{0.733}$	$0.21748 \times 0.733 = 0.15941$	1.443

Steps 3 and 4.

Percentile	Intercept $\times$ Offset	Confidence Interval Lower	Confidence Interval Upper
1	$12.0 \times (1.443)^{\pm 1}$	8.3	17.3
5	$16.8 \times (1.335)^{\pm 1}$	12.6	22.4
10	$20.0 \times (1.265)^{\pm 1}$	15.8	25.3
30	$29.5 \times (1.177)^{\pm 1}$	25.1	34.7
50	$39.0 \times (1.112)^{\pm 1}$	35.1	43.4
70	$49.5 \times (1.177)^{\pm 1}$	42.1	58.3
90	$72.0 \times (1.265)^{\pm 1}$	56.9	91.1
95	$87.0 \times (1.335)^{\pm 1}$	65.2	116.1
99	$123.0 \times (1.443)^{\pm 1}$	85.2	177.5

Steps 5 and 6. The resultant upper and lower confidence interval points are plotted, and smooth curves drawn through these points are shown in Fig. 9-11.

Step 7. All of the points fall within the confidence interval. For a sample of 49 at 95% confidence, we would allow three points, at most, to fall outside the confidence interval.

When using Sturges' Rule, the confidence interval must be adjusted for the effect of grouping. This is readily done by multiplying the offset ratio by the square root of the cell ratio used to group the data.

Example 9-8

Given: The data of Table 9-2 and Fig. 9-8.

Step 1. $g_{y \cdot x}$ is 3.51. From Example 9-1, the cell ratio is known to be 1.9138.

Step 2.

Percentile	$g_{y \cdot x}{}^{k1} \times \sqrt{\text{Cell Ratio}}$	Offset $=$ Antilogarithm
50%	$(3.51)^{0.200} \times \sqrt{1.9138}$	1.777
30 + 70%	$(3.51)^{0.226} \times \sqrt{1.9138}$	1.836
10 + 90%	$(3.51)^{0.326} \times \sqrt{1.9138}$	2.081
5 + 95%	$(3.51)^{0.486} \times \sqrt{1.9138}$	2.543
1 + 99%	$(3.51)^{0.509} \times \sqrt{1.9138}$	2.618

The values of the exponents for $n = 100$ are obtained by linear interpolation from Table 4, Appendix.

Table 9-6. Leakage Current Measurements for Three Independent Samples of Wet Porous Anode Tantalum Capacitors, in Nanoamperes

Sample A			Sample B			Sample C		
19	29	12	46	59	33	70	80	70
34	39	19	44	42	69	42	35	32
44	39	21	44	36	51	48	92	39
49	42	23	109	74	49	41	46	67
50	49	25	105	45	59	55	74	131
59	51	39	183	116	104	52	103	65
103	51	41	49	65	41	24	60	49
14	59	44	29	235	43	59	127	51
22	70	21	179	79	29	30	46	76
24	21	31	41	43	64	39	240	56
24	31	32	40	22	34	29	102	41
29	40	35	92	47	42	126	73	77
34	46	39	19	91	271	35	126	89
39	49	42	173	35	50	60	62	96
69	56	44	65	54	29	42	61	59

Steps 3 and 4.

Percentile	Intercept × Offset	Confidence Interval	
		Lower	Upper
1	0.05 × (2.618)$^{\pm1}$	0.019	0.131
5	0.116 × (2.543)$^{\pm1}$	0.046	0.295
10	0.180 × (2.081)$^{\pm1}$	0.086	0.375
30	0.465 × (1.836)$^{\pm1}$	0.253	0.854
50	0.91 × (1.777)$^{\pm1}$	0.512	1.617
70	1.75 × (1.836)$^{\pm1}$	0.953	3.213
90	4.50 × (2.081)$^{\pm1}$	2.162	9.364
95	7.05 × (2.543)$^{\pm1}$	2.772	17.928
99	16.7 × (2.618)$^{\pm1}$	6.379	43.72

Steps 5 and 6.

The resultant upper and lower confidence interval points are plotted and smooth curves through these points are shown in Fig. 9-8.

Step 7.

All but 2 percent of the initial points fall within the confidence interval so that we accept the grouping and the fitted line at the 95 percent confidence level.

Interpretation of Nonlinear Plots

As with the normal distribution, we may derive plots which flatten out at either or both ends. Flattening of the log-normal distribution has similar causes as for the normal distribution. Two-ended flattening usually represents sorting or selection to a two-sided specification. Flattening at the high end is selection against an upper limit of a specification. Flattening of the low end nearly always indicates a limitation of measurement sensitivity or capability.

Figure 9-9 is an illustration of the effect of measurement equipment sensitivity on a distribution of measurements. The flattening towards the left end was caused by a leakage current measurement kit which lost sensitivity under 20 nanoamperes. This was the noise level of the circuitry in the equipment.

If found that the plot was concave, it would be natural to conclude that the log-normal distribution did not apply. However, it is well known that leakage current for solid tantalum capacitors is log-normally distributed. The equipment used was not suitable for valid measurements of high-quality low-leakage parts.

An S-shaped curve would indicate a bimodal situation, again similar to the normal distribution. Jogged curves would indicate a multimodal situation. These are again the result of mixing raw materials, personnel, equipment, or levels of control. Once again, we caution that such indications are symptoms of important sources of variation which must be removed before numerical estimates can be derived with any validity.

Interpretation of Curved Plots

Curved plots on log-normal paper have fairly straightforward meanings. The convex plots indicate that the data are less skewed than the log-normal assumption and will be better fitted by the normal or chi-square distributions. The concave shape indicates that the data are more skewed than the log-normal and will be better fitted by one of the extreme value distributions. However, if the magnitudes of measurement are quite small, then equipment capability should be questioned as discussed above.

Example of Nonsampling Error

In Chapter 8, we considered the importance of *nonsampling errors* and the need for techniques to discover them. Figure 9-10 represents such a case.

A batch of parts was manufactured for a special test program which consisted of three different kinds of tests. Due to manpower loading, each test was started at a different point in time. However, the batch was partitioned at the time of the first test by random sampling methods so that the three subsamples were expected to be completely inter-comparable. The data for each sample is given in Table 9-6.

A comparison of results was made when all three subsamples had completed initial measurements for the most significant characteristic. The results for each subsample are plotted in Fig. 9-10. These results *do not agree*. Subsamples B and C have a median value which is more than 50% higher than for subsample A and both subsamples also have higher dispersions.

An interesting test, or comparison, of the different test groups can be made using confidence in-

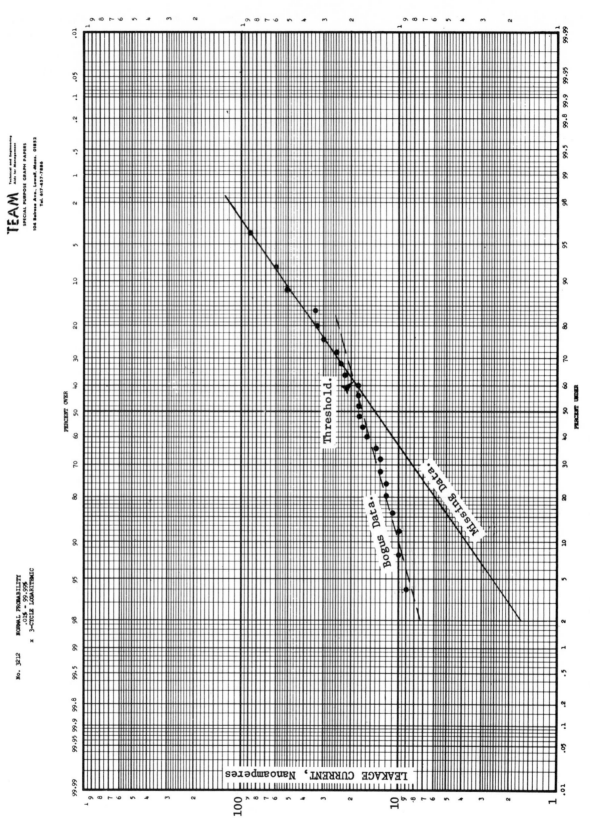

Fig. 9-9.   Probability plot of leakage current measurements of a high-reliability solid tantalum capacitor.

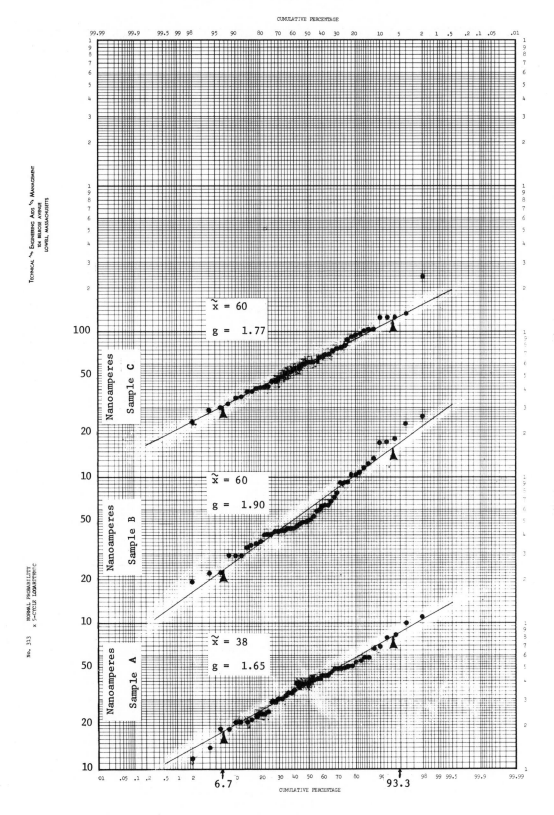

Fig. 9-10.   Probability plots of leakage current measurements for three independent samples of wet porous-anode tantalum capacitors.

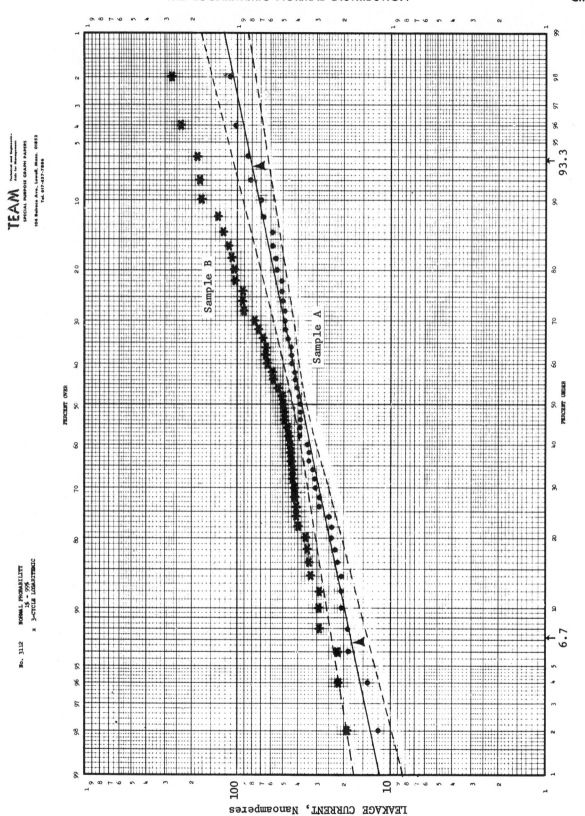

Fig. 9-11.   Comparison of sample A to sample B using probability plots with confidence intervals.

tervals. Figure 9-11 is a re-plot of the data for Sample A showing the confidence interval as determined in Example 9-7. The data for Sample B is plotted as **x**'s against the data plus confidence interval of Sample A. There is *practically no agreement* between the results of these two samples. The numerical results are *different*.

The differences are clearly greater than those for pure sampling error so that further investigation was indicated. The investigation determined that the measurements for subsample A were made in a part of the environmental laboratory area with a closely controlled temperature while subsamples B and C were measured in another part of the environmental area which was not temperature controlled and which contained many high-temperature ovens. The result was that the average ambient temperature was higher and also more erratic, which accounts for the generally higher values of this characteristic, which happens to be temperature dependent. The higher dispersion is due to greater short-time temperature variations.

Therefore, in spite of the fact that each sample was a random representation of the population, the results in comparing two samples were in disagreement. As a result of the subsequent investigation, a reason for the disagreement was found which had nothing to do with the original population which was sampled, which was independent of the actual samples but which altered the results significantly. This is an example of *nonsampling* error. If one does not have the means of detecting and identifying such error, the differences observed in the data might be explained away for the wrong reasons and invalid decisions may result.

Such findings are altogether too frequent in test work. They usually result from a lack of sufficient attention to details. As a consequence, the resultant data may be called biased, contaminated, or otherwise invalid.

A Special Case

One requirement for the log-normal distribution is that the variable of interest be a positively increasing variable. On occasion, one obtains data with both positive and negative values which give goodlooking log-normal plots for either the positive or negative values by themselves. Such data

arise where amounts of change are being studied. In these cases, it is best to obtain the original data and to convert the changes into percentages of the original values. Then a straightforward log-normal plot over the entire range of observation will usually result from the percentage data.

If the nature of the data is such that positive and negative changes have a real and useful physical meaning, then an extreme value probability plot will usually be preferable.

Exercises

9-1. Refer to the data of Exercise 2-1. Using each four consecutive values, obtain 100 products of the four values.

9-2. Using the products from Exercise 9-1, construct histograms similar to Figs. 9-2 and 9-3, using both the observed values as a basis, as well as the theoretically possible values, to determine cell size and endpoints.

9-3. Using the data from the histograms of Exercise 9-2, make probability plots. Estimate the median and geometric dispersion for each probability.

9-4. As a class exercise, tabulate the estimates for each student from Exercise 9-3 against the observed results and against the theoretical results.

9-5. Using the results of Exercise 2-3, obtain 50 results by dividing each 2 consecutive values and multiplying the results of each 2 consecutive quotients.

9-6. Using the products from Exercise 9-5, construct histograms similar to Figs. 9-5 and 9-6, using both observed and theoretical values as a basis for cell sizes and endpoints.

9-7. Using data from the histograms of Exercise 9-6, make probability plots. Estimate the median and geometric dispersion for each probability plot.

9-8. As a class exercise, tabulate the estimates for each student from Exercise 9-7 against the observed results and against the theoretical results.

9-9. Using the probability plot of Exercise 9-3, obtain the confidence interval, plot it, and interpret the results.

9-10. Using the probability plots of Exercise 9-7, obtain the confidence intervals, plot them, and interpret the results.

CHAPTER 10

Engineering Applications of the Log-Normal Distribution

The Log-Normal Life Distribution

The log-normal distribution occurs naturally as a life distribution. In the case of the normal distribution, we were able to derive its properties from simple linearly additive processes. In many practical cases, items with characteristics derived from linear additive processes also wear out by similar processes. For example, automobile tire treads have normally distributed tread depth when new and they wear linearly with the total mileage driven. When wear becomes excessive, blowouts can occur. This is a prime example of a *catastrophic failure* case.

Kao (29), stated that the failure distribution for many mechanical products is log-normal. It is, and for rather simple reasons. First, there is a safety margin which is usually large compared to the variation in the initial value of the variable of interest. For tires, initial variation in tread thickness is a few hundredths of an inch on an initial tread depth of 0.500″ to 0.750″. Blowout failure through the tread typically occurs only after 75 percent or more has worn away. This situation is represented schematically in Fig. 10-1.

In use, wear occurs over some time scale and causes changes to the initial distributions of dimensions of characteristics subject to wear. Wear in tires reduces the average tread thickness. Therefore, the mean tread thickness decreases with the number of miles driven, which is an indirect measure of time. In addition, variations in tire composition or density; variations in conditions of usage such as tire pressure or high speed versus low speed; and variations in environment such as hot or cold weather or paved versus unpaved roads will contribute to variations in the rate of tire wear.

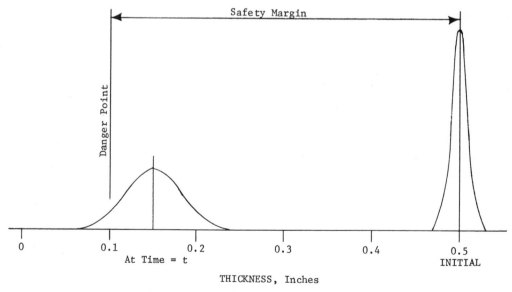

Fig. 10-1. Distributions of tire-tread thickness showing the effects of wear.

Therefore, the variation of tread thickness for a specific mileage point will also increase. The probability of failure of a tire may be assumed to be related to the probability of having a tread depth less than some critical depth, say 3/16ths of an inch. This can be expressed as:

$$p = 1 - F(x) \qquad (10\text{-}1)$$

where:

$p =$ probability of failure
$F(x) =$ probability of exceeding k
$k = k$ factor discussed in Chapter 7.

For the kind of problem stated above, k is determined as follows:

$$k = \frac{(\text{Limit} - \bar{X}_0) \pm \bar{W}_\tau}{\sqrt{\sigma_0^2 + \sigma_{w\tau}^2}} \qquad (10\text{-}2)$$

where:

$Limit =$ some known or assumed critical value. It is the minimum value which is considered safe for adequate performance.
$\bar{X}_0 =$ the mean of the initial distribution of the characteristic of interest.
$\sigma_0 =$ the standard deviation of the initial distribution.
$\bar{W}_\tau =$ the mean of the distribution of change due to wear which has accumulated at time $= t$.
$\sigma_{w\tau} =$ the standard deviation of the change due to wear.

At time 0, $\bar{W}_\tau =$ and, so, the value of (limit $- \bar{X}_0$) is the *safety margin*. The sign of $\bar{W}_\tau$ depends on the value of the initial mean relative to the limit. If $\bar{X}_0$ is greater than the limit, then $\bar{W}_\tau$ is positive; if $\bar{X}_0$ is less than the limit, $\bar{W}_\tau$ is negative. This is consistent with the idea of wearout approaching a safety limit or functional limitation.

The value of $\sigma_{w\tau}$ is rarely determined, but measurements of the dimension of interest after a period of wear will give a combined standard deviation value equal to $\sqrt{\sigma_0^2 + \sigma_{w\tau}^2}$. The value of $\bar{W}_\tau$ is rarely determined directly, either, because measurements at time $= t$ will represent the new dimensional distribution with a mean of $(\bar{X}_0 \pm \bar{W}_\tau)$, However, in serious failure studies, completely new insight is gained when there is also an analysis of the distribution behavior of the dimensional changes due to wear or other forms of degradation.

Let us now consider an alternative form of the same general problem of life distributions. As an example, mating parts such as pistons and piston rings are intended to work in the cylinder of an engine with the piston assembly and the cylinder operating as a paired system. They are designed to fit together with a specified clearance. This clearance is made as small as possible to develop a maximum of power. However, clearance must also be large enough for the piston to move without undue loss of power. This is a *trade-off* situation. The wear of these parts is normally a direct function of the number of strokes of the piston during engine use. In time, wear will occur. Excessive wear will cause loss of compression and a reduction in power. This is usually only a partial operational failure which is also the *malfunction failure case*. This is illustrated in Fig. 10-2.

The mating parts, principally the piston rings and the cylinder walls typically have normally distributed diameters. The distribution of fits, or the clearance, will also be normal. This is because the clearance is just the difference in the two dimensions which is a simple linear additive process. For rings and cylinders, initial variation in the distribution of clearances is only a few ten-thousandths of an inch. Serious loss of compression occurs only after several thousandths of an inch of wear. Once again, we have small initial variation and a large safety margin. In time, the distribution of changes in clearance will have an increasing mean. Variations in properties of the materials of the rings and cylinders, variations in operating speed, and variations in the kind and quality of lubricants used will affect the amount of wear. This will lead to an increasing variation in the wear distribution of the clearance at any specified point in time or mileage.

A Restatement of Wearout Behavior

Real time operation can be better understood by a restatement of Equation 10-2. First, $\bar{W}_\tau$ can be replaced by a statement of the time-dependent reduction of the initial safety margin as: (Limit $- \bar{X}_0)(\pm \rho t)$. Rate of wear, or reduction of the safety margin, is represented by ρ, ρ is positive when $\bar{X}_0$ is less than the limit and negative when $\bar{X}_0$ is greater than the limit. Variance $\sigma_{w\tau}^2$ can be

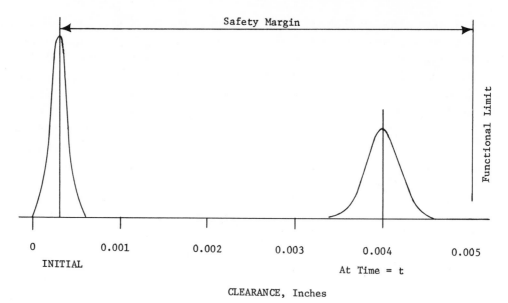

Fig. 10-2.   Distributions of piston-ring clearances showing the effects of wear.

replaced by $\sigma_0{}^2\eta t$. The factor which represents the rate of increase in distributional variation as a function of the initial distribution of the characteristic of interest is η.   Equation 10-2 now becomes:

$$k = \frac{\text{Limit} - \bar{X}_0 + \bar{W}_r}{\sqrt{\sigma_0{}^2 + \sigma_{wr}{}^2}}$$

$$= \frac{(\text{Limit} - \bar{X}_0) + (\text{Limit} - \bar{X}_0)(-\rho t)}{\sqrt{\sigma_0{}^2 + \sigma_0{}^2 \eta t}}$$

$$= \frac{(\text{Limit} - \bar{X}_0)}{\sigma_0} \cdot \frac{(1 - \rho t)}{\sqrt{1 + \eta t}} \qquad (10\text{-}3)$$

In words, this formula states that the safety margin (Limit $-\bar{X}_0$), is linearly reduced over time by the factor $(1 - \rho t)$, and that the initial standard deviation is increased by the factor $\sqrt{1 + \eta t}$. These relationships emphasize that the initial probability of success, represented by the first term of Equation 10-3, is continually modified by the time-dependent behavior of the second term.   The second term represents the effects of wear, and other forms of degradation, on the initial probability of success. Equation 10-3 also states that once something subject to linear wear is placed in use it becomes progressively more failure prone.

Returning now to the earlier discussion of the log-normal distribution as a resultant of random variables combined through multiplication and division operations, we observe that Equation 10-3 contains two sets of division terms, or ratios.

These are: $\dfrac{\text{Limit} - \bar{X}_0}{\sigma_0}$ and $\dfrac{1 - \rho t}{\sqrt{1 + \eta t}}$.

Furthermore, these ratios are subsequently multiplied together. This is directly comparable to the operations performed on the data of Table 6-1 which resulted in Table 9-2 and Figs. 9-5, 9-6, and 9-8.

Extension of Results

Equation 10-3 can be expanded to represent variations in conditions of usage of items during their life span. For instance, many items are subjected to an initial stress, $\bar{X}s$, when first placed in use. Automobile tires may be inflated to different pressures. Tire pressure is known to affect the wearout rate. Piston rings and cylinders may be manufactured from different kinds of alloys to varying surface finish requirements, each of which will affect wear rates. Each of these cases may be considered in a different way.

In the first case, the difference in tire pressures can act like a fixed shift which reduces the safety margin.   Then, (Limit $-\bar{X}_0$) becomes (Limit $-\bar{X}_0 - \bar{X}s$). The pressure difference will also increase the wear rate ρ to ρ_1. $\sqrt{1 + t}$ would change to $\sqrt{1 + \eta t + \mu s}$, where μs represents the contribution to additional variation caused by the applied stress condition.

In the second case, differences in materials or conditions of manufacture can act as multipliers of the wear rate factors, ρ and η. This would change $(1 - \rho t)$ to $(1 - s_1 \rho t)$ and $\sqrt{1 + \eta t}$ to $\sqrt{1 + s_2 \eta t}$. For these kinds of wear processes, it is to be observed that the several factors are what are commonly referred to as *operational acceleration factors*. When these factors are introduced into the terms $(1 - s_1 \rho t)$ and $\sqrt{1 + s_2 \eta t}$ and the value of the resultant ratio is obtained, simple algebraic reasoning will demonstrate that proportional increases in the acceleration factors will not affect failure rate in the same proportion.

Example 10-1

Given: A piston ring-cylinder combination with dimensional relationships that result in $k = 3.00$ at time $= 0$. Test engines are operated at two different test conditions with the relative acceleration intended to be $2/1$. Assume that ρ is known to be 0.0001%/equivalent mile and that η is known to be 0.0001%/equivalent mile. Let s_{11} and s_{21} represent a multiplier of 1 for some standard, or reference, test condition. Let s_{12} and s_{22} represent an acceleration factor of 2 over the standard test condition.

Determine the relative failure probabilities at 1000 and 100,000 equivalent miles. Equivalent miles is used here in place of a time factor. It is the amount of straight operating time which is considered to be equivalent to a specific amount of mileage.

From Equation 10-3, we can establish the following comparative solutions.

For 1000 equivalent miles:

$$k_{11} = 3.00 \frac{1 - s_{11}\rho t}{\sqrt{1 + s_{21}\eta t}}$$

$$= 3.00 \frac{1 - 1 \times 10^{-6} \times 10^3}{\sqrt{1 + 1 \times 10^{-5} \times 10^3}}$$

$$= 3.00 \frac{1 - 0.001}{\sqrt{1 + 0.02}}$$

$$= 2.967$$

$$p_{11} = 0.0015$$

$$k_{12} = 3.00 \frac{1 - s_{12}\rho t}{\sqrt{1 + s_{22}\eta t}}$$

$$= 3.00 \frac{1 - 2 \times 10^{-6} \times 10^3}{\sqrt{1 + 2 \times 10^{-5} \times 10^3}}$$

$$= 3.00 \frac{1 - 0.002}{\sqrt{1 + 0.04}}$$

$$= 2.936$$

$$p_{12} = 0.0016$$

For 100,000 equivalent miles:

$$k_{21} = 3.00 \frac{1 - s_{11}\rho t}{\sqrt{1 + s_{21}\eta t}}$$

$$= 3.00 \frac{1 - 1 \times 10^{-6} \times 10^5}{\sqrt{1 + 1 \times 10^{-5} \times 10^5}}$$

$$= 3.00 \frac{1 - 0.1}{\sqrt{1 + 1}}$$

$$= 1.909$$

$$p_{21} = 0.0282$$

$$k_{22} = 3.00 \frac{1 - s_{12}\rho t}{\sqrt{1 + s_{22}\eta t}}$$

$$= 3.00 \frac{1 - 2 \times 10^{-6} \times 10^5}{\sqrt{1 + 2 \times 10^{-5} \times 10^5}}$$

$$= 3.00 \frac{1 - 0.2}{\sqrt{1 + 2}}$$

$$= 1.386$$

$$p_{22} = 0.0829$$

Now, at 1000 equivalent miles:

$$\frac{p_{12}}{p_{11}} = \frac{0.0016}{0.0015} = 1.066$$

and, at 100,000 equivalent miles:

$$\frac{p_{22}}{p_{21}} = \frac{0.0829}{0.0282} = 2.940$$

In neither case, is the effect on failure probability near 2. In the first case, the ratio is barely different than 1 and in the second case, it is nearly 3.

Since time, or equivalent mileage in this case, is often considered as an acceleration factor, we can examine the effect of an increase in time of a ratio of $100/1$ by comparing the results for each engine at the 1000 and 100,000 equivalent mile points.

Under standard conditions:

$$\frac{p_{21}}{p_{11}} = \frac{0.0282}{0.0015} = 18.8$$

and at twice standard conditions:

$$\frac{p_{22}}{p_{12}} = \frac{0.0829}{0.0016} = 51.8$$

Neither of these cases is very near to the 100/1 ratio for time.

From the preceding example, using apparently simple assumptions, we see that acceleration factors are not the simple relationships that are often looked for. That is, they do not lead to simple failure rate ratios under nominally simple ratios of test exposure. Shooman (38) develops similar examples based on functional relationships of components in electronic circuits.

The non-simple behavior of acceleration factors requires that legitimate failure rate studies must include the means to identify:

1. The correct initial distribution
2. The correct statistical life distribution
3. The proper procedures to partition the several contributions of initial characteristics, effects of usage stresses, effects of usage conditions and environments, and time to the probability of failure. This is because the inherent wear factors and the stress-dependent modifiers of those factors combine to alter the initial values of distribution parameters, particularly the mean and variance, in ways which continually increase the probability of failure.

All of this information is critical to proper understanding of the sources of variations in product behavior. It is important to know the real causes of excess variation so that the correct feedback paths will be followed for product correction and improvement.

Some important considerations in applying the log-normal distribution to life behavior are given by Goldthwaite (16). This reference also contains several useful graphs of the relationships of the log-normal distribution parameters.

Additional Engineering Considerations

From a fundamental engineering basis, the log-normal distribution may be re-presented in more familiar terms. In Chapter 9, we developed the log-normal distribution by using random values from a uniform distribution and by combining those values through multiplication or division operations, or a combination of both. Log-normal distributions with ideal properties will result when random values from a normal distribution are combined by multiplicative operations. For practical purposes, any linear additive distribution in the range from the uniform to the normal distribution will result in a log-normal distribution, when four or more random values are combined multiplicatively.

The multiplication/division development of the log-normal distribution may be readily rewritten into the form: $a/b \times c/d$, where a, b, c, and d each represent an independent random variable. However, combinations of ratios such as a/b and c/d generally represent terms in *rate-dependent processes*. From this perspective, then, we may state that rate-dependent processes should produce output characteristics which are log-normally distributed. Further, if the output characteristics are not log-normal, then there is quite likely something wrong with the process or the measurements of the characteristic which requires investigation.

In the same sense that characteristics arising from linear processes seem to wear or degrade through further linear processes, there is empirical evidence that characteristics arising from rate-dependent processes also wear or degrade by further rate-dependent processes. Under these conditions, the probability of failure is determined from k by direct substitution of the equivalent terms of the log-normal distribution from Equation 9-3 into Equation 10-2 which gives:

$$k = \frac{(\log \text{Limit} - \mu_{l0}) \pm \log \overline{W}\tau_l}{\sqrt{\sigma_{l0}{}^2 + \sigma_w\tau_0{}^2}} \qquad (10\text{-}4)$$

This simplifies to:

$$k = \frac{(\log \text{Limit} - \mu_{l0})(1 - \rho t)}{\sigma_{l0}\sqrt{1 + \eta t}} \qquad (10\text{-}5)$$

Substituting and simplifying:

$$k = \frac{\overline{\dfrac{\text{Limit}}{\tilde{x}}}}{\log g} \cdot \frac{1 - \rho t}{\sqrt{1 + \eta t}} \qquad (10\text{-}6\text{A})$$

$$k = \frac{\text{Limit}}{\tilde{x} \log g} \cdot \frac{1 - \rho t}{\sqrt{1 + \eta t}} \qquad (10\text{-}6\text{B})$$

These equations state that the probability of failure is now based on a ratio of values which is a direct consequence of the underlying multiplicative operations which derive the log-normal distribution. The ratio of the limit to the median changes by the ratio $(1 - \rho t)/\sqrt{1 + \eta t}$. Thus, we have two rates, as defined by the two ratios, which is consistent with the formulation of the log-normal distribution on the basis of $a/b \times c/d$. Finally, the statement of Equation 10-6B permits us to work directly in parameters which are easily derived from probability plots of the Log-Normal Distribution. The limit is a specification; x, the median, is obtained from the 50 percentile and the fitted line; g is the root of specified percentiles; log g is obtained directly from a slide rule or from a table of logarithms.

Example 10-2

Table 10-1 is a sample of data for times to failure due to dielectric breakdown in solid tantalum

Table 10-1. Failure Times for Solid Tantalum Capacitors

(Test terminated at 16,000 minutes. Sample Size = 39 capacitors. 25 capacitors survived at 16,000 minutes.)

Times to Failure, in minutes	
4	654
19	969
65	2450
73	2732
116	5764
166	6010
322	7935

capacitors when exposed to severe overvoltage. Figure 10-3 illustrates a probability plot of this data. Both the dielectric and the solid electrolyte of tantalum capacitors have a number of complex characteristics which are essentially rate-dependent under voltage stress. The combined effect of these characteristics determines the voltage life capability of these capacitors. The so-called leakage current of tantalum capacitors is a measurement which is approximately indicative of the voltage withstanding capability. Leakage current is known to be log-normal in its behavior. Therefore, these parts have the underlying requirements to result in a log-normal life distribution.

Figure 10-3 also shows a confidence interval over the range of the observed data. Since this represents an area within which we could readily expect variation to occur, it also serves to emphasize the high degree of agreement between the observed data and the fitted line. The relationship between the data and the fitted line is as nearly a perfect fit as is possible to observe. This fit is also evidence that the log-normal distribution is ideally representative of this life distribution.

Figure 10-3 further serves to illustrate the large range over which the values of time to failure occur. Failure times were observed from 4 to 8000 minutes. The test was continued to 16,000 minutes and then curtailed. It is of interest to note that only about 37.5 percent of the test sample had failed when the test was terminated. Extrapolation of the fitted line to the 90th percentile, shown as a dashed parallel to the fitted line, gives an estimate that about 10 percent of these capacitors would survive more than 70,000,000 minutes, or about 133 years.

Finally, to improve understanding of life-use behavior, if one observes a log-normal distribution, one should next determine whether the underlying production processes and wear/degradation processes are linear or rate-dependent. If linear, one may be confident that the initial values of the characteristic of interest were normally distributed. If production and wear processes are rate-dependent, then the characteristic was log-normally distributed initially. In addition, the reverse of both preceding statements will be true. That is, if one knows that the initial distribution is normal and that linear wear processes occur, then the life dis-

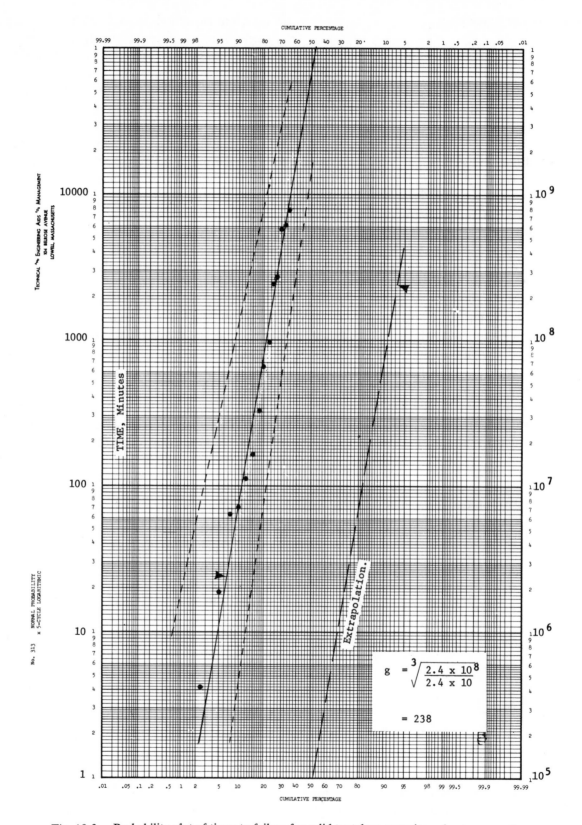

Fig. 10-3.   Probability plot of times to failure for solid tantalum capacitors due to overvoltage.

tribution for this characteristic will be log-normal. Also, if the initial distribution is log-normal and the wear processes are rate-dependent, the life distribution will again be log-normal. Under the stated conditions, if one does not observe a log-normal distribution, then one should investigate to determine the cause(s) which are preventing the results from meeting the expectations.

CHAPTER 11

The Extreme Value Distribution

Background

The term *Extreme Value Statistics* originally came from methods of data analysis which used only the largest or smallest values from sets of data; that is, the *extreme values*. E. J. Gumbel's early work on the analysis of flood data is described in (21). He determined the maximum daily flow rate for major rivers so that 365 flow rates were obtained each year. The largest of these flows within a year was called the *annual flood*. A set of data of the annual floods for a period of years exhibits *extreme value distribution* behavior.

Extreme value distributions are skewed distributions. They may be skewed to the right or to the left, as illustrated in Figs. 11-2, 11-3, 11-4, and 11-5. Right-skewed extreme value distributions occur when the largest extreme value is used, or when the higher order terms in expressions such as Equations 11-7, 11-8, and 11-9 dominate the value of the equation. Left-skewed extreme value distributions occur when the smallest extreme value is used, or where the low order terms in Equations 11-7 through 11-9 dominate. Left-skewed distributions are very common in data from measurements of strength characteristics of materials.

Smallest extreme values are often referred to as the "weakest-link" values. Gumbel develops the theory of extreme values extensively (21) and gives a wide range of applications. Haviland (24) develops the theory around the solution of classical engineering problems and presents many detailed applications in engineering.

Extreme value distributions are obtained from the selection of extreme values such as the heaviest 24-hour rainfall per year at a given location and the highest (or lowest) temperature. Extreme value behavior also occurs in production data, such as the largest (or smallest) quantity during a shift (day) by a specific worker (machine). Extreme value data also occur in traffic counts of motor vehicles per unit time on a given segment of highway, or from counts of the number of telephone calls per unit time on a given switching unit.

Extreme value behavior also occurs for data which are not selected extremes. Botts (5), showed the wider generality of extreme value distributions, with an example of costs due to crop losses in a single year for a mutual crop-hail insurance company. Additional examples are for breakdown voltage of dielectric material in a capacitor, Fig. 11-7; the number of machine stoppages requiring a repair action, Fig. 11-9; and for the tensile strength of aluminum test specimens, Fig. 11-11. There are also published applications using effective gust velocities of aircraft wind loads, distributions of parameter changes in electronic components, and in such surprising situations as the distribution of contributions in church collection envelopes.

Description of the Extreme Value Distribution

The extreme value distribution is also known as the:

1. *Double exponential distribution,* from its cumulative distribution function. See Equation 11-1, below.

2. *Gumbel distribution,* from the contributions of E. J. Gumbel to the formal development of the theory of this distribution.

3. *Type I extreme value distribution,* to distinguish it from the logarithmic extreme value distribution and from the Weibull distribution, which are known respectively as Type II and Type III extreme value distributions.

The cumulative distribution function and the probability density function for the extreme value distribution are given by:

$$\Phi(x) = \int_{-\infty}^{y} e^{-e^{-y}} \qquad (11\text{-}1)$$

$$\phi(x) = \alpha e^{-y - e^{-y}} \qquad (11\text{-}2)$$

under the conditions that:

$$-\infty < y < +\infty \qquad (11\text{-}3)$$

$$y = \alpha(x - \mu_0) \qquad (11\text{-}4)$$

where:

   y = the normalized unit variable, also called the *reduced variate*.

   x = the value of the random variable.

   μ_o = the *mode*, the measure of central tendency for the extreme value distribution.

   α,   when expressed as $1/\alpha$, is the measure of dispersion, called the *Gumbel Slope*.

The probability density function for the extreme value distribution is plotted for the largest extreme value in Fig. 11-1, which shows right-handed skew. The *pdf* for the smallest extreme value is exactly opposite, with the longish tail of the distribution going off to the left. The *mode, μ_0*, which is the measure of central tendency used for the extreme value distribution, occurs at the highest point of the *pdf*. The mode occurs at $y = 0$, as may be seen by inspection of Equation 11-4. The skewness of the extreme value distribution is shown by the dispersion of the pdf around the mode. The nonsymmetry of dispersion is evidenced by the locations of the standard deviation units and the associated percentiles in the scales of Fig. 11-1.

Note that Equation 11-4 is similar to Equations 7-3 and 9-3. The several terms of each equation have the following relationships: y is a normalized unit variable like k; μ_o is used in place of μ and $\tilde{x}$; and $1/\alpha$ is used in place of σ and g.

Equations 11-1 and 11-2 show the double exponential form of the extreme value distribution wherein e is raised to a power twice.

The Origin of an Extreme Value Distribution

The extreme value distribution occurs when a set of random variables is applied to the terms of a polynomial expression, as in the following example:

$$y = f(x^0) + f(x^1) + f(x^2) + f(x^3) + f(x^4) + f(x^5)..) \qquad (11\text{-}5)$$

Compared to the generating equations used for the normal and log-normal distributions, which were linear and first-order terms respectively, the extreme value distribution results from a *power-series accumulation* of the effects of random variables.

Let $f(x^n) = c_n(x^n)$ where c is a constant and x is a random variable giving:

$$y = c_0 x^0 + c_1 x^1 + c_2 x^2 + c_3 x^3 + c_4 x^4 \ldots \qquad (11\text{-}6)$$

We may demonstrate the generation of numerical values for the extreme value distribution by means of a simple physical process. This involves using 900 random values obtained from 100 tosses of nine dice. The random values are contained in Table 11-1, which follows. The identity of each individual die was maintained so that each column in Table 11-1 represents the sequential results for each die. The values in Table 11-1 are grouped by throw and are also numbered 1–9 from left to right for consistent identification.

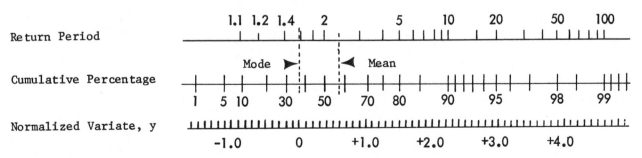

Fig. 11-1. Layout of extreme value scales showing the relationship between the cumulative precentage, the normalized variate, and the return period.

Table 11-1. Individual Values for 100 Throws of Nine Dice

Dice Identification				
1 2 3 4 5 6 7 8 9	1 2 3 4 5 6 7 8 9	1 2 3 4 5 6 7 8 9	1 2 3 4 5 6 7 8 9	1 2 3 4 5 6 7 8 9
Values for 100 Throws				
5 3 2 6 3 2 2 3 1	1 3 5 1 3 3 2 2 5	2 6 3 6 4 2 2 1 4	1 3 3 1 4 4 1 2 3	6 3 2 1 3 5 5 5 3 4
1 5 5 4 2 4 3 5 1	5 5 4 6 6 2 6 4 3	6 1 2 3 4 2 6 2 4	5 1 4 6 4 1 1 6 6	6 4 1 4 4 4 2 3 3
4 4 6 4 4 4 5 2 3	2 5 2 6 1 4 4 1 2	2 3 2 6 1 6 2 6 4	3 6 4 5 3 1 1 4 4	2 6 2 5 2 2 6 6 5
2 6 1 3 3 1 6 3 2	6 5 3 4 6 2 3 3 5	5 5 4 3 6 1 4 1 2	1 2 2 2 5 6 5 6 3	6 1 4 4 2 5 2 2 2
5 5 1 3 6 2 3 3 4	1 5 3 2 4 3 6 2 1	3 6 3 1 6 4 4 3 3	1 5 3 2 3 6 6 6 1	5 5 6 4 6 2 5 5 1
5 5 5 4 5 6 4 1 4	2 2 5 3 2 5 2 2 4	2 6 6 4 4 3 5 6 3	5 5 1 5 5 4 2 6 6	1 5 5 4 2 4 4 6 3
6 1 3 6 4 6 6 2 1	6 4 3 6 3 5 3 1 3	4 3 5 5 3 3 5 3 4	1 4 4 4 3 5 4 3 3	3 2 3 3 1 3 4 5 2
4 5 6 1 4 3 1 1 5	1 6 2 6 3 2 4 2 6	1 3 5 5 5 4 5 2 6	3 1 4 6 2 6 1 3 6	6 2 6 2 6 4 3 4 1
5 2 3 4 5 1 3 3 2	4 6 2 1 4 6 4 6 3	1 4 2 5 1 4 3 1 3	2 1 3 6 2 6 3 4 4	4 4 6 2 2 6 3 4 5
6 3 5 5 1 3 1 2 1	3 2 5 3 2 4 2 3 4	4 1 1 2 2 4 2 2 1	5 2 3 5 1 3 1 1 2	3 6 5 1 1 5 3 6 5
5 5 5 3 5 6 6 6 1	6 6 2 6 2 5 2 6 5	3 5 2 5 3 2 3 5 4	6 2 6 4 2 5 2 2 1	4 5 1 3 6 4 4 1 3
2 6 5 5 2 4 4 1 5	1 4 2 2 1 3 4 5 6	5 2 6 3 2 1 6 2 3	2 1 1 5 1 6 2 4 5	2 1 1 4 3 6 5 1 2
6 4 6 6 4 5 1 4 6	4 1 2 6 3 1 3 2 4	1 4 6 4 5 5 1 6 4	5 1 4 2 1 5 1 6 4	5 2 2 4 1 5 6 4 4
6 4 1 4 3 2 2 6 3	3 2 1 1 3 3 3 2 4	3 3 5 5 4 1 5 5 4	4 6 2 5 5 1 2 1 4	6 3 6 1 3 6 6 1 3
6 2 2 6 2 3 2 3 5	5 5 2 5 2 4 1 4 3	2 4 1 1 5 4 3 1 6	5 5 4 6 5 6 1 6 4	6 5 5 2 1 1 6 5 2
5 2 6 5 4 4 3 3 2	1 2 4 2 2 1 2 1 3	1 6 6 5 3 1 4 3 3	1 5 3 4 2 5 4 4 5	1 2 4 6 5 6 1 4 3
2 2 3 1 1 2 1 3 2	2 4 6 4 5 3 3 5 3	6 6 3 4 4 2 1 3 4	2 2 1 3 4 4 2 6 5	4 4 5 4 4 2 2 1 6
6 3 6 4 3 6 5 6 6	5 3 1 4 2 6 4 5 5	5 5 2 6 1 3 4 6 1	3 6 2 5 1 1 6 6 5	2 4 6 4 2 4 2 2 3
5 1 4 5 1 1 3 1 2	1 2 4 2 5 2 2 3 3	6 2 6 4 3 2 3 3 5	1 1 3 3 6 3 6 5 4	3 1 5 4 2 3 3 5 4
3 1 3 6 2 5 5 4 1	2 1 5 4 3 4 1 5 2	5 2 1 6 2 4 2 5 4	4 4 1 4 5 5 5 6 3	6 4 6 5 4 2 2 4 3

In Equation 11-6, c does not have to be a constant; it may be a random variable. In the direct development of extreme value behavior from polynomial expressions, greater generality and flexibility result when c is used as a random variable. Random values for c have important implications in life/use data analysis which are discussed in Chapters 12 and 15.

A value for each $c_n x^n$ term is obtained by considering both c and x to be random variables, choosing values for the random variables in sequence from Table 11-1, using 1 to 9 and substituting the values so obtained in an appropriate formula similar to Equation 11-6. As an example, consider the following equation:

$$y = x^0 + c_1 x^1 + c_2 x^2 \qquad (11\text{-}7)$$

The first set of five random variables is 5, 3, 2, 6, and 3. Substituting these values in Equation 11-7, we obtain:

$$y = 5 + 3(2^1) + 6(3^2) = 5 + 6 + 54 = 65$$

The results for 100 such substitutions are contained in Table 11-2. These results are called *quadratic sums* because Equation 11-7 was carried out to the square of the x term. That is, in each case, we stopped after we had found the value of y when n in x^n was 2.

Table 11-2. 100 Quadratic Sums (Using Equation 11-7)

65	102	105	82
42	64	52	88
92	141	126	21
35	14	46	54
118	13	34	31
174	26	97	34
105	105	9	8
44	72	60	11
111	55	14	141
26	34	30	175
25	135	42	32
241	53	11	52
18	31	60	20
165	29	14	112
48	16	35	108
24	21	17	117
72	74	126	39
67	34	24	13
32	26	59	33
25	179	43	33
116	42	58	159
56	12	29	88
14	90	125	42
133	36	98	24
57	34	31	110

The results of substitution in Equation 11-7, which are given in Table 11-2, are also shown as a histogram in Fig. 11-2. This histogram has a general resemblance to the histograms obtained for the log-normal distribution shown in Figs. 9-1 and 9-4. However, the data leading to Fig. 11-1 were derived differently. It is particularly interesting to note that these data were obtained from the *addition of successive steps involving multiplication,* that is, *both* addition operations *and* multiplication operations were utilized.

As a further example of generating extreme value data, consider:

$$y = x^0 + c_1 x^1 + c_2 x^2 + c_3 x^3 \qquad (11\text{-}8)$$

This equation is solved by substituting the first seven random variables from Table 11-1, and then solving:

$$y = 5 + 3(2^1) + 6(3^2) + 2(2^3)$$
$$= 5 + 6 + 54 + 16 = 81$$

The results for 100 such substitutions are given in Table 11-3. These results are called *cubic sums* because Equation 11-8 was carried out to the cube of the *x* term; that is, $n = 3$. The histogram for cubic sums is shown in Fig. 11-3.

Table 11-3. 100 Cubic Sums (Using Equation 11-8)

81	477	1401	146
150	439	308	90
592	641	131	213
251	122	62	108
172	45	58	63
558	30	205	74
1041	106	11	56
47	73	810	16
138	805	41	149
29	1330	655	181
49	167	82	352
773	373	203	84
274	37	87	236
219	191	95	760
696	19	39	733
64	646	25	373
207	106	207	789
195	466	408	1093
416	66	75	1329
57	429	47	249
132	298	112	165
488	204	245	104
62	198	130	74
197	198	223	105
313	169	139	126

Table 11-4. 100 Quartic Sums (Using Equation 11-9)

84	963	1407	389
155	1207	933	858
754	3233	5315	219
299	203	548	1983
940	47	1433	1343
814	192	253	76
1403	7902	59	2556
672	1097	8606	1552
186	1291	57	405
31	1336	659	1717
1299	7963	3832	2852
1097	616	6683	3834
290	3925	599	3986
2094	1215	607	2040
698	35	363	1219
576	1414	106	454
288	349	612	805
2787	4216	3533	2117
902	98	318	1410
825	434	127	329
388	784	1392	489
1000	284	407	1400
1598	202	1666	236
213	2698	1503	1385
556	3919	1435	450

Similarly:

$$y = x^0 + c_1 x^1 + c_2 x^2 + c_3 x^3 + c_4 x^4 \qquad (11\text{-}9)$$

Substitution of the nine random values from Table 11-1 results in:

$$y = 5 + 3(2^1) + 6(3^2) + 2(2^3) + 3(1^4)$$
$$= 5 + 6 + 54 + 16 + 3 = 84$$

Table 11-4 lists 100 results. These results are called *quartic sums* because *x* is raised to the fourth power. The histogram for Table 11-4 is illustrated in Fig. 11-4.

It is instructive to compare Figs. 11-2, 11-3, and 11-4 on the basis of an equal number of cell groupings. In all three figures, the relative density is greatest at the low end of the plot and decreases markedly towards the high end. The relative concentration increases as the number of terms used to compute the extreme value data is increased from five to nine. In addition, the tail to the right becomes relatively thinner and longer as more terms are used. The range of values covered increases by about a factor of five times for each additional term which is included. Note also, that the last three cells contain only about 5 percent of the

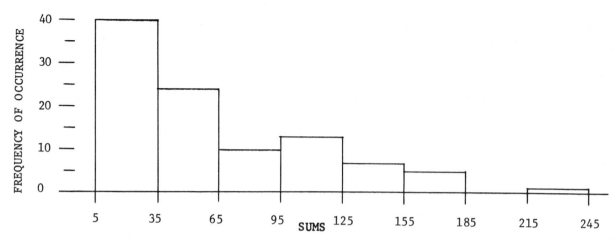

Fig. 11-2. Histogram of quadratic sums obtained as solutions to $y = x^0 + c_1 x^1 + c_2 x^2$ using values from Table 11-1.

total distribution. Extreme value distributions include quite extreme values in a natural way.

Data Presentation

Data for an extreme value distribution can be rearranged into a normal-appearing histogram by using cell ratios, as with the log-normal distribution. The main difference in appearance is that the tails of the rearranged Extreme Value Distribution are not as thin as those usually found for the normal and the rearranged log-normal distribu-

tions. It is preferable to use histograms which show skew, because a skewed appearance is characteristic of extreme value distributions. Therefore, the steps of obtaining the number of cells using Sturges' Rule, cell sizes, balancing of cell endpoints and cell endpoint definition are used identically as for the normal distribution.

Extreme Value Probability Paper

The layout and design features of extreme value probability paper are different from those of normal

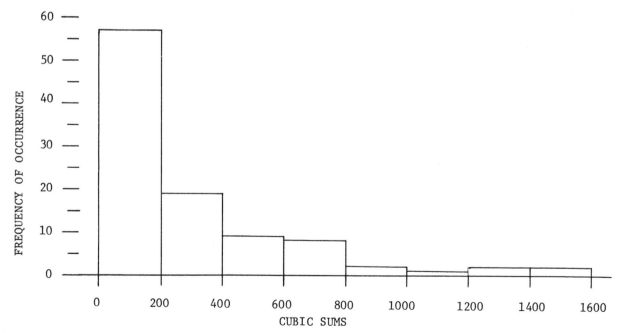

Fig. 11-3.   Histogram of cubic sums obtained as solutions to $y = x^0 + c_1 x^1 + c_2 x^2 + c_3 x^3$
using values from Table 11-1.

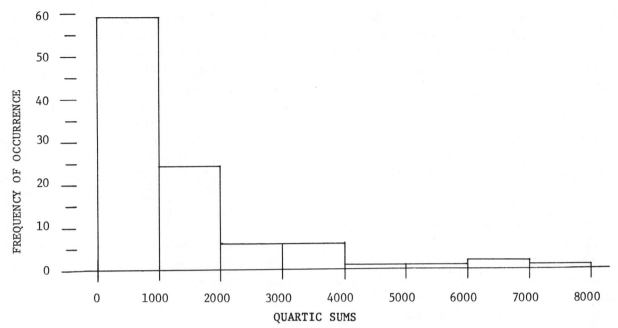

Fig. 11-4.   Histogram of quartic sums obtained as solutions to $y = x^0 + c_1 x^1 + c_2 x^2 + c_3 x^3 + c_4 x^4$
using values from Table 11-1.

and log-normal probability papers. Figure 11-1 shows the three scales used on extreme value probability paper. The uniform scale of the normalized unit variable, y, is shown at the bottom. The scale for cumulative percentage is shown in the middle. The spacing of the cumulative percentage scale is made to correspond to the shape of the extreme value distribution which is highly compressed for low values and increasingly more spread out for high values. The peak of the distribution at the mode occurs at the 36.79% point which is much less than the 50% point of the normal and log-normal distributions.

The top scale, which is usually located along the top edge of the grid, is the *return period scale*. This is a nonuniform scale which increases in value

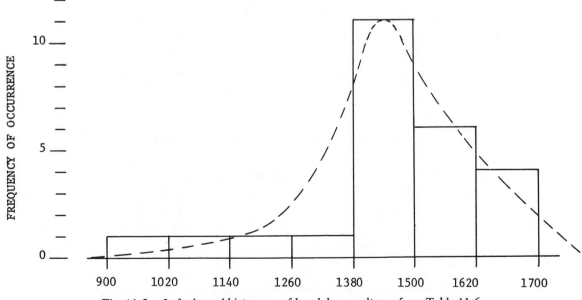

Fig. 11-5.   Left-skewed histogram of breakdown voltages from Table 11-6.

from left to right. The value on this scale is equal to $1/(1-p)$, where p is the cumulative probability. Due to the statistical behavior of the extreme value distribution, the return period has a unique interpretation. For any value of x, one may obtain the intercept with a best-fit line and project vertically to the return period scale. The value of the return period is interpreted as the sample size of additional items or observations required to have a 50% chance of observing another value equal to, or larger than, the value of x which is of interest. See Example 11-2 and Fig. 11-9.

The vertical axis, for the value of the variable of interest, is linear. A dashed vertical line shows the location of the mode, and a second dashed line locates the mean. The intersections of the two dashed verticals with a best-fit line are used to estimate the values of the mode and the mean.

Extreme Value Probability Plots

The sequence of data arrangement is important for extreme value data. In the histograms of Figs. 11-2 through 11-4, the peak is to the left side for positively skewed data. In Fig. 11-5, the peak is towards the right for negatively skewed data. Positively skewed data are arranged conventionally;

that is, from the smallest value up to the largest. Negatively skewed data are arranged from the largest value down to the smallest value.

Tables 11-5 and 11-6 show the data arrangement for the positive and negative skew cases respectively. Frequency cumulation and the values for the cumulative percentage plotting are obtained as for the normal distribution. The procedure for obtaining the best-fit line is also the same as for the normal distribution. In Figs. 11-6 and 11-7, we can see the probability plots for each table on extreme value probability paper.

Estimation of Extreme Value Distribution Parameters

On extreme value probability paper, the fitted straight line equation is:

$$x = \mu_0 + y/\alpha \qquad (11\text{-}10)$$

where:

x = the value of the extreme valued variable.
μ_0 = the value of the mode.
y = the value of the normalized variate for a specified percentile.
$1/\alpha$ = the *Gumbel slope* in x,y units.

The mode μ_0 is estimated directly from the intersection of the dashed vertical line at the modal

Table 11-5. Data Arrangement for Quadratic Sums (From Table 11-2)

Cell Interval	Mid-Point	Cumulative Occurrences	Cumulative Percentage Plotting
5.0 to 34.9	20	1 to 39	0.99 to 38.6
35.0 to 64.9	50	40 to 64	39.6 to 63.2
65.0 to 94.9	80	65 to 74	64.3 to 73.2
95.0 to 124.9	110	75 to 87	74.1 to 86.1
125.0 to 154.9	140	88 to 94	87.1 to 93.1
155.0 to 184.9	170	95 to 99	94.1 to 98.0
185.0 to 214.9	200		
215.0 to 244.9	230	100	99.01

Table 11-6. Data Arrangement for Breakdown Voltages

Cell Interval	Mid-Point	Cumulative Occurrences	Cumulative Percentage Plotting
1620 to 1739	1680	1 to 4	3.85 to 15.4
1500 to 1619	1560	5 to 10	19.25 to 38.5
1380 to 1499	1440	11 to 21	42.35 to 80.9
1260 to 1379	1320	22	84.7
1140 to 1259	1200	23	88.3
1020 to 1139	1080	24	92.2
900 to 1019	960	25	96.15

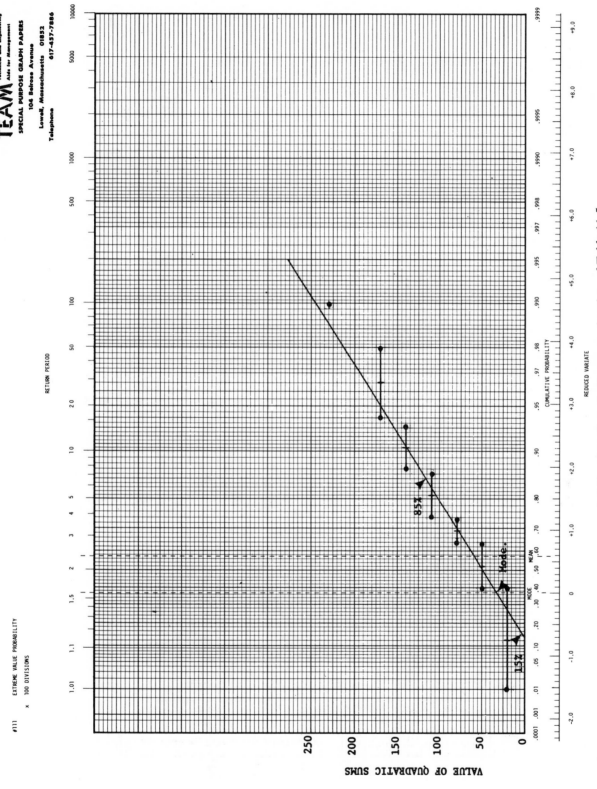

Fig. 11-6. Probability plot of quadratic sums, using data of Table 11-5.

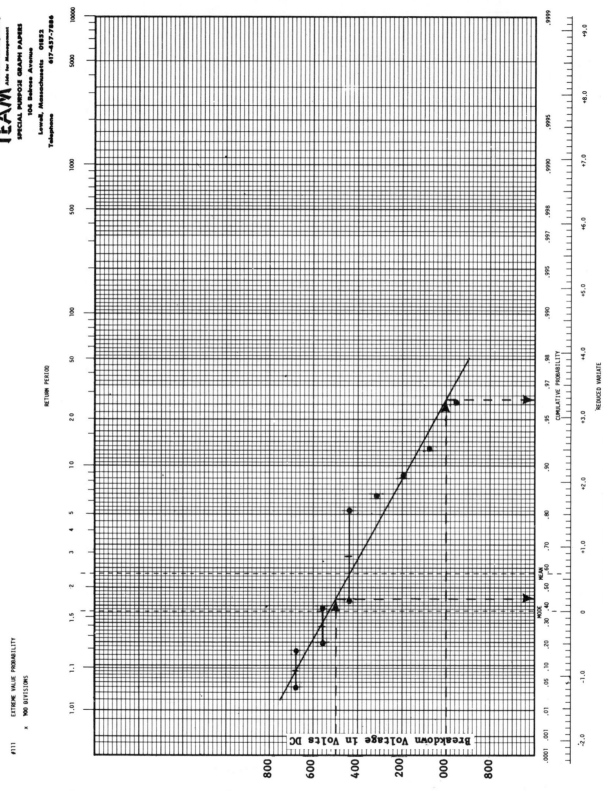

Fig. 11-7. Probability plot of breakdown voltages, using data from Table 11-6.

location and the best-fit straight line representing the plotted data. The value y is used in the same manner as k is with the normal and log-normal distributions except that y requires special tables for the related probability points. Tables for y are given in (18) and (19). The y scale on extreme value probability paper eliminates the need of tables in most extreme value data analysis problems. The Gumbel slope, $1/\alpha$, is determined by subtracting the value of x at the 15% vertical from the value at the 85% vertical and then dividing by 2.457:

$$1/\alpha = \frac{p_{0.85} - p_{0.15}}{2.457} \qquad (11\text{-}11)$$

Probability Statements about the Extreme Value Distribution

The area under the curve in Fig. 11-8 between the mode and $\pm 1\sigma$ is about 73%; $\mu_0 \pm 2\sigma = 92.6\%$; and $\mu_0 \pm 3\sigma = 97.9\%$. The percentages included by the $k\sigma$ intervals under the extreme value curve are different from the percentages included for the same intervals under the normal distribution curve because of the skewness of the extreme value distribution. However, once again we take advantage of being able to read probability statements directly from probability plots, using the cumulative percentage scale.

Example 11-1

The data arrangement for a study of machine stops per shift is given in Table 11-7. The data is plotted in Fig. 11-9. Parameter estimates are:

$\mu_0 = 5.9$

$$1/\alpha = \frac{9.40 - 4.55}{2.457} = \frac{4.85}{2.457} = 1.97$$

Table 11-7. Data Arrangement for Machine Stops per Shift

Machine Stops	Cumulative Occurrences	Cumulative Percentage Plotting
3	1 to 6	1.09 to 6.52
5	7 to 35	7.61 to 38.0
7	36 to 65	39.0 to 70.8
9	66 to 80	71.9 to 87.0
11	81 to 88	88.0 to 95.8
13	89 to 90	96.9 to 97.9
15	91	98.9

The regression equation for the best-fit straight line is then:

$$x = 5.9 + 1.97y \qquad (11\text{-}12)$$

Example 11-2

Using the probability plot of Fig. 11-7: What percentage of the breakdown voltages occurred between 1000 and 1500 volts? What percentage of breakdown voltages was less than 1000 volts?

The percentage of breakdown voltages greater than 1500 volts is 44% and the percentage greater than 1000 volts is 96.2%.

The percentage between 1000 and 1500 volts is $96.2 - 44 = 62.2\%$.

The percentage less than 1000 volts is $100.0 - 96.2 = 3.8\%$.

Applications of the Return Period

We have already considered that the return period represents an estimate of probable sample sizes required to observe certain specified events. This is best understood from examples of applications.

Example 11-3

Using the probability plot of Fig. 11-9 determine the following:

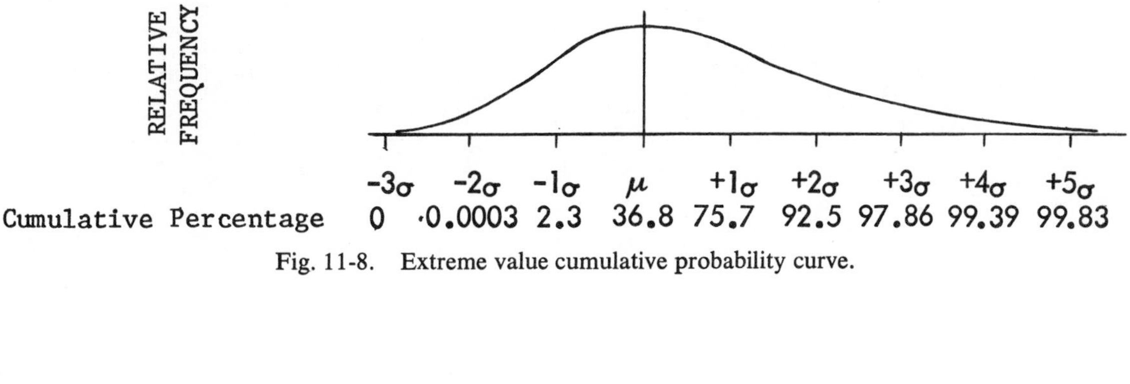

	-3σ	-2σ	-1σ	μ	$+1\sigma$	$+2\sigma$	$+3\sigma$	$+4\sigma$	$+5\sigma$
Cumulative Percentage	0	·0.0003	2.3	36.8	75.7	92.5	97.86	99.39	99.83

Fig. 11-8.   Extreme value cumulative probability curve.

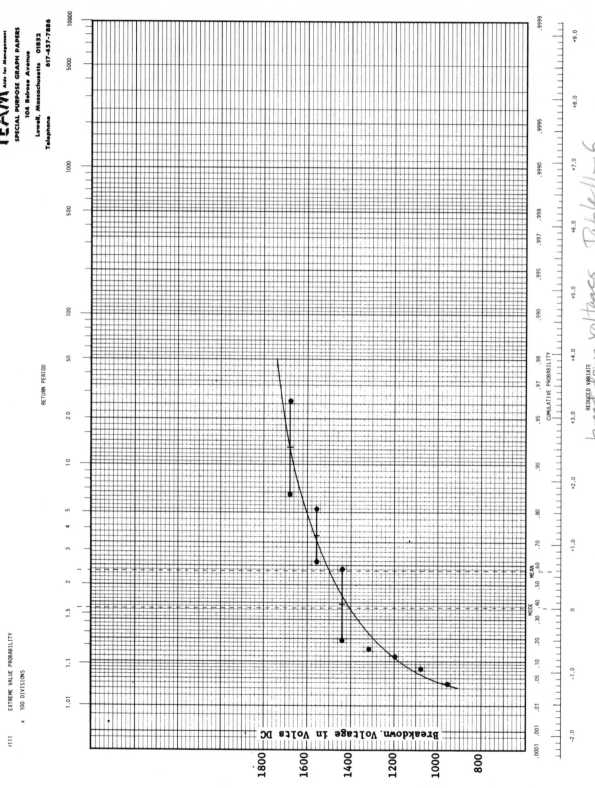

Fig. 11-9. Probability plot of machine stops per shift, using data from Table 11-8.

A. What is the return period for 6 stops per shift?

Start at 6 on the scale for machine stops, project to the right to intersect with the best-fit line and, then, project vertically to the return period scale. The return period value is just less than 2. This means that 6 or more stops per shift will occur every two shifts, on the average.

B. In a normal work week of five shifts, what is the estimate of the peak work load for repairmen likely to be?

Start at 5 on the Return Period scale, drop vertically to the best-fit line and project to the stops scale at the left, which results in a value of about 9 stops. This means there is a 50 percent chance of having one shift during a week in which 9 or more stops occur.

C. In the analysis of maintenance personnel requirements, it is often required to determine the amount of staffing needed to handle the 90% level of stoppages. How is this determined?

In this case, project vertically from the 90% point to the best-fit line and then left to the stops scale, which indicates a value of about 10 stops. Therefore, staffing would be based on a capability of handling 10 stops per shift.

D. With staffing for the 90% stoppage level, how often would the capability of the staff be exceeded?

Project the 90% point to the return period scale, which gives a value of ten shifts. This means that the capability of the staff would likely be exceeded once every two weeks, on the average.

Further Estimates from Extreme Value Probability Plots

At times it is desirable to determine the values of the mean and the standard deviation of an extreme value distribution. This is accomplished by estimating the mode and the Gumbel slope from an extreme value probability plot and then multiplying by correction factors which Gumbel called *expected values.* Expected values vary with sample size. Appendix Table A-5 contains the correction factors for the expected values of means and standard deviations of samples from 15 to 1000. Values for the mean and standard deviation are calculated by substitution in the following equations:

$$\bar{x} = \mu_0 + \overline{y(N)}/\alpha \qquad (11\text{-}13)$$

where:

$\overline{y(N)}$ is the value of the *expected mean,* Table A-5.

$$s_x = \sigma(N)/\alpha \qquad (11\text{-}14)$$

where:

$\sigma(N)$ is the value of the *expected standard deviation,* from Table A-5.

Example 11-4

Using Fig. 11-6, we obtain estimates of $\mu_0 = 32$ and $1/\alpha = 46$. Determine the mean and standard deviation.

From Appendix Table A-5, for $n = 100$, we find $\overline{y(N)} = 0.56$ and $\sigma(N) = 0.206$. By substitution in Equations 11-13 and 11-14, we obtain:

$$\bar{x} = 32 + 0.56(46) = 57.8$$

$$s_x = 0.206(46) \quad\quad = 9.5$$

Interpretation of Extreme Value Probability Plots

As was the case for the normal and log-normal distributions, a linear plot on extreme value probability paper is a first condition for obtaining valid parameter estimates.

Nonlinear extreme value plots have the same interpretation as for the normal and log-normal probability plots. Nonlinearity indicates that the lot from which the sample was taken has been sorted, inspected or truncated for one reason or another. A step pattern indicates mixed sources of input.

Convex plots indicate that the data are less skewed than the expected extreme value behavior and may be better fitted by a chi-square distribution paper. There is one convex plot which is an important exception in extreme value probability plots. If the direction of skew was not determined initially by a frequency tally or a histogram, then a plot which is flat at the high end may indicate that the plotted data actually have skew in the opposite direction to that assumed in making the initial data arrangement. When opposite skew is suspected, the data should be rearranged and replotted in the opposite order. A convex plot obtained from the data of Table 11-6 by purposely inverting the order is shown in Fig. 11-10. Com-

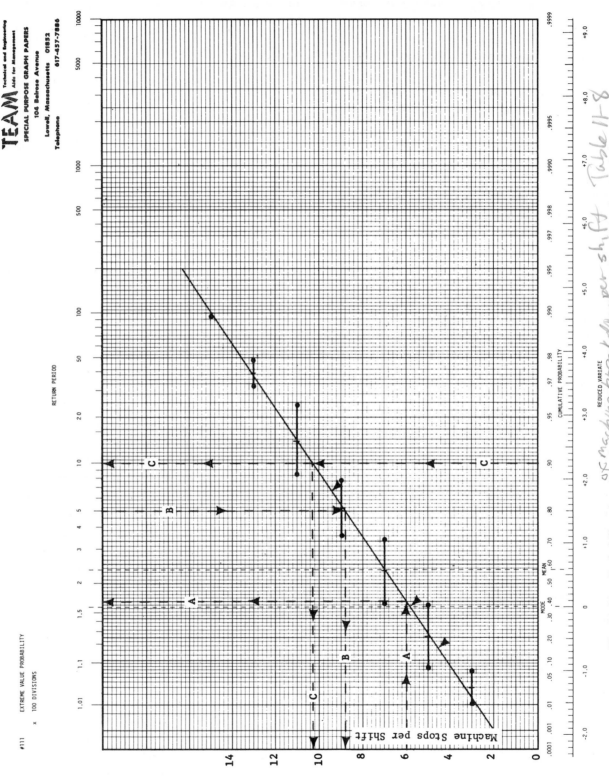

Fig. 11-10.   Probability plot of breakdown voltages, using data from Table 11-6 in inverse order.

or Machine Breakdown per shift Table 11-8

Table 11-8. Ultimate Tensile Strengths of 30 Specimens of 2014-T6
Aluminum Tested at −423°F (Units in KSI.)

101.0	99.8	99.3	98.6	97.9	97.6
100.8	99.6	99.2	98.4	97.9	95.8
100.6	99.6	98.8	98.2	97.8	95.2
100.2	99.4	98.8	98.1	97.6	93.6
100.2	99.4	98.7	98.0	97.6	92.8

pare this to Fig. 9-7, which is a correct plot of the same data.

Concave plots indicate that the data are more skewed than the extreme value distribution and may be better fitted by logarithmic extreme value or Weibull probability papers.

Confidence Intervals for Extreme Value Plots

Confidence intervals for extreme value probability plots are obtained in a manner similar to those for normal and log-normal plots. The extreme value line falls within:

$$y = \bar{L} \pm k_2 \frac{(|1/\alpha|)}{\sqrt{n}} \qquad (11\text{-}15)$$

where:

k_2 is a factor similar to k for the normal distribution;

$\dfrac{|1/\alpha|}{\sqrt{n}}$ is equivalent to s_y.

Values for k_2 are given in Appendix Table A-6. The values of k_2 for the largest and second largest values need not be divided by $\sqrt{n}$. The k_2 factor alone is sufficient to determine the two largest values.

The procedure for obtaining confidence intervals is:

Step 1. Obtain the Gumbel slope estimate, $1/\alpha$, from the fitted line.

Step 2. Multiply $1/\alpha$ by the k_2 factors from Appendix Table A-6, and then divide by $\sqrt{n}$. For the largest and second largest values, perform only the multiplication by k_2. The values so obtained are *offset values*.

Step 3. Using the line fitted to the plotted data, estimate the intercept of the fitted line with the lines for the preselected cumulative percentage plotting positions from Appendix Table A-6.

Step 4. Add and subtract the offset values obtained in Step 2 from the intercept values from Step 3.

Step 5. Plot the results from Step 4.

Step 6. Connect the points plotted in Step 5 with a faired curve.

Step 7. Since Appendix Table A-6 is based on 95 percent confidence, the confidence interval resulting from Steps 1–7 should enclose 95 percent of the plotted points.

The procedure for obtaining confidence intervals is illustrated in Example 11-5 and Fig. 11-11, using the data given in Table 11-8.

Example 11-5

The ultimate tensile strengths for 30 specimens of 2014-T6 aluminum when tested at −423°F are contained in Table 11-8. The data are tabulated in order from the largest value to the smallest. This is an example of a smallest extreme value distribution.

The cumulative percentage–plotting is obtained from $(n_i \times 100\%)/(n+1)$. $(1 \times 100\%)/(30+1)$ yields about 3.22% per item. The strength data are plotted by individual value in Fig. 11-11. From the fitted line, we obtain the estimates:

$$\mu_0 = 99.2$$

$$\frac{1}{\alpha} = \frac{96.4 - 100.2}{2.457} = \frac{-3.8}{2.457} = -1.54$$

The negative value of the Gumbel slope results because these data are plotted from largest to smallest. The 85% point is therefore less than the 15% point. This is seen in the slope of the fitted line in Fig. 11-11. The offset values, however, are calculated using the absolute value of the Gumbel slope because the vertical offsets around the fitted line will be both plus and minus distances.

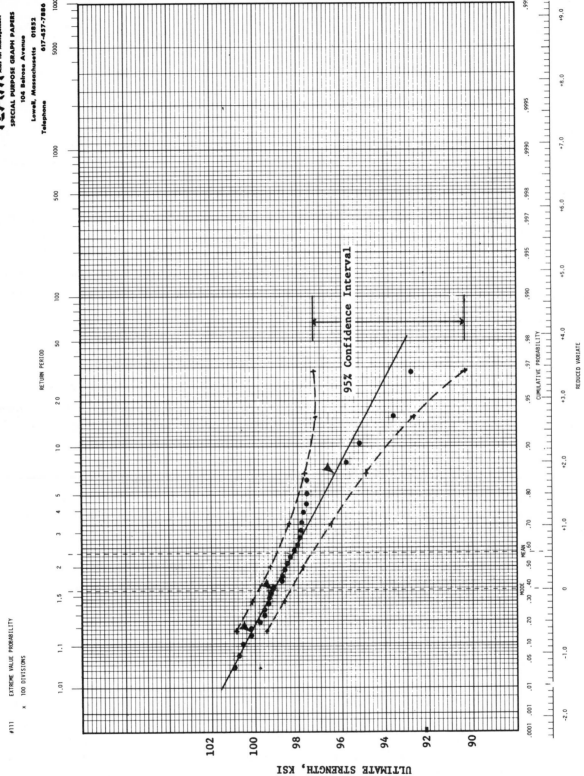

Fig. 11-11. Extreme value probability plot. Ultimate tensile strength for 2014-T6 aluminum at −423°F with 95 percent confidence intervals.

Percentile	$|1/\alpha|$	$\sqrt{n}$		$\times\ k_2$	Offset
15%	$|1.54|$	$\div\ \sqrt{30}$	$= 0.280$	$\times 2.51$	$= 0.7$
30%				0.280×2.54	$= 0.7$
50%				0.280×2.89	$= 0.8$
70%				0.280×3.67	$= 1.0$
85%				0.280×5.17	$= 1.4$
2nd Largest Value				$|1.54| \times 1.51$	$= 2.3$
Largest Value				$|1.54| \times 2.28$	$= 3.5$

The offsets are added to and subtracted from the fitted line by eye and then used to draw in the confidence interval which is shown as a dotted line in Fig. 11-11. All of the plotted points fall inside the control lines; therefore, an extreme value fit is accepted.

The confidence interval for the largest value can be extrapolated to provide estimates at values beyond those observed. To do this, the end of the flared confidence interval is projected from that point parallel to the fitted line. This is illustrated in Fig. 12-2.

Exercises

11-1. a. Using the values from Table 11-1 *in reverse order,* obtain the quadratic sums for the first 24 sets of values.

b. Arrange the data and construct the probability plot.

c. Fit the best straight line and obtain estimates of the extreme value parameters. State the equation for the fitted line.

d. Calculate the offsets for the confidence intervals and plot.

11-2. a. Using the values from Table 11-1 *in reverse order,* obtain the quartic sums for the first 49 sets of values.

b. Arrange the data and construct the probability plot.

c. Fit the best straight line and obtain estimates of the extreme value parameters. State the equation for the fitted line.

d. Calculate the offsets for the confidence intervals and plot.

11-3. a. Using the first 24 values from Table 3-1 for the Before sample, arrange the data, construct the probability plot, estimate the parameters, and obtain the confidence intervals.

b. Using the first 24 values from Table 3-1 for the After sample, arrange the data and construct the probability plot on the same sheet as Exercise 11-3 a, above.

c. Discuss the differences in results.

11-4. a. Using the values from Table 3-3, Lot #1, arrange the data, construct the probability plot, estimate the parameters and obtain the Confidence Intervals.

b. Plot the data from Table 3-3, Lot #2, on the same sheet and discuss the results.

CHAPTER 12

Engineering Applications of the Extreme Value Distribution

Examples of the Smallest Extreme Value Distribution

In Chapter 11, we stated that the strength properties of materials were well represented by extreme value distributions. The breakdown voltage of an electronic capacitor is a measure of the dielectric strength, or the property of preventing electric currents from flowing under an applied voltage stress. Figure 11-5 is an example of a breakdown voltage distribution which is of the smallest extreme value type. The tensile strength of aluminum at low temperature is another example of a smallest extreme value distribution, as shown in Fig. 11-11. Figure 12-1 is a comparison of the percent elongation in a textile yarn taken from the data of Table 3-4.

Figure 12-1 is an application of the use of confidence intervals to compare test results on material obtained from two different sources. The calculations for Gumbel slope and offsets for the confidence interval are shown in Table 12-1. After the confidence interval is drawn around the plot of the data from Source A, it is very apparent that there are no grounds for comparison between the elongation characteristics of the two sources of yarn. The yarn with greater elongation will result in better resilience in carpeting applications.

Examples of the Largest Extreme Value Distribution

Example 11-3 and Fig. 11-9 illustrate the use of the return period in an industrial engineering problem for largest extreme value data. The same approach can be used to establish equipment requirements for an assured amount of output and to determine inventory levels against specified contingencies.

Table 12-1. Calculations for Confidence Interval for Fig. 12-1

$$1/\alpha = \text{Gumbel slope} = \frac{P\,0.85 - P\,0.15}{2.457} =$$

$$\frac{1.44 - 2.59}{2.457} = -0.468$$

$$|1/\alpha| \div \sqrt{n} = |-0.468| \div \sqrt{49} = 0.0668$$

Cumulative Percentage Plotting Positions	Multiply	By	To Obtain Vertical Offset
15%	0.0668	2.51	0.17
30	"	2.54	0.17
50	"	2.89	0.19
70	"	3.67	0.24
85	"	5.17	0.34
Second Largest Value	0.468	1.51	0.71
Largest Value	"	2.28	1.07

Figure 12-2 uses confidence intervals to compare successive batches of an electrolytic capacitor for differences in electrical loss known as dissipation factor. Calculations for Gumbel slope and the offsets based on Lot #1 are given in Table 12-2. The two distributions appear to become different after the 60% point. All of the points for Lot #2 are outside of the confidence interval of Lot #1, starting with the 68% point. The upper 40% of the points for Lot #2 look like a jog pattern similar to Fig. 5-8. Subsequent investigation disclosed that part of Lot #2 had been accidentally damaged in processing. Precautions were then taken to prevent similar damage in the future.

Extrapolation of Extreme Value Confidence Intervals

In testing many kinds of electronic components, we are interested in determining how stable some

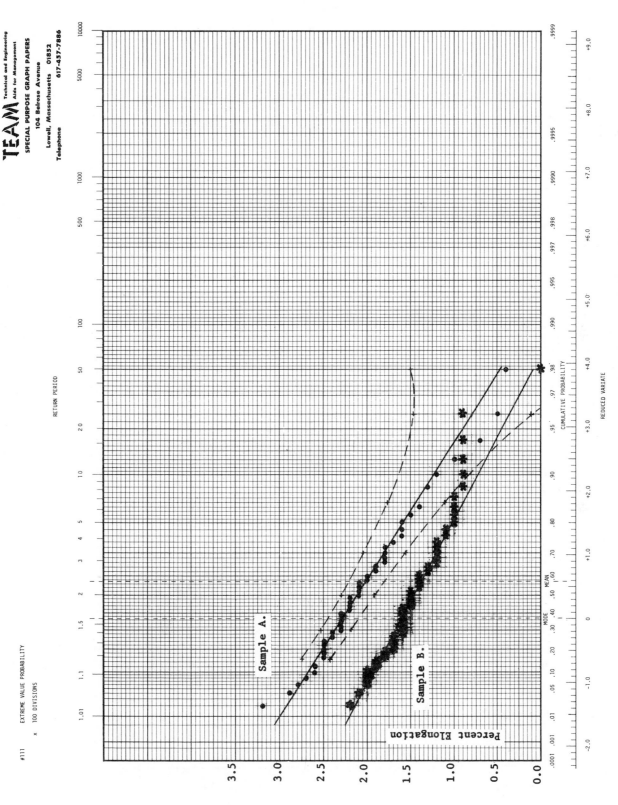

Fig. 12-1.   Comparison of two yarn samples for elongation in tension.

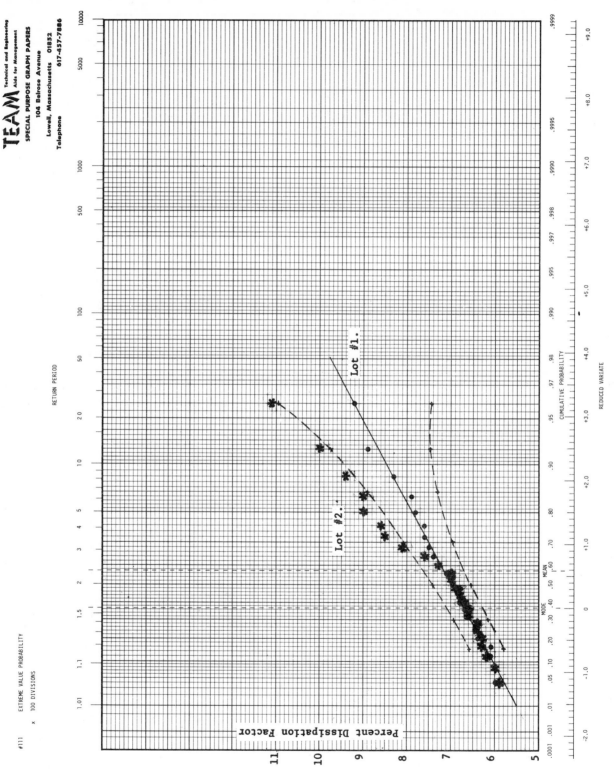

Fig. 12-2.   Comparison of two samples of electrolytic capacitors for electrical loss.

Table 12-2. Calculations for Confidence Interval
for Fig. 12-2

$$1/\alpha = \frac{8.15 - 6.20}{2.457} = 0.7936$$

$$|1/\alpha| \div \sqrt{n} = |0.7936| \div \sqrt{24} = 0.162$$

Cumulative Percentage Plotting Positions	Multiply	By	To Obtain Vertical Offset
15%	0.162	2.51	0.41
30	"	2.54	0.41
50	"	2.89	0.47
70	"	3.67	0.59
85	"	5.17	0.84
Second Largest Value	0.7936	1.51	1.20
Largest Value	"	2.28	1.81

important characteristic is. For example, with resistors we would like to know how stable the resistance value remains under some condition of applied power. Stability is frequently determined by measuring a sample of parts, testing under specified conditions for a designated period of time, re-measuring the parts after the test, and calculating the difference in the measured value of the characteristic of interest.

Figure 12-3 is a plot of the resistance change in a 100 ohm metal-film resistor, with an original purchased tolerance of 1%, resulting from a 1,000-hour life test at full-rated conditions. The confidence interval is shown as a faired curve out to the last observed point. The confidence interval is extrapolated simply by drawing straight lines through the offset points for the smallest (or largest) value parallel to the best-fit line. The extrapolated confidence interval will yield estimates of information not readily available from the observed data.

A typical requirement for stability of metal-film resistors under the conditions stated above is that no resistor should change more than 5% from its initial value. For a 100 ohm resistor, this is equal to 5 ohms change. The smallest extreme value plot of Fig. 12-3 indicates that the more likely direction of excessive change will be in the negative direction *even though* the largest observed negative change during the life test was only −0.6 ohms. Extrapolation of the best-fit line results

in the estimate that less than 0.01% of similar parts would fail under the specified life test conditions. Extrapolation of the lower confidence limit results in an estimate that not more than 0.06% would fail at the 97.5% confidence level, since the lower bound of a 95% confidence interval is at the 97.5% level. The preceding determination is more informative than that of a conventional test evaluation which would present the results shown in Fig. 12-3 as a simple statement: "No part failures occurred in 24 parts tested under specified conditions."

The two most serious problems in quality control and reliability testing today are time and money. To ship materials as soon as possible on an economic basis, quality assurance tests are abbreviated, both in time and in sample size tested. With small sample sizes, it is customary to require zero failures. When the test is completed successfully, one typically knows only that a sample of x parts was tested for time, t, under specified conditions with zero failures occurring. This is a low confidence procedure and, therefore, a low assurance procedure. Batch-to-batch, lot-to-lot, week-to-week, and other sources of variation are completely submerged.

By contrast, the simple analysis of key change data, such as that for Fig. 12-3, yields estimates of statistical parameters such as the mode, Gumbel slope, and projected failure rate. Test-by-test variability in a product can be analyzed, evaluated, and monitored, using variables control charts of parameter estimates. See (10), (11), (17), (21), (32), and (41) for discussion and examples of statistical control charts. The use of control charts of key statistics in addition to the conventional lot test results can provide a predetermined level of assurance of statistically controlled output.

Extreme Value Behavior in Life Testing

Some characteristics of electronic components are naturally extreme value distributed, and the changes in measured values are also observed to be extreme value distributions. It is known that the sums and differences of extreme value distributions are also extreme value distributions. We have already commented that normally distributed

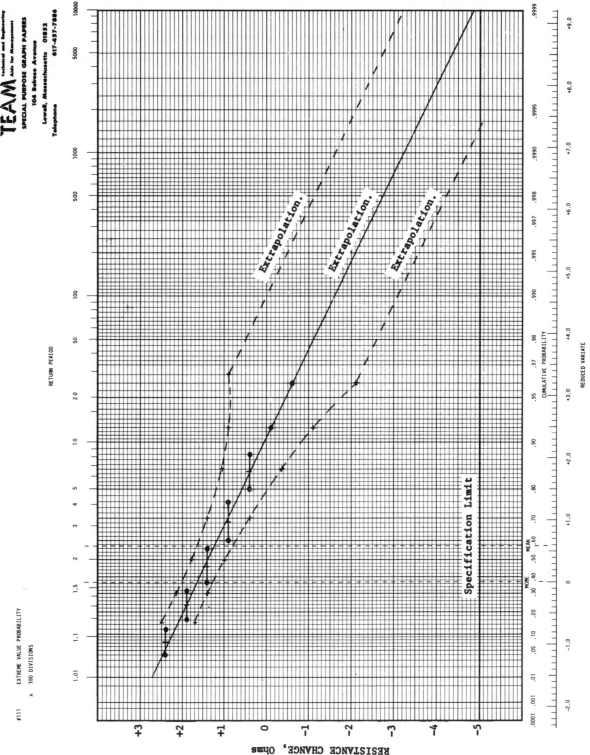

Fig. 12-3.   Extreme value probability plot for changes in resistance value of a 100 ohm, 1 percent tolerance resistor during a 1000-hour life test showing 95 percent confidence intervals and extrapolated estimates.

characteristics wear out by linear processes and that log-normally distributed characteristics wear out by rate-dependent processes, and now we observe that extreme valued characteristics appear to wear out by extreme value processes. An example is given below.

An important characteristic of a transistor is the current gain, or amplification ratio of the output signal in the emitter circuit to the input signal in the base circuit. Usually, it is only necessary to know that the current gain is greater than some ratio which can be determined indirectly by measuring the amount of base current required to cause a fixed emitter current. As a result, low values of base current indicate "good" transistors and values of base current above some specified value indicate "bad" transistors.

Figure 12-4 shows a family of lines fitted to actual data points for the distribution of base current at various stages of a transistor life test. The individual data points are omitted for clarity. Line 0 is the best-fit line representing the initial distribution of base current measurements. Each subsequent line represents the distribution of measurements after a test step. Each test step was 24 hours. The transistor was operated with 150 milliwatts of power dissipation in the first step and the power dissipation was raised by 50 milliwatts after each 24-hour step was completed.

Lines 0, 1, 2, and 3 are relatively close together and are nearly parallel, which indicates that little, if any, change has taken place, because it was also known that measurement repeatability error was about ±0.25 milliamperes. After Step 3, the lines become increasingly steep. This means that the variation between individual transistors is increasing, although the modal value is not increasing by very much. Table 12-3 contains the values of the mode and Gumbel slope for each line in Fig. 12-4. The table shows that after Step 8 the mode has increased by only 64%, but the Gumbel slope has increased by 206%. The rate of increase for the slope is more than three times the rate for the mode. The increase in slope, indicating increasing individual variation, is obviously the more important measure of potential failure.

After the first few steps, the lines appear to rotate about a common point near the 10th percentile. The later lines drop below the lines of the earlier steps at the low end of the plot. Thus it appears that some parts are "improving." The idea of improvement is misleading. If the random terms in a polynomial expression representing an extreme value process are truly random, then some of the terms will have values less than 1 or will take on negative values. In either case, some final values will become smaller than the corresponding initial value. Such behavior is a significant indicator of extreme value changes to initially extreme value-distributed characteristics. Some observers have commented that such behavior represents the effect of mixed distributions, but this is not necessarily so.

Differential Equations and Extreme Value Distributions

Linear differential equations with constant coefficients occur frequently in chemistry and theoretical physics. These equations have the general solution:

$$y = \sum c_n e^{r_n x} \qquad (12\text{-}1)$$

where: $\qquad n = 1, 2, 3 \ldots . n$

Expanding Equation 12-1, we obtain:

$$y = c_1 e^{r_1 x} + c_2 e^{r_2 x} + c_3 e^{r_3 x} + \ldots . \qquad (12\text{-}2)$$

Equation 12-2 can be rewritten more conveniently as:

$$y = e^{x_1} + e^{x_2} + e^{x_3} + e^{x_4} \ldots . \qquad (12\text{-}3)$$

Table 12-3. Values of Distribution Parameters from Fig. 12-4

Fitted Line	Mode	Gumbel Slope
0	0.49	0.140
1	0.44	0.123
2	0.55	0.180
3	0.58	0.185
4	0.64	0.232
5	0.68	0.303
6	0.70	0.365
7	0.74	0.383
8	0.80	0.430

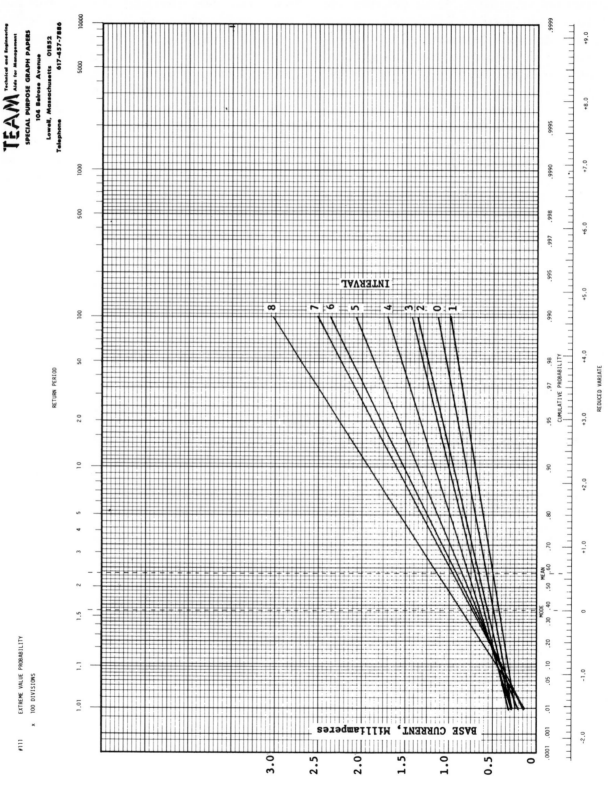

Fig. 12-4. Family of fitted lines at equal exposure intervals.

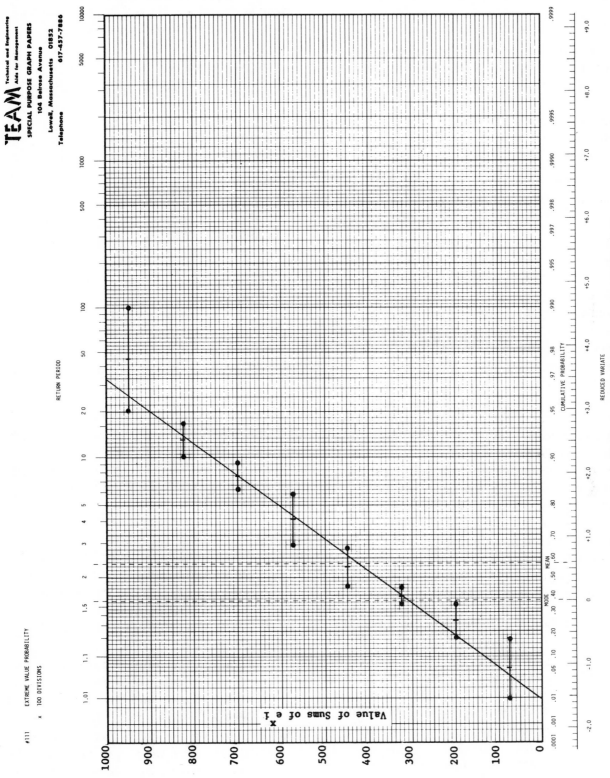

Fig. 12-5.   Probability plot of sums of e^{x_1}. (x_i from Table 6-1.)

where: y = the value of the variable of interest

x_n = the value of a random variable

c_n is taken as a common constant.

The values for the random variables, x_n, may be taken from Table 6-1. These sets of values were obtained from tosses of dice. When the values of the random variable are substituted in Equation 12-3, we obtain solutions for y. For example, using the values from the first line of Table 6-1, we obtain:

$$y = e^3 + e^2 + e^6 + e^3 = 20 + 7 + 403 + 20 \doteq 450$$

Values from the second line yield:

$$y = e^5 + e^5 + e^4 + e^2 = 148 + 148 + 55 + 7 = 358$$

Table 12-4 contains the results of 100 such substitutions. Figure 12-5 is the probability plot for this data. This plot is quite similar to the one of Fig. 11-6, although it was obtained in a different way.

The individual terms in Equation 12-3 are called *transcendental terms* and the equation is called a *transcendental equation*. The transcendental form is basically only a mathematical restatement of the polynomial form used to generate the extreme value distribution in Equation 11-6. However, since we have now shown that extreme value behavior arises from *both* algebraic equations involving polynomial terms and also from exponential equations with transcendental terms, we have illustrated the great generality of extreme value behavior.

It is of interest to note that Equation 12-3 involves only *addition* of the transcendental terms. The transcendental e is raised to the *power* of a random variable. In the form of Equation 12-3,

Table 12-5. Data for Base Currents of Transistors Subjected to Temperature Step Stressing in Equal Temperature Steps

Initial Readings	After Step 1	After Step 2	After Step 3
0.56	0.62	1.75	1.70
0.34	0.48	0.86	0.94
0.55	0.54	0.76	1.50
0.71	0.74	1.40	2.50
0.50	0.72	1.00	1.75
0.32	0.30	0.34	0.38
0.53	1.60	2.35	2.30
0.50	0.52	0.86	1.30
0.78	1.32	4.10	3.40
0.40	0.52	0.63	0.86
0.60	1.75	3.60	3.80
0.70	1.35	1.90	2.60
0.79	0.92	1.35	2.80
0.56	0.65	0.96	1.65
0.86	0.73	1.00	1.35
0.60	0.83	1.02	1.37
0.46	0.43	0.56	0.71
0.58	0.64	1.05	1.62
0.50	0.72	1.18	0.91

the extreme value distribution is obtained through the operation of *addition* of terms involving *exponentiation*. The transcendental form is particularly useful in deriving the logarithmic extreme value distribution within a framework of relatively simple and logical mathematical steps.

Exercises

12-1. a. Using the data of Table 12-5, construct the probability plots for each set of readings, estimate the parameters and construct the confidence intervals.

    b. Using the parameter estimates, plot all 4 lines as in Fig. 12-4.

    c. Compare the results between each pair of readings; that is, between Initial and Step 1, Step 1 and Step 2, Step 2 and Step 3.

    d. Based on the comparisons of Exercise 12-1.c, what would you say about the effect of temperature on these transistors? Consider both changes from step-to-step and from start-to-finish.

Table 12-4. Sums of e^{x_1} Using Values from Table 6-1

450	191	882	97	50	465	822	324	473	575
358	1010	85	515	166	708	72	438	157	80
567	562	434	626	567	916	434	661	67	72
446	627	626	171	119	132	33	372	708	446
574	230	830	196	1010	426	312	208	755	307
755	183	916	448	359	614	79	975	230	614
481	498	337	184	50	33	661	533	85	312
515	834	465	468	822	498	85	562	562	520
230	468	213	434	473	208	218	486	446	213
320	183	20	177	557	434	226	421	260	661

CHAPTER 13

The Logarithmic Extreme Value Distribution

Background

The logarithmic extreme value distribution stands in the same relationship to the extreme value distribution as the logarithmic normal distribution does to the normal distribution. That is, the normalized unit variable for the log-extreme value distribution is obtained by a simple logarithmic transformation of the unit variable of the extreme value distribution.

Logarithmic extreme value distributions are highly skewed, frequently covering many orders of magnitude of the variable. Selected extremes from log-normal distributions are log-extreme value distributions. The most common use of the log-extreme value distribution is in the statistics of particle sizes, where it is better known as the Rosin-Rammler Distribution. Log-extreme value distributions also occur with ratios of identically distributed variables; from the average of n mutually independent random vectors — that is, from problems in Brownian motion or random walks; and in measurements of electronic and hydrological phenomena.

Description of the Logarithmic Extreme Value Distribution

The Logarithmic Extreme Value Distribution is also known as:

1. Type II Extreme Value Distribution: one of the extreme value classifications established by E. J. Gumbel to distinguish it from the extreme value distribution and the Weibull distribution.

2. Rosin-Rammler Distribution: named after two men who made significant applications of this distribution to sizing coal and other materials.

The cumulative distribution function and the probability density function for the Logarithmic Extreme Value Distribution are given by:

$$\Pi(x) = \int_0^x \exp -(\mu_o/x)^k \qquad (13\text{-}1)$$

$$\pi(x) = -k(\mu_o/x)^{k-1} \exp -(\mu_o/x)^k \qquad (13\text{-}2)$$

under the conditions that:

$$o < x < \infty$$

$x =$ the value of the random variable.
$\mu_o =$ the mode.
k, when expressed as $1/k$, is the measure of dispersion, called the *Geometric Gumbel Slope, g'*

The relationship between Type I and Type II extreme value distributions is established by the identity:

$$(\mu_o/x)^k = e^{-\alpha(x-\mu_o)} \qquad (13\text{-}3)$$

Taking logarithms and rearranging, we obtain:

$$k(\log \mu_o - \log x) = -\alpha(x - \mu_o) \qquad (13\text{-}4)$$

$$-k(\log x - \log \mu_o) = -\alpha(x - \mu_o)$$

and

$$k = \alpha$$

where $1/\alpha$ is the Gumbel slope of the Type I extreme value distribution.

Equation 13-4 states simply that the logarithms of a logarithmic extreme value distribution are extreme value distributed. This is completely analogous to the relationship of the log-normal to the normal distribution. Using the same logic as for the log-normal distribution, we can obtain a formula for convenience of calculation by appropriate substitutions:

$$x = \mu_o (g')^y \qquad (13\text{-}5)$$

μ_o = the value of the mode of the log-extreme value distribution.

g' = the geometric Gumbel slope, $1/k$.

y = normalized unit variable, as in Chapter 11.

Equation 13-5 states that the variable, x, equals the mode multiplied by the dispersion raised to a power representing the probability of occurrence.

The Origin of a Logarithmic Extreme Value Distribution

Equation 12-3 gave the transcendental form for generating extreme value distributions. This equation can be rewritten as:

$$y = \exp(x_1 + x_2 + x_3 + x_4 \ldots) \qquad (13\text{-}6)$$

The logarithmic extreme value distribution is generated from an equation which is obtained by direct substitution of multiplication for addition of the exponents, giving:

$$y = \exp(x_1 \cdot x_2 \cdot x_3 \cdot x_4 \ldots) \qquad (13\text{-}7)$$

Equations 13-6 and 13-7 are in one-to-one correspondence to the addition and multiplication operations on random variables which produce the normal and log-normal distributions. The difference is that the addition and multiplication operations for extreme value cases are applied to random variables when used as *exponents in a transcendental equation.* Although products of polynomial terms will generate logarithmic extreme value distributions, substitution of the equivalent transcendental terms accentuates the fundamental importance of the operations of addition and multiplication in the mathematical expressions describing underlying physical processes. Consequently, the general considerations relating the log-normal distribution to the normal distribution are also applicable to the relationships of logarithmic extreme value distributions to extreme value distributions.

Example 13-1

Given: The data of Table 9-1.

Table 9-1 contains the products of four values of a random variable obtained by throwing four dice and counting the spots showing for each die. Each product in the table is substituted in Equation 13-7, resulting in 100 values for y. The first and second values are:

$$y_1 = e^{108} = 108 \log_{10} e = 108(0.43429) = 8.01 \times 10^{46}$$

$$y_2 = e^{200} = 200 \log_{10} e = 200(0.43429) = 7.23 \times 10^{86}$$

The values so obtained are contained in Table 13-1 which has been arranged in order of increasing magnitude. A plot of these values is given in Fig. 13-1 on extreme value probability

Table 13-1. Ordered Values of $e^{\Pi x_1}$ Using the Πx_1 from Table 9-1

5.46×10	4.31×10^{15}	1.14×10^{26}	1.30×10^{52}	1.94×10^{130}
1.48×10^{2}	4.31×10^{15}	1.14×10^{26}	1.30×10^{52}	1.94×10^{130}
4.03×10^{2}	4.31×10^{15}	1.14×10^{26}	1.30×10^{52}	1.94×10^{130}
4.03×10^{2}	4.31×10^{15}	6.24×10^{27}	1.94×10^{54}	9.42×10^{138}
2.98×10^{3}	2.38×10^{17}	1.98×10^{31}	3.46×10^{62}	2.22×10^{156}
2.98×10^{3}	2.38×10^{17}	1.98×10^{31}	3.46×10^{62}	2.22×10^{156}
1.63×10^{5}	2.38×10^{17}	3.73×10^{32}	3.46×10^{62}	2.22×10^{156}
8.89×10^{6}	3.49×10^{19}	3.73×10^{32}	1.39×10^{65}	7.25×10^{162}
6.57×10^{7}	7.02×10^{20}	5.54×10^{34}	2.42×10^{83}	7.25×10^{162}
6.57×10^{7}	7.02×10^{20}	5.54×10^{34}	2.42×10^{83}	5.88×10^{166}
4.85×10^{8}	7.02×10^{20}	1.22×10^{39}	7.23×10^{86}	4.12×10^{187}
4.85×10^{8}	7.02×10^{20}	1.22×10^{39}	7.23×10^{86}	2.89×10^{208}
2.65×10^{10}	7.02×10^{20}	4.93×10^{41}	6.42×10^{93}	2.89×10^{208}
2.65×10^{10}	5.18×10^{21}	4.93×10^{41}	6.42×10^{93}	2.89×10^{208}
2.65×10^{10}	2.83×10^{23}	4.93×10^{41}	6.42×10^{93}	3.30×10^{234}
2.65×10^{10}	2.83×10^{23}	4.93×10^{41}	5.20×10^{97}	1.42×10^{250}
2.65×10^{10}	2.83×10^{23}	2.69×10^{43}	1.70×10^{104}	1.42×10^{250}
1.07×10^{13}	1.14×10^{26}	8.01×10^{46}	1.70×10^{104}	3.77×10^{260}
1.07×10^{13}	1.14×10^{26}	8.01×10^{46}	1.70×10^{104}	3.77×10^{260}
7.90×10^{13}	1.14×10^{26}	1.30×10^{52}	1.19×10^{125}	4.92×10^{312}

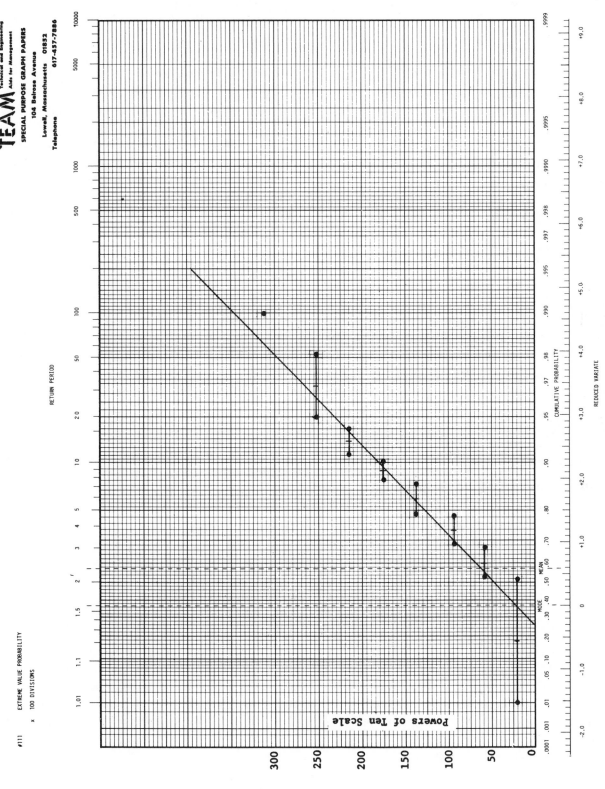

Fig. 13-1.   Probability plot. Data of Table 13-1.

Table 13-2. Data Arrangement for Product Values
from Table 13-1

$\left(\text{Number of Cells} = 8\right.$

$\left.\text{Cell ratio} = \dfrac{4.92 \times 10^{312}/5.46 \times 10^{1}}{8} = 7.40 \times 10^{38}\right)$

Cell Interval	Mid-Point	Cumulative Occurrences	Cumulative Percentage Plotting
5.46×10 to 4.03×10^{40}	$10^{20.5}$	1 to 52	0.99 to 51.8
4.04×10^{40} to 2.98×10^{79}	$10^{59.5}$	53 to 68	52.5 to 67.2
2.99×10^{79} to 2.20×10^{118}	$10^{93.5}$	69 to 79	68.2 to 78.2
2.21×10^{118} to 1.63×10^{157}	$10^{137.5}$	80 to 87	79.2 to 86.1
1.64×10^{157} to 1.20×10^{196}	$10^{176.5}$	88 to 91	87.1 to 90.1
1.21×10^{196} to 8.97×10^{234}	$10^{215.0}$	92 to 95	91.1 to 94.1
8.98×10^{234} to 6.64×10^{273}	$10^{253.5}$	96 to 99	95.1 to 98.1
6.65×10^{273} to 4.92×10^{312}	$10^{292.5}$	100	99.01

paper using powers of ten for the variable scale. Calculations and data arrangement are given in Table 13-2. The most obvious feature of this plot is the enormous range of the variable, y, obtained from solving Equation 13-7. Values for y range over several hundreds of *orders of magnitude*. This example is presented to emphasize an important feature of the logarithmic extreme value distribution: this distribution is virtually unlimited to the right — that is, in the magnitude of the values which it can assume.

Logarithmic extreme value distributions more commonly occur over number ranges which are more restricted than those obtained from Equation 13-7. They occur more often in the form:

$$y = \exp\{(x_1/x_2)(x_3/x_4)\ldots(x_{n-1}/x_n)\} \quad (13\text{-}8)$$

The form of Equation 13-8 occurs in the crushing of solid materials such as coal, rock, gravel, etc., in accordance with the "theory of breakage." For a given crushing process, breakage theory assumes that particle dimensions at any stage of the breaking process are in proportion to the dimensions at the preceding stage. Therefore, size distributions of material after a sequence of breaking processes are based on the statistical products of a series of ratio-related results.

Data Presentation

For data presentation, Sturges' Rule is used as in Chapter 3; cell sizes are determined by ratios

as in Chapter 9; and the determination of cell endpoints and cell balancing are also done as in Chapter 9.

Logarithmic Extreme Value Probability Paper

This paper has the same probability scale as extreme value probability paper. The vertical scale for the variable is logarithmic instead of linear. The scales for the reduced variate and the return period are identical to those for extreme value probability paper and are used in the same way. The vertical lines for the mode and the mean are similar except that they refer to the values of the logarithms of the variable of interest.

Logarithmic Extreme Value Probability Plots

Sequence of data arrangement has the same sense for log-extreme value probability plots as for extreme value plots. Positively skewed data are arranged from smallest to largest, and negatively skewed data are arranged from largest to smallest. The slope of the best-fit line is positive for positively skewed data and negative for negatively skewed data. Curvature of the plot can indicate that the data have been plotted in the opposite sense.

Frequency cumulation is done as before and the best-fit line is obtained by dividing the points above and below the line.

Estimation of Parameters

As usual, one requires a good straight-line fit in order to make valid estimates of the log-extreme value parameters. The equation for the straight line was given in Equation 13-5. The value of μ_o is estimated from the modal line and the best-fit line, while y is used for the extreme value distribution and g' is obtained by dividing the value of x at the 85% vertical by the value at the 15% vertical and then taking the 2.457th root of the quotient because the difference between the 15th and 85th percentiles is 2.457 units on the scale of the normalized variate y.

$$g' = (x_{0.85}/x_{0.15})^{1/2.457} \quad (13\text{-}9\text{a})$$

or

$$g' = \text{antilog} \frac{\log x_{0.85} - \log x_{0.15}}{2.457} \quad (13\text{-}9\text{b})$$

Probability Statements about the Logarithmic Extreme Value Distribution

The area under the curve in Fig. 11-8 in the interval of $\mu_o(g')^{\pm y}$ is about 73%; $\mu_o(g')^{\pm 2y}$ is 92.6%; and $\mu_o(g')^{\pm 3y}$ is 97.9%. These are the same percentages as for the extreme value distribution except that the value of the variable of interest is now in logarithms. Using the above relationships, we can once again obtain probability statements directly from the cumulative percentage scale of the probability plots.

The return period scale is used identically as for the extreme value distribution, as illustrated in Example 11-3.

Interpretation of Plots

The usual conclusions apply when one obtains a satisfactory straight-line fit with 95% or more of the plotted points falling within the confidence interval. Nonlinear plots can generally be interpreted as for the other distributions. There is not sufficient working information available for logarithmic extreme value distributions to give meaningful rules for the interpretation of curved plots. This is due to the sensitivity of logarithmic extreme value distributions to small variations in the input values of the input generating functions. Therefore, if one expects logarithmic extreme value behavior but obtains an erratic looking plot, all underlying assumptions should be reviewed and all significant inputs should be examined independently for irregular changes in level and dispersion.

Confidence Intervals

Confidence intervals for the logarithmic extreme value distribution are obtained by combining the results of Equations 9-8 and 11-14, giving

$$y = \overline{L} \cdot g'^{\pm k_2} \qquad (13\text{-}10a)$$

for the second largest and largest values,

and

$$y = \overline{L} \cdot g'^{\pm k_2(n^{-1/2})} \qquad (13\text{-}10b)$$

for the other recommended percentiles in Appendix, Table A-6.

$\overline{L}$ = the median position of the best-fit line at a specified percentile.

g' = the geometric Gumbel slope.

k_2 is as given in Appendix, Table A-6.

n is the sample size.

When grouped data is used and has been arranged with cell ratios, the exponent for g' in Equation 13-10b must be multiplied by the square root of the cell ratio, $\sqrt{r_c}$, where r_c is as defined in Chapter 9, in order to correct for the effect of grouping the data. Note that there is no confidence interval derived for the second largest and largest values because these values are now incorporated in their respective cell endpoints.

Example 13-2
Given: The initial readings data of Table 13-3.
Required: Obtain the parameter estimates and the confidence intervals.

Table 13-3. Data for Leakage Current (ICBO) of Transistors Subjected to Temperature Step Stressing in Equal Temperature Steps

Initial Readings	Leakage Current in Microamperes		
	After Step 1	After Step 2	After Step 3
1.01	3.60	0.65	64.0
1.99	0.97	1.90	162.0
1.14	1.30	1.44	88.5
1.03	0.72	1.55	130.0
1.69	1.72	4.18	57.5
1.63	5.05	10.80	14.2
1.36	1.66	2.92	6.8
0.90	1.53	1.44	57.5
1.64	1.18	87.0	172.0
1.75	6.42	13.20	36.5
1.52	7.00	9.30	9.8
1.21	1.33	23.30	190.0
1.32	5.95	8.22	27.4
1.45	3.61	2.47	400.0
1.18	1.63	2.50	1.1
2.32	10.50	16.10	25.6
1.20	1.06	1.48	287.0
3.75	2.43	3.50	1140.0
1.00	9.05	236.0	590.0

Procedure:

Step 1. Arrange the data in ascending order and plot the data as shown in Fig. 13-2.

Step 2. Construct the best-fit line and obtain the value of the mode, $\mu_o = 1.24$; and the 15th and 85th percentiles which are 1.01 and 2.02

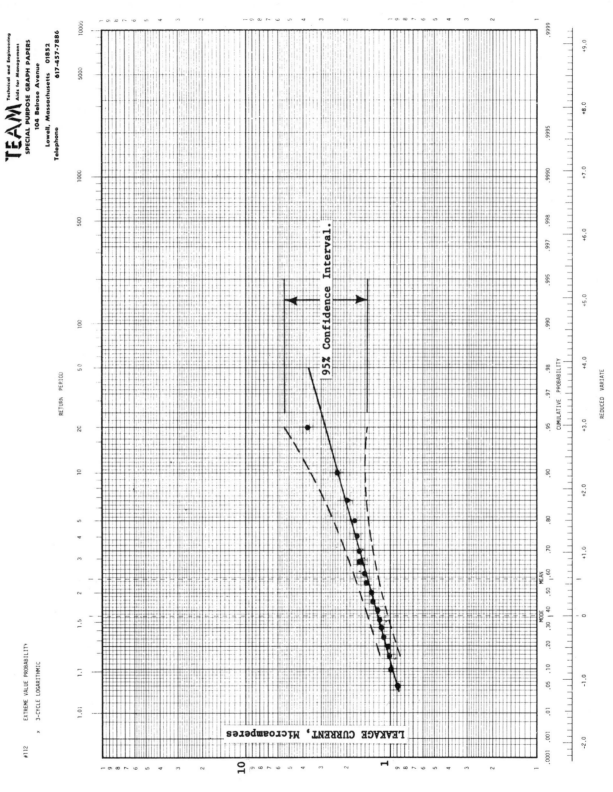

Fig. 13-2.   Probability plot of transistor leakage current, using initial readings from Table 13-3.

microamperes, respectively, giving:

$$g' = \text{antilog } \frac{\log 2.02 - \log 1.01}{2.457}$$

$$= \text{antilog } \frac{0.301}{2.457} = \text{antilog } 0.123 = 1.326$$

Step 3. Calculate the values for the confidence interval. At the 15% point, the intercept with the best-fit line is 1.01. The value of g' was determined to be 1.326 in Step 2. Using k_2 for 15% from Appendix Table A-6, we divide k_2 by the square root of the sample size, n. That is, $2.51/\sqrt{19} = 0.577$, which is the power to which g' is raised. This is best calculated by taking logarithms and antilogarithms:

$$0.577 \log 1.326 = 0.577 \times 0.12254 = 0.07071$$

antilogarithm $0.07071 = 1.177 = $ offset ratio

The value for the intersection of the 15% and best-fit lines is now multiplied and divided by the offset ratio to obtain the upper and lower confidence limits. Results for Example 13-2 are tabulated below:

Percentile	Intercept with Best-fit Line	$g'^{k_2(n-1/2)}$	Offset Ratio	Confidence Interval Lower	Confidence Interval Upper
15	1.01	$1.326^{0.577}$	1.18	0.86	1.19
30	1.18	$1.326^{0.581}$	1.18	1.00	1.39
50	1.36	$1.326^{0.661}$	1.20	1.13	1.64
70	1.63	$1.326^{0.842}$	1.27	1.29	2.07
85	2.02	$1.326^{1.18}$	1.40	1.45	2.84
		g'^{k_2}			
Second largest	2.3	$1.326^{1.51}$	1.53	1.50	3.52
Largest	2.8	$1.326^{2.28}$	1.90	1.47	5.43

Step 4. The confidence intervals are plotted in Fig. 13-2 with a smooth curve fitted to the values calculated in Step 3. The fit of this data to the best-fit line and within the confidence interval is excellent.

Application of the Logarithmic Extreme Value Distribution

As stated earlier, the most common application of log-extreme value distributions is to the prob-

lem of sizing coals and other particulate materials. See (3), (34), (38), (44), and (46) where it is called the Rosin-Rammler distribution. In this class of applications, the behavior of size data is identical to that of the smallest extreme value distribution. That is, the data must be arranged from the largest to the smallest value. This occurs naturally for sizing data. Particulate materials such as coal, sand, gravel, ores, and powders are classified by sifting them through a series of screens. The screens range from coarse to fine with the mesh space decreasing in assigned steps. The amount of material which remains on the screen after sifting is weighed and is normally reported as a percentage of the initial weight of the sample, or *percent residue*.

Table 13-4. Percent Residue from Three Different Grindings of Ruhr District Lean Coal

Particle Diameter	Sample A	Sample B	Sample C
Microns	Residue, percent		
200	16.2	1.1	0.2
150	27.2	3.2	0.3
120	38.6	9.6	1.5
88	48.6	18.5	7.1
75	54.0	25.1	12.4
60	60.7	34.3	19.7
40	74.9	53.5	36.2
20	88.0	78.4	63.9

Example 13-3

Given: The data of Table 13-4 with the fineness distributions for a German coal ground to three different levels of pulverization.

Required: Parameter estimates for the three samples.

Procedure:

Step 1. Plot the data and obtain the best-fit lines as in Fig. 13-3.

Step 2. Determine the modal values for particle size from the intersection of the best-fit line and the vertical for the mode.

Step 3. The geometric Gumbel slope, g', is obtained by rearranging Equation 13-9 b to simplify

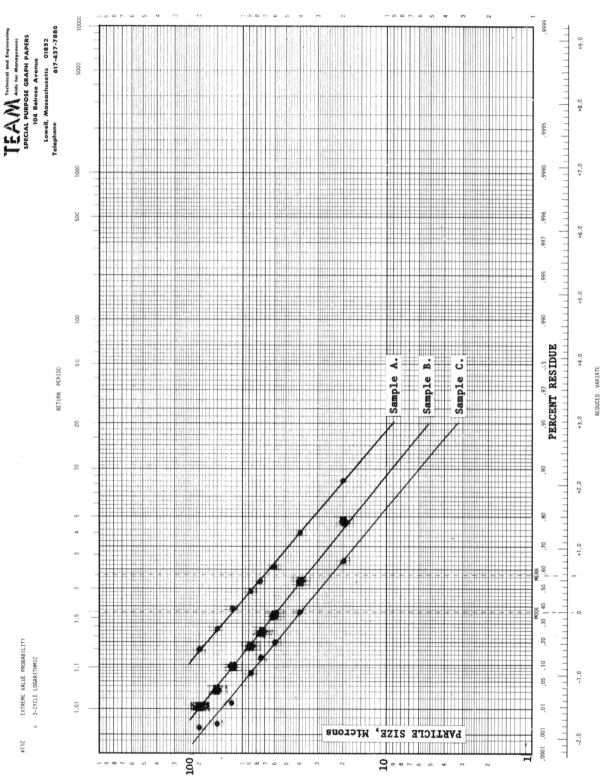

Fig. 13-3.　Probability plots of fineness measurements of a lean coal from the Ruhr district in Germany.

computations by eliminating negative logarithms:

$$g' = - \text{antilog} \frac{\log x_{0.15} - \log x_{0.85}}{2.457}$$

For Sample C, this gives:

$$g' = - \text{antilog} \frac{\log 67 - \log 8.5}{2.457}$$

$$= - \text{antilog} \frac{0.8966}{2.457}$$

$$= - \text{antilog} \, 0.365$$

$$= -2.32$$

Results: Estimates for the three samples are given below:

	Sample A	Sample B	Sample C
Mode	118 microns	57 microns	40 microns
g'	2.37	2.28	2.32

COMMENT: It is obvious that continued pulverization reduces the particle size. The dispersion shows a tendency to decrease slightly. However, g' is frequently treated as if it were a constant. The values obtained for g' vary for different materials and for different crushing processes. For coals, the values of the mode and g' are used in studies of combustion efficiency.

Exercises

13-1. a. Using the data of Table 13-3, construct the probability plots, estimate the parameters, and obtain the confidence intervals.

b. Using the parameter estimates, plot the four lines as in Fig. 12-4.

c. Compare the results between each pair of readings.

d. Based on the comparisons of Exercise 13-1 c, discuss the effect of temperature on leakage current. Use step-to-step and start-to-finish comparisons.

The Weibull Distribution

Background

This distribution has been named after W. Weibull of Sweden, who published applications to the particle size of fly ash and strength of materials, see (54). J. H. K. Kao popularized the Weibull distribution with application to the failure behavior of electronic components and systems, as explained in (28), (29), (30), and (31). Mugeles and Evans developed a modified form of this distribution to describe the distribution of droplet sizes in sprays (38), which they call the "upper-limit" equation. Berretoni showed a wide range of applications in corrosion testing, industrial engineering, and sales analysis, see (4).

Description of the Weibull Distribution

The Weibull distribution is also known as the Type III extreme value distribution, to distinguish it from the extreme value and logarithmic extreme value distributions.

The cumulative distribution for the Type III extreme value distribution is:

$$P(x) = \int_0^x \exp\left[-\left(\frac{\omega - x}{\omega - \mu_o}\right)^k\right] \qquad (14\text{-}1)$$

where: $-\infty < x < \omega$

x = the value of the random variable
μ_o = the mode
$1/k$ is the measure of dispersion
ω = some limiting value

By transposing the quantity in parentheses and changing the limits of integration, we obtain a more useful form of Equation 14-1:

$$P(x) = \int_0^x \exp\left[-\left(\frac{x - \omega}{\mu_o - \omega}\right)^k\right] \qquad (14\text{-}2)$$

where: $o < x < \infty$

The Weibull failure distribution is:

$$F(x) = 1 - P(x)$$
$$= 1 - \int_0^x \exp\left[-\frac{(x-\gamma)^\beta}{\alpha}\right] \qquad (14\text{-}3)$$

The more conventional symbols for the Weibull distribution are obtained using the following substitutions:

$$\alpha = (\mu_o - \omega)^\beta$$
$$\beta = k$$
$$\gamma = \omega$$

The probability density function is then:

$$f(x) = \frac{\beta}{\alpha}(x-\gamma)^{\beta-1} \exp\left[-\frac{(x-\gamma)^\beta}{\alpha}\right] \qquad (14\text{-}4)$$

Referring back to Equation 14-1, the relationship between the Type I and Type III extreme value distributions is established by the identity:

$$\left(\frac{\omega - x}{\omega - \mu_o}\right)^k = e^{-\alpha(x-\mu_o)} \qquad (14\text{-}5)$$

Taking logarithms and rearranging, we obtain:

$$-k \log\left(\frac{x - \omega}{\mu_o - \omega}\right) = -\alpha(x - \mu_o) \qquad (14\text{-}6)$$

Once again, we find that $k = \alpha$. The quantities in parentheses in Equation 14-6 are not simply related anymore. On the left, the difference between the variable and the limiting value is divided by the difference between the mode and the limiting value. The difference between the mode and the limiting value is a constant, and so the value of $(x - \omega)$ is *scaled* in units of $(\mu_o - \omega)$. The symbols in Equation 14-3 are assigned the following meanings:

α is the scale parameter
β is the shape parameter
γ is the location parameter

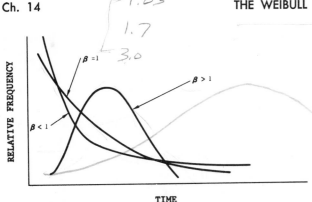

Fig. 14-1. Variation in Weibull distribution shapes with different values of *beta*. Adapted from Reference (4).

The scale, shape, and location parameters do not have direct counterparts to the measures of central tendency and dispersion which are characteristic of the two-parameter distributions with which we dealt previously. All three Weibull parameters can affect the measure of central tendency and it is the ratio of β/α that affects the dispersion. In order to treat Weibull data in a conventional two-dimensional graphical form, the location parameter, γ, is effectively eliminated by means which will be discussed in the section on gamma correction.

Figure 14-1 illustrates the appearance of the Weibull distribution. The scale parameter, α, controls the amount of skewness, or spreading from left to right. Next, β controls the shape — this is illustrated for three general value ranges of β. The location parameter, γ, establishes the position of the left end of the distribution. This is also sometimes called a threshold parameter,

because it represents a stress level or a time before which no failures can occur.

Figure 14-2 shows the relationship between the Weibull distribution and failure rate behavior. From this, it is seen that β is the most interesting parameter. For $\beta > 1$, the failure rate is increasing with time. When $\beta = 1$, the failure rate is constant and is the condition corresponding to the exponential failure case. For $\beta < 1$, the failure rate is decreasing with time.

The Origin of a Weibull Distribution

There is no simple way to generate experimental Weibull variates as there was for study of preceding distributions. Hahn and Shapiro (22), give a useful method of obtaining synthetic Weibull variates from tables of random uniform variates which are similar to Tables 6-1 and 11-1. The derivation of Hahn and Shapiro involves more effort in calculating than that used in earlier chapters of this book, but it is useful for Monte Carlo simulation of the Weibull distribution with electronic computers. Their formula for obtaining random Weibull variates, y', is:

$$y' = -\alpha\{\ln(1 - R_u)\}^{1/\beta} \qquad (14\text{-}7)$$

where:

  y' is the random Weibull variate
  α and β are the scale and shape parameters
  R_u is a random uniform deviate.

However, if we let $\ln(1 - R_u) = x$, then $(1 - R_u) = e^x$. This shows that $(1 - R_u)$ is similar to the exponential terms used to generate the Type I and Type II extreme value distributions in Chapters 11 and 13. Equation 14-7 is one operational order more complicated, due to the need to raise to the power $1/\beta$.

Design and Layout of Weibull Probability Paper

Weibull probability paper, (30) and (43), is based on a double logarithmic transformation of Equation 14-3 after transposing and inverting:

$$1 - F(x) = \exp-\frac{(x - \gamma)^\beta}{\alpha} \qquad (14\text{-}8)$$

$$\frac{1}{1 - F(x)} = \exp\frac{(x - \gamma)^\beta}{\alpha}$$

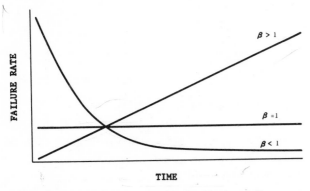

Fig. 14-2. Variation in Weibull distribution failure rates with different values of *beta*. Adapted from Reference (4).

$$\ln \ln \frac{1}{1 - F(x)} = \beta \ln (x - \gamma) - \ln \alpha$$

which is in the linear form: $y = mx + b$.

The values of $y = \boxed{\ln \ln \dfrac{1}{1 - F(x)}}$ comprise the right-hand vertical scale of Weibull paper which is shown in Fig. 14-3. The values of $\ln (x - \gamma)$ are given in the top horizontal scale. These scales are known as the auxiliary scales.

Two direct reading scales are provided to facilitate data plotting. A left vertical scale permits direct plotting of *percent failure,* which is properly interpreted as "cumulative percentage equal to or less than the observed value." A bottom horizontal scale permits direct plotting of the value of the observed stress level or time to failure.

Note that the direct reading scales are reversed from the orientation which has been used on other probability papers. This relationship is used because this format was first presented by Kao (30), and has been widely followed in the literature of Weibull applications. Weibull probability papers are available with failure rate scales of 0.0001%, 0.01%, and 1.0% to 99.9% combined with stress/time scales of 3, 5, and 7 logarithmic cycles.

Data Preparation and Plotting

Data for Weibull plotting will be expressed either as the time (stress) to failure for individual test items or as a time (stress) level at which the number of test failures are observed and recorded. For example:

CASE I

Time to Failure by Test Item

1st failure at t_1

2nd failure at t_2

mth failure at t_m

CASE II

Parts Failed per Readout Time

x_1 parts failed by t_1

x_2 parts failed by t_2

x_m parts failed at t_m

For reasons which will be considered later, it is desirable to have a minimum of seven data points to plot. If this cannot be achieved, an absolute minimum of five points should be used.

Two useful rules to follow in order to satisfy such an objective is to require at least seven failed parts when time or stress is monitored on an individual basis or to schedule seven readout points when monitoring occurs only at specific times. For tests with planned maximum durations of, for example, 1,000 hours or 1 million cycles, the interim readouts are most efficiently scheduled by successively halving the allowed maximum duration; that is, $\frac{1}{2}$, $\frac{1}{4}$, $\frac{1}{8}$, . . . etc.

In Case I situations, we know the time to failure for each individual failure occurrence. This data may be tabulated (as percent failed) as specific times in a frequency table. Cumulative frequencies and cumulative percentages are determined as shown in Chapter 4. Each failure is then plotted at its cumulative percentage plotting and respective time (stress) to failure. The Weibull line is found most easily by using the last plotted point as the reference for a straightedge and dividing the remaining points into two equal parts above and below the line. Grouped data for Case II is handled similarly. This is illustrated in Tables 14-1 and 14-2.

Table 14-1. Data for Case I

Time — Hours		Failures		
Actual	Gamma Corrected	Actual	Cumulative	Plotting Percentage
0.5	0.0	1	1	2.4
11.3	10.8	1	2	4.9
25.3	24.8	1	3	7.3
53.0	52.5	1	4	9.8
113.8	113.3	1	5	12.2
206.5	206.0	1	6	14.6
464.5	464.0	1	7	17.0
572.5	572.0	1	8	19.5
		$n = 40$		

Gamma Correction

As stated previously, the Weibull distribution is effectively reduced to a two-parameter distribution by making an initial correction in the data for the location parameter, γ, by subtracting the value for time to first failure from all subsequent failure times. Many authors recommend making such a

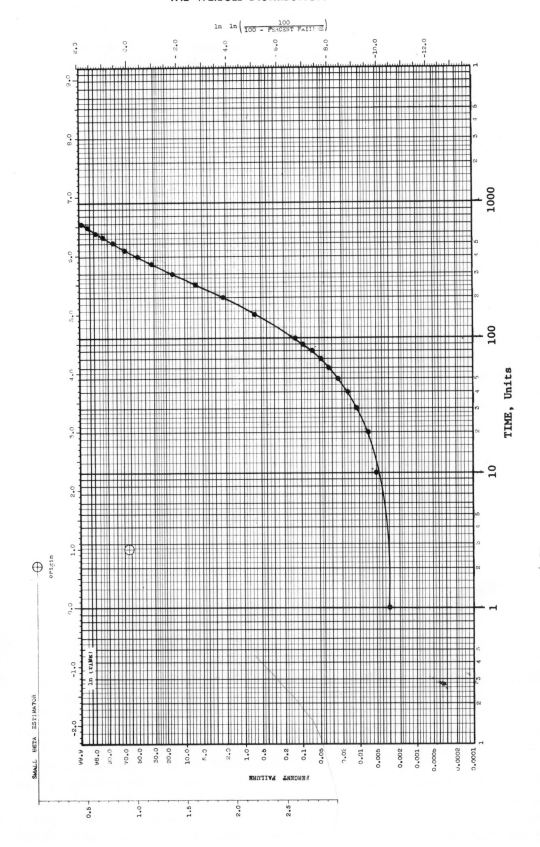

Fig. 14-3. Identification of Weibull paper scales and nomenclature.

Weibull plot of solutions of Eq. 14-6 as given in Table 14-5

Table 14-2. Data for Case II

Time — Hours		Failures		
Actual	Gamma Corrected	Actual	Cumulative	Plotting Percentage
1	. . .	0	0	. . .
24	18.4	4	4	9.8
72	66.4	2	6	14.6
168	162.4	1	7	17.0

$$n = 40$$

$$\hat{\gamma} = \hat{t}_1 = \frac{4(1) + 24}{4 + 1} = \frac{28}{5} = 5.6$$

correction to help linearize the Weibull line. This is thought to improve the ability to estimate the parameters of the distribution from the auxiliary scales on the Weibull paper. However, see the discussion under Interpretation of Curved Plots (p. 130) for precautions against making gamma corrections which obscure the real meaning of the data.

In Case I, the most efficient estimate for gamma, $\hat{\gamma}$, is the actual time at which the first failure is recorded; that is, $\hat{\gamma} = t_1$. For stress other than time, the value of stress causing the first failure is used.

For Case II, the estimate for γ is derived from the grouped data as follows:

$$\hat{\gamma} = \hat{t}_i = T_{(i-1)} + \frac{n_i T_{(i-1)} + T_i}{n_i + 1} \qquad (14-9)$$

where:

$\hat{t}_i$ is the *estimated* time to first failure
n_i is the number of failures occurring in the interval
T_i is the time of a given readout
$T_{(i-1)}$ is the time of the previous readout when > 0.

The original data are now adjusted by subtracting $\hat{\gamma}$ from each of the t_i's in Case I and $\hat{t}_1$ from the t_i's of Case II.

Tables 14-1 and 14-2 illustrate data preparation and adjustment for Cases I and II.

Estimation of Parameters

Estimation of γ has already been covered.

Figure 14-3 shows all of the scales on Weibull probability paper and the names and locations of the principal axes. The Weibull line, estimated or fitted by calculation, is used to estimate the parameters α and β.

To estimate α, the scale parameter, the Weibull line is extended to the 0.0 ordinate. This also corresponds to time 1 on the Time Scale. The intersection of the Weibull line and the 0.0 ordinate is projected horizontally to the extreme right-hand scale for y. The intercept of the horizontal line and the y scale gives an estimate of $-1n/\alpha$. By using a table of natural logarithms or a slide rule, α is then determined.

In order to estimate β, the shape parameter, it is necessary to construct an auxiliary line, parallel to the Weibull line, which passes through a circled point at the intersection of the principal ordinate and the principal abscissa. This line is also extended to the 0.0 ordinate and is then projected horizontally to the extreme right-hand scale. The numerical value on this scale is the estimate of β. Since this scale tends to be compressed, the Weibull paper illustrated has an additional auxiliary scale called the Small Beta Estimator in the upper left-hand corner of the paper. This is utilized by drawing a parallel to the Weibull line through the point marked "origin." Parameter β may then be read, with good two-decimal discrimination, directly from the vertical scale farthest to the left.

Figure 14-4 illustrates the plotting of the data of Tables 14-1 and 14-2, the fitting of the Weibull lines, and the estimation of the Weibull parameters. The example given, shows results of life tests on a transistor operated at two different levels of life-test exposure. Condition 2 is more severe than Condition 1. This is shown by the relative locations of the two Weibull lines. Condition 2 also has a higher failure rate than Condition 1. In addition, α_2 is smaller than α_1, indicating a more compact distribution — that is, that the failures occur closer together under Condition 2. Parameter β_2 is smaller than β_1, which can be interpreted as meaning that more failures are occurring earlier and fewer later for Condition 2 as compared to Condition 1. In this example, the times to first failure happen to be opposite to what one would expect. Time to first failure *appears* to be smaller for the lower stress

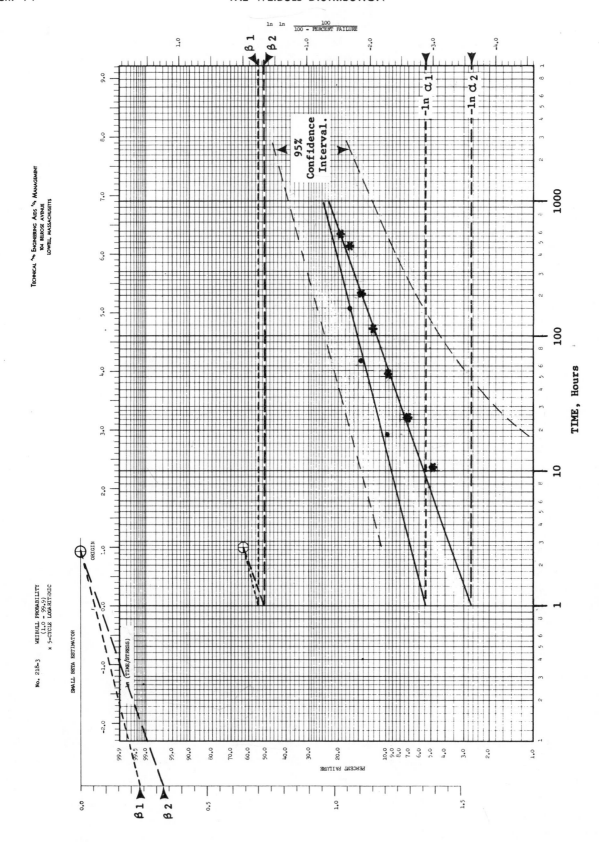

Fig. 14-4. Wiebull plot comparison of life-test results of two samples of transistors operated at two different power levels.

condition. This is not necessarily true because, with the use of grouped data in Condition 2, the estimation of t_1 contains a linearity assumption which results in a tendency to estimate somewhat too high.

Interpretation of Linear Plots

Linear plots can have more than one interpretation, due to the generality of the Weibull distribution in fitting data. As discussed in Estimation of Parameters, p. 128, β's > 1 indicate failure rates which are increasing with time (see Fig. 14-2). When $\beta = 1$, the failure rate is constant. When $\beta < 1$, failure rates decrease with time, as is shown in Fig. 14-2.

Confidence Intervals

As with the other distributions which we have considered, one can also derive confidence intervals for data which display Weibull distribution behavior. It is important to consider that since the Weibull distribution has properties which permit it to be fitted to many kinds of data, it is a more general distribution than some of the other distributions we have studied. This results in quite wide confidence intervals, because we pay for increased generality with decreased precision.

In Appendix, Table A-7 gives the percentage values to be used as offsets at preselected percentiles of the Weibull distribution. Near the center of the distribution, even over the range of the 10–90 percentile values, the convergence is rather slow, with increases in sample size. It is only in the tails of this distribution that large divergence occurs. The values in this table are not exact; they have been rounded off to be consistent with plotting capability on Weibull paper.

The dotted line in Fig. 14-4 illustrates the use of confidence intervals for the data of Case I. Two points are of interest: first, the limits are relatively wide as compared to the spread of the observed data; second, the data for Case II happen to be completely contained within the confidence interval for Case I. This situation would, of course, permit an interpretation of the data of Case II as not being significantly different from the data of Case I. This is further evidence that what we have

gained in generality has been lost in ability to establish precise limits of discrimination.

Interpretation of Curved Plots

Curved Weibull plots arise primarily from plots of non-Weibull data. One common example is illustrated in Fig. 14-5. This is the case of a normally distributed variable shifting uniformly toward a limit which defines or causes failure. This is derived from Equation 10-3 with:

$\overline{X}_0 = 0$; $\sigma_0 = 1$; $\rho = 0.0025$; $\eta = 0$ and Limit $= 4.00$, giving

$$k = \frac{(4.00 - 0)}{1} \times \frac{(1 - 0.0025t)}{1 + 0t} \quad (14\text{-}10)$$

Solutions for this equation are given in Table 14-3.

Table 14-3. Solutions to Equation 14-10

t	k	Percent Failing		t'
		Original	Screened	
		$p \times 100\%$	$p \times 100\%$	
1	3.99	0.003	$\cdots$	$\cdots$
10	3.90	0.005	$\cdots$	$\cdots$
20	3.80	0.007	$\cdots$	$\cdots$
30	3.70	0.011	$\cdots$	$\cdots$
40	3.60	0.016	$\cdots$	$\cdots$
41	3.59	0.017	0.001	1
50	3.50	0.023	0.007	10
60	3.40	0.034	0.018	20
70	3.30	0.048	0.032	30
80	3.20	0.069	0.053	40
90	3.10	0.097	0.081	50
100	3.00	0.13	0.114	60
140	2.60	0.47	0.454	100
150	2.50	0.62	0.604	110
200	2.00	2.27	2.25	160
250	1.50	6.68	6.66	210
300	1.00	15.87	15.85	260
350	0.50	30.85	30.83	310
400	0.00	50.00	49.98	360
450	-0.50	69.15	69.13	410
500	-1.00	84.13	84.11	460
550	-1.50	93.32	93.31	510
600	-2.00	97.73	97.71	560
650	-2.50	99.38	99.36	610
700	-3.00	99.87	99.85	660

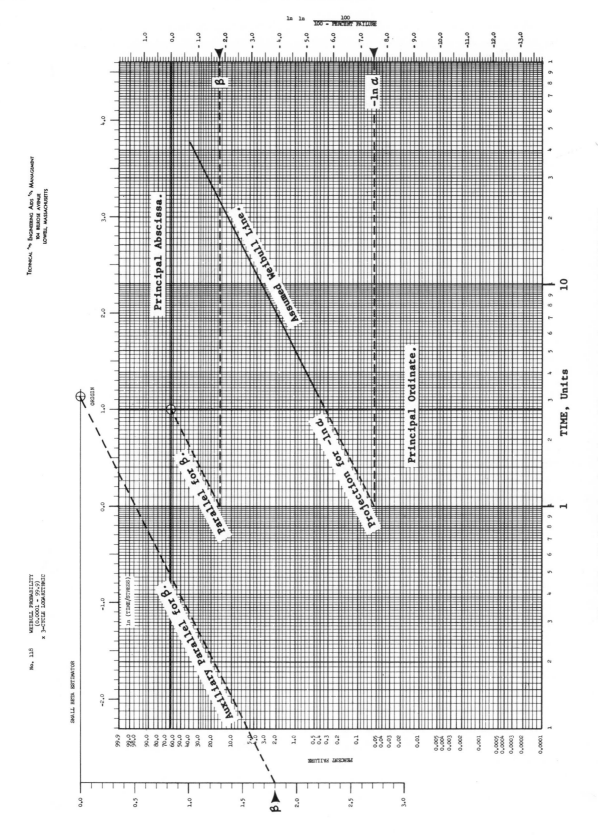

Fig. 14-5. Weibull plot of solutions of Equation 14-6, as given in Table 14-5.

Illust. of Weibull paper scales & nomenclature

Table 14-4. Failure Times for Solid Tantalum Capacitors under Accelerated Conditions. Times to Failure Given in Minutes

	Sample A[†]	Sample B[†]	Sample C[†]	Sample D[†]
1.	0.73	39	0 *	0.07
2.	1.55	154	0 *	0.87
3.	2.75	492	0 *	1.53
4.	4.03	581	0 *	3.00
5.	4.37	1022	0.02	3.35
6.	6.70	2326	0.05	4.07
7.	10	3016	0.20	6.23
8.	21	3606	0.75	6.23
9.	46	3756	2	8.53
10.	50	4018	26	8.62
11.	57	6368	34	9.23
12.	69	6506	135	9.92
13.	102	7426	236	13
14.	126	8422	320	13
15.	142	8966	424	16
16.	143	9241	550	19
17.	157	· · ·	640	20
18.	167	· · ·	1434	23
19.	· · ·	· · ·	1887	25
20.	· · ·	· · ·	· · ·	26

[†] $n = 39$ for all samples.

* These parts failed as voltage was being increased to start the test. Since the planned test voltage was not reached, no elapsed time is credited to these parts.

This is an example of a product characteristic where the variation in the initial distribution is process- and materials-dependent but, where once established initially, the lifetime behavior is a relatively constant change from the initial characteristic for all items. This is an important form of behavior to identify.

Probability Statements about the Weibull Distribution

The methods used for other distributions to obtain probability statements also work for the Weibull distribution. To obtain the percentage of items which will fail by a certain time or stress level, simply project up to the Weibull line, and then left to the percent failure scale. To obtain the percentage of items which will fail between two

points in time or between two different stress levels, project both values of the variable of interest up to the Weibull line, and left to the percent failure scale. Subtract the smaller percent failure from the larger to obtain the difference. Alternatively, to obtain the value of time or stress at which some predetermined percent failure will occur, simply enter the graph from the percent failure scale, project right to the Weibull line, and then down to the variables scale.

Exercises

14.1. Table 14-4 lists the individual times to failure for four different samples of a solid tantalum capacitor under various accelerated test conditions.

   a. Plot any two of the four data sets without, and with, gamma correction.

   b. Estimate α and β for each plot.

   c. Obtain and plot the confidence intervals.

14-2. Table 14-5 lists the number of failures observed for two samples of a metal film resistor to

Table 14-5. Failure Counts for Metal Film Resistors under Different Test Conditions. Cumulative Number of Failures at Each Readout Time is Shown

Time, Hours	Use Condition	Acceptance Condition
25	0	0
50	0	0
75	0	0
100	0	0
125	0	0
250	0	0
500	0	1
1000	0	25
1500	1	31
2000	1	40
3000	1	49
4000	2	57
5000	2	61
6000	3	66
7000	8	72
8000	12	77
	$n = 302$	$n = 190$

one particular definition of failure. One sample was tested at standard acceptance test conditions and the other sample was tested at use conditions.

    a. Plot both data sets without, and with, gamma correction.

    b. Estimate α and β for each plot.

    c. Obtain and plot the confidence intervals.

    d. Compare the results of 14-2 a and 14-2 b, and discuss the impact of the choice of test conditions on test results.

CHAPTER 15

Further Consideration of the Weibull Distribution

Application to Life Testing

Since the Weibull distribution is of particular interest in describing life distributions, we can develop another interesting derivation based on Equation 10-3 for the log-normal distribution. Weibull distributions occur most readily from Type I extreme value distributions in much the same manner in which normal distributions result in log-normal life distributions. Equation 10-3 can be restated in terms of Type I extreme value parameters:

$$y = \alpha_0 (\text{Limit} - \mu_0) \cdot \frac{(1 - \rho t)}{\sqrt{1 + \eta t}} \qquad (15\text{-}1)$$

where:

Limit is a maximum specified value which can be allowed

μ_0 is substituted directly for $\bar{X}_0$

α_0 is substituted for $1/\sigma_0$

ρ is a factor which represents rate of increase of the mode

η is a factor which represents increase of variation

t is time of operation

y is the normalized variate for all extreme value distributions.

The practical results of this equation are illustrated by an example derived from the data of Table 12-3. Over the times observed, the mode, μ, increased from 0.49 to 0.80. This is an average of about 8% per unit time. This results in a reduction of the safety margin by 2 percent. The Gumbel slope increases from 0.140 to 0.430, or about 26 percent. Using $\mu_0 = 0.49$, $1/\alpha_0 = 0.14$, Limit = 2.50, $\rho = 0.02$, and $\eta = 0.26$, we obtain the following:

$$y = \frac{(2.50 - 0.49)}{0.14} \cdot \frac{(1 - 0.02)t}{\sqrt{1 + 0.26t}} \qquad (15\text{-}2)$$

Results for typical values are tabulated in Table 15-1 and illustrated in Fig. 15-1. These results show an excellent fit on the Weibull probability paper.

Table 15-1. Solutions of Equation 15-2

t	y	$1 - p$	$p \times 100\%$
5	8.5194	0.99983	0.017
10	6.0529	0.9976	0.24
20	3.4600	0.9690	3.10
30	1.9353	0.8654	13.46
40	0.8499	0.6520	34.80
50	0.0000	0.3679	63.21
60	− 0.7049	0.1322	86.78
70	− 1.3108	0.0246	97.54
80	− 1.8449	0.0018	99.82

Equation 15-2 and the results displayed in Fig. 15-1 serve to demonstrate once again that acceleration factors are realistically of the form of a ratio such as: $(1 - \rho t)/\sqrt{1 + \eta t}$. This results in nonlinear accelerations as conditions change. Again, we emphasize that it is important to obtain detailed data about changes in the typical value and in the variation of a distribution during use or stress in order to understand life and wear characteristics properly.

Effects of Stress and Failure Definition

The stress levels used to test parts and materials influence the value of Weibull parameters. Figure 15-2 shows the results of estimates of Weibull parameters from life tests of diodes in a wide matrix of conditions. The time to first failure, γ, occurs earlier as stress increases. The Weibull slope, β, increases with stress level. In this context, the increase in β may be interpreted as an increase in the rate of failure after initial onset.

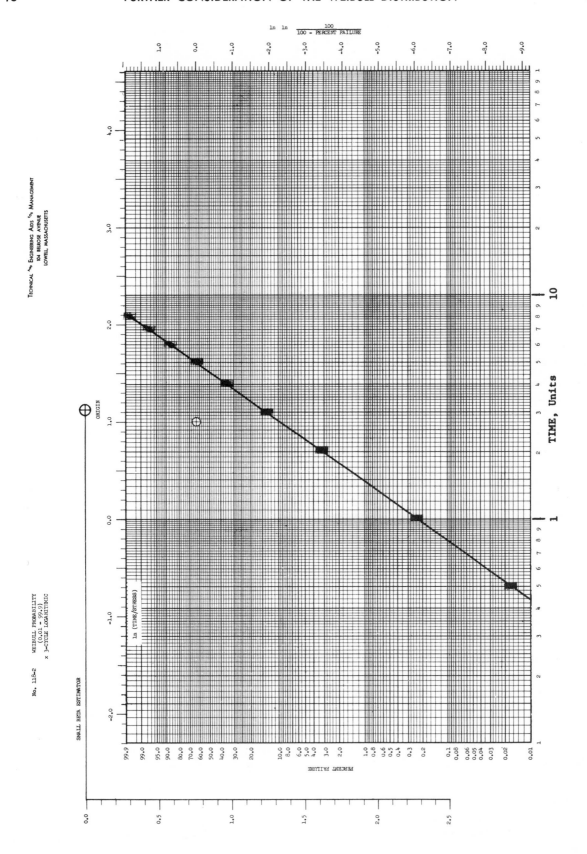

Fig. 15-1.   Weibull plot of solutions of Equation 15-1, using data of Table 15-1.

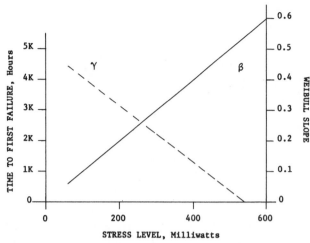

Fig. 15-2.   Graph of the variation of Weibull parameters with variations in stress level.

Both of these results are intuitively reasonable. Increasing stress causes failures sooner and faster.

The definition of a failure is also important in affecting the estimates of time to first failure, γ. As the definition of failure is located further away from the limits of original distribution, estimates of γ become larger — this is intuitively acceptable. There is also an effect on the Weibull slope. As the time to first failure increases, the points on the Weibull plot are crowded relatively closer together, thus tending to cause β to increase. Generally, however, if the inherent failure distribution has a failure rate which is increasing with time, where $\beta > 1$, then the β's will become larger than the initial estimate. If the β's are less than 0.5, they will increase but will tend to stay smaller than 1.0.

These results are illustrated in Fig. 15-3.

Additional Uses of the Weibull Shape Parameter, β

Weibull β values can be used as clues to underlying distribution functions, when one is searching for a properly descriptive distribution. This kind of information is highly dependent on the origin of the data plotted.

For individual distributions of *measured variable parameters* with the bottom scale representing the value of the variable of interest, the following interpretations are possible:

1. $\beta = 1$ represents the exponential distribution.
2. $\beta = 2$ represents the Rayleigh distribution.
3. $\beta = 5$ represents the normal distribution.

For distributions of *lifetime characteristics* which represent times to failure in response to stress, degradation, or deterioration where failure is defined as exceeding some specified limit, the values of β may be interpreted as follows:

4. $\beta = 1$ is the exponential distribution with constant failure rate.
5. $\beta = 3$ is the log-normal distribution with normal wearout.

Furthermore, when one is dealing with life distributions *and the raw data* is acceptably linear without any need of a gamma correction, the value of β may be used as a clue to the time-dependent behavior of ρ and η in Equation 15-1. The response of the wear factors with time may be estimated as follows:

6. $\beta = 3$ to 4, ρ and η vary directly with t.
7. $\beta = \sim 2$, ρ and η vary approximately as $\sqrt{t}$.
8. $\beta < 1$, ρ and η vary approximately as $\log t$.

Figure 15-4 illustrates the results of the foregoing, using the three different time functions as modifiers of the stress factors in Equation 15-2.

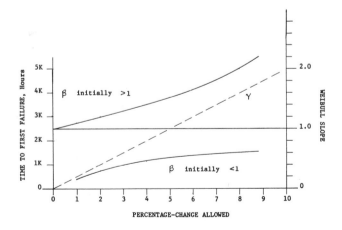

Fig. 15-3.   Graph of the variation of Weibull parameters with variations in failure definition.

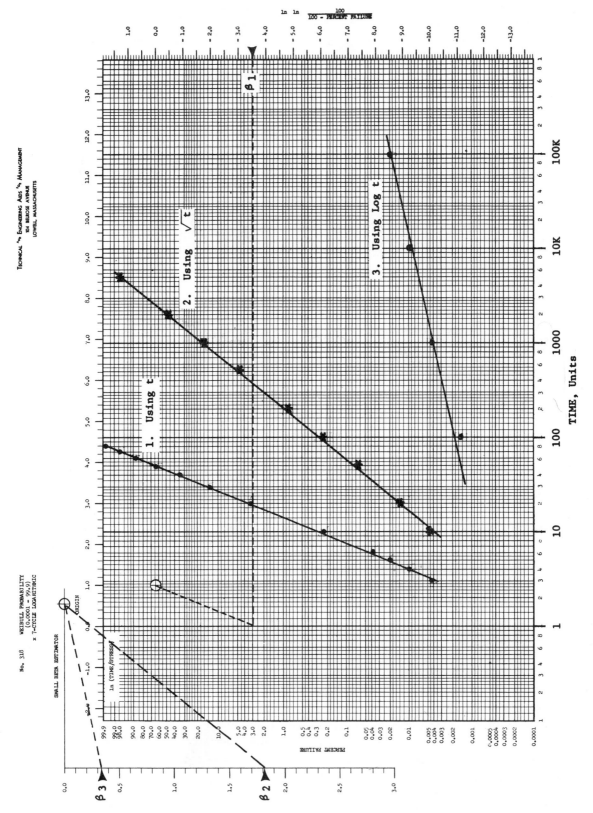

Fig. 15-4.   Wiebull plot of solutions of Equation 15-2, using t, $\sqrt{t}$, and log t.

Mixed Weibull Effects

Various authors, notably Kao, (29), and Berretoni, (4), have presented examples of "mixed Weibull effects," in which the premise is that more than one cause of failure is present. In addition, each cause of failure has a different characteristic time to failure pattern. This is illustrated in Fig. 15-5 for data of Table 15-2. In such cases,

Table 15-2. Failure Data for Stepping Switch

Number of Steps, in 1000's*					
to 1st Miss	to 2nd Miss	to 1st Miss	to 2nd Miss	to 1st Miss	to 2nd Miss
61	3000+	2968	3500	4000	5000+
2364	3206+	22	5000+	3000+	3000+
2889	2976	3000+	3000+	3000+	3000+
485	3000+	1901	2005	3000+	3000+
1933	3000+	1556	1858	1108	1595
2009	3000+	281	2900	3500	5000+
2754	3000+	616	5000+	237	1891
3276	3837	2047	2101	2453	3000+
659	1293	90	3000+	1173	2426
5000+	5000+	3000+	3000+	1359	1640
1971	2233	4600	5000+	2297	2301
4242	5000+	2248	5000+	1746	1956
4400	5000+	2721	3000+	3000+	3000+
5000+	5000+	3200	3600	11	3700
76	2296	2840	2904	2205	5100
313	4225	1753	1825	2705	2716
3000+	3000+				

*NOTES: 1. A number of parts were removed from test at 3,000,000 steps due to time limitations. Those parts which had only 0 or 1 miss are shown as 3000+ in the '1st-Miss' column. 2. The test was terminated at 5,000,000 steps. Parts which had either 0 or 1 miss at this point are shown as 5000+ in the '1st-Miss' column.

the data are segregated into two groups and the parameters of each group are estimated separately. However, we will not develop the estimation procedures, because if more than one cause of failure is present, this can only be established by a careful program of failure analysis. In such a case, each subgroup, as determined by the failure analysis results, should be plotted independently. The parameter for each subgroup is then determined as in Chapter 14. If there is not a careful verification that more than one failure mode exists, then caution is indicated in using the procedures recommended in (4) and (29).

There are other explanations for the graphical appearance of the mixed effect. One is that a non-Weibull distribution has been plotted. Figure 15-6 illustrates this. Data from a test program were plotted on Weibull paper and showed a "mixed Weibull" result. However, postmortem failure analysis which was applied to these failed parts did not disclose any change in the failure mechanism as time increased.

In this case, the "mixed Weibull" effect is similar to a convex plot on other probability papers which may indicate that the wrong probability paper has been used to plot the data. The data plotted in Fig. 15-6 are those of Table 10-1, which gave an excellent log-normal plot in Fig. 10-3.

To date, on the basis of empirical evidence, a concave plot on Weibull paper may be a good clue to mixed Weibull effects. However, as we have stated, it is more correct to use data which have been separated by adequate failure analysis. A convex plot is a good clue that the Weibull assumption is not appropriate for the data which have been plotted.

The same pattern as that observed for mixed Weibull effects has also been derived from a normal distribution in which the mean is approaching a limit and the standard deviation is increasing by the same percentage. In this case, the mixed Weibull is not a Weibull function at all; it is a known normal distribution. The change in slope on the Weibull plot is caused by a shift in the dominance of the mean in affecting the value of the probability of failure to the influence of variation within the distribution on the probability of failure. This leads directly to the log-normal distribution as discussed in Chapter 10.

Some Important Cautions in the Analysis and Interpretation of Life Test Data

Figure 14-5 serves to illustrate a frequently overlooked problem. Many kinds of tests are conducted with only one or two readout points. These tests could not identify behavior such as the distribution in this figure. In addition, within any decade interval of time, the data in this figure are almost linear. This emphasizes the importance of obtaining at least five, and preferably seven, readout points when attempting to establish the nature of an underlying distribution.

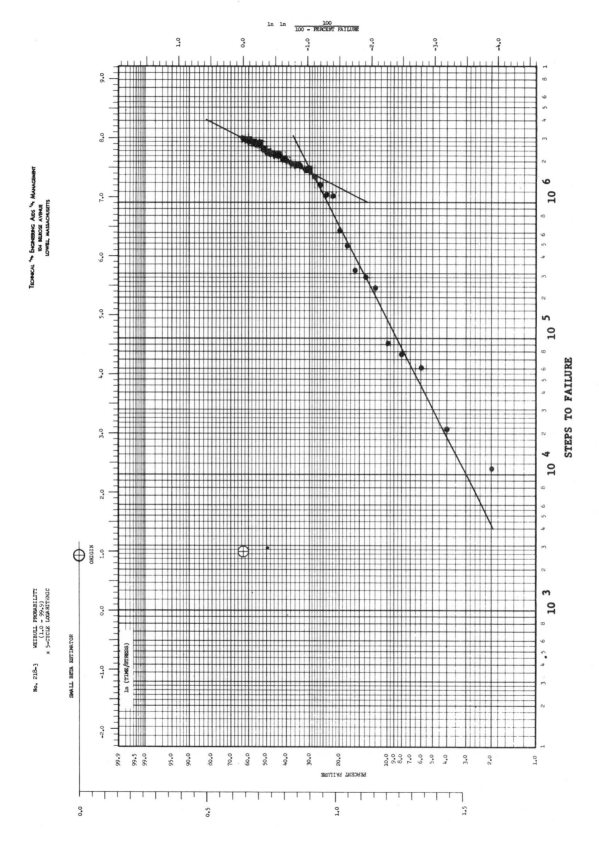

Fig. 15-5.   Weibull plot showing "mixed Weibull effects," using 1st-miss data from Table 15-2.

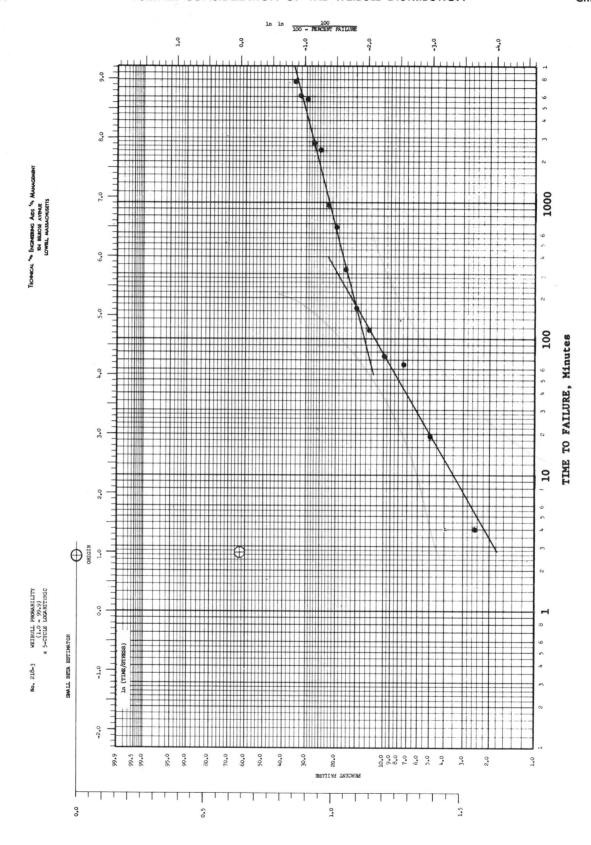

Fig. 15-6.   Weibull Plot showing the results of plotting the wrong distribution on Weibull paper. Data from Table 10-1.

To further complicate matters in the identification of distributions, activities such as screening, selection, sorting, truncation, bake-out, burn-in, and stabilization cycling modify the original distribution. Let us examine the change in the life distribution shown in Fig. 14-5 which would occur if parts were subjected to life test and then screened after 40 hours of exposure (which occurs in some military specifications). Table 14-4 shows the resultant percent failure after the results of the first 40 hours are subtracted from the original distribution values. If a customer were to perform his own life test, then his test times would be those shown under t'. A plot of the customer's life test results would be as in Fig. 15-7. This plot is much more linear than Fig. 14-5 over the interval from 1 to 100 time units. At later times, there is relatively little difference in these distribution plots.

Let us now assume that data were taken only at 30 and 100 time units and that Weibull behavior was assumed. If these data were extrapolated to determine the cumulative failures at 1,000 time units, then one would estimate about 53% failure. However, in terms of the original distribution and the screened distribution, more than 99% failure would have been experienced by about 600 time units. If one were interested in maintaining spare parts or replacement parts, the improper Weibull estimate would call for stock to cover about 47% replacement at 1,000 time units, while the actual underlying distribution would require more than 99% replacement at about 600 time units.

Therefore, it is strongly recommended that an adequate number of data points be used when attempting to determine any distribution. Further, *all data* intended for Weibull analysis should be checked initially in the raw form before *any* adjustments or corrections are applied. The existence of any consistent curvature should be suspect. This is similar in concept to the indications of curved plots as discussed in Chapter 5. The present instance is simply another case of look before you leap.

Curvature can be easily checked by laying a straightedge across the first and last plotted points and assessing the camber of the plotted points by eye. The general pattern exhibited in Figs. 14-5 and 15-7 can be used as an approximate guide. A further test can be made by re-plotting the data. For instance, the data for Fig. 14-5 will plot correctly on normal probability paper.

Design Considerations Arising from the Weibull Distribution

The Weibull distribution, due to its generality, has been shown to have many possible interpretations. In order to make correct interpretations, it is important to know the source of the data used for analysis, and also associated data such as test conditions, failure definitions, and failure analysis results, in order to interpret the behavior of the plot of the observed data correctly.

The generality of the Weibull distribution is also due to its direct propagation from Type I extreme value distributions. At the system usage level, extreme value behavior can occur even though the initial distributions are not extreme value types. As an example, if one starts with a single type of part, it is normal to find that such a part is used in different applications. As a consequence, one or more of the following situations can occur:

1. Some parts may be misapplied, leading to unplanned-for environmental stresses, $f(e)$, which in fact exceed the design limits of the parts.
2. Parts are used at a variety of load conditions which represent a spectrum of use from low- to high-stress applications, $f(a_i)$.
3. Parts may be inadvertently overstressed in such ways as:
   a. Errors in design consideration, $f(\epsilon_d)$
   b. Unplanned random variation in applied stresses, $f(\epsilon_s)$
   c. Unplanned-for, or unsuspected, environmental factors, $f(\epsilon_e)$.

In situation 1, some fraction of the initial distribution, $f(d)$, will be overstressed by $f(e)$ for each system manufactured, and the weakest parts will fail soonest. This is a classic case of the distribution of smallest extreme values. Thus,

$$\text{Failure Rate} \sim e^{f(d)} + e^{f(e)} \qquad (15\text{-}3)$$

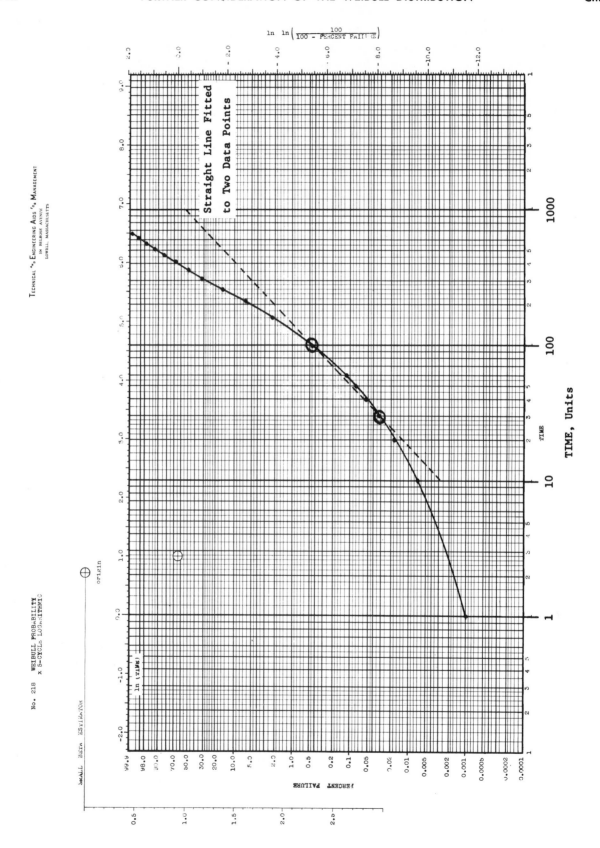

Fig. 15-7.   Weibull plot of data of Table 15-4 when truncated by removing all failures earlier than 40 hours.

As shown in Equation 13-6, this is a basic Type I extreme value distribution.

In the case of situation 2, the parts are effectively divided into a number of subpopulations, each of which operates under different conditions. Failure will normally occur more frequently in the higher stress groups. Stated somewhat differently, there will be a contribution to failure rate deriving from the initial parameter distribution, $f(d)$; a contribution from the planned distribution of stress conditions (environments), $f(a_i)$, and, on occasion, a contribution from the response of a distribution characteristic to some set of environmental factors, known as interaction. This can be symbolically stated as:

$$\text{Failure Rate} \sim e^{f(d)} + e^{f(a_1)} + e^{f(a_2)} + e^{f(a_3)}$$
$$+ \ldots + \sum e^{f(d \cdot a_i)} \qquad (15\text{-}4)$$

In situation 3, we are dealing with 2, plus one or more factors of ignorance such as design error, e_d; uncompensated stress variation, e_s; and unplanned for environmental factors, e_e. These factors lead to:

$$\text{Failure Rate} \sim e^{f(d)} + e^{f(a_i)} + e^{f(\epsilon_d)} + e^{f(\epsilon_s)}$$
$$+ e^{f(\epsilon_e)} + 25 \text{ or more interaction terms} \qquad (15\text{-}5)$$

This is again a basic extreme value form.

Therefore, just the typical conditions of application and misapplication lead to fractional populations in terms of the original distribution and the exposure of random elements of that distribution to variable stresses. These conditions can then be stated in terms which lead directly to the expectation of extreme value behavior of the fractional populations. Finally, with the addition of time as a variable, one can anticipate a wide variety of situations which lead to Weibull life behavior.

Alternatively, the following conditions should be expected to lead to the log-normal failure distribution:

1. Normally distributed input parameters, as previously discussed

2. Ideally, only a small range of stress conditions

3. Ideally, only small variations in environments

4. Trivially small, or nonexistent, error terms.

The first three requirements need no elaboration. Requirement 4 implies that well-known and well-defined design criteria are expected to be associated with log-normal failure distributions. There is a further implication in the four preceding conditions: they also represent general characteristics of a mature process or product.

In summary, the preceding discussion leads to the following expectations of life distributions for basically engineering reasons when applied to assemblies and systems of any complexity. When the design is new and subject to relatively wide variations in component characteristics and internal stresses and environments, the Weibull distribution should be most expected. When a design is more mature, components are better controlled, and stresses and environments are better known and allowed for, the log-normal failure distribution is more likely.

Exercises

15-1. a. Make a Weibull plot of the number of steps to second miss, using the data of Table 15-2. Use only those values *below* 3000.

b. Estimate the Weibull parameters and plot the confidence intervals.

c. Plot the balance of the data, using a different symbol, and ignoring the +'s where they occur.

d. Discuss the fit of the balance of data to the confidence intervals based on the first set of points plotted. Are these later values consistent with earlier values? Is there any indication that these data will appear to be mixed?

CHAPTER 16

Reciprocal Functions

Background

Another category of skewed distributions arises from measurements of characteristics which naturally occur as reciprocals. Reciprocals are often used when a measurement has a reciprocal relationship to another characteristic. For instance, in high-frequency radiation it is simpler to measure frequency than wavelength; we can determine wavelength from frequency, since wavelength = 1/frequency, which results in a skewed distribution for wavelength.

In reaction kinetics, terms are of the form:

$$\text{Reaction Rate} = \exp -Q/R(1/T_1 - 1/T_2)$$

Q is the activation energy, usually assumed to be a constant. R is the universal gas constant. The variable terms, then, are reciprocals, $1/T_A$, with T_A being absolute temperature in degrees Kelvin.

It has not been possible to find functions that yield reciprocal distributions directly. While reciprocal measurements usually have a skewed distribution, Hald (23) notes a special case where reciprocals will be normally distributed if the variables in the denominator of the reciprocal terms are normally distributed and have a small variance. However, this requires a large numerical value for the denominator — say, greater than 100 — with a variance not greater than about 10 percent of the value of the denominator. One difficulty with reciprocals is that as the value of the denominator decreases, the reciprocal value rapidly approaches infinity. This fact is reflected in the reciprocal scale of Fig. 16-1. The spacing of scale intervals increases quite slowly for high values but very rapidly for low values.

Design and Layout of Reciprocal Paper

The scale in Fig. 16-1 ranges from 0 to 1, where $0 = 1/\infty$ and $1 = 1/1$. As shown in the figure, values beyond 100 are practically unobtainable on this basis. However, the reciprocal scale has one very useful property. It is invariant to multiplication. Thus, a scale running from 1–100 is adequate. Figure 16-1 shows the values of the scale which occur from *multiplying* the scale by 2, 5, and 100. As a consequence, it is easy to accommodate any range of values of a variable suspected of behaving reciprocally.

Data Preparation and Plotting for Normal Probability Reciprocal Paper

One useful combination of a reciprocal scale is with a normal probability scale. Table 16-1 gives data for the pulse rate of 99 persons in beats per second. When this data was grouped, as in Table 16-2, and plotted on normal probability paper, the plot was concave. Since the reciprocal of pulse rate is pulse duration, the data were graphed on normal

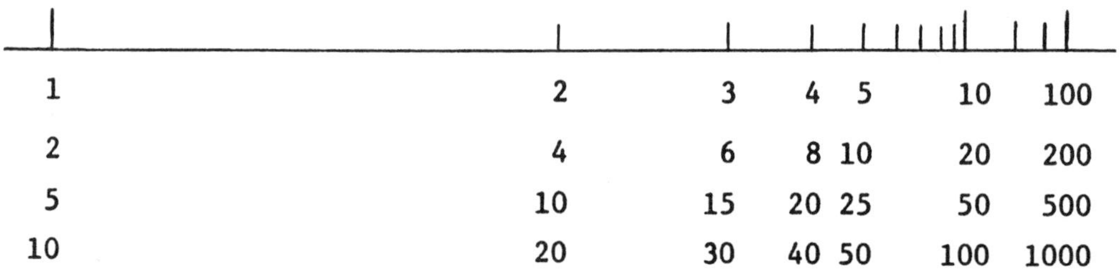

1		2	3	4	5	10	100
2		4	6	8	10	20	200
5		10	15	20	25	50	500
10		20	30	40	50	100	1000

Fig. 16-1. Layout of a reciprocal scale showing scale adjustments obtained by simple multiplication.

Table 16-1. Values of Pulse Rate in Beats per Second

92	92	109	78	71	65	93	78	86	82	100
85	61	82	68	70	70	77	77	83	71	77
69	75	100	89	105	70	74	64	60	65	71
92	60	61	62	92	103	74	81	74	72	75
78	79	91	89	84	132	73	78	86	97	80
63	78	67	96	84	79	81	81	73	72	78
71	73	92	114	79	84	115	107	78	70	88
82	147	92	78	79	69	73	84	67	71	81
89	56	72	139	73	70	80	92	78	80	70

reciprocal paper. The results are shown in Fig. 16-2. The fitted straight line was obtained by the same methodology as for a normal distribution (see Chapter 8).

The straight-line fit is acceptable. However, it is now preferable to find cells and cell endpoints based directly on the reciprocal values. Estimation of distribution parameters (mean, standard deviation, etc.) is thereby improved.

Example 16-1
Given: Data of Table 16-1.
Required: Obtain cell endpoints in terms of reciprocal values.
Procedure:

Step 1. For a sample size of 99, Fig. 3-1 indicates that about 8 cells should be used.

Step 2. Obtain the maximum and minimum values from Table 16-1, 147, and 56; then calculate their reciprocals: 0.0068 and 0.0178.

Step 3. Divide the difference in reciprocals by the required number of cells: $(0.0178 - 0.0068)/8$ yielding 0.00137; use 0.0014.

Step 4. The cell endpoints become 0.0068 — 0.0081; 0.0082 — 0.0095; 0.0096 — 0.0109, etc.

Table 16-2. Grouped Data of Table 16-1
Arranged for Plotting

Cell Interval	Mid-Point	Cumulative Occurrences	Cumulative Percentage Plotting
54–65	60	1 to 10	1% to 10%
66–77	72	11 to 42	11% to 42%
78–89	84	43 to 77	43% to 77%
90–101	96	78 to 90	78% to 90%
102–113	108	91 to 94	91% to 94%
114–125	120	95 to 96	95% to 96%
126–137	132	97	97%
138–149	144	98 to 99	98% to 99%

Table 16-3. Reciprocal Grouping of Table 16-1
Data for Plotting

Cell Interval	Mid-Point	Cumulative Occurrences	Cumulative Percentage Plotting
56–60	58	1 to 3	1% to 3%
61–65	63	4 to 10	4% to 10%
66–72	69	11 to 29	11% to 29%
73–81	77	30 to 62	30% to 62%
82–91	86.5	63 to 78	63% to 78%
92–104	98	79 to 91	79% to 91%
105–122	113.5	92 to 96	92% to 96%
123–147	135	97 to 99	97% to 99%

These are converted back to the original scale of pulse beats, giving: 147 — 123; 122 — 105; 104 — 92, etc.

Step 5. For convenience, the cell endpoints are tabulated from smallest to largest, the frequencies and also the cumulative percentage plotting as in Table 16-3, are obtained.

Step 6. Plot the data and fit the best line, as in Fig. 16-3.

Parameter Estimation from Linear Plots

There is no need to perform individual calculations to obtain reciprocal values for plotting. The reciprocal scale on the paper allows us to graph the data in direct units. Therefore, normal reciprocal paper is another instance of a time-saving application.

Our data are now displayed as reciprocals. In Fig. 16-3, at the 50 percent point, we obtain a value of 80 beats per minute. Converted to its reciprocal form, this yields $1/80 = 0.0125$ minutes of pulse duration. The reason for this is that the units were transformed from beats per minute to minutes per beat. The values at 6.7 percent and 93.3 percent are also found and, again, the reciprocals of these values are taken. At 6.7 percent, we have 63, and, at 93.3 percent, we have 108; $1/63 = 0.0159$, and $1/108 = 0.0093$. The standard deviation of the distribution of reciprocals is evaluated by the general method previously given:

$$(0.0159 - 0.0093)/3 = 0.0066/3 = 0.0022.$$

The corresponding estimates from Fig. 16-2 are a mean of 0.0123 beats per minute and a standard deviation of 0.0023. The differences between the

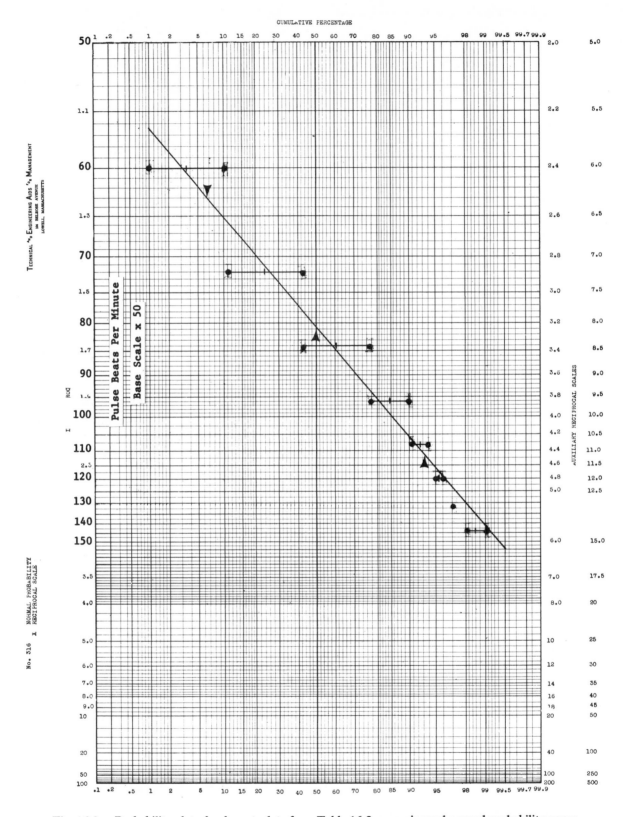

Fig. 16-2.   Probability plot of pulse-rate data from Table 16-2, on reciprocal normal probability paper.

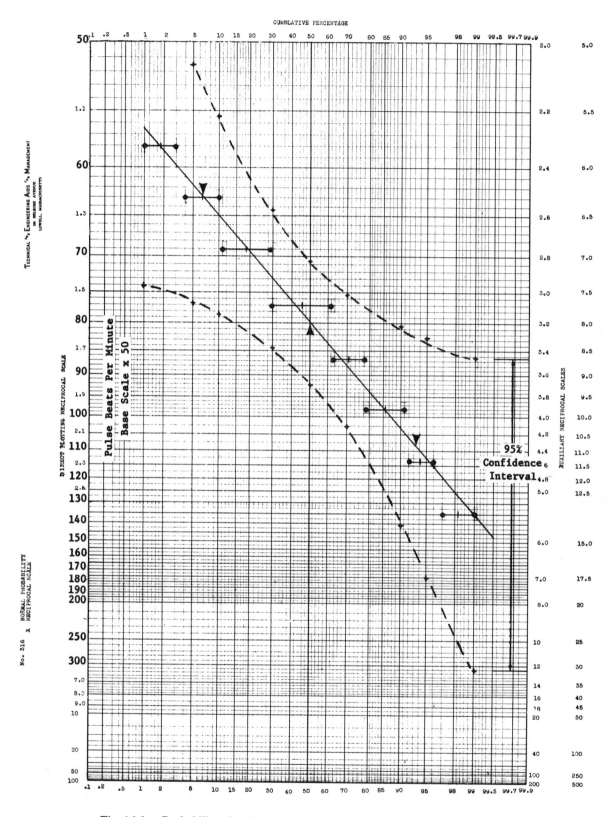

Fig. 16-3.   Probability plot of pulse-rate data using cells based on reciprocals and
showing the 95 percent confidence interval.

two sets of estimates are small. However, note that the estimate of the mean from Fig. 16-3, 80 beats per minute, is closer to the accepted value of 78 beats per second, which is considered normal for pulses, than is the estimate of 81 from Fig. 16-2. Further, note that the estimate of the standard deviation from Fig. 16-3 is smaller than that of Fig. 16-2, which is indicative of a better fit to the data. Also, the best line of Fig. 16-3 passes closer to the middle of more data groups, which can be taken as a qualitative indication of a better fit to the data.

Confidence Intervals

Confidence intervals may be obtained straightforwardly by obtaining the proper intercepts from the fitted line, taking reciprocals, applying the factors from Appendix Table A-4, and taking reciprocals a second time to obtain values in the original number scale. The values obtained are plotted above and below the best-fit line. The points so obtained are connected by a smooth line to define the confidence interval.

Example 16-2
Given: The probability plot of Fig. 16-3. The sample standard deviation is 0.0022, and the cell interval is 0.0014.
Required: Obtain the confidence interval.
Procedure:

Step 1. Obtain the intercepts of the best-fit line and percentiles indicated in Appendix Table A-4.

The results are shown in Table 16-4, Column 1. Note that only those percentiles within the actual range of the data are used.

Step 2. Take the reciprocals of the intercepts shown in Column 1. These results are shown in Table 16-4, Column 2.

Step 3. For the percentiles used in Column 1, obtain the appropriate factors from Appendix Table A-4. Note that the entries for sample size in Table A-4 go from 90 to 120. The sample size observed is 99. The values given in Column 3 were obtained by linear interpolation.

Step 4. Multiply the standard deviation, $s_{y \cdot x}$, by the square root of the number of units per cell. For this example, $s_{y \cdot x} = 0.0022$. The cell interval is 0.0014 which means that 14 *units* per cell were used. The product of $0.0022 \times \sqrt{14} = 0.00823$. The factors of Column 3 are multiplied by 0.00823 and the results are given in Column 4.

Step 5. The values of Column 4 are added to and subtracted from the values of Column 2 to obtain the values for the confidence interval in reciprocal units.

Step 6. Reciprocals of the values in Column 5 are taken to obtain values for the confidence interval in the original number scale. These values are given in Column 6.

Step 7. The values of Column 6 are plotted as in Fig. 16-3. Faired curves are fitted to the plotted points to obtain the confidence interval which is shown by the dashed lines.

Table 16-4. Data and Calculations to Obtain the Confidence Interval for Fig. 16-3

Column 1. Intercept at Indicated Percentile		Column 2. Reciprocal of Col. 1.	Column 3. Factors from Appendix Table A-4	Column 4. Col. 3. × 0.00823	Column 5. Col. 2. ± Col. 4.	Column 6. Reciprocal of Col. 5.
1%	56.5	0.01770	0.509	0.00419	0.01351–0.02189	74.0–45.7
5%	61.8	0.01618	0.386	0.00318	0.01300–0.01936	76.9–51.6
10%	65.0	0.01538	0.326	0.00268	0.01270–0.01806	78.7–55.4
30%	73.0	0.01370	0.226	0.00186	0.01184–0.01556	84.5–64.3
50%	80.0	0.01250	0.200	0.00165	0.01085–0.01415	92.2–70.7
70%	88.0	0.01136	0.226	0.00186	0.00950–0.01322	105.3–75.6
90%	103.0	0.00971	0.326	0.00268	0.00703–0.01239	142.2–80.7
95%	112.5	0.00889	0.386	0.00318	0.00571–0.01207	175.1–82.8
99%	135.0	0.00741	0.509	0.00419	0.00322–0.01160	310.6–86.2

Recognizing the Applicability of Reciprocal Functions

When one is searching for a probability paper to fit a set of data, it is quite possible that reciprocal data will have been tried on log-normal and on extreme value probability paper. The data of Table 16-1 will give quite acceptable results on both. Therefore, one does not often recognize a need for reciprocal probability papers. However, if it is known that a set of data came from a process with a known reciprocal relationship, then such paper is the grid of choice for graphing the results.

Thresholds in Data

We have earlier considered the location parameter for the Weibull distribution and eliminated the need of working with a three-parameter function by making the gamma correction. This was, in effect, a simple subtraction of time to first failure from all subsequent failure times and operating with the residual times. The time or stress level before which no failures occur or before which no failures are *assumed* to occur is called a *threshold value*. As with the Weibull distribution, sometimes it is of interest to determine threshold values in data. These values are then used to adjust the data in order to improve the fit of data to a specific probability paper. Hald (23) illustrates the determination of thresholds for the log-normal distribution, and Diviney and David (10), illustrate a graphical method for the reciprocal normal distribution.

Such adjustments and transformations are considered to be licit only within the context of a specific problem. Good general rules have already been given for the requirements of choosing a proper underlying distribution. Successful determination of thresholds requires specialized knowledge in such fields as chemical thermodynamics, economics, biology, and psychology, where thresholds do occur that require knowledgeable interpretation. Therefore, no generalization will be offered in this book.

Arhennius Plots

The so-called Arhennius function is of the form $y = e^{Q/T}$. Q is again the activation energy and T is the Kelvin temperature. A useful method of handling this function is by taking logarithms: $\log y = Q(1/T)$, with Q taken as a constant. This reduction will plot linearly on a paper that has a logarithmic scale versus a reciprocal Kelvin temperature scale.

Failure rates for many electronic components and insulation materials have been found to follow this relationship. The data for failures in a temperature step-stress test at constant power is given for two transistor types in Table 16-5 and the plots are given in Fig. 16-4. These plots are made against the oven temperature, which is increased in equal amounts from step to step. On the basis of these plots, transistor A would appear to have a higher failure rate than transistor B, by an average of half again more at any given temperature.

Common Errors

The results of Fig. 16-4 also illustrate an all too common misuse of graph paper to present test results. The temperature used for plotting was that of the test oven. This procedure is incorrect because it fails to recognize that, during operation, electronic components consume power which generates internal heat. The internal heat causes an additional temperature rise above that of the test oven. Therefore, knowledge of the internal temperature is important since the actual operating temperature has a direct influence on the failure mechanisms which occur. For transistors, the significant internal temperature is that of the junction between the base and emitter portions of the transistor.

Table 16-5 includes information on the junction operating temperatures for both the Type A and Type B transistors. The junction temperatures are now plotted against the failure percentage in Fig. 16-5. Compared to the results of Fig. 16-4, interpretation and conclusions are now reversed. In Fig. 16-4, the Type B transistor appears to have a lower failure percentage than the Type A transistor for any given test-oven temperature. In Fig. 16-5, the Type B transistor is seen to have approximately double the failure percentage for any given junction temperature. This is caused because the Type B transistor dissipates less internal heat than the

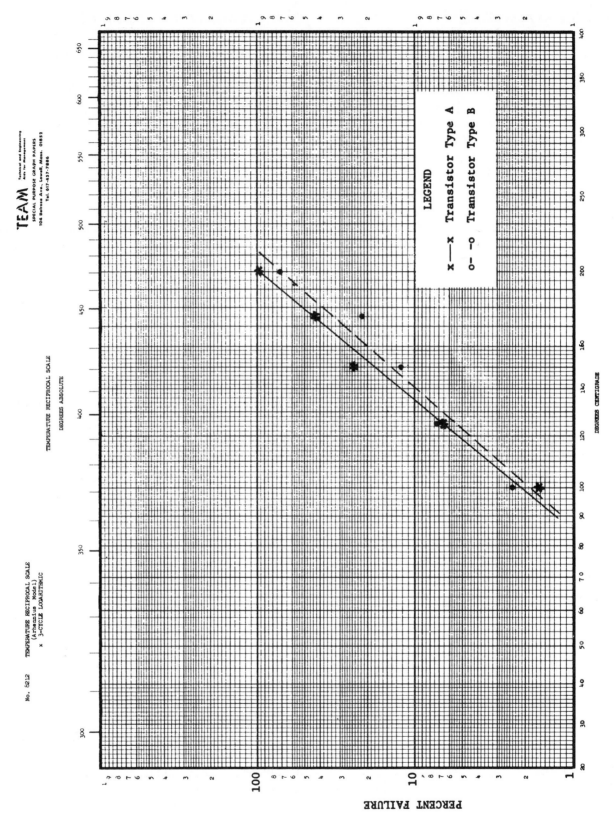

Fig. 16-4.   Arhennius plot of transistor failure percentages versus test-oven temperature.

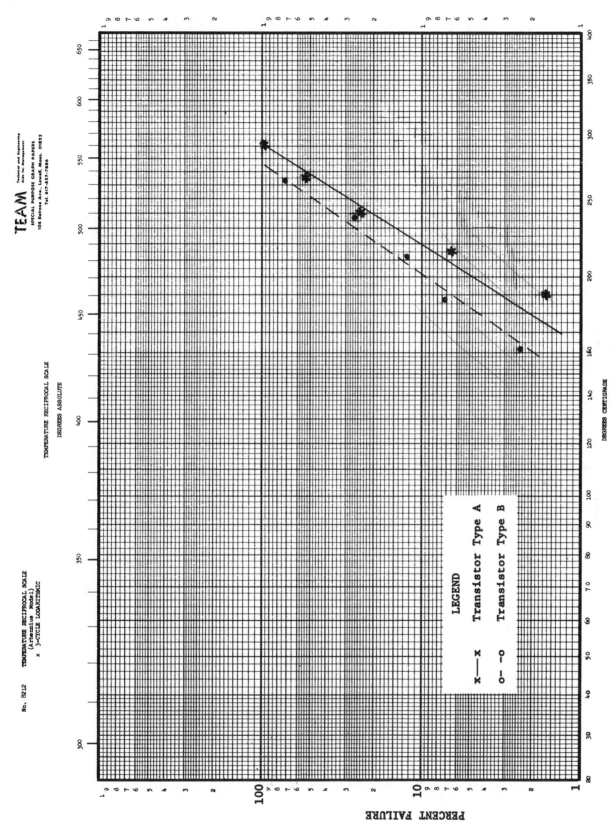

Fig. 16-5.   Arhennius plot of transistor failure percentages versus junction operating temperatures.

Table 16-5. Step-Stress Failure-Rate Data for Two Transistor Types

Test Oven Temp., °C	Type A Transistor			Type B Transistor		
	Number of Failures	Cumulative Plotting Percentage	Junction Temp., °C	Number of Failures	Cumulative Plotting Percentage	Junction Temp., °C
100	1	1.6	190	1	2.4	162
125	4	6.6	215	3	7.2	187
150	15	24.6	240	5	12.2	212
175	32	52.4	265	11	26.8	237
200	60	98.4	290	29	70.7	262
TOTAL, n:	60			40		

Type A transistor. Therefore, the Type B transistor runs hotter at any given oven temperature, the electrochemical reactions which can cause failure occur at a faster rate, and so more failures occur for the Type B transistor.

Another Arhennius Application

It has also been found that some measurable characteristics of products change as a function of exposure to temperature and follow Arhennius relationships. Table 16-6 gives data for the average ohmic change for a number of different samples of resistors of metal film resistors operated for 8,000 hours with the internal operating temperature of the film as indicated. This data is plotted in Fig. 16-6.

Such figures are useful in design work when adequate test data are available. Individual plots, such as Fig. 16-6, can be made for each of a number of operating times of interest. Then, on the basis of knowing, or being able to assume the internal operating film temperature, the behavior of this

type of part can be estimated for various combinations of time and other operating conditions.

Extension of Distribution Concepts

In earlier chapters, we have usually worked with the results of one set of measurements taken under a specified set of conditions at a single point in time. However, we may wish to know not only how a variable is distributed under one set of conditions, but also how the variable behaves under several sets of related conditions. A typical example is the variation in behavior of a part, or a system, over a range of possible operating temperatures.

Table 16-7 gives results for the change in capacitance of a liquid electrolytic capacitor. A sample of 49 parts was used. The maximum, the mean, and the minimum percentage change from a 25°C reference reading at each test temperature is given, and is also plotted in Fig. 16-7.

Since both positive and negative changes occur in such tests, this graph paper is designed to accommodate the related plotting of these changes. The

Table 16-6. Resistance Change and Failure-Rate Data for a Metal Film Resistor

Operating Temperature, °C	Time of Observation, in Hours							
	1000		2000		4000		8000	
	Change in Resistance, Ohms	Percent Failing	Change in Resistance, Ohms	Percent Failing	Change in Resistance, Ohms	Percent Failing	Change in Resistance, Ohms	Percent Failing
126	+ 20	0.23	+ 75	1.1	+ 150	1.9	+ 100	2.8
139	+ 80	0.6	+ 140	2.9	+ 220	5.0	+ 360	7.2
153	+ 140	1.6	+ 220	8.0	+ 310	14.0	+ 620	19.4
178	+ 680	8.0	+ 1060	38.1	+ 1720	66.6	+ 3610	88.7
182	+ 560	10.3	+ 960	35.0	+ 1450	43.6	+ 2405	80.5
193	+ 1670	88.7	+ 2240	90.0	+ 3310	81.1	+ 6490	92.2
221	+ 3330	100	+ 6740	100	+ 8500	100	+ 29740	100

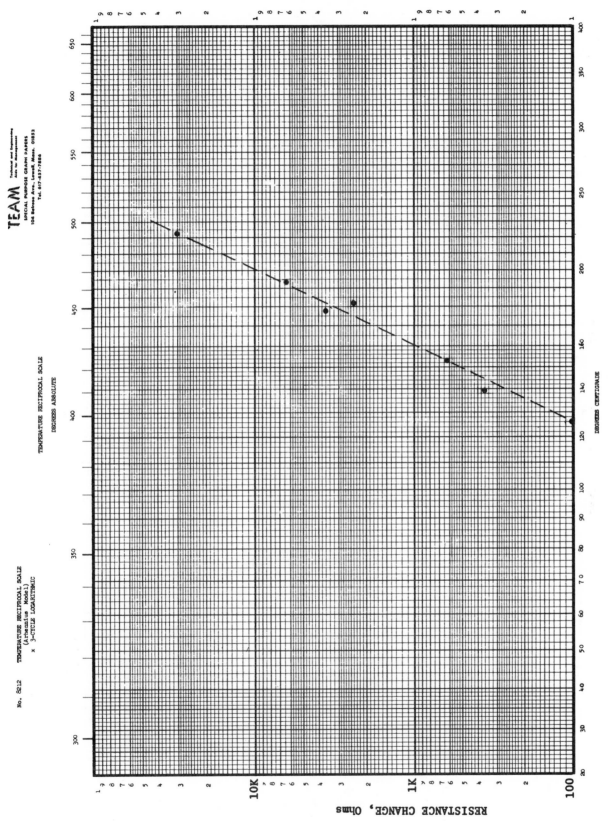

Fig. 16-6. Arhennius plot of resistance change versus metal-film operating temperature at 8000 hours.

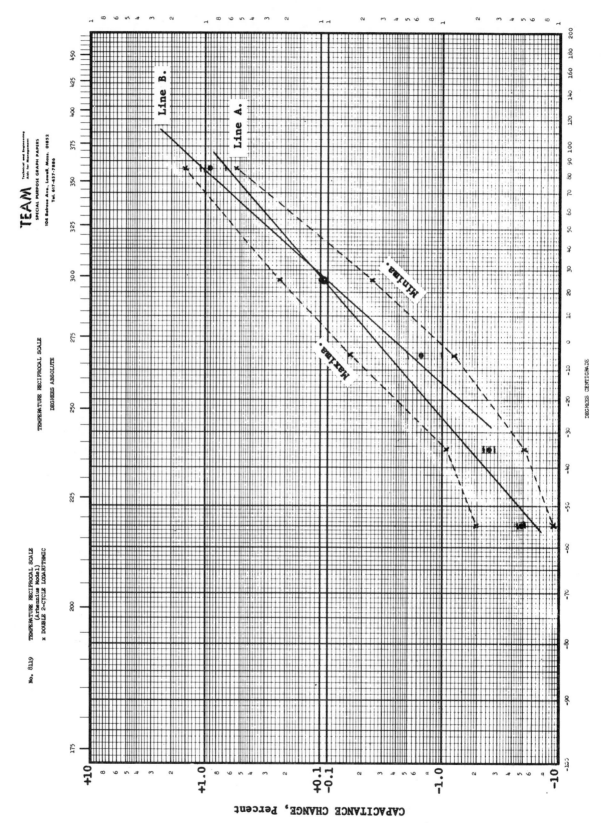

Fig. 16-7. Double Arhennius plot of capacitance change versus temperature variation.

Table 16-7. Capacitance Change During Low and High Temperature Exposure

	Percent Capacitance Change from Reference Capacity Value.					
	Step 1. + 25° C	Step 2. − 55° C	Step 3. − 35° C	Step 4. − 5° C	Step 5. + 25° C	Step 6. + 85° C
	Percent					
Maximum	Reference	− 1.98	− 1.09	− 0.16	+ 0.23	+ 1.51
Mean	Reference	− 4.78	− 2.54	− 0.74	+ 0.08	+ 0.93
Minimum	Reference	− 9.40	− 5.10	− 1.26	− 0.22	+ 0.54

bottom half represents the percentage decrease from reference; the upper half represents an increase. The circle represents the reference condition. One convention must be observed in this kind of plotting: the lines on either side of the middle should be set at the same value, 0.1 in this case. If all the +85°C values had been greater than 1.0 percent, for instance, the scales should still be valued identically to preserve correct proportional relationships.

The fitted line, A, is drawn using the 25°C reference condition as a zero point. This line should also fall between the plotted maximum and minimum values. The maximum points are now connected together as are the minimum points. Since the maxima and minima represent estimates of the 1 and 99 percent points, the lines connecting the max-min points are a 98 percent envelope of the observed results.

Another Case of Non-Sampling Error

Ideally, the envelope should be approximately symmetrical about the fitted line. In this case, it is not. At the lower end, it appears to be "out-of-line." This was caused by freezing of the electrolyte. Therefore, the two lower test conditions are not valid for this part and, if used, would bias interpretation of the purely temperature response characteristics of this part.

Ignoring the two lowest points, Line B is now fitted to the data with correspondingly better symmetry in reference to the max-min envelope.

Another Case of Measurement Limitations

In the required test sequence, the parts are given initial measurements. Then they are placed in a cold chamber to obtain the −55°C readings, raised successively to −35°C, −5°C, +25°C and +85°C, with readings at each point. At 25°C, we are repeating the equivalent of initial conditions. However, the envelope at +25°C shows that we do not reproduce the initial readings absolutely identically. The envelope at this point is ±0.25 percent, around zero. This is also a good measurement of the probable test error at each other point as well.

The estimate of measurement error may be added to and subtracted from the mean percentage change at each test point. This will assist in judging the placement of the fitted line. It will also test the validity of certain sets of readings. Since Line B was drawn through the three upper points within the measurement error interval, it is now very clear that something different has occurred at −35°C and −55°C — which, of course, was due to the electrolyte freezing.

Table 16-8. Capacitance Change During Low and High Temperature Exposure

	Percent Capacitance Change from Reference by Step.					
	Step 1. + 25° C	Step 2. − 55° C	Step 3. − 35° C	Step 4. − 5° C	Step 5. + 25° C	Step 6. + 85° C
	Percent					
Maximum	Reference	− 3.35	− 2.42	− 0.72	− 0.11	+ 1.11
Mean	Reference	− 3.54	− 2.48	− 0.84	− 0.17	+ 0.97
Minimum	Reference	− 3.83	− 2.52	− 0.94	− 0.22	+ 0.88

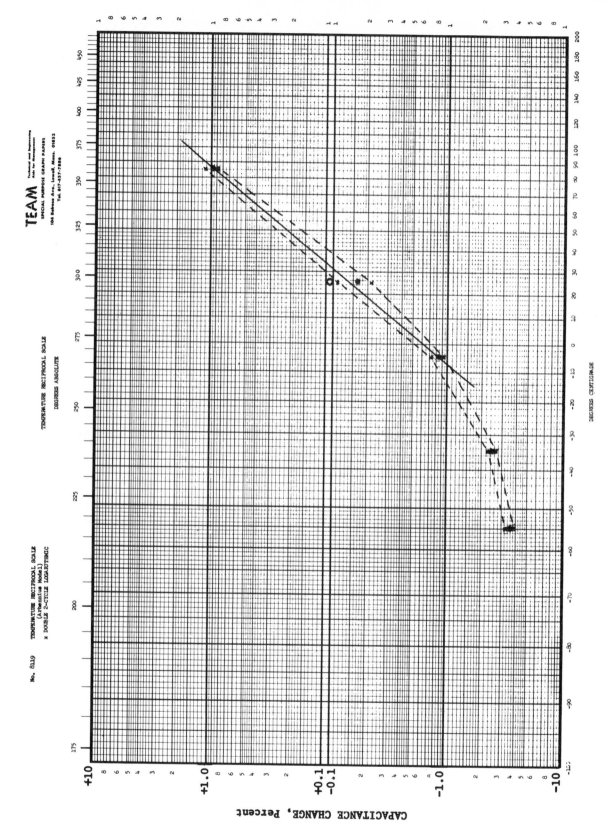

Fig. 16-8. Double Arhennius plot of capacitance change versus temperature variation, showing effects of test errors.

More About Non-Sampling Error

Another set of temperature response data is given in Table 16-8 for a sample of nine parts of a second type of electrolytic capacitor.

This data is shown in Fig. 16-8. In this case, at +25°C, the max-min envelope does not even include zero. This is a significant indication of sampling errors due to mistakes during testing or to poor test procedures. As with curvature and nonlinearity in single distribution plots, evidence of nonsampling error requires action. The sources of such errors must be eliminated in order to obtain valid data. If data are not valid, analysis is of little value. Invalid data lead to invalid conclusions and recommendations which, in turn, lead to useless decisions.

Exercises

16-1. Table 16-9 gives measurements of the times between pulses generated in a pulse-forming network.

Table 16-9. Time Between Pulses in a Pulse-Forming Network

Time, in Milliseconds		
2.7	2.8	2.3
2.4	2.2	2.4
2.6	2.5	2.6
1.9	2.3	2.6
3.7	2.9	2.4
2.9	2.2	2.0
2.7	2.3	2.2
2.2	3.1	2.3

a. Prepare the data and plot the results on reciprocal normal probability paper.

b. Obtain estimates of the 10, 50, and 90 percentiles.

c. Calculate the nominal frequency of the pulse source using the relationship: frequency = 1/pulse duration.

d. Estimate the nominal tolerance of the frequency source by use of the differential between the 10 and 90 percentiles.

16-2. Table 16-3 gives data on percent failure for a metal film resistor by levels of operating temperature at four separate total test times.

a. Prepare Arhennius plots for any two test times and plot the data on the same sheet.

b. Compare the results and discuss the apparent effect of time and temperature on percent failure.

16-3. Table 16-3 also gives values of resistance change for the same four test times as the percent failure data.

a. Prepare Arhennius plots for the same two test times as used in Exercise 16-2 and plot the results on the same sheet.

b. Compare the results and discuss the apparent effect of time and temperature on the amount of resistance change.

c. Compare the plot of Exercise 16-3 to the plot of Exercise 16-2. Discuss similarities or dissimilarities in the overall appearance of the results.

CHAPTER 17

The Gamma Distribution

Background

The gamma distribution is a generalized factorial function leading to a family of essentially extreme value functions which is usually bounded at 0 by defining that values less than 0 are excluded. However, the bound may be at some value of x greater than 0. In such a case, the value of x is once again a threshold value. For practical problems with the gamma distribution, the threshold may be stated in terms of a specific minimum number of events, such as a minimum inventory level, or the time between arrivals of a public transit vehicle.

Description of the Gamma Distribution

Like many distributions, the gamma distribution is known by various names; some of the more common aliases are:

1. The Pearson Type III distribution (used in mathematical statistics)
2. The Erlang distribution (used in queuing theory and waiting-line problems)
3. The Chi-Square distribution (a common special case derived by specific restrictions on the distribution parameters)
4. The Maxwell distribution (another special case, from statistical mechanics, derived by specific restrictions on the distribution parameters)
5. Fisher's Z-statistic
6. Snedecor's F-statistic
7. Student's t-statistic.

Using the arrangement of Hahn and Shapiro (22), the cumulative distribution function and the probability density function are given by:

$$F(x; n, \lambda) = \frac{\lambda^n}{\Gamma(n)} \int_0^x t^{(n-1)} e^{-\lambda t}\, dt \qquad (17\text{-}1)$$

$$f(x; n, \lambda) = \frac{\lambda^n}{\Gamma(n)} x^{(n-1)} e^{-\lambda x} \qquad (17\text{-}2)$$

where:

$x \geq 0$. These functions are zero elsewhere.
The time required for n events to occur at a rate, λ, is $f(x; n, \lambda)$.
t is the time of observation.
n is a value representing some event or number of events which constitute an expected, or desired, result.
λ is the mean rate at which individual events occur.
x is a random variable representing the average time between individual occurrences of the event n.
Γ is the gamma function.

For the gamma distribution, n represents a quantity fixed by specified circumstances. For instance, if material is ordered in specified quantities, or lot sizes, then n is the lot size. If some kind of action such as inspection, maintenance, calibration, or adjustment is specified after a fixed amount of usage, then n is the number of times the item may be placed in service before the specified activity must occur.

By comparison, λ is caused by circumstances and has various representations. In the case of materials usage, it is a relatively constant rate of usage per unit time, such as λ items per week. In the case of service functions, it can represent the mean usage rate or mean frequency of use, for example, λ times a day.

The random variable, x, has different connotations under the conditions given above. In the first case, it is the time elapsed for the consumption of a lot or, more realistically, the time between reorder points. In the second case, it is the elapsed time during which the frequency of usage leads to the need for a service function to be performed.

Under practical circumstances, n is a value which should be known by definition of the use situation; λ is a mean rate of usage which may or may not be known; and x is a random time variable.

When n is restricted to an integer value, the gamma distribution is referred to as the Erlang distribution; this is used in queuing or waiting-line theory. Applications can involve waiting for service of demands for telephone service on a switchboard, the number of customers arriving in a store, or the number of machines needing repair.

Design and Layout of Chi-Square/Gamma Probability Paper

The same probability paper can be used to plot both the gamma distribution and its special case, the chi-square distribution. This paper was first developed for the chi-square distribution before its applicability to the more general gamma distribution became known. The paper was subsequently retitled to describe its dual usage.

The top scale on a chi-square/gamma probability paper gives the value of the chi-square distribution which corresponds to the probability points of the lower scale. This is readily converted for use with the gamma distribution by the simple relation: $\chi^2 = 2\eta$. The use of this scale will be discussed later.

The linear vertical scale is used to plot observed values of x.

Chi-square/gamma probability paper for $n = 1$ appears similar to extreme value probability paper. In fact, the low end of the scale is more compressed than for the Type I extreme value scale. At about $n = 2$, the two scales are nearly identical. As n approaches 5, the gamma distribution is nearly equivalent to the log-normal distribution. For n approaching 15, the gamma distribution approaches the normal distribution.

Figure 17-1 shows the probability scales for $n = 1$, 2, and 5 against the Type I extreme value and normal probability scales.

Some Preliminary Considerations in Gamma Plotting

Data preparation and plotting are done in the same way for the gamma distribution as for the normal and extreme value distributions.

Due to the transition in the shape of the gamma distribution across the entire spectrum of shapes which we have previously considered, gamma papers should only be used when there are known technical grounds to expect gamma distribution behavior. The conditions of the problem under consideration will be important clues. Such conditions would be a specification of one or more limiting events, a usage or recurrence rate, or a time dependency.

Gamma papers should not be used to obtain arbitrary data fits. In this case, the possibilities of the normal and extreme value families should be exploited because of their more systematic interpretations.

When there are sound reasons for using the gamma distribution assumption in choosing a probability paper, there is additional pertinent information to be determined before a proper choice of a specific paper type can be made. These are:

1. Can the value η be defined from known definitions or physical constraints? The value of η then indicates the type of gamma paper to use.

2. Is λ known to be a constant, or nearly constant? If λ is not at least nearly constant, then the gamma distribution should not be used.

Generation of the Gamma Distribution

The uniform distribution which we first considered in Chapter 6 leads directly to the gamma distribution under specified rules of operation. These rules are different from those of the other distributions which we have considered. Once again, dice are convenient function generators to study the behavior of this distribution.

If we now refer to Table 6-1 dice data, we can establish the minimum operating rules for the gamma distribution. For the dice, there are six faces with each face representing only one possible outcome, a value from 1 to 6. If we choose one particular value for observation, η becomes 1, automatically. Any one value from 1 through 6 may be used. Since there are six possible values, the frequency of occurrence to be expected is $\frac{1}{6}$. This is the value for λ. With a specific value, such

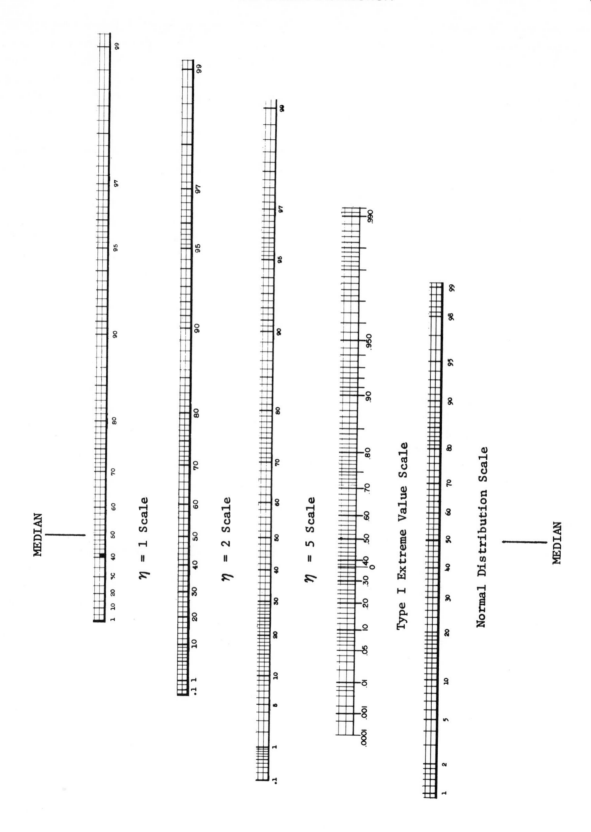

Fig. 17-1. Comparison of Gamma Distribution Scales to Type I Extreme Value and Normal Distribution Scales.

as 4, we can then obtain values for x, the time between the occurrences of η; that is, the occurrence of a 4.

Example 17-1

In Table 6-1, we use the first column in each group, then the second column, etc. We count the number of successive throws required to obtain a 4. The first 24 such sequences are given in Table 17-1.

Table 17-1. Waiting Times for a 4 to Appear on Throws of a Die

3	5	12	1	3
5	5	13	2	5
5	12	2	19	18
1	4	7	3	1
13	2	8	14	

The number of tosses between 4's are also called waiting times for 4's to appear. These data are shown ordered and plotted in Fig. 17-2.

Parameter Estimation from Linear Plots

Estimates of the parameters of the gamma distribution are readily obtained from the probability paper using the top scale.

The mean, μ, of the gamma distribution occurs at η. Therefore, for Fig. 17-2, $\eta = 1$; $\chi^2 = 2\eta = 2$. Locate 2 on the top scale and drop down to the fitted line and project to the x scale at the left. This gives a value of $\eta = 7.2$ for the mean.

λ is estimated from the slope of the fitted line by substituting in:

$$\lambda = \frac{\chi_2^2 - \chi_1^2}{2(x_2 - x_1)} \qquad (17\text{-}3)$$

where:

x_2 and x_1 are two convenient values on the x scale: χ_2^2 and χ_1^2 are the projections of x_2 and x_1 on the top scale and 2 is the proportionality constant between x^2 and η.

From Fig. 17-2, $\lambda = \dfrac{3.36 - 1.60}{2(12 - 6)} = \dfrac{1.76}{12} = 0.147$

μ, η and λ are related quite simply:

$$\mu = \frac{\eta}{\lambda} \qquad (17\text{-}4)$$

Therefore, λ can also be estimated after μ is determined without use of Equation 17-3.

The variance of this distribution is given by:

$$V = \frac{\eta}{\lambda^2} \qquad (17\text{-}5)$$

Example 17-2

Again using Table 6-1 for our data, we can obtain data to illustrate the gamma distribution for $\eta = 2$. We can define the joint event for $\eta = 2$ as requiring a 1 followed by a 2. The probability of occurrence of either event is known to be $\frac{1}{6}$. The joint probability is the product of the individual probabilities or $\frac{1}{6} \times \frac{1}{6} = \frac{1}{36}$. The waiting times for the 1-2 event are given in Table 17-2.

Table 17-2. Waiting Times for a 1-2 Combination to Appear on Throws of a Die

34	16	102
36	27	25
23	3	30
22	2	21
20	10	

The results from Table 17-2 are plotted in Fig. 17-3. Parameter estimates are

$$\mu = 26 \text{ and } \lambda = \frac{10.90 - 3.20}{2(80 - 20)} = \frac{7.70}{120} = 0.064$$

Discussion of Parameter Estimates

Table 17-3 tabulates the theoretical and actual results obtained from Examples 17-1 and 17-2.

The estimate of μ for $\eta = 1$ misses by $+20\%$ and for $\eta = 2$ by -27.7%. The estimates for λ are off by -12.6% and $+16.4\%$, respectively.

Table 17-3. Comparison of Theoretical and Actual Parameter Estimates Using Data from Examples 17-1 and 17-2

	Example 17-1. $\eta = 1$	Example 17-2. $\eta = 2$
μ — Theoretical	6.0	36.0
μ — Actual	7.2	26.0
Difference	$+ 20.0\%$	$- 27.7\%$
λ — Theoretical	0.166	0.055
λ — Actual	0.147	0.064
Difference	$- 12.6\%$	$+ 16.4\%$

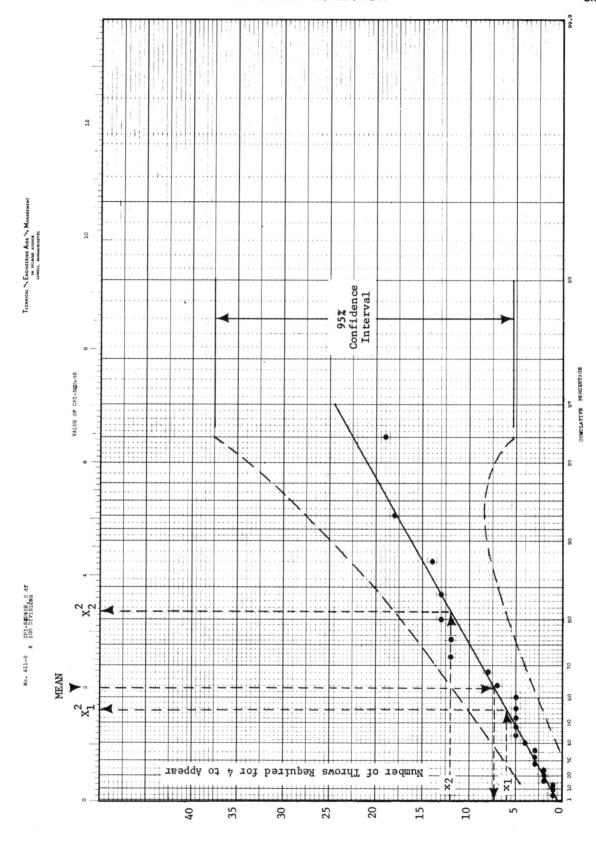

Fig. 17-2.   Gamma probability plot of waiting times for 4's to appear in throwing dice.

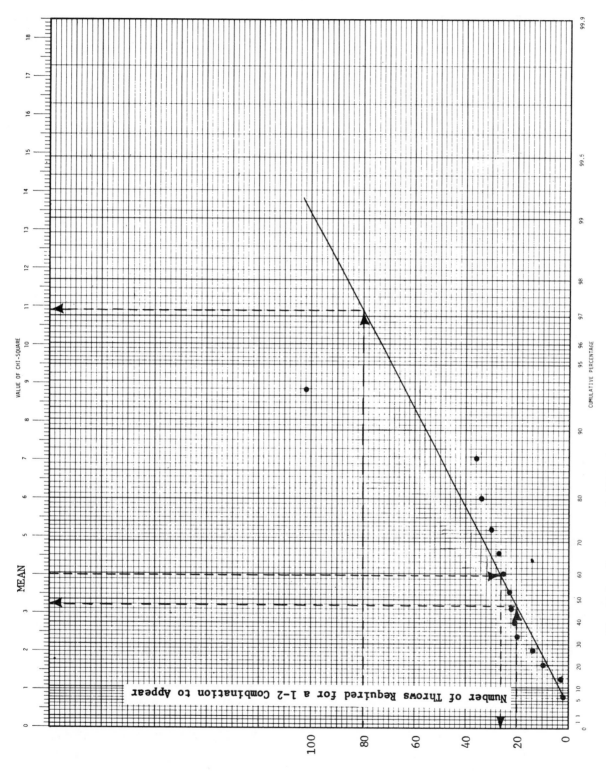

Fig. 17-3.   Gamma probability plot of waiting times for a 1 followed by a 2 in throwing dice.

It may be seen from Equation 17-5 that the variance increases directly with η and inversely as the square of λ. Since sample size does not enter into the variance, the variance is independent of sample size.

Although it is not directly obvious from Equation 17-5, an increase in η will normally be accompanied by a decrease in λ. At least, in the sense used above, an increase in η represents an increase in complexity of the description of the event. The increase in complexity will normally be accompanied by a decrease in the frequency of occurrence which results in a smaller value for λ.

Therefore, on a simplistic basis, we should normally expect the variance to increase greatly as the index, η, of the gamma distribution increases. However, many practical problems involving the gamma distribution are stated in terms which make λ greater than 1. This keeps the variance term to relatively small values.

Confidence Intervals

Confidence intervals for the gamma distribution can be derived with a method similar to that for extreme value distributions with a slight modification. From Equation 17-5, the variance is given as $V = \eta/\lambda^2$. The standard deviation is then $\sigma = \sqrt{\eta/\lambda^2}$. The standard deviation is used in place of the Gumbel slope and is to be corrected by the factor in Table A-5[1] for expected standard deviation. Then the rest of the procedure given in Example 11-3 is applicable. This is illustrated for the data of Table 17-1 and Fig. 17-2.

Example 17-3

From Example 17-1, we have $\eta = 1$, $\lambda = .147$, and $\eta = 24$.

$$\sigma = \sqrt{\frac{1}{.147^2}} = 6.9388$$

For $n = 24$, Table A-5 gives $\sigma(N) = 1.0864$.

$$\frac{\sigma}{\sigma(N)} = \frac{6.94}{1.0864} = 6.39$$

[1] In Appendix.

Percentile	$\sigma/\sigma(N) \div \sqrt{24}$	$\times k_2$	Offset from Best-fit Line
15%	$6.39 \div \sqrt{24} =$	$1.30 \times 2.51 =$	3.26
30%		$1.30 \times 2.54 =$	3.30
50%		$1.30 \times 2.89 =$	3.76
70%		$1.30 \times 3.67 =$	4.77
85%		$1.30 \times 5.17 =$	6.72
Second Largest		$6.39 \times 1.51 =$	9.65
Largest Value		$2.68 =$	17.12

A Non-time-related Application

Equation 17-1 specifies the gamma distribution as time-dependent. However, the case of $\eta = 1$ has also been found to be applicable to data which measure the response of a group of individuals to some stimulus. In such applications, $\eta = 1$ represents the single individual responding; λ represents the mean rate at which individuals respond; and x represents the total number of responses per individual.

In studies of reader response to advertising, there are several key questions. One question often asked is: "Do readers who respond quickly after publication show a different degree of interest than those who respond later?" The reason for this question is the assumptions that those readers who respond quickly:

1. Take the publication under consideration seriously
2. Read the publication soon after receiving it
3. Have specific purposes for using the publication as a guide in their work.

The corresponding assumptions applicable to those who respond more slowly are:

1. They have less serious interest in the publication.
2. They read the publication "when they get to it."
3. They are less specific in their utilization of the publication in their work.

From the preceding sets of assumptions, it can be conjectured that the quick responder would request fewer items of information since it is believed that he reads the publication more fre-

Table 17-4. Frequency Tallies of Numbers of Items of Information
Requested on Reader Response Cards from a Technical Journal

Number of Items	Offering of New Catalogue		Comparison of Advertisements*	
	Early	Late	Item X	Item Y
1	THL III	III	THL	IIII
2	THL THL II	IIII	III	III
3	THL II	THL I	I	THL
4	THL II	THL	THL	II
5	THL THL II	IIII	II	THL I
6	THL II	IIII	II	IIII
7	I	III		
8	III	I		
9		IIII	I	
10	II		III	II
11	I		I	I
12		II		
13			I	
14			II	I
15				
16		I		
17				
18	I		I	
19			I	
20	I	I		
21		I		I
	$n = 62$	$n = 39$	$n = 28$	$n = 29$

* To be used for Exercise 17-4.

quently and with specific motives. By contrast, the slow responder would be expected to request more items since he may read the publication less often and, probably, with less specific interests.

Example 17-4
Given: Table 17-4 lists data for samples of the number of responses to a journal advertisement. The "early" sample is from the first week's response after reader response cards start to come in. The "late" sample is from response cards received six weeks later. The data is presented in the form of frequency tallies showing the total number of items of information requested by the individuals returning the reader response card.
Question: Is there any reason to believe that the response is different between the early and late responses?
Procedure: Data for the "early" sample is plotted in Fig. 17-4. The best-fit line is drawn through the plotted points. The parameter estimates obtained are:

$$\mu = 4.5$$

$$\lambda = \frac{5.32 - 2.30}{2(10 - 5)} = \frac{3.02}{10} = 0.302, \text{ use } 0.3$$

$$\sigma = \sqrt{\frac{1}{0.3^2}} = \frac{1}{0.3} = 3.33$$

The confidence interval is obtained as shown below:

For $n = 62$, Table A-5 gives $\sigma(N) = 1.177$.

$$\frac{\sigma}{\sigma(N)} = \frac{3.33}{1.177} = 2.84$$

Percentile	$\sigma/\sigma(N) \div \sqrt{62}$		$\times k_2$		Offset from Best-fit Line
15%	2.84 ÷ 7.88	=	0.36 × 2.51	=	0.91
30%			0.36 × 2.54	=	0.92
50%			0.36 × 2.89	=	1.04
70%			0.36 × 3.67	=	1.33
85%			0.36 × 5.17	=	1.86
Second Largest			2.84 × 1.51	=	4.29
Largest Value			2.84 × 2.68	=	7.61

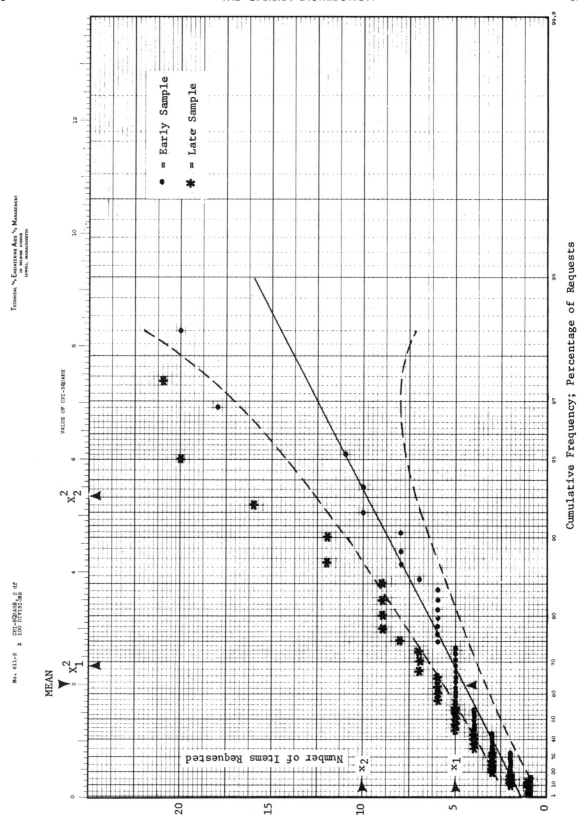

Fig. 17-4. Gamma probability plot of numbers of items requested on reader response cards from a technical journal.

Only two points fall outside the 95 percent limits for a sample of 62 where a maximum of three points could be allowed. Therefore, the fitted line is assumed to represent this data reasonably.

Data for late sample of 39 responses are plotted as crosses superimposed on the plot for early responses. But 25 out of 39 points fall outside the confidence interval; all of the points which fall out are above the upper confidence limit. Therefore, we readily conclude that the later responses have a higher number of requests for information.

Another question raised in the evaluation of advertising is: "Was there a difference in impact, as measured by response, between two different ads, or the same ad placed at two different points in time?" The approach used in Example 17-4 can also be used to investigate this question. Exercise 17-4 gives data on the comparison of responses to one advertisement portraying one item of product and a second advertisement portraying a second, and different, product item.

Exercises

17-1. a. Use the data from Table 6-1, as before, for some value other than a 4, and obtain the waiting times for the number which you choose.
   b. Prepare the data, plot, estimate the parameters, and determine the confidence interval.

c. Tabulate the various parameter estimates in class and discuss.

17-2. a. Again using Table 6-1 as a source, for some combination other than 1-2, obtain the waiting times for the number pair which you choose.
   b. Prepare the data, plot, estimate the paramaters, and determine the confidence interval.
   c. Tabulate the various parameter estimates in class and discuss.

17-3. a. Using Table 11-1 for more data, take each three adjacent columns and define a specific triplet such as 1-1-1 or 2-3-4. Obtain the waiting times for the triplet which you choose. This will be an example of $\eta = 3$.
   b. Prepare the data, plot, estimate the parameters, and determine the confidence interval.
   c. Tabulate the various parameter estimates in class and discuss.

17-4. a. Use the data for comparison of advertisements in Table 17-4. Plot the data for Item X, estimate the parameters, and obtain the confidence intervals.
   b. Plot the data for Item Y, using a different symbol, on the same graph. Compare the results to those for Item X and discuss the agreement or the disagreement.

CHAPTER 18

The Chi-Square Distribution

Description of the Chi-Square Distribution

The chi-square distribution is derived from the gamma distribution as a special case when $\lambda = \frac{1}{2}$ and n is a multiple of 2.

Let:
$$n = \frac{f}{2} \qquad (18\text{-}1)$$

Then
$$\chi^2 = \frac{1}{2^{f/2}\,\Gamma(f/2)}\,(x)^{(f/2)-1}e^{-x/2} \qquad (18\text{-}2)$$

where:
> f is known as the degrees of freedom and Γ is the gamma function.

The degrees of freedom parameter for the chi-square distribution is determined by the *number of independent variables* used to obtain a value for x. The independent variables must be in the form of unit normal random variables as defined in Chapter 7, using the symbol k. This is discussed further below.

In spite of the nearly identical mathematics of the gamma and chi-square distributions, the origin of each in practical terms is quite different, almost surprisingly so. The gamma distributions have an inherent time dependence and lead naturally into waiting-time problems. By contrast, the chi-square distribution has wide physical applicability in dimensional problems.

Under an important generalization, the chi-square distribution, with its one parameter (degrees of freedom) represents the sum of n factors in a vector space, where n represents the index of the n-fold vector space. Here, in Equation 18-2, n is substituted for f in order to retain the conventional mathematical meaning for n in vector mathematics.

When $n = f = 1$ degree of freedom, we have the distribution of a single normal unit random variable which operates according to the Square Law:

$$\chi^2_{1df} = \left(\frac{x_i - \bar{x}}{\sigma_x}\right)^2 \qquad (18\text{-}3)$$

For $n = f = 2$ degrees of freedom, we have the distribution of the sum of two equal random variables which are squared. This is better known as the *bivariate normal distribution* and can be expressed as:

$$\chi^2_{2df} = \left(\frac{x_i - \bar{x}}{\sigma_x}\right)^2 + \left(\frac{y_i - \bar{y}}{\sigma_y}\right) \qquad (18\text{-}4)$$

This is also an application of a joint and equal statistical distribution between two variables in Cartesian coordinates.

A further extension of the chi-square distribution is:

$$\chi^2_{3df} = \left(\frac{x_i - \bar{x}}{\sigma_x}\right)^2 + \left(\frac{y_i - \bar{y}}{\sigma_y}\right)^2 + \left(\frac{z_i - \bar{z}}{\sigma_z}\right)^2 \qquad (18\text{-}5)$$

This is an extension of unit vectors into three-dimensional space. When particle velocities are represented, this particular form of the chi-square distribution is known as the *Maxwell distribution*. On a macroscopic basis, problems in three-dimensional space apply to projectiles, aircraft, astronomy, and spacecraft. Particle velocities in gases or quantum mechanics represent instances of submicroscopic applications. Note that this distribution could also be called the *tri-variate distribution*.

Extensions to 4-fold or higher spaces have applications in space-time problems and in complex probability functions. Such applications will be left to the imagination and mathematical ingenuity of the reader, since they are beyond the scope of this work.

In a more specialized way, the chi-square distribution is also applicable to distributions of the values of the variance for a series of samples of equal size. Such distributions of values arise in the analysis of variance from factorial experiments. In this application, the degrees of freedom to be used are $n - 1$, where n is the established sample size per cell or replicate.

Utilization of Chi-Square/Gamma Probability Paper

Data preparation and plotting are done as for the normal and extreme value distributions. The design and layout of these papers has been covered in Chapter 17.

Parameter estimates are obtained from:

$$\mu = \frac{f/2}{1/2} = f \qquad (18\text{-}6)$$

$$V = \frac{f/2}{1/4} = 2f \qquad (18\text{-}7)$$

$$\sigma = \sqrt{2f} \qquad (18\text{-}8)$$

These results show that the mean is that value corresponding to the degrees of freedom of the chi-square paper which gives a straight-line fit and that the variance is twice the value of the mean.

Confidence intervals are obtained in the same way as for the gamma distribution.

Applications

Table 18-1 gives data for four samples of 24 each of normal unit variates. Also shown are the squares of these values.

Figure 18-1 shows the results for Sample A, which is the square of one normal unit variate.

Figure 18-2 shows the results for Sample A+B which is the sum of squares of two normal unit variates.

Figures 18-3 and 18-4 illustrate the results for Samples A+B+C and Samples A+B+C+D, respectively, for the cases of squares of three and four normal unit variables.

Table 18-1. Four Samples of Normal Unit Random Variates with the Squares and the Consecutive Sums of Squares Obtained by Adding the Results of Each Sample to the Total of All Preceding Samples

Sample 1		Sample 2		Sample 3		Sample 4		Sums of		
A		**B**		**C**		**D**		A + B	A + B + C	A + B + C + D
x_1	x_1^2	x_2	x_2^2	x_3	x_3^2	x_4	x_4^2			
0.0	0.0	− 0.3	0.09	0.0	0.0	0.9	0.81	0.09	0.09	0.90
− 0.3	0.09	− 0.6	0.36	1.5	2.25	1.8	3.24	0.45	2.70	5.94
0.9	0.81	0.0	0.0	− 0.9	0.81	0.9	0.81	0.81	1.62	2.43
0.5	0.25	1.2	1.44	− 0.1	0.01	0.3	0.09	1.69	1.70	1.79
2.3	5.29	1.6	2.56	0.5	0.25	1.0	1.00	7.85	8.10	9.10
1.8	3.24	− 0.6	0.36	− 0.4	0.16	− 0.3	0.09	3.60	3.76	3.85
− 0.4	0.16	1.6	2.56	0.1	0.01	− 0.2	0.04	2.72	2.73	2.77
0.0	0.0	0.6	0.36	0.4	0.16	1.5	2.25	0.36	0.52	2.77
1.2	1.44	− 0.5	0.25	0.6	0.36	− 0.4	0.16	1.69	2.05	2.21
1.3	1.69	− 0.2	0.04	− 0.1	0.01	0.0	0.0	1.73	1.74	1.74
0.0	0.0	− 0.8	0.64	1.9	3.61	0.3	0.09	0.64	4.25	4.34
− 0.6	0.36	0.6	0.36	− 0.7	0.49	0.3	0.09	0.72	1.21	1.30
− 0.1	0.01	0.0	0.0	0.0	0.0	− 0.2	0.04	0.01	0.01	0.05
0.9	0.81	− 0.9	0.81	1.5	2.25	0.5	0.25	1.62	3.87	4.12
0.4	0.16	0.6	0.36	0.5	0.25	0.5	0.25	0.52	0.77	1.02
0.6	0.36	0.6	0.36	1.1	1.21	− 0.1	0.01	0.72	1.93	1.94
− 0.5	0.25	− 1.2	1.44	0.9	0.81	0.8	0.64	1.69	2.50	3.14
0.2	0.04	− 0.5	0.25	− 1.0	1.00	− 1.0	1.00	0.29	1.29	2.29
0.4	0.16	0.5	0.25	− 0.4	0.16	− 2.1	4.41	0.41	0.57	4.98
0.3	0.09	0.8	0.64	0.4	0.16	0.3	0.09	0.73	0.89	0.98
0.3	0.09	− 1.5	2.25	0.2	0.04	0.6	0.36	2.34	2.38	2.74
0.9	0.81	− 0.1	0.01	1.0	1.00	− 0.4	0.16	0.82	1.82	1.98
0.1	0.01	0.1	0.01	− 0.4	0.16	2.4	5.76	0.02	0.18	5.94
0.5	0.25	0.1	0.01	− 1.7	2.89	1.5	2.25	0.26	3.15	5.40

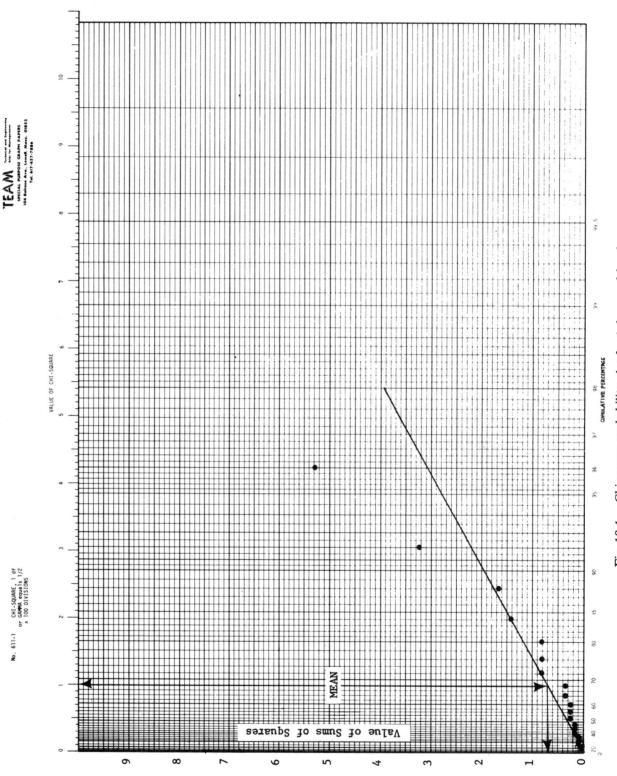

Fig. 18-1.   Chi-square probability plot for 1 degree of freedom.

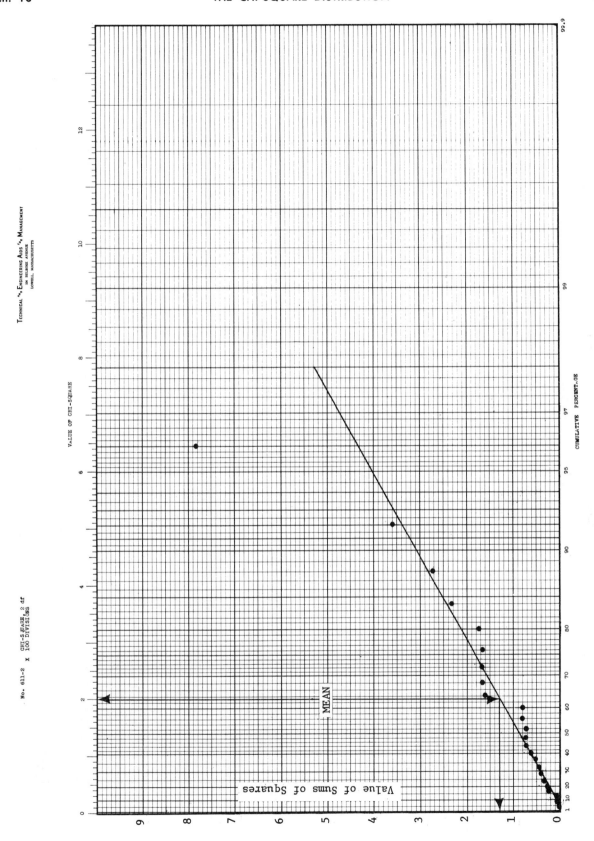

Fig. 18-2. Chi-square probability plot for 2 degrees of freedom.

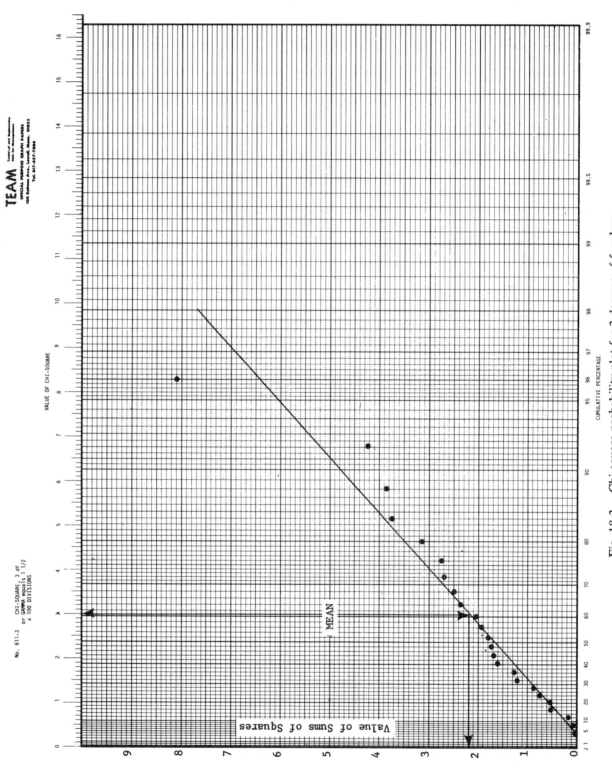

Fig. 18-3. Chi-square probability plot for 3 degrees of freedom.

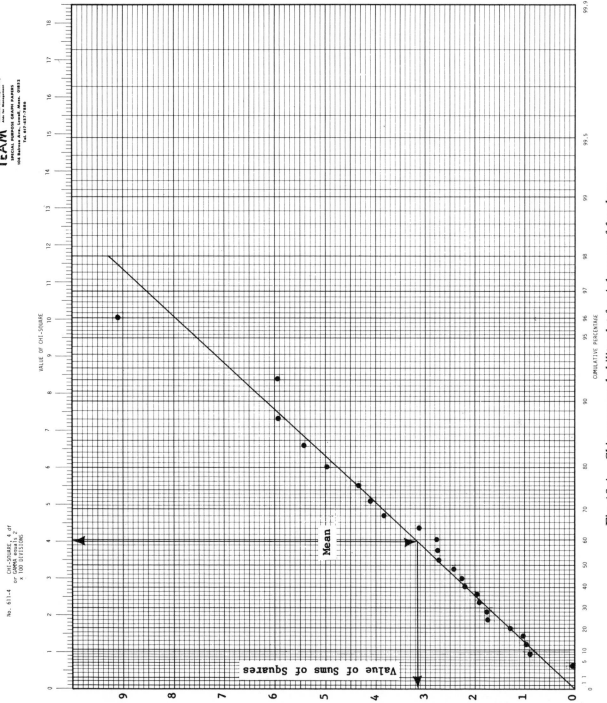

Fig. 18-4. Chi-square probability plot for 4 degrees of freedom.

Table 18-2. Four Samples of Normal Random Variables with the Squares and the Consecutive Sums of Squares Obtained by Adding the Results of Each Sample to the Total of All Preceding Samples

Sample 1		Sample 2		Sample 3		Sample 4		Sums of		
A		B		C		D				
x_1	x_1^2	x_2	x_2^2	x_3	x_3^2	x_4	x_4^2	A + B	A + B + C	A + B + C + D
17	289	16	256	11	121	16	256	545	666	906
12	144	16	256	15	225	11	121	400	625	746
13	169	16	256	15	225	15	225	425	650	875
16	256	17	289	21	441	19	381	745	1186	1566
19	361	17	289	16	256	11	121	650	906	1027
15	225	12	144	20	400	13	169	369	544	733
17	289	14	196	8	64	17	289	485	549	838
9	81	12	144	17	289	14	196	225	514	710
13	169	17	289	17	289	13	169	458	747	916
15	225	14	196	18	324	16	256	421	745	1001
11	121	12	144	16	256	12	144	265	521	665
12	144	12	144	10	100	15	225	288	388	613
14	196	14	196	13	169	13	169	392	561	730
20	400	16	256	16	256	13	169	656	912	1081
14	196	11	121	15	225	13	169	317	542	711
20	400	15	225	15	225	16	256	625	850	1106
15	225	8	64	13	169	12	144	289	458	602
11	121	17	289	23	529	14	196	410	939	1135
11	121	14	196	15	225	14	196	317	542	738
12	144	11	121	11	121	10	100	265	386	486
10	100	11	121	21	441	17	289	221	662	951
7	49	13	169	13	169	15	225	218	387	612
9	81	13	169	18	324	11	121	250	574	695
10	100	12	144	9	81	14	196	244	325	521
16	256	17	289	11	121	16	256	545	666	922
15	225	17	289	14	196	17	289	514	710	999
15	225	10	100	16	256	15	225	325	581	806
18	324	10	100	20	400	13	169	424	824	993
14	196	21	441	18	324	14	196	637	961	1157
17	289	16	256	15	225	17	289	545	770	1059
18	324	22	484	13	169	20	400	808	977	1377
13	169	17	289	12	144	21	441	458	602	1043
16	256	12	144	10	100	20	400	400	500	900
14	196	17	289	7	49	11	121	485	534	655
7	49	6	36	12	144	15	225	85	229	454
12	144	13	169	5	25	11	121	313	338	459
7	49	13	169	19	361	13	169	218	579	748
9	81	9	81	10	100	13	169	162	262	431
16	256	19	361	10	100	17	289	617	717	1006
16	256	13	169	15	225	10	100	425	615	750
7	49	13	169	13	169	13	169	248	417	586
19	361	13	169	13	169	18	324	530	699	1023
10	100	16	256	17	289	16	256	356	645	901
15	225	16	256	15	225	15	225	481	506	731
18	324	10	100	20	400	17	289	424	824	1113
16	256	19	361	10	100	10	100	617	717	817
19	361	16	256	13	169	15	225	617	786	1011
17	289	14	196	10	100	15	225	485	585	810
9	81	21	441	13	169	13	169	522	691	860

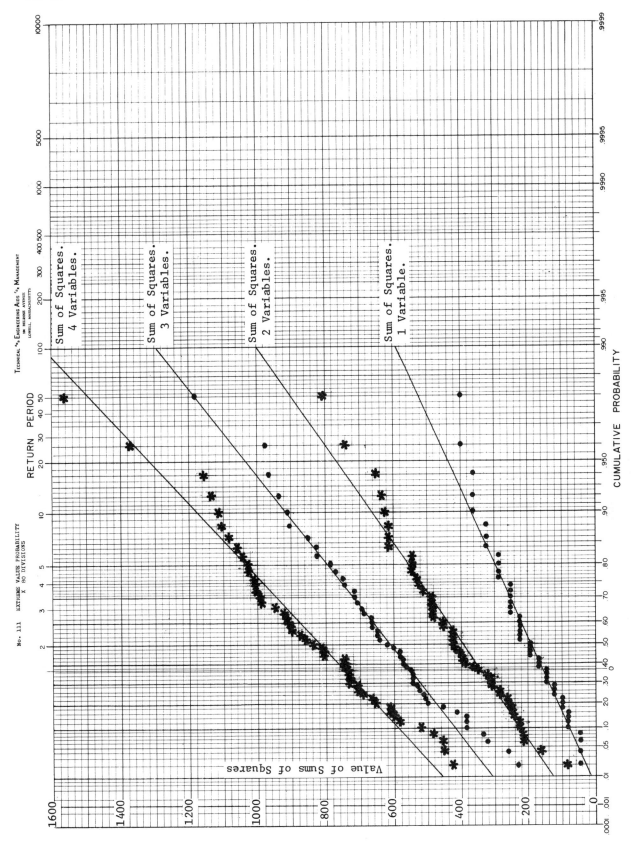

Fig. 18-5.   Type I extreme value probability plots for sums of squares of normal random variables.

The results of Figs. 18-1 through 18-4 illustrate some basic properties of chi-square distributions. The four samples used are all random selections from a table of unit variates. Therefore, each sample should have approximately the same mean and variance. When we combine these samples *by addition,* the values of the mean and variance should increase directly with the degrees of freedom; that is, the mean and variance for 2 *df* should be twice the values obtained for 1 *df*. Results from Figs. 18-1 through 18-4 are compared below:

Degrees of Freedom	Mean	Variance
1 *df*	0.7	1.4
2 *df*	1.3	2.6
3 *df*	2.2	4.4
4 *df*	3.15	6.3

All four results above are in an approximate arithmetic progression. Chi-square distributions, then, when added together are still chi-square distributions. When two or more chi-square distributions are added, the values of the distribution parameters, μ and V, are also obtained directly by addition. This result is identical to the results obtained by adding normal distributions together.

Relationship of the Type I Extreme Value Distribution

In the earlier discussion of the physical origin of chi-square distributions, the restriction was made of requiring the squares of unit normal variables. Data are rarely obtainable in this form and tedious calculations are thus required to derive this form. The more general case would be that of squares of a normally distributed random variable. Table 18-2 gives results of four samples of normally distributed data obtained from the sum of face counts of four dice thrown at a time. Also given are the squares and the sums of squares of samples A, A+B, A+B+C and A+B+C+D. These results

are plotted in Fig. 18-5. The fit of these data on extreme value paper is very good. This is useful because we now have only the restriction of equal independent random variables.

The results shown in Fig. 18-5 illustrate a special relationship between the chi-square distribution and the Type I extreme value distribution. Each distribution can accommodate data from sums of squares, but the squares for the chi-square distribution must be normalized. Alternatively, the Type I extreme value distribution is ideal for handling square law data directly. Square law data is typically found in problems dealing with acceleration, energy, and power as well as multidimensional vectors. In such applications, the Type I extreme value distribution becomes a special case of a polynomial given by:

$$y = \sum_{i=1} c_i x_i^2 \tag{18-9}$$

Exercises

18-1. Use data for Sample D of Table 18-1. Prepare a distribution plot for chi-square with 1 degree of freedom — fit a line, and estimate the mean and variance.

18-2. Use data for Samples D and C to prepare a distribution plot for chi-square with 2 degrees of freedom — fit a line, and estimate the mean and variance.

18-3. Use data for Samples D, C, and B for chi-square with 3 degrees of freedom — fit a line, and estimate the mean and variance.

18-4. Tabulate the results for Exercises 18-1 through 18-3 — compare the results, and discuss.

18-5. Tabulate the results for the entire class, obtain the average of the estimates for the mean and variance for each degree of freedom — plot, compare these results, and discuss.

CHAPTER 19

Hazard Plotting for Incomplete Data and Failure Data with Different Causes

Background

The term *hazard plotting* is uninformative and misleading. To some people it has an immediate connotation of bad news, as if to imply that one is analyzing an undesirable or risky situation. This is an unfortunate accident of nomenclature. The term *hazard function* originated in the statistical analysis of instantaneous failure rate. This is the failure rate in a population at a specified level of stress, or at a specified time. More generally, the mathematical development refers to a probability of occurrence of any result (event) after some sequence of applied stress (time) has occurred. A hazard function is simply an algebraic statement of the relationship of two probability functions: the density function and the survival function, which are defined below.

Dr. Wayne Nelson of the Research and Development Center of the General Electric Company has developed detailed graphical methods for both the analysis of data which is "incomplete," and for data which includes more than one mode of failure concurrently. Since the graphical methods were derived from the mathematics of the hazard function, they are called hazard plotting and analysis methods.

In earlier chapters, we have used the cumulative distribution function of various distributions to arrive at probability plots of data. The resultant plots are described by statements such as: We have a probability, $F(x)$, of observing values equal to or less than the value x; or, we expect to observe $100 \cdot F(x)$ percent failure up to the point x. That is, $F(x)$ is the probability of occurrence of an observation below x; $[1 - F(x)]$, then, is the probability of nonoccurrence. In time-to-failure studies,

$[1 - F(x)]$ is the probability of survival beyond point x.

Suppose, instead, that we wish to know the probability of failure of items that have survived up to point x, in some additional increment, $x + \Delta x$. This is obtained with the hazard function which is defined by:

$$h(x) = \frac{f(x)}{1 - F(x)} \tag{19-1}$$

$h(x)$ = the hazard function
$f(x)$ = the probability density function
$F(x)$ = the cumulative distribution function
$1 - F(x)$ = the survival function.

In words, the hazard function is the ratio of the density function to the survival function.

Earlier chapters have also been predicated on two important assumptions: First, that we have the values of *all* the observations in a sample; that is, the sample is *complete*. Second, for life data, that we have *all* the times to failure up to some point in time and have no reason to expect any future change in the *kind* of failure distribution which we are observing. Sometimes, however, neither of the two stated assumptions is valid. Typically, this is true when some data is missing or when life tests are not run for equal times on all units in a sample, resulting in incomplete data.

In life tests of units, incomplete data can occur in several ways. For example, a sample of units is placed on life test for some intended period. Before completion of the intended test time, part of the sample is removed to make room for some new units, while the balance of the *original* sample remains to complete the intended test. Units are also put into service on different dates and run

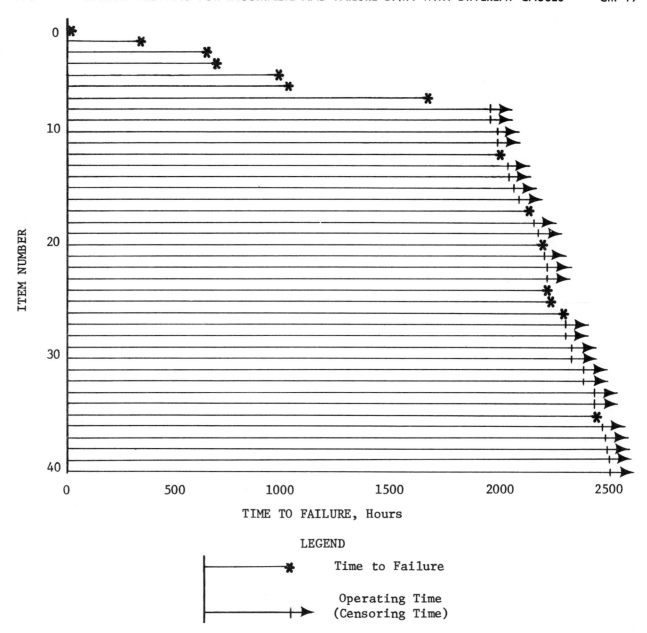

Fig. 19-1.   Ordered display of times to failure and operating time without failure; from Nelson, Reference (41).

indefinitely with analysis performed from time to time, while still other units have not yet failed and continue in service.

The situations above lead to data which are called *arbitrarily censored data;* that is, the times at which units are removed from test are *arbitrary* and the removal times are called *censoring times.* Such data is also called *randomly* or *multiply censored data.* One important restriction is that the censoring times and the censored units must be statistically independent of the failure times of the removed units.

Figure 19-1 illustrates a set of arbitrarily censored data.   Forty units were placed on test. The times of failures are shown with an asterisk. Times of removal for items which are still good are shown with a vertical dash and an arrow.   These data are shown in order of increasing time.   Since time to failure is the variable of interest, the times of removal of good units represents "missing" times to failure; that is, it is known only that the failure times of the removed units are beyond their observed removal times.

Until recently, the analysis of arbitrarily censored data has been a highly subjective and arbitrary affair, but the new development of hazard plotting papers to treat arbitrarily censored data is a major contribution toward a systematic and orderly treatment of such data. In addition, as will be described later, these techniques have important applications in situations in which time is not the variable of interest. However, for convenience, terminology appropriate to life data analysis is used to describe the mechanics of hazard plotting.

Dr. Nelson presented detailed developments of hazard plotting papers and methods in (40) and (41). The author is grateful to both Dr. Nelson and the General Electric Company for permission to adapt certain material from these references for use in this chapter.

Description of Hazard Functions

The hazard function is also known as:

1. The instantaneous failure rate of a distribution of time to failure

2. The conditional failure rate ✓

3. The intensity function

4. The force of mortality.

Hazard plotting is based on the concept of the instantaneous failure rate of a distribution of time to failure. The instantaneous failure rate, $h(x)$, is called the hazard function and is defined in Equation 19-1. Then the quantity $\Delta \cdot h(x)$ is the expected proportion of units of age x that will fail in the time interval, Δ, from x to $x + \Delta$. The cumulative hazard function $H(x)$ of a distribution is the integral of the hazard function from time zero up to time x:

$$H(x) = \int_0^t h(x)\, dx = -\ln[1 - F(t)] \quad (19\text{-}2)$$

The relationship between the cumulative distribution function and the cumulative hazard function for a distribution can be rewritten as:

$$F(x) = 1 - e^{-H(x)} \quad (19\text{-}3)$$

The scales on hazard papers for the various underlying distributions are constructed so that the corresponding cumulative hazard functions, $H(x)$, plot against the value of x as straight lines. The basic relationship between the cumulative probability, $F(x)$, and the cumulative hazard, $H(x)$, can be seen on all hazard papers. Thus, the cumulative hazard scale is completely equivalent to the cumulative probability scale. It is a convenient alternative scale against which to plot arbitrarily censored data. Using the basic relationship of Equation 19-2 between the cumulative hazard function and the cumulative distribution function, we obtain the cumulative hazard function for various distributions by substitution of the appropriate standardized cumulative distribution function.

For the normal distribution, the cumulative hazard function is:

$$H(x) = -\ln\left[1 - \Phi\left(\frac{x - \mu}{\sigma}\right)\right] \quad (19\text{-}4)$$

where:

$\Phi\left(\dfrac{x - \mu}{\sigma}\right)$ is the standardized normal variable of Equation 7-3.

For the log-normal distribution:

$$H(x) = -\ln\left[1 - \Phi\left(\frac{\log x - \mu_l}{\sigma_l}\right)\right] \quad (19\text{-}5)$$

where:

$\Phi\left(\dfrac{\log x - \mu_l}{\sigma_l}\right)$ is the standardized log-normal variable of Equation 9-3.

For the exponential distribution:

$$H(x) = x/\Theta \quad (19\text{-}6)$$

which is a linear function of x.

For the Weibull distribution:

$$H(x) = (x/\alpha)^\beta \quad (19\text{-}7)$$

which is a power function of x.

For the extreme value distribution:

$$H(x) = \exp(x - \mu_o)/\alpha \quad (19\text{-}8)$$

which is an exponential function of x.

Theoretical cumulative hazard functions for each of these distributions are shown in Fig. 19-2. Since the scales of hazard plotting papers are de-

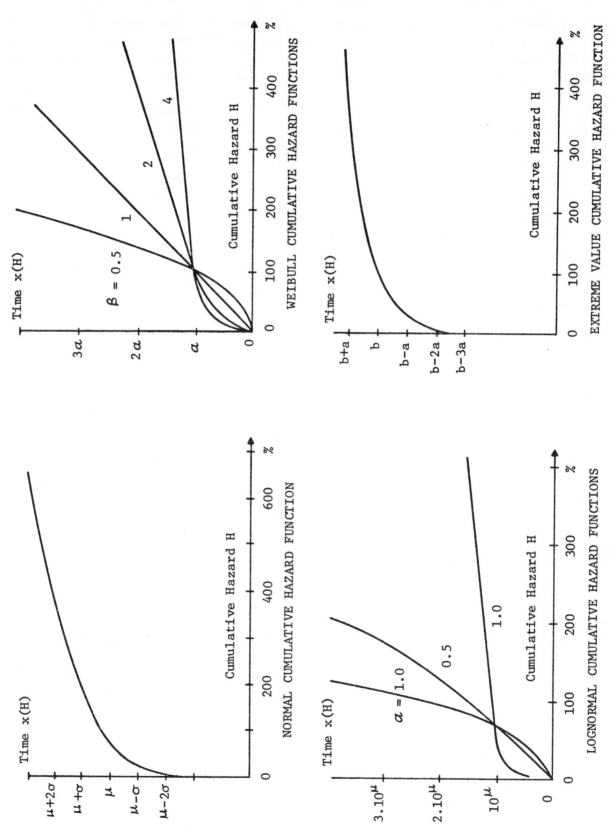

Fig. 19-2.   Theoretical cumulative hazard functions; from Nelson, Reference (40).

rived so that the relationship between the variable, x, and the cumulative hazard value for a given distribution is linear, comparison of a plot of a sample cumulative hazard function made on rectangular-grid graph paper to the shapes of the theoretical cumulative hazard functions can be used to make a choice of which hazard plotting paper to use for a first try at fitting the data.

The basic principle underlying plotting on hazard paper is essentially the same as that for plotting on probability paper. A cumulative distribution function on probability paper is a straight-line function of time, stress, or other variable. Similarly, a cumulative hazard function on hazard paper is a straight-line function of the variable of interest. In either case, one is plotting a *sample* cumulative function which is an *approximation* of the *actual* cumulative function of the population from which the sample was obtained.

Another way of looking at this is the following: For a complete sample of n failure times, there is a probability of $1/n$ associated with each failure time. A histogram of the failure times and their probabilities approximates the probability density of the distribution from which the times are taken. Then the sample cumulative distribution function, based on the sum of the probabilities, approximates the theoretical cumulative distribution function, which is the integral of the probability density. Because it smooths the data better than does the sample histogram, the sample cumulative distribution function is used. Similarly, for an arbitrarily censored sample of failure times, there is a *conditional* probability of $1/K$ associated with each failure time which is the proportion of the K items that experienced an observed age and then failed at that time. The histogram of failure times and their conditional probabilities approximates the instantaneous failure rate or hazard function of the distribution from which the times are taken. The sample cumulative hazard function, based on the sum of the conditional probabilities, then approximates the theoretical cumulative hazard function, which is the integral of the instantaneous failure rate. The sample cumulative hazard function is used because it smooths the data better than a histogram.

Relationship of Hazard Plotting Papers to Probability Papers

Hazard plotting papers are equivalent to probability papers; therefore, details of data arrangement, cell designation, and plot interpretation (discussed in earlier chapters) apply. The principal difference is that observations are plotted against cumulative hazard values rather than cumulative probability values. This requires one additional simple step in data arrangement.

The advantages of hazard plotting papers compared to probability papers are:

1. The capability of readily handling arbitrarily censored data
2. Easy determination of instantaneous failure rate
3. The ability to obtain standard probability statements directly from an auxiliary probability scale on the hazard paper
4. Computational effort is less with hazard plotting than with any other method for analysis of multiply censored data

Hazard plotting papers are available for normal, log-normal, Type I extreme value, exponential, and Weibull distributions (Figs. 19-3 through 19-7). Choose the kind of hazard paper to use on the same basis governing the choice of other probability papers. If existing information indicates that a certain distribution is expected to provide an adequate fit to the data, then the hazard paper for that distribution should be used. If the underlying distribution is unknown, then Fig. 19-2 may be used to evaluate data plots made on rectangular coordinate paper to assist in choosing the correct hazard paper. Visually compare the plot on rectangular paper to the curve shapes in Fig. 19-2, and choose the curve shape which most seems to resemble the shape of the trial plot. Skill in these shape comparisons will improve with experience.

Description of Hazard Plotting Papers

Hazard plotting papers all have a bottom horizontal scale for cumulative percent hazard. The normal, Type I, extreme value, and exponential hazard papers have linear vertical scales for the measured variable. The log-normal and Weibull hazard papers have logarithmic vertical scales. Each hazard paper also has an auxiliary top scale for cumulative probability. It reads from left to right, as on cumulative probability papers. The cumulative probability scale is keyed to the cumulative hazard scale and has exactly the same appearance as on a cumulative probability paper. Thus, the probability scales on hazard plotting papers may be used in the same manner as they are with cumulative probability papers.

The Weibull hazard paper has an additional scale for estimating the Weibull shape parameter value, β. This is used in conjunction with the reference point. As with conventional Weibull paper, draw a parallel to the fitted data line through the reference point up to the right, intersecting the shape parameter scale, to obtain the Weibull shape parameter estimate.

Data Preparation

Data are prepared for hazard plotting in the following way:

Step 1. Order the n values in the sample from smallest to largest without regard to whether they are *observed* or *censored* values. In the list of ordered values, the observed data are each marked with a common symbol to distinguish them from the censored values (see Fig. 19-1).

If some observed and censored items have the same value, they should be listed in a random order.

Step 2. Number the ordered values in *reverse* order with n assigned to the smallest data value, $n - 1$ to the second, etc. The numbers so obtained are called K values, or reverse order numbers.

Step 3. Obtain the corresponding hazard value for each *observed* value and record it. The hazard value for an observed value is 100 divided by its K value. Censored values do not have a corresponding hazard value.

Hazard values are obtained from Table A-8[1]. This table lists the hazard value for all K values from 1 through 200.

Step 4. For each observed value, calculate the corresponding cumulative hazard value. This is

[1] In Appendix.

the sum of the hazard values of that observed value and of all preceding observed values.

Step 5. Plot each observed value against its corresponding cumulative hazard value on the hazard paper for the appropriate distribution. If there is no reason to choose a particular distribution, plot the data on rectangular coordinate paper and compare the sample cumulative hazard function with those in Fig. 19-2. On the basis of the best comparison, choose the appropriate hazard plotting paper.

Step 6. Proceed to analyze the plot as for conventional probability plots:

a. Examine the plot for linearity, nonlinearity, curvature, and for peculiar data values. If any such occur, investigate to determine the causes, or reexamine your assumptions in choosing a paper.

b. If the plot appears to be linear, fit a straight line to the data.

c. Parameter estimates are obtained as with probability papers by utilizing the cumulative probability scale at the top of the hazard plotting paper.

Example 19-1
Given: The data of Table 19-1. This data is adapted from Herd (25). The data are operating times on 50 electronic systems. For failed systems these are operating times to failure. Some systems were removed from test prior to failure and the total observed operating time without failure is given for these systems. The failed systems are identified by an asterisk.

The data in the table are listed in the order of increasing time. Operating times for unfailed systems are known as the censoring times for those systems.

Steps 1 and 2. The ordered data are numbered in reverse order from 50 down to 1. The reverse order number for a system is its K value.

Step 3. Hazard values are obtained from Table A-8 for each time corresponding to a system failure. The first system failure has $K = 50$, which gives a hazard value of $100/50 = 2.00$; the second failure has $K = 49$ with a hazard value of $100/49 = 2.04$, etc.

Table 19-1. System Failure, Operating Times, and Hazard Calculations

Reverse Order	Hours	Hazard	Cumulative Hazard	Reverse Order	Hours	Hazard	Cumulative Hazard
50	1843*	2.00	2.00	25	4301		
49	2243*	2.04	4.04	24	4326		
48	2513*	2.08	6.12	23	4347		
47	2564*	2.13	8.25	22	4373*	4.55	58.83
46	2704*	2.17	10.42	21	4387*	4.76	63.69
45	2792*	2.22	12.64	20	4398*	5.00	68.69
44	3024*	2.27	14.91	19	4455*	5.26	73.95
43	3171*	2.33	17.24	18	4466		
42	3385			17	4520*	5.88	78.93
41	3392*	2.44	19.68	16	4525		
40	3468*	2.50	22.18	15	4561		
39	3488*	2.56	24.74	14	4587*	7.14	86.97
38	3535			13	4599*	7.69	94.66
37	3605*	2.70	27.44	12	4639*	8.33	102.99
36	3709*	2.78	30.22	11	4721*	9.09	112.08
35	3811			10	4727*	10.00	122.08
34	3830*	2.94	33.16	9	4767*	11.11	133.19
33	3851			8	4822*	12.50	145.69
32	3905			7	5013*	14.29	159.98
31	3979*	3.23	36.39	6	5130		
30	4014*	3.33	39.72	5	5208*	20.00	179.98
29	4069*	3.45	43.17	4	5296*	25.00	204.98
28	4125*	3.56	46.73	3	5472*	33.33	238.31
27	4132*	3.70	50.43	2	5859*	50.00	288.31
26	4219*	3.85	54.28	1	6042		

* Denotes failure.

Step 4. The cumulative hazard values are obtained by adding each consecutive hazard value to the sum of all of those hazard values which occur on the preceding failed systems. For example, the first hazard value is 2.00. The cumulative hazard is also 2.00. The second hazard value is 2.04; the cumulative hazard is $2.00 + 2.04 = 4.04$. The third hazard value is 2.08; the cumulative hazard is then $4.04 + 2.08 = 6.12$, etc.

Step 5. A plot of the times to failure versus their cumulative hazard values is first made on rectangular coordinate paper. Such a plot for these data is shown as an insert in Fig. 19-3. After comparing this plot with the curves in Fig. 19-2, normal hazard paper appears to be a reasonable choice for further plotting.

Step 6. The data from Table 19-2 are now plotted on normal hazard paper as shown in Fig. 19-3. A best-fit line is obtained in the same manner as given earlier for probability papers. The best-fit line is also drawn in on Fig. 19-3.

Step 7. Parameter estimates are obtained through use of the probability scale located at the top of the grid in the same manner as described for the normal distribution in Chapter 8. The estimate for mean time to failure in this case is obtained from the intersection of the 50 percent line with the best-fit line:

Mean time to failure = 4280 Hours.

The standard deviation is obtained using the 6.7 and 93.3 percent points and dividing the difference in these values by 3:

Standard deviation $= (5800 - 2700)/3 = 1033$.

Note: Sometimes hazard plots do not cover the range of 6.7 to 93.3 percent. In such cases, it is convenient to estimate the standard deviation directly from the difference between the 16 percent and 50 percent points. This difference is equal to one standard deviation unit.

Comment: Figure 19-3 illustrates a frequent problem which occurs in plotting life test data.

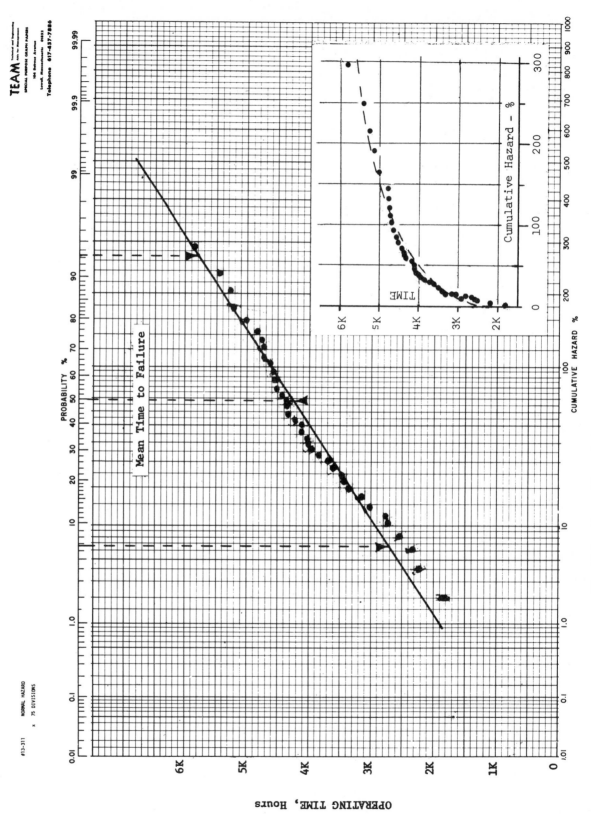

Fig. 19-3.   Normal hazard plot of system operating times to failure.

Although the best-fit line is a reasonable fit to these data for many purposes, the points cross the line only twice. Whether the points are above or below the best-fit line, there are simply too many points in a row, on either side, to be considered as random behavior. Actually, this situation is quite similar to the one shown in Fig. 5-8. In the example of Fig. 5-8, we observed the results of mixing outputs from two different machines. In the present example, we are concerned with times to failure instead of mechanical dimensions. Each failure must have some cause. The pattern of behavior demonstrated in Fig. 19-3 may result from the combined effect of several competing modes of failure. Failure modes are said to be *competing* when each failure mode is an independent cause of failure with its own distribution of times to failure. When a unit can fail for any one of several causes, it is inappropriate to lump all of the failures together indiscriminately. When more than one failure mode is suspected, further engineering analysis is required to determine the different modes.

In order to avoid the risk of drawing incorrect conclusions due to irregular plots caused by competing modes of failure, it is strongly recommended that specific information on individual modes of failure be obtained. Analysis of competing modes of failure is greatly facilitated by the use of hazard plotting papers. Such analyses are discussed in Examples 19-2 through 19-4.

Example 19-2
Given: Data of Table 19-2 for all failures and cumulative hazard values. These data are adapted from Weaver and Scarlett (52). Normalized operating times are given for a miniature integrating gyro used in a classified military program.

Step 1. Order the data and number them in reverse, as shown.

Step 2. Obtain the hazard value for each K.

Step 3. Calculate the cumulative hazard values.

Step 4. Make the rough plot of time to failure versus cumulative hazard values. This is illustrated in Fig. 19-4.

Comment: At first glance, one would be tempted to accept the rough plot as nearly linear, with some

variations. However, on the basis of plotting against the rectangular coordinates, one must assume the exponential distribution in order to accept a plot as linear. The exponential distribution represents a *uniform* failure rate *starting from time 0;* therefore, in using 0 as a fixed point, the data are divided into an upper and lower half by the solid line. This results in two separate groupings, one of 17 consecutive points above the line and one of 14 consecutive points below the line. In Chapter 5, it was stated that runs of 11 or more points on one side of the line are highly significant indicators of nonrandom behavior. In this example, we have *two* such runs; therefore, we cannot easily accept the assumption of random variation about the fitted line which, for this example, represents the exponential distribution. This problem is analyzed in greater detail with methods described in the next section.

The Assessment of Competing Failure Modes

In Example 19-2, we found that there is a problem in deciding which hazard plotting paper to use. A common cause for this indecision is that often only gross failure data is obtained; that is, one counts only the total number of failures or observes only the cumulative percent failure. This ignores the important fact that failures can occur for more than one reason. Some kinds of failure have completely different origins. For example, in an automobile, a broken drive shaft, poor ignition timing, or faulty brakes are not part of the same chance-cause system of failure — they are all different and competing failure modes.

In failure data, each identifiable cause of failure has its own time-to-failure distribution. The examples of mathematical operations used to generate different statistical distributions in earlier chapters also represent different classes of failure modes: physical, chemical, etc. In order to understand failure distributions in terms of competing failure modes, it is necessary to obtain as much detailed information as possible on the kinds of failure which are occurring, as well as the associated physical, environmental, and use factors involved, because each failure mode can have its own statistically independent failure distribution.

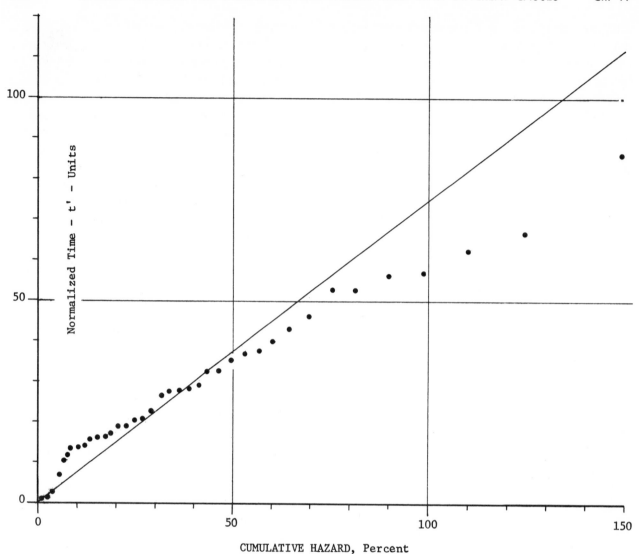

Fig. 19-4.   Hazard plot for normalized times to failure for a miniature integrating gyro.

In Example 19-2, the data are more revealing if each failure mode is examined separately.   It was known from prior experience that it was not correct to combine data for both catastrophic and degradation-type failures, since the catastrophic failures were due to mechanical malfunction, while the degradation failures were electrical in origin.   A more appropriate method of handling such data is given in the following example.

Example 19-3
Given: The data of Table 19-2.   The data in this table also give the separate classifications of cata-

strophic failures and the corresponding cumulative hazard values, as well as the degradation failures and their cumulative hazard values.   Cumulative hazard values are determined independently for each mode of failure.   In order to accomplish this, when determining the hazard value for one mode of failure, all failures for the other class are treated as censoring times.   This is done because the individual failure modes are known, or assumed to be, independent.   Then, a failure for one mode can be treated in the same way as any random unit removal from test where all other failure modes are concerned.   The time to failure for the failing

Table 19-2. Normalized Times, t'; Failure Classifications; and Hazard Calculations

Reverse Order	t'	Hazard Value	Cum. Hazard	Cum. Hazard Cat. Fail.	Cum. Hazard Degr. Fail.	Reverse Order	t'	Hazard Value	Cum. Hazard	Cum. Hazard Cat. Fail.	Cum. Hazard Degr. Fail.
77	0.8C	1.30	1.30	1.30		38	30.5				
76	0.9					37	32.7D	2.70	43.78	19.99	26.57
75	0.9					36	32.8C	2.78	46.56		
74	1.0D	1.35	2.65		1.35	35	33.8				
73	2.0					34	34.1				
72	2.7					33	34.1				
71	3.3D	1.41	4.06		2.76	32	35.3	3.12	49.68		29.69
70	6.8D	1.43	5.49		4.19	31	36.7				
69	7.1					30	37.1D	3.33	53.01		33.02
68	7.6					29	37.5D	3.45	56.46		36.47
67	9.4					28	37.9				
66	10.3					27	39.5				
65	10.6C	1.54	7.03	2.84		26	39.5				
64	13.9D	1.56	8.59		5.75	25	39.9D	4.00	60.46		40.47
63	14.0C	1.59	10.18	4.43		24	41.3				
62	14.2	1.61	11.79		7.36	23	42.9D	4.35	64.81		44.82
61	14.7					22	43.8				
60	15.8D	1.67	13.46		9.03	21	46.1D	4.76	69.57		49.58
59	15.9C	1.69	15.15	6.12		20	51.1				
58	16.0D	1.72	16.87		10.75	19	51.1				
57	16.7C	1.75	18.62	7.87		18	51.1				
56	17.1					17	52.9C	5.88	75.45	25.87	
55	17.3					16	53.0C	6.25	81.70	32.12	
54	17.3					15	53.3				
53	17.3					14	53.6				
52	17.7					13	55.6				
51	18.4C	1.96	20.58	9.83		12	56.1	8.33	90.03		57.91
50	18.5D	2.00	22.58		12.75	11	57.0D	9.09	99.12		67.00
49	19.5					10	62.1				
48	20.0					9	62.2D	11.11	110.23		78.11
47	20.2D	2.13	24.71		14.88	8	63.2				
46	20.3D	2.17	26.88		17.05	7	66.5C	14.29	124.52	46.41	
45	22.9D	2.22	29.10		19.27	6	84.9				
44	26.0D	2.27	31.37		21.54	5	85.5				
43	27.5D	2.33	33.70		23.87	4	86.0D	25.00	149.52		103.11
42	27.8C	2.38	36.08	12.21		3	86.3				
41	27.9C	2.44	38.52	14.65		2	117.0				
40	29.0					1	127.4				
39	29.2C	2.56	41.08	17.21							

C — Catastrophic failure; D — Degradation failure.

mode is also a running time *without failure* for all other modes, since none of them had caused failure up to that time.

Data for catastrophic failures is analyzed first.

Steps 1–3. Same as in Example 19-2.

Step 4. The rough plot of time versus hazard is fairly linear, therefore exponential hazard paper is used for plotting the data. The rough plot is shown as an insert in Fig. 19-5.

Step 5. Plot the data on exponential hazard paper and draw a best-fit line. This is shown in Fig. 19-5.

Note: Equation 19-3 gives the relationship between cumulative probability and cumulative hazard. For small values of the hazard function, that is, less than 10 percent, a satisfactory approximation is obtained by:

$$F(x) \simeq H(x) \qquad (19\text{-}9)$$

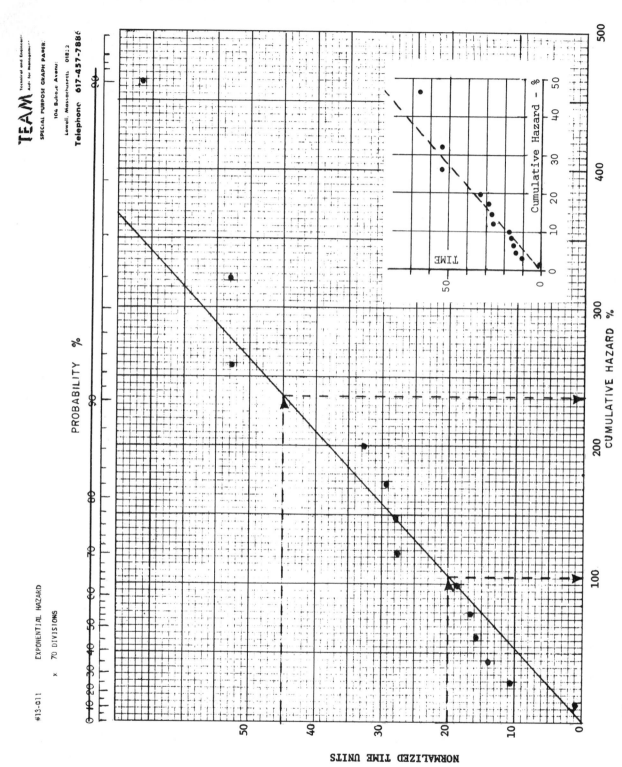

Fig. 19-5   Exponential hazard plot of normalized times to failure for catastrophic failures of a miniature integrating gyro.

This can also be interpreted conveniently for small values as:

Cumulative Probability $\simeq$ Cumulative Hazard

(19-10)

Step 6. The plot in Fig. 19-5 was made by multiplying the scale units for the cumulative hazard scale by 10. Therefore, since the upper cumulative probability scale is not applicable, the relationships given in Equations 19-9 and 19-10 are used.

The constant hazard rate or failure rate is determined by using any convenient time value. Project from the time value scale horizontally to the fitted line, and then vertically, down to the cumulative hazard scale to obtain the corresponding cumulative hazard value. The failure rate is determined from:

$$\text{Failure rate} = \lambda = \frac{H}{t} \qquad (19\text{-}11)$$

In this example, the failure rate is 23.7/45 = 0.53% /unit time.

The failure rate is used to obtain the mean time to failure from:

$$\text{Mean time to failure} = \frac{l}{\lambda} \qquad (19\text{-}12)$$

For this example, we have an estimate of 1/0.0052 = 188 time units.

Example 19-4

Given: The data of Table 19-2.
Required: Analyze the degradation failures.

Steps 1–3. Same as in Example 19-2.

Step 4. The rough plot of time versus hazard suggests a log-normal distribution; therefore, log-normal hazard paper is used for plotting the data. The rough plot is shown as an insert in Fig. 19-6.

Step 5. Plot the data on log-normal hazard paper and draw a best-fit line. This is shown in Fig. 19-6.

Step 6. The median time to failure is obtained at the 50 percent point and is estimated to be 59.5 normalized time units. The geometric dispersion, g, is obtained from the ratio 59.5/22.5 = 2.65.

Note: In Step 6, a different method of estimating geometric dispersion was used than that which was given in Chapter 8. This is because data were not available over the interval of 6.7 to 93.3 percent,

therefore, an alternative method was employed. This is simply taking the ratio of the 50 percent point to the 16 percent point which gives the geometric dispersion directly, without the need for taking roots.

Comment: The first three points in Fig. 19-6 may appear to be out of line. Much of this appearance is due to the scale of two logarithmic cycles on the vertical axis. However, it is also possible that these points represent a particular failure mode. For the presented data, the only differentiation which has been made is between catastrophic and degradation failures. However, within each classification of failure, there may be several specifically different causes of failure. Further engineering effort is needed to gain insight on this.

Example 19-5

Given: The data of Table 19-3. These are simply Monte Carlo data generated to illustrate the extreme value hazard function.

Steps 1–3. Same as in Example 19-2.

Step 4. The rough plot of time versus cumulative hazard has a curvature similar to that for extreme value plots in Fig. 19-2. The rough plot is shown as an insert in Fig. 19-7.

Step 5. Plot the data on extreme value hazard paper and draw a best-fit line. This is shown in Fig. 19-7.

Step 6. Extreme value distribution parameters may be obtained directly from the plot of Fig. 19-7 in the same manner as in Chapter 11. The modal time to failure is obtained from the intersection of the 37 percent and the fitted line. For this example, we obtain 925 hours. The Gumbel slope may be obtained from the 85 and 15 percent lines. This gives (1059 − 825)/2.457 = 234/2.457 = 95.

Applications of Hazard Plotting to Service and Warranty Problems

Besides determining the kind of failure distributions which are occurring in a product and the kinds of failure which occur, hazard plots have further value. Service and repair activities must carry inventories of spare parts and replacement units. If the inventory level is too low, then all

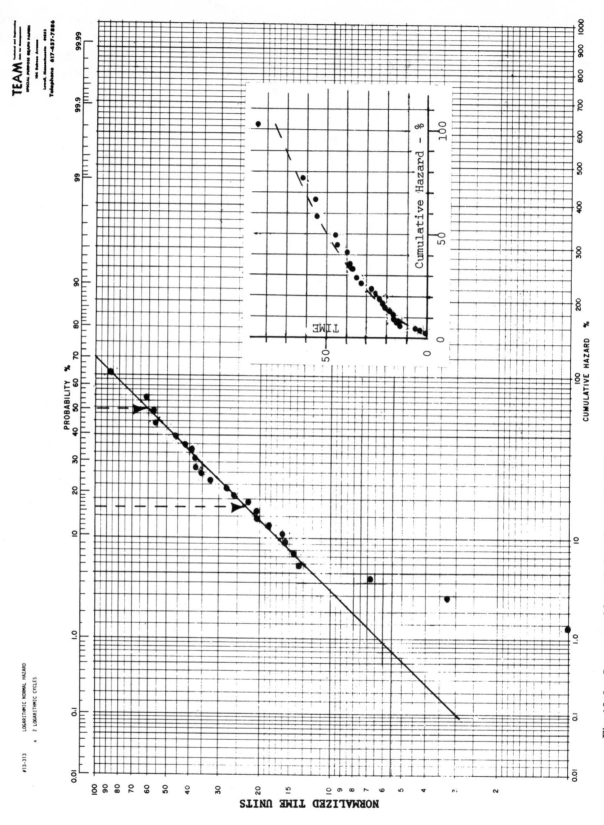

Fig. 19-6.   Log-normal hazard plot of normalized times to failure for degradation failures of a miniature integrating gyro.

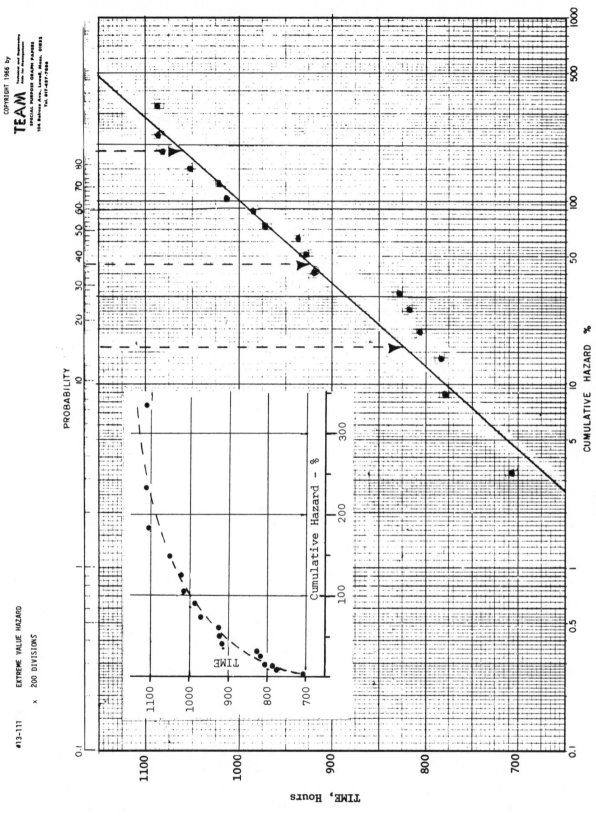

Fig. 19-7.   Extreme value hazard plot of Monte Carlo data.

Table 19-3. Monte Carlo Extreme Value Data and Hazard Calculations

Reverse Order	Time, Hours	Hazard	Cum. Hazard	Reverse Order	Time, Hours	Hazard	Cum. Hazard
100	0			14	890		
to	to	No Failures		13	909		
26	668			12	911		
25	700			11	920*	9.09	40.71
24	708*	4.17	4.17	10	926*	10.00	50.71
23	708			9	936*	11.11	61.82
22	739			8	972*	12.50	74.32
21	773*	4.76	8.93	7	985*	14.29	88.61
20	782*	5.00	13.93	6	1014*	16.67	105.28
19	796			5	1022*	20.00	125.28
18	806*	5.56	19.49	4	1051*	25.00	150.28
17	817*	5.88	25.37	3	1108*	33.33	183.61
16	829*	6.25	31.62	2	1111*	50.00	233.61
15	851			1	1115*	100.00	333.61

* Denotes failure.

of the demands for service and repair cannot be met. If the inventory is excessive, then unnecessary costs are incurred. Also, the appropriate kind and amount of spares inventory is determined by the mixture of age of units in service. Hazard analysis can give greater insight to such problems. This is illustrated in the following example:

Example 19-6

Given: The hazard plot of Fig. 19-7. For those parts which have survived to 750 hours, what is the probability of failure during the next 150 hours; that is, between 750 and 900 hours?

Step 1. Enter the time scale at each of the two times of interest. Project horizontally to the fitted line and project vertically down to the cumulative hazard scale to get the corresponding cumulative hazard value for each time. This is illustrated in Fig. 19-7.

Step 2. Take the difference between the two cumulative hazard values found in Step 1. This gives $35.5 - 7.5 = 28$ percent.

Step 3. Enter the cumulative hazard scale at 28 percent and project vertically to the probability scale to get a probability of failure of about 24.5 percent.

Comment: The result of Step 3 indicates that one should be prepared to repair or replace about 25 percent of the items currently in service with

age 750 hours during the next following 150 hours. This example illustrates the capability of obtaining direct estimates of failure probabilities for parts of any age and how such estimates can be applied to inventory requirements.

Comment: The results of Step 3 can be reformulated into a reliability statement. That is, the reliability for the next 150 hours of parts which have already survived 750 hours of life is:

$$100\% - 24.5\% = 75.5\%$$

The following two examples illustrate the use of hazard plotting to determine the behavior of a single failure mode, the evaluation of the effects of a purposeful engineering change, and the determination of the resultant failure distribution on a warranty problem.

Example 19-7

Given: The data of Table 19-4. This table gives the cycles to failure for one specific failure mode of a small electric appliance in a development program.

Steps 1–3. Same as in Example 19-2.

Step 4. The rough plot of time versus hazard suggests a Weibull plot. The rough plot is shown as an insert in Fig. 19-8.

Step 5. Plot the data on Weibull hazard paper and draw a best-fit line. This is shown in Fig. 19-8, as Line I.

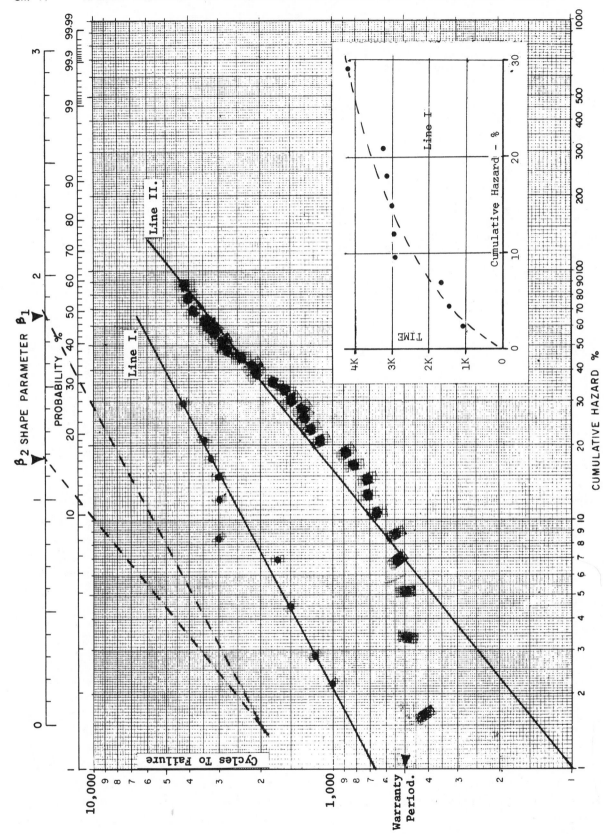

Fig. 19-8.   Weibull hazard plot of cycles to failure for failure mode (A) of a small electric appliance.

Table 19-4. Cycles to Failure for Failure Mode (A) and Hazard Calculations

Reverse Order	Cycles	Hazard	Cum. Hazard	Reverse Order	Cycles	Hazard	Cum. Hazard	Reverse Order	Cycles	Hazard	Cum. Hazard
46	1015*	2.17	2.17	31	3462*	3.23	20.88	16	4132	$\cdots$	$\cdots$
45	1430	$\cdots$	$\cdots$	30	3508	$\cdots$	$\cdots$	15	4161	$\cdots$	$\cdots$
44	1493*	2.27	4.44	29	3532	$\cdots$	$\cdots$	14	4246*	7.14	29.02
43	1624	$\cdots$	$\cdots$	28	3550	$\cdots$	$\cdots$	13	4252	$\cdots$	$\cdots$
42	1680*	2.38	6.82	27	3579	$\cdots$	$\cdots$	12	4256	$\cdots$	$\cdots$
41	1877	$\cdots$	$\cdots$	26	3719	$\cdots$	$\cdots$	11	4275	$\cdots$	$\cdots$
40	2615	$\cdots$	$\cdots$	25	3727	$\cdots$	$\cdots$	10	4317	$\cdots$	$\cdots$
39	2961*	2.56	9.38	24	3773	$\cdots$	$\cdots$	9	4318	$\cdots$	$\cdots$
38	2974*	2.63	12.01	23	3976	$\cdots$	$\cdots$	8	4323	$\cdots$	$\cdots$
37	3009*	2.70	14.71	22	3904	$\cdots$	$\cdots$	7	4334	$\cdots$	$\cdots$
36	3075	$\cdots$	$\cdots$	21	3978	$\cdots$	$\cdots$	6	4349	$\cdots$	$\cdots$
35	3174	$\cdots$	$\cdots$	20	3984	$\cdots$	$\cdots$	5	4393	$\cdots$	$\cdots$
34	3244*	2.94	17.65	19	3995	$\cdots$	$\cdots$	4	4441	$\cdots$	$\cdots$
33	3264	$\cdots$	$\cdots$	18	4103	$\cdots$	$\cdots$	3	4486	$\cdots$	$\cdots$
32	3424	$\cdots$	$\cdots$	17	4112	$\cdots$	$\cdots$	2	4589	$\cdots$	$\cdots$

* Denotes failure.

Step 6. Draw a second line parallel to the best-fit line through the heavy dot near the left edge of the paper and extend this line through the shape parameter scale at the top of the paper. This gives a direct estimate of the Weibull beta, β_1. The value in this case is 1.82, which indicates that the failure rate is increasing with time. This is a classical "wearout" situation.

Comment: This example will be further discussed with the following example as another application of hazard plotting.

Example 19-8

Given: The data of Table 19-5. This table gives the cycles to failure for the same failure mode analyzed in Example 19-7. However, in this case the data are from tests run before a purposeful engineering change was introduced to increase the number of cycles before failure for this specific cause.

Steps 1–3. Same as in Example 19-2.

Steps 4–5. These are omitted. Since the previous data were plotted on Weibull hazard paper, these data are also plotted on the same graph in order to observe whatever contrast exists.

Step 6. A best-fit line is drawn, Line II, and the parallel through the heavy dot gives an estimate of β_2, 1.18.

Comment: The most obvious contrast is that Line I indicates many more cycles of operation before failure occurs than does Line II. It is evident that the engineering change which was introduced was successful.

The plot for Line I is a good Weibull fit. The estimate of 1.82 for β_1 suggests that the wear factors for this failure mode, after engineering changes, probably vary with the square root of time (see Chapter 14). The fact that β_1 is considerably greater than 1 is also evidence that a wearout failure mode is present.

The plot for Line II crosses the fitted line only twice, so there is some suspicion about the validity of the fit of Line II. There may be more than one cause for these failures disguised under the identity of one designated failure mode. The estimate of 1.18 for β_2 is close enough to 1 so that the distribution of this failure mode is nearly exponential. This is indicative of the presence of more than one failure mode on a random additive basis.

Comment: A final consideration is that the appliance which was evaluated is sold with a warranty of 500 cycles. It is obvious from Line II that this one failure mode alone would cause the failure of an estimated 7 percent of the appliances before the expiration of the warranty. This is unacceptably high. The real success of the engineering change

Table 19-5. Cycles to Failure for Failure Mode (A) before Engineering Change

Reverse Order	Cycles	Hazard	Cum. Hazard	Reverse Order	Cycles	Hazard	Cum. Hazard	Reverse Order	Cycles	Hazard	Cum. Hazard
64	45	...	...	43	1321*	2.33	25.12	22	3483	...	...
63	148	...	...	42	1342*	2.38	27.50	21	2552	...	...
62	378	...	...	41	1489*	2.44	29.94	20	3688	...	...
61	412*	1.64	1.64	40	1585	...	...	19	3830*	5.26	68.78
60	437	...	...	39	1588*	2.56	32.50	18	3855	...	...
59	470	...	...	38	1738	...	...	17	3892	...	...
58	487*	1.72	3.36	37	1789*	2.70	35.20	16	3901	...	...
57	496*	1.75	5.11	36	2070	...	...	15	3937	...	...
56	535*	1.79	6.90	35	2113*	2.86	38.06	14	3985	...	...
55	546*	1.82	8.72	34	2157*	2.94	41.00	13	4004*	7.69	76.47
54	649*	1.85	10.57	33	2203	...	...	12	4006		
53	687	...	...	32	2432*	3.12	44.13	11	4017*	9.09	85.56
52	703*	1.92	12.49	31	2433	...	...	10	4056	...	...
51	713*	1.96	14.45	30	2757	...	...	9	4129	...	...
50	816*	2.00	16.45	29	2762*	3.45	47.58	8	4137	...	...
49	881*	2.04	18.49	28	2899*	3.57	51.15	7	4319	...	...
48	1103	...	...	27	3008	...	...	6	4368	...	...
47	1117*	2.13	20.62	26	3164*	3.85	55.00	5	4395	...	...
46	1238*	2.17	22.79	25	3319	...	...	4	4413	...	...
45	1312	...	...	24	3380*	4.17	59.17	3	4693	...	...
44	1312	...	...	23	3412*	4.35	63.52	2	4816	...	...
								1	5448	...	...

* Denotes failure.

which was introduced is measured by the indication that warranty failure percentage for this failure mode would now be less than 1 percent under a 500 cycle warranty, as shown by Line I.

Further Analysis of Mixed Failure Causes with Hazard Plots

Failure data often contain a mixture of causes, or *modes,* of failure. Such "mixed" data result when more than one factor can contribute to failure under similar operating conditions. For example, an automobile tire may fail due to an early blowout (weak carcass), from a puncture (by a nail), by a slow leak (defective valve), or through excessive wear (poor abrasion resistance of the tread stock). Each of these failures occurs for a different reason. As another example, a storage battery may fail due to a short circuit (separator failure) which consumes the energy in the battery; the electrolyte may evaporate (dry battery) which reduces its available energy; or, the battery may age ("sulphate") and consume the internal materials which generate the energy. Again, such failures occur for quite

different and causally unrelated reasons. As a last example which does not involve life data, consider a simple system composed of a wire connection attached to a terminal. Failure may occur as the simple separation of the wire from the terminal at the point of attachment, or the wire may break at some other point.

In situations involving mixed failure modes, in addition to the different reasons underlying each failure mode, the times to failure or breaking strength at failure, when classified by the appropriate failure mode, frequently have different statistical distributions. Under such conditions, one is usually tempted to sort out the data by individual modes creating several separate sub-samples with one sub-sample assigned to each cause.

For instance, if we had three categories of failure modes, the analysis of Mode A by itself ignores all of the data for Modes B and C. However, the data for Modes B and C actually contain positive information about Mode A. That is, we know that up to the time or point of failure at which Modes B and C had occurred, Mode A *had not* occurred. If we can assume that Modes A, B and C are statistically *independent* of each other, then, in the analysis of any *single* failure mode, we can treat the data for the other causes simply as censored values.

The following examples will illustrate hazard analysis for both a variable other than time and for mixed failure modes.

Example 19-9

Given: The data of Table 19-6. This table gives the breaking strength at failure for wire bonds made in a semi-conductor. The wire bonds are diffusion "welds" of one end of a fine wire to a metallized area on a semi-conductor wafer. This is followed by bonding the other end of the fine wire to a terminal post. Strength of the bond is determined by pulling the connecting wire until failure of some type occurs. Two classifications of failure are recorded: 1. The wire separates from the metallized area (the diffusion weld fails in tension), or it separates from the terminal and is called a *lifted bond*; or, 2. the wire breaks (structural tensile failure).

Table 19-6. Values of Breaking Strengths of Wire Bonds and Hazard Calculations

Reverse Order	Breaking Strength, Milligrams	Hazard Value	Cumulative Hazard		
			All Failures	(LB)	(WB)
23	0 LB	4.35	4.35	4.35	
22	0 LB	4.55	8.90	8.90	
21	550 LB	4.76	13.66	13.66	
20	750 WB	5.00	18.66		5.00
19	950 LB	5.26	23.92	18.92	
18	950 WB	5.56	29.48		10.56
17	1150 WB	5.88	35.36		16.44
16	1150 LB	6.25	41.61	25.17	
15	1150 LB	6.67	48.28	31.84	
14	1150 WB	7.14	55.42		23.58
13	1150 WB	7.69	63.11		31.27
12	1250 LB	8.33	71.44	40.17	
11	1250 LB	9.09	80.53	49.26	
10	1350 WB	10.00	90.53		41.27
9	1450 LB	11.11	101.64	60.37	
8	1450 LB	12.50	114.14	72.87	
7	1450 WB	14.29	128.43		55.56
6	1550 LB	16.67	145.10	89.54	
5	1550 WB	20.00	165.10		75.56
4	1550 WB	25.00	190.10		100.56
3	1850 WB	33.33	223.43		133.89
2	2050 LB	50.00	273.43	139.54	
1	3150 LB	100.00	373.43	239.54	

LB — Lifted Bond; WB — Wire Breaks.

Each failure mode requires greatly different action for correction. In Table 19-6, the failure classification is shown along with the breaking strength data.

Steps 1–3. Use all of the data in Table 19-6, irrespective of cause of failure, and proceed as in Example 19-2.

Step 4. Since we are dealing with breaking strength data, extreme value hazard paper is a reasonable choice for a first attempt to fit the data. The rough plot will, therefore, not be necessary.

Step 5. Plot the data on extreme value hazard paper. This is shown in Fig. 19-9. A dashed line is shown in this plot instead of a fitted straight line. The dashed line shows a jog similar to jogs caused by mixed distributions as discussed in Chapter 5.

Comment: Since two classifications of failure causes were used, one has reason to be sensitive to the possibility of competing failure modes. This example and Fig. 19-9 are illustrations of such competing effects.

Example 19-10

Given: The data of Table 19-6.

Required: Construct extreme value hazard plots for each mode of failure.

Steps 1–3. Same as in Example 19-2.

Step 4. Omit. See Step 4 of Example 19-9.

Step 5. Plot the data for each failure mode separately on extreme value hazard paper as shown in Fig. 19-10. The fitted line for lifted bonds is shown as a solid line, and wire breaks are represented as a dashed line.

Comment: Each plot is a reasonably good fit and the jog is gone. This also indicates that the separation of the data on the basis of failure modes is meaningful. The two fitted lines cross at about the 45th percentile, approximately the same point where the jog in Fig. 19-9 occurs.

Comment: Note the important difference between the plots of individual failure modes. Each plot is an acceptable extreme value hazard plot by itself, exhibiting little difference in values for the mode, the median, or the mean. The significant

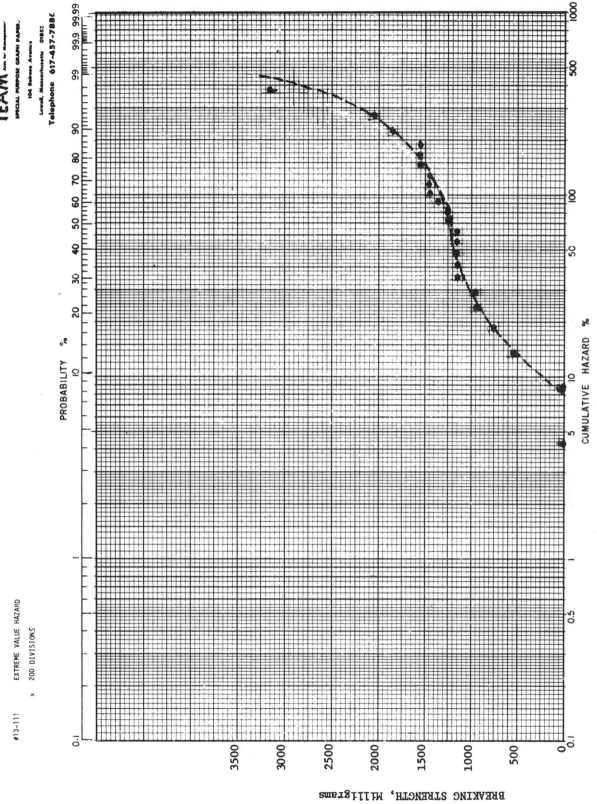

Fig. 19-9.   Extreme value plot of breaking strengths of wire bonds in a semiconductor.

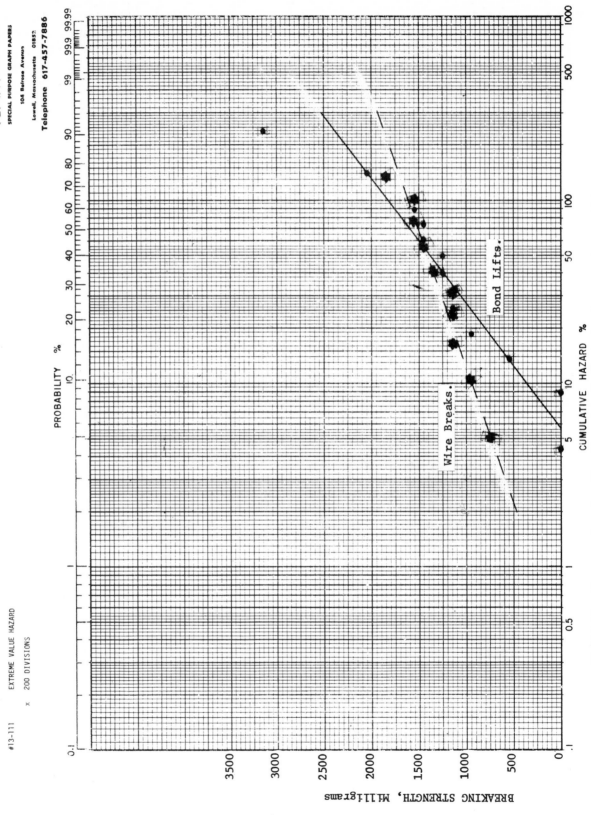

Fig. 19-10.   Extreme value plot of breaking strengths of wire bonds, comparing bond lifts to wire breaks.

difference is in the value of the Gumbel slope. The Gumbel slope is 259 for wire breaks. For lifted bonds, the slope is 559, more than twice as great. This means that the bond attachment strengths (weld strengths) are more highly variable than the wire-breaking strengths.

Comment: In this particular product, 99 percent of the individual items are intended to exceed 500 milligrams in strength. It is obvious that as long as the cause of lifted bonds is allowed to exist, the objective of having 99 percent of the bond strengths greater than 500 mg will not be met, since lifted bonds make up about 12 percent of the failure values below the 500-mg level. On the other hand, if lifted bonds are eliminated, the problem is almost solved, since only about 2 percent of the wire breaks are less than 500 mg. This is an illustration of the use of hazard plotting to identify and to estimate the individual effects of failure modes, and the expected or probable results if failure mode elimination is successful.

Exercises

Note: In all of the following exercises, make the hazard calculations, determine the most appropriate hazard plot, and estimate whichever of the following distribution parameters is appropriate for the hazard function which was determined:

    a. Mean
    b. Mode
    c. Median
    d. Standard deviation
    e. Weibull slope
    f. Gumbel slope

19-1. Use Table 19-7

19-2. Use Table 19-8

19-3. Use Table 19-9

19-4. Use Table 19-10

19-5. Use Table 19-11

19-6. Use Table 19-12

19-7. Use the data of Table 19-13 for two combined failure modes.

Table 19-7. Generator Fan Failure Data

Reverse Order of Failure	Operating Hours to Fan Failure	Reverse Order of Failure	Operating Hours to Fan Failure	Reverse Order of Failure	Operating Hours to Fan Failure
70	4,500*	46	32,000	23	61,000
69	4,600	45	34,500*	22	63,000
68	11,500*	44	37,500	21	64,500
67	11,500*	43	37,500	20	64,500
66	15,600	42	41,500	19	67,000
65	16,000*	41	41,500	18	74,500
64	16,600	40	41,500	17	78,000
63	18,500	39	41,500	16	78,000
62	18,500	38	43,000	15	81,000
61	18,500	37	43,000	14	81,000
60	18,500	36	43,000	13	82,000
59	18,500	35	43,000	12	85,000
58	20,300	34	46,000*	11	85,000
57	20,300	33	48,500	10	85,000
56	20,300	32	48,500	9	87,500
55	20,700*	31	48,500	8	87,500*
54	20,700*	30	48,500	7	87,500
53	20,800*	29	50,000	6	94,000
52	22,000	28	50,000	5	99,000
51	30,000	27	50,000	4	101,000
50	30,000	26	61,000	3	101,000
49	30,000	25	61,000*	2	101,000
48	30,000	24	61,000	1	115,000
47	31,000*				

* Denotes failure.

a. Determine if the two failure modes should be analyzed separately.

b. If the two modes should be analyzed sep-

arately, then make the hazard calculations for each mode and determine the appropriate hazard plot for each one.

Table 19-8. System Operating Times

Reverse Order	Operating Hours	Reverse Order	Operating Hours	Reverse Order	Operating Hours
50	2081*	33	3891*	16	4529*
49	2498*	32	3971	15	4575*
48	2564*	31	3999*	14	4596*
47	2662*	30	4061*	13	4610
46	2769	29	4079*	12	4679*
45	2895*	28	4129*	11	4721*
44	3098*	27	4201*	10	4737*
43	3352*	26	4291*	9	4819*
42	3386*	25	4304*	8	4830
41	3404*	24	4328*	7	5035
40	3468*	23	4362	6	5134*
39	3514	22	4384*	5	5273*
38	3586*	21	4393	4	5415*
37	3659*	20	4488	3	5757*
36	3769	19	4461*	2	5935*
35	3815*	18	4469*	1	6433*
34	3845*	17	4522		

* Denotes failure.

Table 19-9. Monte Carlo Data

Reverse Order	Operating Hours	Reverse Order	Operating Hours	Reverse Order	Operating Hours	Reverse Order	Operating Hours
100	0	75	105*	50	227	25	700*
99	1	74	108	49	240	24	708
98	4	73	112	48	250*	23	708*
97	6	72	126	47	251*	22	739
96	7*	71	130	46	252	21	773
95	8	70	131	45	252*	20	782
94	12*	69	138*	44	255*	19	796
93	15	68	140	43	263*	18	806
92	21*	67	144*	42	272*	17	817
91	24	66	145*	41	287	16	829
90	25	65	149	40	288*	15	851*
89	35	64	158*	39	303*	14	890*
88	37*	63	174	38	323	13	909*
87	42*	62	177*	37	351	12	911*
86	43	61	179	36	355	11	920
85	45	60	186	35	393*	10	926
84	50	59	189	34	405	9	936
83	55*	58	196	33	445*	8	972
82	59	57	196	32	513*	7	985
81	67	56	205	31	535*	6	1014
80	73	55	209	30	536	5	1022
79	78	54	209*	29	581*	4	1051
78	83*	53	217	28	607*	3	1108
77	91*	52	217	27	616*	2	1111
76	102	51	218*	26	668*	1	1115

* Denotes failure.

Table 19-10. System Failure Data

Reverse Order	Operating Hours	Reverse Order	Operating Hours	Reverse Order	Operating Hours	Reverse Order	Operating Hours
100	46*	75	129*	50	155	25	192
99	46	74	129	49	155	24	192
98	46	73	129	48	156*	23	192
97	46	72	137*	47	156	22	205*
96	46	71	137	46	156	21	205
95	72*	70	137	45	156	20	205
94	72	69	146*	44	156	19	212*
93	72	68	146	43	157*	18	212
92	87*	67	146	42	157	17	212
91	87	66	146	41	157	16	233*
90	87	65	146	40	158*	15	233
89	90*	64	146	39	158	14	233
88	90	63	146	38	158	13	261*
87	90	62	146	37	165*	12	261
86	94*	61	146	36	165	11	261
85	94	60	148*	35	165	10	293*
84	94	59	148	34	176*	9	293
83	94	58	148	33	176	8	293
82	94	57	152*	32	176	7	293
81	121*	56	152	31	192*	6	293
80	121	55	152	30	192	5	293
79	121	54	153*	29	192	4	293
78	126*	53	153	28	192	3	293
77	126	52	153	27	192	2	293
76	126	51	155*	26	192	1	293

* Denotes failure.

Table 19-11. Values of Breaking Strengths of Wire Bonds

Reverse Order	Strength, in Milligrams	Reverse Order	Strength, in Milligrams	Reverse Order	Strength, in Milligrams
23	0 LB	15	1150 LB	7	1450 WB
22	0 LB	14	1150 WB	6	1550 LB
21	550 LB	13	1150 WB	5	1550 WB
20	750 WB	12	1250 LB	4	1550 WB
19	950 LB	11	1250 LB	3	1850 WB
18	950 WB	10	1350 WB	2	2050 LB
17	1150 WB	9	1450 LB	1	3150 LB
16	1150 LB	8	1450 LB		

LB — Lifted Bond; WB — Wire Breaks.

Table 19-12. Breaking Strength Data, in Milligrams

Reverse Order	Strength, in Milligrams	Reverse Order	Strength, in Milligrams	Reverse Order	Strength, in Milligrams
25	550*	16	1550	8	2050
24	750*	15	1550	7	2050
23	1050	14	1550*	6	2050
22	1050*	13	1650	5	2050*
21	1050*	12	1850	4	2050*
20	1250	11	1850	3	2250
19	1250	10	1950	2	2450
18	1350	9	1950*	1	2550
17	1550				

* Denotes bond life failure.

Table 19-13. Failure Data on Small Appliance

Reverse Order	Cycles	Reverse Order	Cycles	Reverse Order	Cycles	Reverse Order	Cycles
110	45	82	1588	54	3424	27	4103
109	148	81	1624	53	3462–B	26	4112
108	378	80	1680–B	52	3484	25	4129
107	412	79	1738	51	3508	24	4132
106	437	78	1789	50	3532	23	4137
105	470	77	1877	49	3550	22	4161
104	487	76	2070	48	3552	21	4246–B
103	496	75	2113	47	3597	20	4252
102	535	74	2157	46	3688	19	4256
101	546	73	2203	45	3719	18	4275
100	649	72	2432	44	3727	17	4317
99	687	71	2433	43	3773	16	4318
98	703	70	2615	42	3830	15	4319
97	713	69	2757	41	3855	14	4323
96	816	68	2762	40	3876	13	4349
95	881	67	2899	39	3892	12	4368
94	1015–B	66	2961–B	38	3901	11	4384
93	1103	65	2974–B	37	3904	10	4395
92	1117	64	3008	36	3937	9	4398
91	1238	63	3009–B	35	3978	8	4413
90	1312	62	3075	34	3984	7	4441
89	1312	61	3164	33	3985	6	4486
88	1321	60	3174	32	3995	5	4596
87	1342	59	3244–B	31	4004	4	4693
86	1430	58	3264	30	4006	3	4800
85	1489	57	3319	29	4017	2	4816
84	1493–B	56	3380	28	4056	1	5448
83	1585	55	3412				

B — Failure due to cause B.

CHAPTER 20

Binomial Functions

Introduction

In Chapter 2, we introduced the binary distribution, which was based on a system which can assume only one of two states or conditions. We further restricted the binary system by requiring that each state occur with equal frequency; that is, on a 50-50 basis. We now generalize the binary system by removing the restriction of equal frequency and say that the two states may occur with any relative frequency. This permits us to work with *proportional systems* called *binomial distributions,* which deal with questions such as: What proportion of adults over 30 are college graduates? or, What percentage of all automobile registrations are for Mustangs?

This leads us to consider some properties of *counted data.* In order to count, we must deal with discrete items which are enumerated one at a time; that is, as *discrete units.* To obtain proportions from counted data, we must even count in a special way; that is, we count the number of objects, c, which have a defined property, and we count the number of objects, $n - c$, which do not have the defined property. An alternative method of obtaining a proportion is to select a sample of n objects from a large collection of objects (population) and to count only those objects, c, having a defined property. The number of objects not having the property is obtained simply by subtraction, giving $n - c$ directly.

All of the distributions which were considered in earlier chapters are classed as *continuous distributions* which means that the values obtained through the operation of random processes may take on any possible value of the variable of interest over its range of behavior. We pass on now to a class of distribution behavior which is called *discrete* in that we obtain data as whole number counts of discrete objects. As a consequence, the variables are not a continuum and can proceed only by steps of 1 or more counts at a time. Such data occur naturally as a result of inspection operations, such as 5 defective items in a sample of 100. Under normal decision rules used, we do not obtain $4\frac{7}{8}$ or $5\frac{1}{3}$ defectives because an item either has a specific property or it lacks this property. Note that the continuous distributions were generated from discrete distributions by applying stipulated mathematical operations. Examples were given involving the binary distribution with only two possible states and the uniform distribution for several possible states which were illustrated by coin-tossing and dice-throwing experiments.

However, there are a number of important and interesting problems which occur in the form of counted data that are best handled by the binomial distribution. All such problems are solvable through mathematical manipulation, but the majority of these problems are solved much more quickly and simply through the use of binomial plotting papers.

Binomial plotting papers consist, basically, of a square-root scale on both the horizontal and vertical axes. Binomial plotting papers are not probability papers in the cumulative probability sense, even though one common format is called binomial probability paper (BIPP). It is more correct to say that the binomial papers permit comparisons of observed and expected binomial behaviors. Binomial plotting papers are also adaptable to the analysis of cumulative binomial data with important applications in reliability analysis and forecasting.

Description of the Binomial Distribution

The binomial distribution is based on the *binomial proportion, p,*

$$p = \frac{c}{n} \qquad (20\text{-}1)$$

where:

p is the binomial (observed) proportion.
c is the count of objects with a specified property.
n is the sample size.

In some cases, p is referred to as the *probability of success* because the definition for c is based on some desired result, which is referred to as a successful, or desirable, outcome. For example, c may be the number of heads in a toss of n coins; the number of students who obtain honor marks in a class of n students; the number of sales made in n calls; or the number of passengers on a Boeing 707 flight from New York to San Francisco with n seats. When a binomial system is considered to be reproducible, or consistent, over a period of time, p is treated as a constant system parameter. Actually, p behaves more like the mean or mode of other distributions, since it will vary somewhat in a series of repeated observations, or *trials*.

When p is considered as a constant probability of success, the probability of observing r, or fewer, successes in m trials of *equal sample size* is given by the cumulative distribution function:

$$Pr(x \le r) = F(r; p, m)$$
$$= \sum_{x=0}^{r} \binom{m}{x} p^x (1-p)^{(m-x)} \qquad (20\text{-}2)$$

The probability of exactly x successes in m independent trials is the probability density function, given by:

$$f(x; p, m) = \binom{m}{x} p^x (1-p)^{(m-x)} \qquad (20\text{-}3)$$

where:

x is the random variable, the number of occurrences.
r is a designated number of occurrences
p is the probability of success in an individual trial
m is the number of independent trials

and $\quad \binom{m}{x} = \dfrac{m!}{x!(m-x)!} \qquad (20\text{-}4)$

$m! = 1 \cdot 2 \cdot 3, \ldots, m$, the factorial expansion

with $\quad 0! = 1$, by definition.

The value obtained from Equation 20-4 is called the *binomial coefficient*. Interpretation of the bi-

nomial distribution is based on the binomial coefficient. The probability of success at any one trial is defined by p, but there are m trials. The number of successes, x, can occur in a combination of ways. For example, if $p = 1/3$, then in three trials, p is true if any of the following sequences occurs: *xoo; oxo; oox*. However, the following sequences are also possible: *ooo; xxo; xox; oxx*; and *xxx*. But Equation 20-4 states that for x to occur in one out of three trials, then: $3!/1!(3-1)! = 3 \cdot 2 \cdot 1/1(2 \cdot 1) = 3$. That is, x can occur in only 1 of 3 ways which was shown as *xoo; oxo*; and *oox* above. Therefore, the binomial coefficient defines the number of combinations (permutations) which result in success out of all the possible combinations which can occur.

The common part of the right-hand portion of Equations 20-2 and 20-3 can therefore be stated as: the probability that something will happen is the product of the number of ways in which it can occur, multiplied by the probability that it will occur x times, multiplied by the probability that it will not occur $(m-x)$ times.

Discussion of Binomial Nomenclature

Equations 20-2 and 20-3 imply that we know, in advance, what p really is. However, in reality, we are more often in the situation of trying to determine what a reasonable estimate, or approximation, for p may be. We are likely to have data on the results of m trials (experiments). In this case, the estimate for the mean of the binomial distribution for proportions is:

$$\bar{p} = \text{the estimate of } p \qquad (20\text{-}5)$$

where:

$\bar{p}$ is the mean of the p's observed in m trials.
and p is the binomial proportion as defined in Equation 20-1.

The estimate for the standard deviation is:

$$\sigma_{\bar{p}} = \sqrt{\bar{p}(1-\bar{p})/n} \qquad (20\text{-}6)$$

However, we are usually dealing with samples from populations whose true proportions are not always known. In this case, it is simpler to work directly with the observed data, which consists of

c and n. The standard deviation can then be estimated from:

$$\sigma_{\bar{p}} = \sqrt{c(1 - c)/n} \qquad (20\text{-}7)$$

The numerators of the terms under the radicals in Equations 20-6 and 20-7 can be restated as ratios; that is:

$\bar{p}/(1 - \bar{p})$ is called a *binomial split*

$c/(n - c)$ is called a *paired count*

A binomial split is simply the *proportion,* or *percentage,* of items having a specified characteristic divided by the proportion, or percentage *not having* the specified characteristic. The paired count is the *number* of items having a characteristic divided by the number of items' *not having* the characteristic. These relationships are used to simplify binomial plotting.

When n is relatively large and either $np \geq 5$ or $n(1 - \bar{p}) \geq 5$, the binomial distribution is an approximately normal distribution with a mean of np and a standard deviation of:

$$\sigma_{n\bar{p}} = \sqrt{n\bar{p}(1 - \bar{p})} \qquad (20\text{-}8a)$$

$$\sigma_{n\bar{p}} = n\sigma_{\bar{p}} \qquad (20\text{-}8b)$$

Description of Binomial Plotting Paper

Figure 20-1 illustrates a binomial plotting paper. Both axes are ruled to the square root of the indicated values. The vertical scale is labeled the *c scale* since c is usually plotted on the vertical axis. The horizontal scale is labeled the *n scale* but could just as readily be labeled the *n − c scale* since either of these values is plotted against this axis. This illustration shows the left vertical scale extending to 50 and the bottom horizontal scale extending to 100. The right vertical scale goes to 5000 and the top horizontal scale goes to 10,000. Due to the square root relationship, binomial plotting paper scales can be expanded or contracted readily by multiplying or dividing by 100, depending on the numbers involved. In addition, the vertical and horizontal scales may be used interchangeably.

To represent a proportion on binomial plotting paper, say $p = .25$ or $25/100$, plot the binomial split at $25/100 − 25$, or $25/75$ and connect it to the origin. This line, then, represents all samples with $p = .25$.

At the lower left corner is a scale labeled confidence bounds. Values are shown for 2.5%, 10%, 40%, 60%, 90%, and 97.5% confidence. The difference between any pair gives the value of the confidence interval in percentage. For example, between the 97.5% and 2.5% points we have a 95% confidence interval. If the 2.5% and 97.5% points are now used as origins from which lines are drawn parallel to the line representing a given proportion, then the 95% confidence region is defined. This is illustrated in Fig. 20-1 by the dashed lines.

The confidence scale may be used as is, *only with* the left vertical and bottom horizontal scale. See Examples 20-3 and 20-4 for modification.

Types of Binomial Problems

Case 1: Comparison of one or more observed (experimental) proportions to a standard or expected proportion.

Example 20-1
Given: An expected proportion based on past records; $p = .25$, as in Fig. 20-1.
Question: If we obtained counts represented by the following three sample results: 13/30, 18/65, and 18/90, would they represent the expected proportion with 95% confidence?
Procedure: Simply plot the paired counts $c/(n − c)$: $1.^{13}\!/_{17}$, $2.^{18}\!/_{47}$, $3.^{18}\!/_{72}$ at the coordinates representing the sampling results. Samples 2 and 3 fall inside the confidence interval, but Sample 1 falls outside. Therefore, there is reason to believe that there is something different about Sample 1.

Comment: This is the simplest of all applications for binomial plotting paper. This method is useful for assessing sampling results under several typical operating conditions such as:

a. When production quantities vary widely, most sampling plans require widely different sample sizes. Figure 20-1 shows a method for quick interpretation of results against a work standard independently of the lot disposition achieved through sampling.

b. In job shops, quantities are often both variable in lot size and sporadic as to time of occurrence. Usually, such jobs will also be subject to

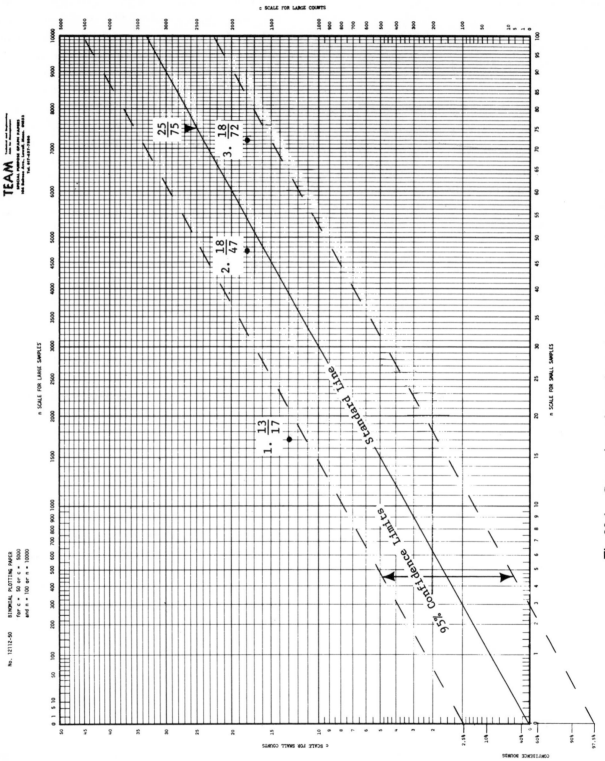

Fig. 20-1.   Comparison of several sample proportions to a standard.

100 percent inspection. The method of Fig. 20-1 is a quick check on the consistency of performance of any job run against a desired or standard level for that kind of job.

c. In comparing several machines and/or operators running the same kind of job, inspection results of individual outputs can be quickly compared to the desired performance standard.

Case 2: Comparison of two proportions, standard unknown. Here we have the situation of results from two different samples which may represent different sources of supply, different machines, different personnel, and different times of occurrence. Without having a standard of reference, we wish to ask if the two samples are comparable.

If the two samples have equal proportions, then $p_1 = p_2$ or $c_1/n_1 = c_2/n_2$. This leads to a simple method of evaluation based on the requirement that the c's should be in direct proportion to their sample sizes.

Example 20-2
Given: 28 resistors were read on each of two different resistance bridges, designated as A and B. Each B reading was subtracted from its corresponding A reading with the following results: There were 7 minus results and 21 plus results.
Question: Is there a difference in the distribution of plus and minus results at the 95% confidence level? This may also be stated as: Is the ratio of 7/28 different from a 50/50 split?
Procedure: If there is no difference between the bridges, the differences observed between the two readings should be only random error. If the error is random, we would expect nearly the same number of pluses as minuses. This is completely analogous to the arguments for the binary distribution in coin tossing.

Therefore, we assume a binomial split of 50/50 as representing no difference between the results. This is plotted in Fig. 20-2. The paired count is $7/(28 - 7) = 7/21$. This is shown plotted as x in Fig. 20-2. Since it falls outside the 95% confidence interval, we then assume that there is a real difference between the pluses and minuses.
Comment: This type of example is sometimes classed as a Case 1 example. Since we must make certain assumptions — in this case, the equivalence

of the bridges — the standard is not really known. Subsequent investigation of the results of this example disclosed that each bridge had been calibrated differently and one bridge did, in fact, read higher than the other. This was corrected quite easily.

This example is an application of the binomial distribution to a comparison of any two systems which are expected to be comparable. The classification of results was simply by plus and minus. However, as discussed in Chapter 2, any of the paired classifications of a binary system may be analyzed in the same way.
Note: If there were any "tied" results; that is, identical readings on each bridge, the number of ties should be subtracted from n before taking the paired count.

Example 20-3
Given: Students from each of two schools were given the same standardized examination. Outstanding students were cited for achievement. The number of citations for School A was 22 out of 300 students and for School B, there were 12 citations out of 400 students.
Question: Is there any difference between the performance of students in the 2 schools at the 95% confidence level?
Procedure: Take the ratio of the smaller sample size to the larger sample size. In this case, we have $n_A/n_B = 300/400$. This will serve in lieu of a standard; it is shown in Fig. 20-3. Next, take the ratio of results c_A/c_B or 22/12. The plot for this point is outside the 95% confidence interval, so there is some reason to believe that School A achieved higher than School B, since the plotted point is above the confidence interval. Had the point been below, then School A would have achieved less than School B.
Comment: This procedure is an example of a common question based on two-sided intercomparisons. It is applicable to any pair of results where c_1, n_1, c_2, and n_2 are known.

Case 3: Comparisons of several proportions, standard unknown.

Example 20-4
Given: Batting averages for the 1968 season of the top hitters from each American League team with 450 or more at bats, Table 20-1.

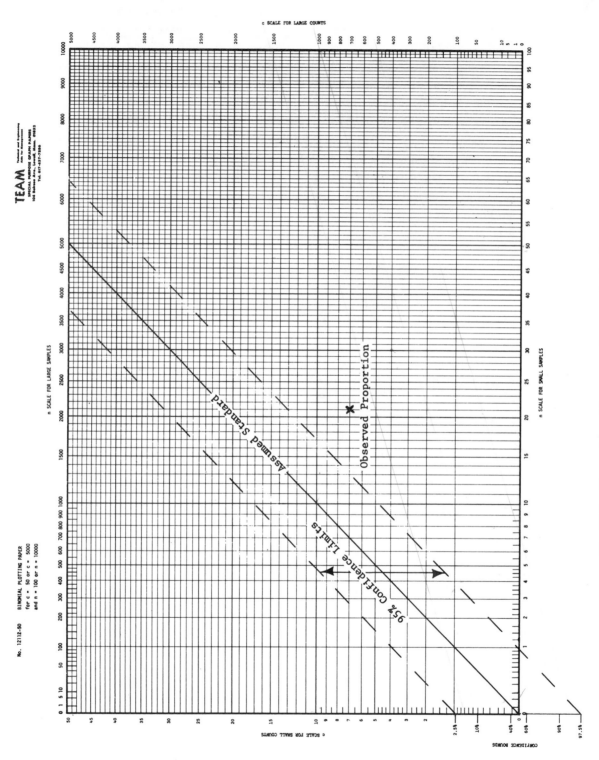

Fig. 20-2.   Comparison of two proportions; standard unknown.

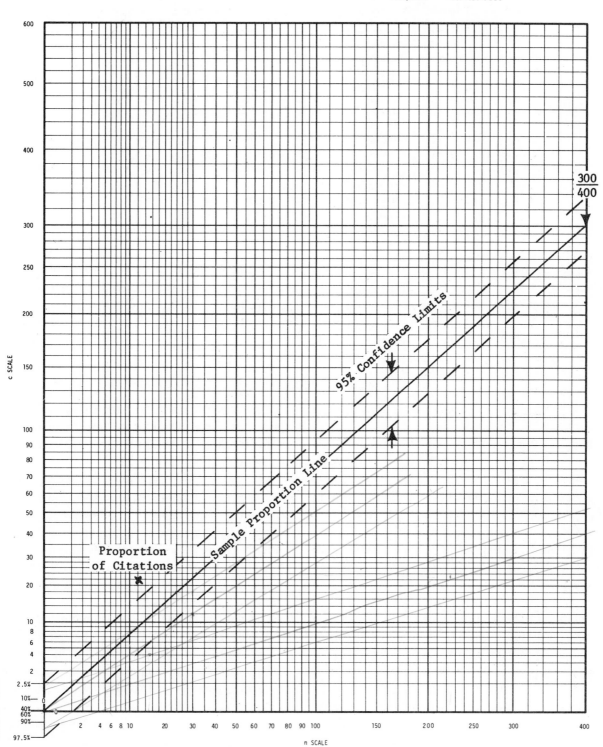

Fig. 20-3.   Comparison of two schools for performance in a standardized examination.

Table 20-1. Batting Records for the Player with the Highest
Batting Average with more than 450 At-Bats on Each
American League Team

Player	Team	At-Bats	Hits	No Hits	Hits From:
B. Robinson	Baltimore	608	154	454	Right Side
Yastrzemski	Boston	539	162	377	Left Side
Davalillo	California	519	144	375	Left Side
Davis	Chicago	456	122	334	Right Side
Cardenal	Cleveland	582	150	432	Right Side
Horton	Detroit	512	146	366	Right Side
Oliva	Minnesota	470	136	334	Left Side
White	New York	577	154	423	Switch
Cater	Oakland	504	146	358	Right Side
F. Howard	Washington	598	164	434	Right Side
	TOTALS	5365	1478	3887	
Hits from:					
Right Side		3260	882	2378	
Left Side		1528	442	1086	
Switch		577	154	423	

Question: Is there any difference between the top hitters of each team at the 90% confidence level?

Procedure: Obtain the total of at-bats and hits: $p = 1478/5365 = .275$. The binomial split is then .275 to .725. This line is shown in Fig. 20-4.

Note: The 90% confidence interval is obtained by direct measurement, using the *midpoint* between 2.5% and 10% and 90% and 97.5% points. This gives the 5% and 95% confidence bounds resulting in the 90% confidence interval.

Then, each paired count of hits versus no-hits is plotted individually for each batter. Two points fall outside the 90% confidence interval. On the high side is Yastrzemski who won the AL batting title. At the 90% confidence level, he was better than the other top hitters in the league. On the low side was B. Robinson. The interpretation here is that he was a significantly weaker hitter than were all the other team leaders at the 90% confidence level.

Comment: The utilization of sports data has a twofold purpose. First, we have a clear application of pure counts; that is, so many hits in so many times at bat. Second, over the course of a baseball season, there are many random variables at work: time of year, time of day, weather conditions, temperature, individual health, and attitude. These factors are many and complex, and lead naturally into binomial results.

The same kind of analysis can be applied readily to groups of workers, machines, processes, test groups in experiments, and human population subgroups in cultural, social, or economic studies.

Case 4: Comparison of several proportions, greatly different sample sizes.

Example 20-5

This is similar to Example 20-4, except that there the paired counts were quite similar. This method, however, is still very applicable even when the paired counts vary widely.

Given: Table 20-1 also shows the hitting side for each hitter. There are six right-hand batters, three left-handers, and one switch hitter.

Question: Is any one style of batting better than another at the 90% confidence level?

Procedure: Since the same data is involved as for Example 20-4, the same p is used as in the previous example.

The data of Table 20-1 is summarized for the new categories of classification of hitting style.

The paired counts for each hitting style are plotted in Fig. 20-5 against the p line and 90% confidence interval. Hitting style does not show a significant advantage.

Note: Figure 20-5 also illustrates the adaptability of scales on binomial plotting papers. In order to include the range of observed data, the bottom

$c =$
$n = 30$

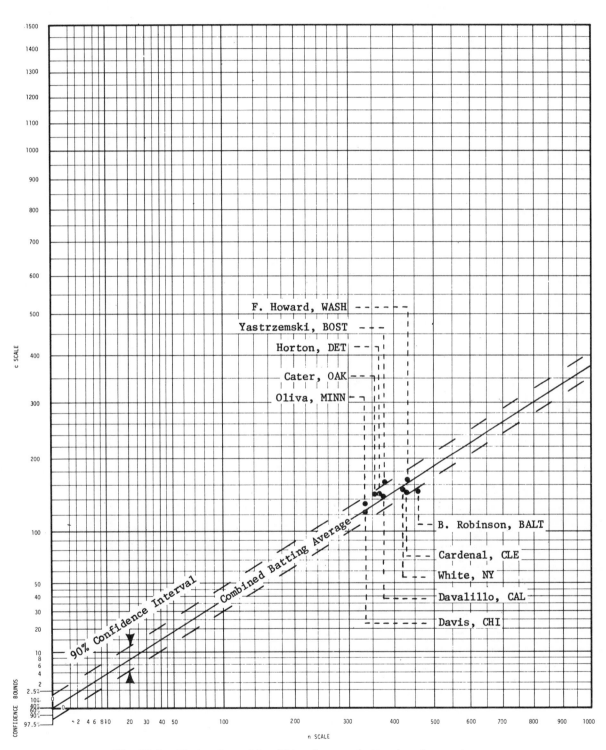

Fig. 20-4. Comparison of top hitters from each American League team.

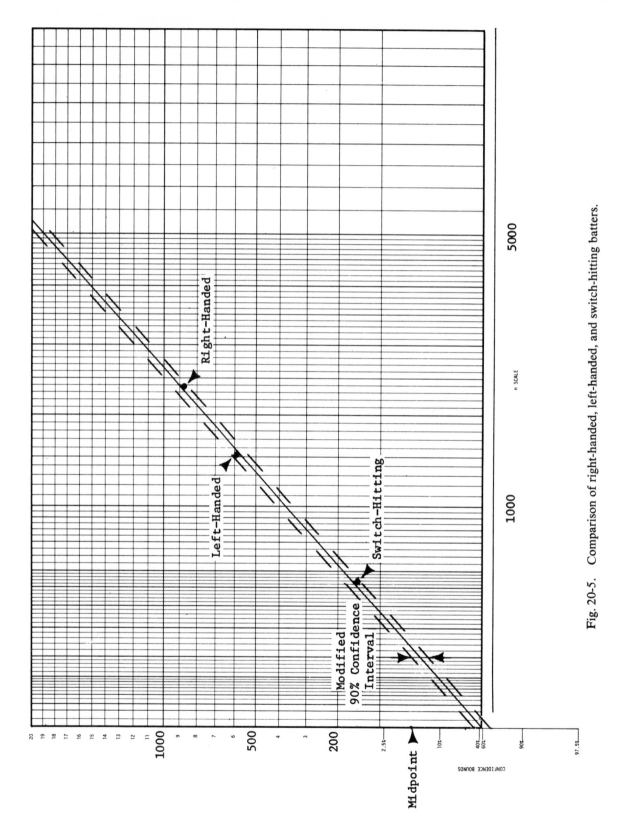

Fig. 20-5.   Comparison of right-handed, left-handed, and switch-hitting batters.

Table 20-2. Final Standings of American and National League
Baseball Teams at End of 1968 Season

American League				National League			
Team	Won	Lost	Pct.	Team	Won	Lost	Pct.
Detroit	103	59	.636	St. Louis	97	65	.599
Baltimore	91	71	.562	San Francisco	88	74	.543
Cleveland	86	76	.534	Chicago	84	78	.519
Boston	86	76	.531	Cincinnati	83	79	.512
New York	83	79	.512	Atlanta	81	51	.500
Oakland	82	80	.506	Pittsburgh	80	82	.494
Minnesota	79	83	.488	Los Angeles	76	86	.469
California	67	95	.414	Philadelphia	76	86	.469
Chicago	67	95	.414	New York	73	89	.451
Washington	65	96	.404	Houston	72	90	.444

scale has been divided by 100 and the vertical scale has been multiplied by 100, giving a paper with a range of 2000 × 10,000 from paper scaled 20 × 1,000,000.

The confidence intervals are obtained in two steps. First, the 5% point is located at the midpoint between the 2.5% and 10% points. Since the values on the vertical scale have been expanded by a factor of 100, the increments have been reduced by 100. However, since this is a square-root scale, the actual displacement is only $1/\sqrt{100}$ or 1/10 of the original distances. Therefore, use 1/10 of the distance from 0 to the 2.5 − 10% midpoint to locate the new 5% confidence bound. Measure the same distance below 0 to obtain the 95% bound. Then, the difference 95% − 5% gives the new 90% confidence interval.

Further discussion of binomial plotting paper, theory, continuity corrections, and additional applications are given by Mostellor and Tukey (37); Hicks (26); Satterthwaite (45); and Wallis and Roberts (51).

Detailed development of the binomial distribution may be found in Dixon and Massey (11); in Hald (23); and in Feller (15).

Exercises

20-1. Compare the following proportions to an assumed standard of $p = 0.4$ at the 95% confidence level: 24/39, 21/44, 11/36, 17/46, 22/41, 11/46, 25/60, 40/76, 18/55 and 26/69. Are there any proportions which you believe to be different from the standard? Why?

20-2. A city of 75,000 population reported a total of 166 cases of death due to lung cancer during a single year. Another city of 18,000 population reported a total of 26 deaths due to lung cancer. Is there a significant difference between these two cities in the death rate for lung cancer at the 95% confidence level?

20-3. Table 20-2 gives the final standings of each team in the American and National leagues. Compare all of the teams within each league. Is there any reason, at the 95% confidence level, to believe that the Number One team was better than the other teams in the league? Were there any teams that appeared to be unusually low in performance?

CHAPTER 21

Bradley Binomial Plotting Paper

Introduction

Due to the wide range of applicability of the binomial distribution, the binomial plotting papers described in Chapter 20 are not always adaptable to the most convenient graphical solutions. G. J. Bradley, now of the Raytheon Company, developed a valuable transformation of the binomial distribution. This transformation was used to prepare a new kind of plotting paper now called Bradley binomial plotting paper. With this paper, it is possible to solve many problems in terms of the binomial proportion, p, without having to convert to binomial splits or paired counts. In addition, it is possible to obtain the standard deviation of the binomial distribution directly and to obtain predetermined confidence intervals easily.

Description of Bradley Binomial Plotting Paper

Figure 21-1 is an example of Bradley binomial plotting paper. On the extreme right is a scale labeled Sample Size — n. To the left of the sample-size scale is a grid. The grid is graphical representation of Bradley's transformation of the relationship of the observed proportion, p, to the sample standard deviation, σ_p. The bottom horizontal scale of the grid is the p scale and the value goes from 0 to 0.5. The top horizontal scale of the grid is the $q = (1 - p)$ scale with values from 0.5 to 1.0. The left vertical scale of the grid is the scale for sample standard deviation, σ_p. This scale is uniformly graduated. The subscript p is omitted in the nomenclature of the Bradley paper.

To the left of the p,σ grid is a set of scales for several preselected confidence levels. The confidence level scales are derived from the σ scale simply by multiplying σ by the appropriate k factor which represents the indicated confidence level based on the normal approximation defined in Equation

20-8. The confidence level value is given across the top of this set of scales. At the bottom, the values for significance level are given, from the relationship: Significance level = 1 — confidence level.

The p,σ grid has a heavy curved line running from the origin at 0,0 upward to the right. This represents the condition that $np = 5$. Only those data which occur to the right of the $np = 5$ line may be validly solved in terms of the binomial distribution. Data points which occur to the left of the $np = 5$ line are usually caused by very small sample sizes or by very small values for p. Data under these conditions are not correctly solved by the binomial distribution. Generally, these problems must be solved by use of the hypergeometric or multinomial distribution functions.

At the top of the paper are two additional scales which are labeled, respectively, Correction Factor and Sample-to-Lot ratio. These scales are used to correct estimates of distribution parameters under the conditions that:

1. Sampling occurs without replacement
2. The proportion of the lot used as a sample size exceeds 20 percent of the total lot quantity.

With the binomial plotting paper described in Chapter 20, it was possible to change scale ranges to accommodate different sample sizes. The scale changes used the square root-relationship of the basic scales so that multiplication and division of the scale values was easily accomplished. This advantage is not applicable to the Bradley binomial plotting papers. Therefore, Bradley papers are required for a number of scale ranges in order to accommodate a wide range of sample sizes.

Figure 21-1 illustrates a sample-size scale range of 10–1,000. Figure 21-2 covers the range of 50–

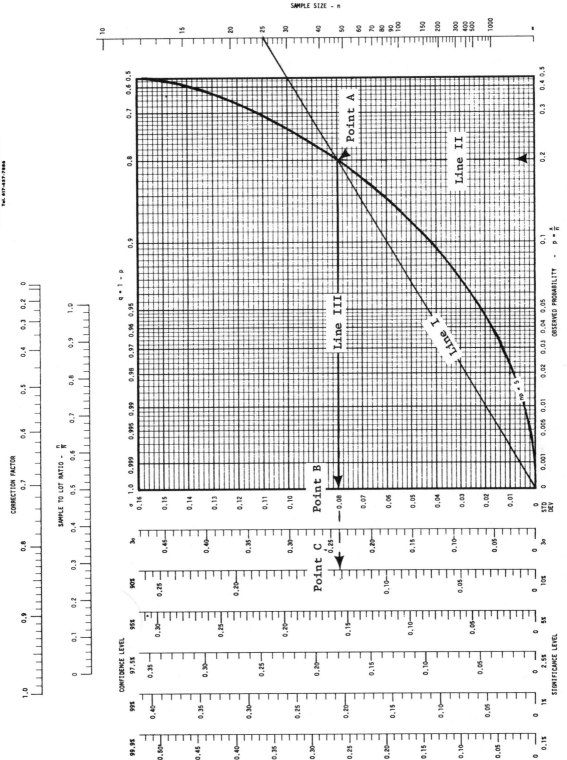

Fig. 21-1.   Determination of a confidence interval for an observed proportion.

5,000; Fig. 21-3 covers 250–25,000; and Fig. 21-5 goes from 1,000 to 1,000,000. Due to the layout of the σ scale with respect to the sample-size scale, it is generally preferable to use that paper with a scale arrangement which gives the steepest slope to a line from the origin to the sample size scale using the sample size involved in the problem.

Applications of Bradley Binomial Papers to Binomial Problems

Case 1: Using an observed proportion, estimate the range of future results.

Example 21-1
Given: A girl-watcher observed 25 consecutive women as they passed by his girl-watching post and observed that 5 had red hair.
Required: An estimate of the 90 percent confidence interval for the number of redheads that the girl-watcher would observe in many additional samples of 25 observations.
Procedure: First, calculate

$$p = \frac{c}{n} = \frac{5}{25} = 0.2$$

Second, draw a line on Bradley binomial plotting paper from the origin at 0,0 to 25 on the sample-size scale at the far right, as shown in Fig. 21-1 by Line I.

Third, find the intersection of Line I and the line for $p = 0.2$, Line II. This is shown at A.

Note: This point is right on the $np = 5$ line, so it may be used.

Fourth, point A is projected horizontally to the σ scale, Line III. The value for σ_p is at point B and is found to be 0.08.

Fifth, obtain estimates of the distribution parameters:

$n \times p = 25 \times 0.2 = 5$ redheads, on the average

$n \times \sigma_p = 25 \times 0.08 = 2$

Sixth, to obtain the 90 percent confidence interval around the average of 5, extend Line III to the 90 percent confidence scale where we obtain the appropriate value for $k\sigma_p$ of 0.131 as shown at C.

Seventh, then:

$$n \times k\sigma_p = 25 \times 0.131 = 3.3$$

The 90 percent confidence interval is therefore 5 ± 3.3, or 1.7 to 8.3. Since the girl-watcher is counting individuals, it is more practical to round off this result to 2 and 8. That is, with 90 percent confidence, the girl-watcher would expect to observe from 2 to 8 redheads in repeated samples of 25 observations.

Comment: The principles of this example apply equally well to results of a first sample of observations of any phenomena. This example illustrates how to make estimates of the likely range of results to be expected for some future time until more experience is obtained. Such estimates are valuable even if not precise. They can serve as guidelines for evaluation of data from activities which typically do not represent long-run situations. Some examples of such areas of application are in comparing successive results of development testing, prototype evaluation, and pilot line-runs. The estimates so obtained are also useful for judging the success, or lack thereof, of early production runs as compared to engineering development results.

Example 21-2
Given: The attendance at a monthly meeting of an organization with a membership of 400 members was 75 attendees.
Required: Based on the observed attendance, what is the 97.5 percent confidence interval for attendance at future meetings?
Procedure:

First, calculate

$$p = \frac{c}{n} = \frac{75}{400} = 0.1875$$

Second, draw the line from 0,0 to $n = 400$, Line I, Fig. 21-2.

Third, find the intersection of Line I and $p = 0.1875$, A. This point is well to the right of $np = 5$, so it may be used.

Fourth, project point A to the 97.5 percent confidence scale. Line III at point B indicates that $\sigma_p = 0.0192$.

Fifth, the estimates of the distribution parameters are:

$$n \times p = 400 \times 0.1875 = 75$$

$$n \times \sigma_p = 400 \times 0.0192 = 7.68$$

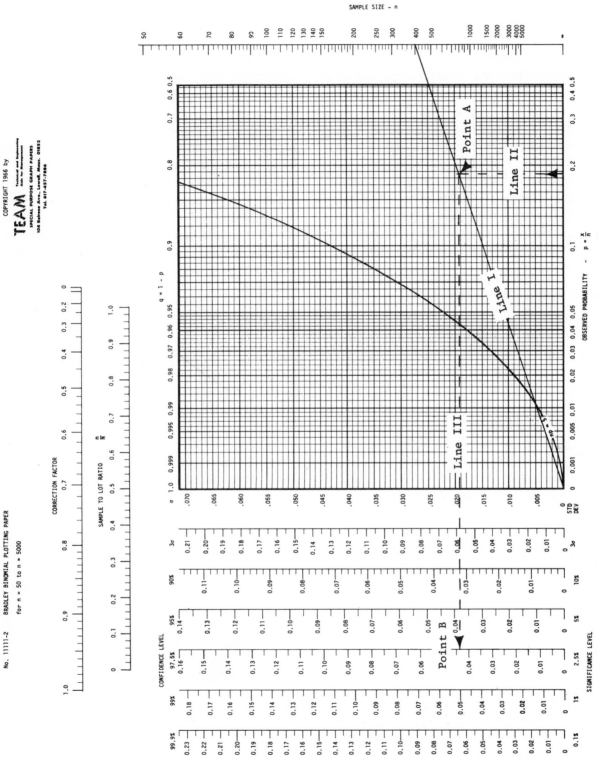

Fig. 21-2.   Prediction of meeting attendance using an observed proportion.

Sixth, Line III at point C indicates that $k\sigma_p = 0.044$.

Seventh, $n \times k\sigma_p = 400 \times 0.044 = 17.6$, say 18.

The 97.5 percent confidence interval is therefore 75 ± 18, or 57 to 93.

Comment: This kind of application has pertinence when refreshments are to be served and it is desired to avoid excessive costs and offense to members. This class of problem has broader scope when applied to cafeteria usage at a school or at an industrial plant; to serving meals on airlines; and to estimating load factors on transportation facilities. One caution is that such estimates are often invalid when special events, rainy days, holidays, and vacation times occur. These situations require independent determination of their own parameters.

Case 2: To determine the correct sample size for a particular evaluation.

Example 21-3
Given: We wish to obtain estimates of the proportion of occurrences with no more than a 4 percent absolute error with 95 percent confidence.
Required: The minimum sample size required to hold the error at or below the desired limiting error with the stated confidence.
Procedure: The method used is the opposite of that for Case 1; that is, we work this class of problem backwards.

First, an absolute error of 4 percent may be stated as $\epsilon = k\sigma_p = 0.04$.

Second, since we wish 4 percent as a *maximum* error under any conditions, we must use the maximum value for σ_p which occurs at $p = 0.5$, since we do not have any stated process average.

Third, in Fig. 21-3, enter the 95 percent confidence scale at a value of 0.04, point A.

Fourth, project A to the right, Line I, until it intersects $p = 0.5$, Line II, point B.

Fifth, draw a line from 0,0 through point B until it intersects the sample-size scale, point C, which is at $n = 600$. Therefore, a sample size of 600 is the minimum sample size which should be used in order to have 95 percent confidence of controlling the error at or below the 4 percent level.
Comment: Many experiments and evaluations wind up in an indeterminate state because sampling

error is allowed to be larger than the effects which one really wishes to measure. To put it differently, we may sometimes be interested in determining if some specific effort has resulted in a desired result. The effort could be a sale, an advertising campaign, a corrective action, or a new process. The desired result would be an increase in business and profits or a reduction in defective production or customer complaints. If some prespecified amount of improvement occurs, then the effort expended would be judged to have been effective. The test error should be smaller than the amount of improvement which we wish to demonstrate. A rough rule of thumb taken from economic considerations is that the error should be less than half of the minimum amount of change to be demonstrated. This is illustrated with some variations in the following examples:

Example 21-4
Given: The sales department of a particular company has a historical average of obtaining contracts for 20 percent of the proposals which they submit to potential customers. A training program was instituted which included instruction in effective writing, proposal preparation, and contract negotiation principles. This program would be considered to be successful if the percentage of contracts obtained increased by a 20 percent margin over the previous results.
Required: The minimum number of additional proposals which must be submitted before a 20 percent increase in acceptance can be demonstrated with 95 percent confidence.
Note: The confidence level scales on Bradley binomial paper are based on symmetrical intervals around the mean of the distribution. That is, a 90 percent confidence interval includes the range of values from the 5 percent to the 95 percent points of the distribution. Therefore, when we are dealing with a one-sided question such as: "How many trials do we need to demonstrate an increase?" a successful demonstration must give a value greater than the value of the 95 percent point. Although we are outside the 90 percent confidence interval, we are also at a value greater than the 95 percent value of the distribution. Consequently,

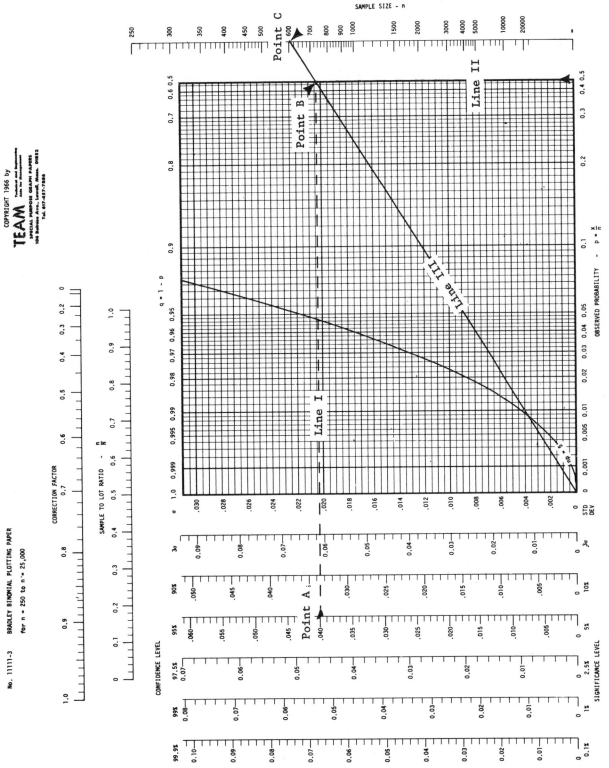

Fig. 21-3.   Determination of the proper sample size required to control experimental error.

we actually have 95 percent or more confidence that an increase has occurred.

Procedure:

First, the required increase to be demonstrated is 20 percent of 20 percent, or 4 percent absolute increase. If the error is to be one-half of 4 percent, then the required $\epsilon = \leq 0.02 = k\sigma_p$.

Second, $p = 0.2$, since this is the established process average.

Third, in Fig. 21-4, enter the 90 percent confidence scale at a value of 0.02, point A, for the reason noted above.

Fourth, project A to the right, Line I, to intersect Line II at B.

Fifth, draw a line from 0,0 through point B to intersect the sample-size scale at point C, which gives a value of 1100.

Comment: Most managers will revolt at a requirement of 1100 observations to demonstrate a point. The simple argument is that a sample of this size takes too long to accumulate. However, under certain circumstances alternative decisions may be determined from the same graph.

Example 21-5

Given: The same situation as in Example 21-4.

Required: The appropriate decision points to demonstrate increases as high as 30 percent, 40 percent, and 50 percent, or absolute increases of 6, 8, and 10 percent.

Procedure:

First, we can now allow ϵ's of 0.03, 0.04, and 0.05.

Second, a $p = 0.2$ is still used as in Example 21-4.

Third, in Fig. 21-4, enter the 90 percent confidence scale at the values 0.03, 0.04, and 0.05.

Fourth, project from each value above, to intersect Line II.

Fifth, draw lines from 0,0 through the intersection of each ϵ line and Line II to the sample-size scale. The required sample sizes to demonstrate the required levels of improvement are 490, 275, and 175 additional proposals, respectively. These results can be interpreted as follows: If p is approximately 0.26 after 490 additional proposals; or, if p is 0.28 after 275 proposals; or, if p is 30 percent af-

ter 175 proposals, then there has been an increase in successful proposal work with 95 percent confidence.

Comment: The same methodology can be applied to the evaluation of decreases in rework, scrap, rejections, and defects after an operations change, process improvement, machine overhaul, or operator training program has been completed.

Case 3: Comparison of two proportions.

Example 21-6

Given: A screw machine operation has had a historical record of producing 0.4 percent defective items. The screw machine was rebuilt. Inspection of the first 3000 parts produced after rebuilding found only 2 defectives.

Required: To determine if rebuilding the machine improved it. Normally, such determinations are based on $\pm 3\sigma$ intervals rather than on the use of percentage confidence intervals.

Procedure:

First, draw the line from 0,0 to $n = 3000$, Line I in Fig. 21-5.

Second, project from the intersection of Line I and $p = 0.004$, Line II, to the 3σ scale and obtain the value of 0.0031 at B.

Third, the $\pm 3\sigma$ interval from an historical basis would then be 0.0040 ± 0.0031, or 0.0009 to 0.0071 for a sample of 3000.

Fourth, the observed $p = \dfrac{2}{3000} = 0.00067$. Since p is less than the historical lower 3σ limit, we are highly confident that rebuilding the machine resulted in a real improvement.

Case 4: Adjustment of parameter estimates for lot depletion.

Example 21-7

Given: A school with 500 students: 200 students are picked at random for a physical fitness test, and 56 students fail it.

Required: Estimates of the results if the entire school were tested and the 99 percent confidence interval for the number of students who would be expected to fail the test. (Use charts in Fig. 21-6.)

Procedure: First,

$$p = \frac{56}{200} = 0.28$$

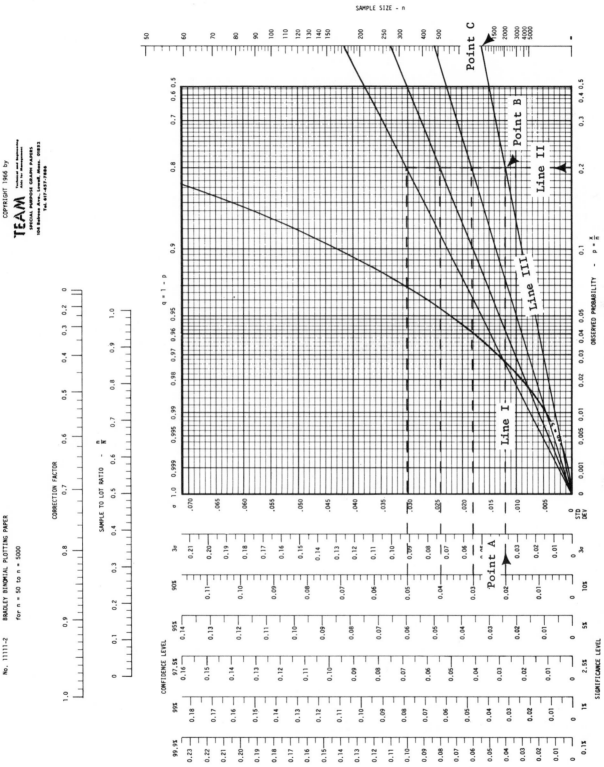

Fig. 21-4.   Evaluation of improvement in contract proposal work.

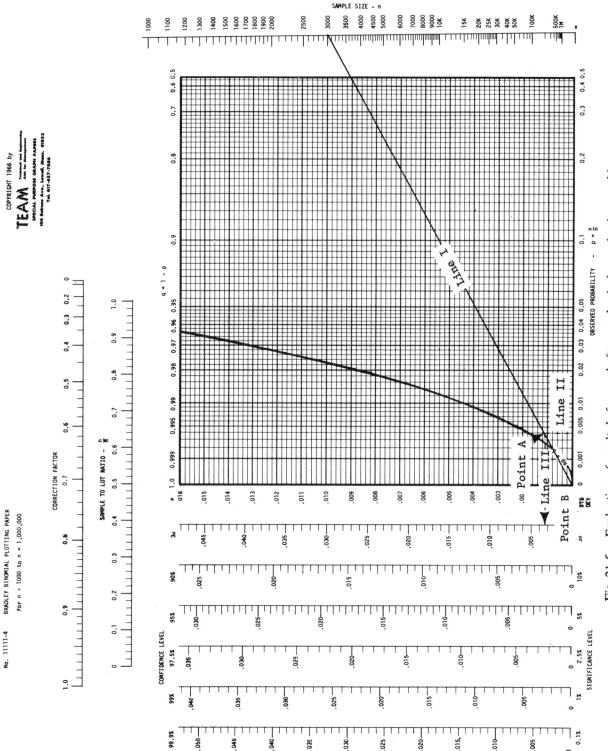

Fig. 21-5. Evaluation of results before and after overhaul of a production machine.

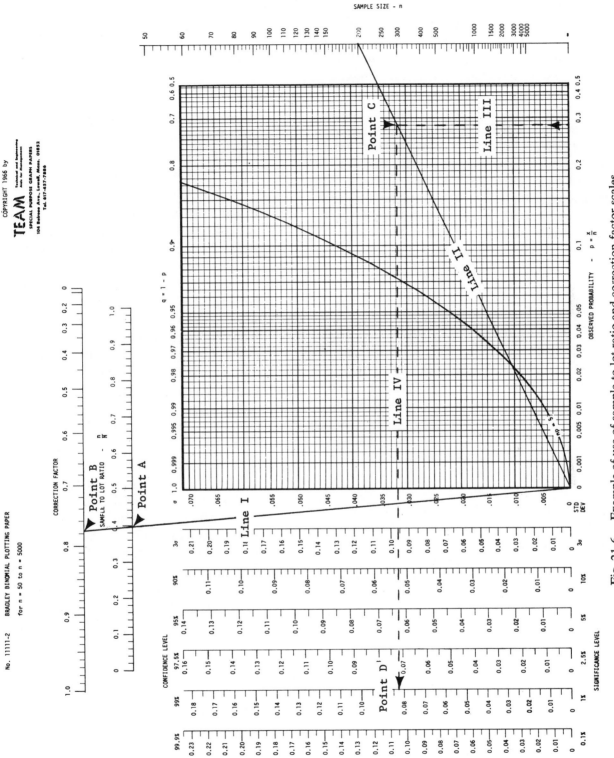

Fig. 21-6.   Example of use of sample-to-lot ratio and correction-factor scales.

Note: In this case of sampling without replacement, we have a fairly limited population, the 500 students in the school. Any one student, who represents a particular score value in the fitness test, is chosen only once, so that the value which he represents does not recur randomly thereafter. In addition, the sample of 200 students represents 40 percent of the total student population for that school. Therefore, the estimate for σ_p requires correction. The correction factor is readily obtained from Bradley binomial plotting paper by use of two auxiliary scales labeled Sample to Lot Ratio and Correction Factor. After the corrected estimate for σ_p is obtained, the remaining procedure is similar to that in Examples 21-1 and 21-2.

Second, determine the sample to lot ratio:

$$\frac{n}{N} = \frac{200}{500} = 0.4$$

Third, draw a line from the origin at 0,0 upward through the value 0.4, point A, on the Sample-to-Lot Ratio Scale and extend this line, Line I, until it intersects the correction factor scale at Point B.

Fourth, draw the line from the origin to $n = 200$, Line II, and find the intersection with $p = 0.28$, Line III, at Point C.

Fifth, project C to the 99 percent confidence scale with Line IV to obtain the value of $k\sigma_p = 0.082$.

Sixth, the sample estimate, $k\sigma_p$, is adjusted by multiplying by the correction factor, 0.775, yielding $0.082 \times 0.775 = 0.064$, which is now the school population estimate, $k\sigma_p'$.

Seventh, the confidence interval is obtained for the school population. In order to accomplish this, we must use $N = 500$:

$$N \times p = 500 \times 0.28 = 140$$

$$N \times k\sigma_p' = 500 \times 0.064 = 32$$

Then, 140 ± 32 gives 108 to 172 for the 99 percent confidence interval of the number of students in the entire school who would fail to pass the physical fitness test.

Exercises

21-1. Obtain the required confidence intervals for the following proportion:
   a. 18/55 at 90 percent
   b. 26/69 at 95 percent
   c. 40/76 at 99 percent

21-2. In a city of 75,000 population, 166 cases of death due to lung cancer occurred in a single year. What is the 95 percent confidence interval for expected deaths in future years?

21-3. We wish to obtain estimates of an unknown proportion with no more than a 1 percent absolute error with 95 percent confidence. What is the minimum sample size required to hold the error at or below the desired limit with the required confidence?

21-4. Use the data of Exercise 20-2. Consider the first city as the norm. Is the death rate in the second city significantly different at the 3σ level?

21-5. In a high school with 476 seniors, 125 members of the senior class are chosen at random to take a special college aptitude test. There were 85 students who were considered to have achieved satisfactory, or better, scores on the test. If the entire senior class were tested, what is the 95 percent confidence interval for the number of students who would be expected to achieve the satisfactory level, or better?

CHAPTER 22

Engineering and Other Applications of Binomial Plotting Paper

Introduction

Some interesting and useful applications of binomial plotting papers have been developed by Dr. P. S. Olmstead. His major contribution is a fine tutorial paper, "Stochastic Evaluation of Reliability" (42). As a result of this paper, special formats of binomial plotting papers were recommended to facilitate the evaluation of high reliability, that is, low-failure-rate systems and components. The types of data most susceptible to such analysis are usually derived from life tests or system operational data.

In previous uses of the binomial function, we have dealt largely with the analysis of binomial proportions and their relationship to one another or to some standard or expected proportion. In the analysis of binomial proportions there is an important assumption which was not stated: the sample data so analyzed comes from stable, or consistent, processes which are generally assumed to be in a reasonable state of control.

In the case of stochastic, or continuous, evaluation of reliability, there is a different assumption. This assumption is that high-reliability components or systems are usually subject to repeated improvements and refinements. This eliminates the assumption of a stable process. As a result of continued improvement, high-reliability products should show continual improvement until some optimum is reached. This condition is sometimes called *product maturity*. After product maturity is achieved, then it is possible to revert to an assumption of a stable process.

Binomial Plotting Paper for Stochastic Evaluation

Binomial plotting papers for stochastic evaluation are square-root ruled, as are regular binomial

plotting papers. The basic difference is that a small number range is used for the c scale and a large number range for the n scale. A typical example of scale combinations is illustrated in Fig. 22-1 with a c scale range of 20 and an n scale of 1,000,000. This set of scales permits evaluation of failure rates of 0.002 percent, or less. Lines which represent equal failure rates for cumulatively plotted data are simply radials starting at the origin and terminating at the upper or right-hand edge of the grid. Radials are illustrated in Fig. 22-1 for values of 0.005, 0.002, 0.001, and 0.0005 percent. If plotted data tend to cross and recross any one of these lines, then the value of that line would be the demonstrated failure rate.

A special use of radials is developed from a recommendation of the Darnell Report (9). The recommendation was that reliability testing and evaluation be conducted in such a way as to answer the question: "What is the demonstrated failure rate with 90 percent confidence?" This is readily accomplished by constructing radials through the point which represents the 90 percent confidence bound which is located at the lower left corner of the binomial plotting paper. The radials are constructed parallel to the position which they would have if constructed through the origin by the use of parallel rules or triangles. A set of relocated radials is illustrated in Fig. 22-2 for the same values which were used in Fig. 22-1.

The freehand line A drawn in Fig. 22-2 is representative of the cumulative behavior of a high-reliability product which has been successfully subject to failure analysis and corrective action feedback. The net result is a period of continued improvement. Improvement is usually indicated by the plotted data successively crossing the radials

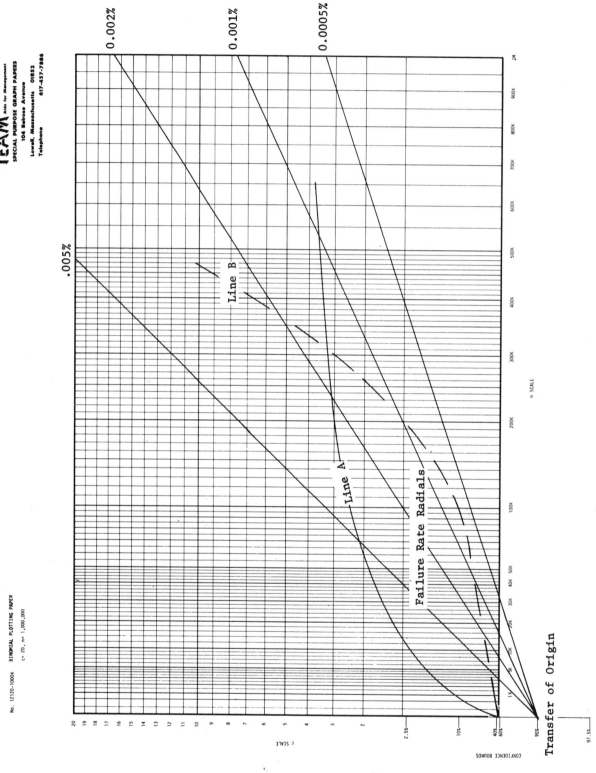

Fig. 22-1. Example of a binomial plotting paper adapted for the stochastic evaluation of data.

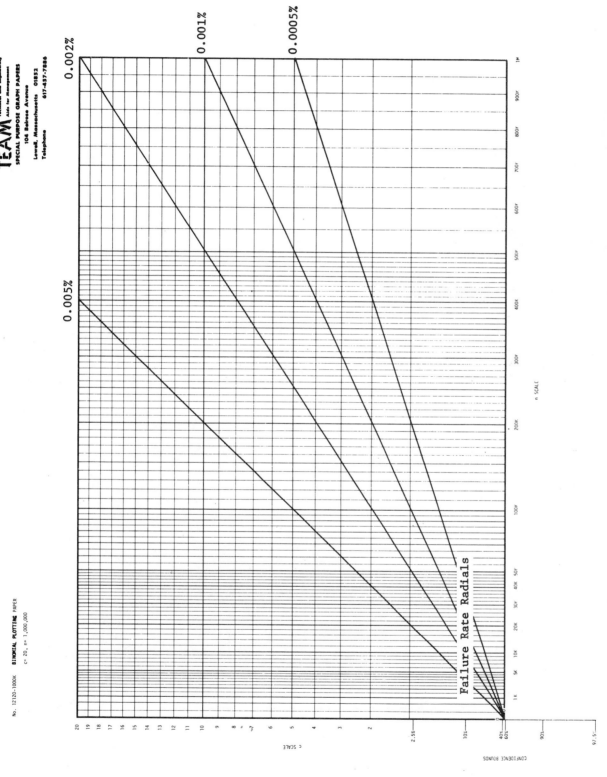

Fig. 22-2.   Example of binomial plotting paper with 90 percent confidence radials.

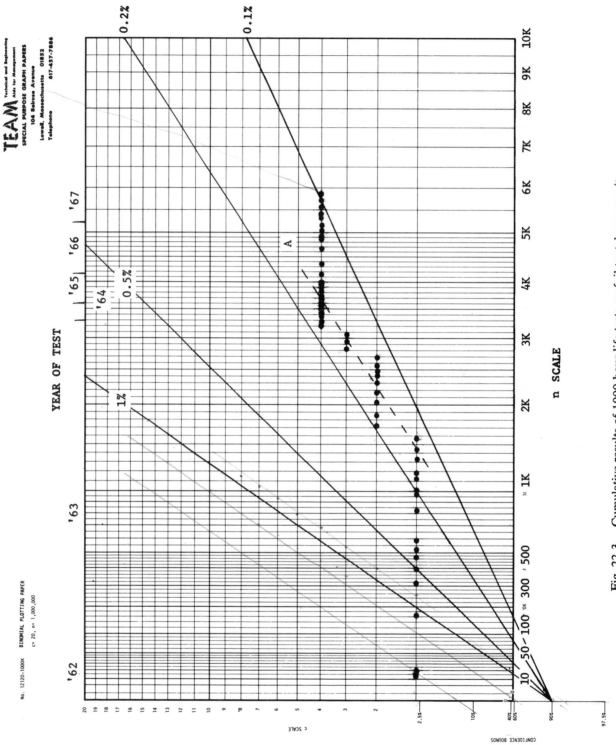

Fig. 22-3.   Cumulative results of 1000-hour life tests on foil tantalum capacitors.

in a left–to–right direction. Conversely, the free-hand line, *B*, is representative of a product which is getting worse with time; indicated by crossing radials from bottom to top.

Using Binomial Plotting Paper
for Stochastic Evaluation

As data are obtained from successive lot tests, we accumulate information in terms of the number of failures per test, c_i, and the sample size per lot, n_i, where i is $1, 2, 3, \ldots$, representing the successive lot samples. For stochastic binomial plotting, the data are cumulated by adding the results of each lot to the total of all preceding plots. In the case of the failure counts, c_i, we plot $(c_i + 1)$. The 1 is added because binomial data with a small value of p are distributed approximately as chi-square with $2(c + 1)$ degrees of freedom. Failure rate is obtained from $2(c + 1)/2n$ so that plotting of the cumulative test results is a graphical demonstration of the achieved failure rate at any point in time. The plotted data representing failure in combination with properly relocated radials permit direct statements about a demonstrated failure rate at a specified confidence level without additional computation.

Example 22-1

Given: The data of Table 22-1 for the results of 1000–hour life tests conducted on foil tantalum capacitors.

Table 22-1. Results of Life Tests on Tantalum Capacitors Operated at 85°C and Rated Voltage for 1000 Hours

Lot No.	No. Tested	Cum. No. Tested	No. Failed (c)	Cum. (c+1)
1	15	15	0	1
2	2	17	0	1
3	150	167	0	1
4	150	317	0	1
5	75	392	0	1
6	75	467	0	1
7	50	517	0	1
8	150	667	0	1
9	150	817	0	1
10	150	967	0	1
11	150	1117	0	1
12	75	1192	0	1
13	150	1342	0	1
14	75	1417	0	1
15	150	1567	0	1

Table 22-1 (Continued).

Lot No.	No. Tested	Cum. No. Tested	No. Failed (c)	Cum. (c+1)
16	(Not used)			
17	150	1717	1	2
18	150	1867	0	2
19	150	2017	0	2
20	150	2167	0	2
21	150	2317	0	2
22	75	2392	0	2
23	75	2467	0	2
24	75	2542	0	2
25	150	2692	0	2
26	150	2842	1	3
27	75	2917	0	3
28	150	3067	0	3
29	150	3217	1	4
30	75	3292	0	4
31	80	3372	0	4
32	50	3422	0	4
33	75	3497	0	4
34	32	3529	0	4
35	50	3579	0	4
36	50	3629	0	4
37	50	3679	0	4
38	50	3729	0	4
39	80	3809	0	4
40	80	3889	0	4
41	50	3939	0	4
42	32	3971	0	4
43	200	4171	0	4
44	315	4686	0	4
45	200	4886	0	4
46	50	4936	0	4
47	125	5061	0	4
48	125	5186	0	4
49	125	5311	0	4
50	125	5436	0	4
51	125	5561	0	4
52	125	5686	0	4
53	125	5811	0	4

Required: Plot and interpret the data.

Procedure:

Step 1. Table 22-1 shows the cumulative total of failures plus 1 and the cumulative total of samples tested.

Step 2. The data are plotted in Fig. 22-3 as well as the 90 percent confidence radials for 1.0, 0.5, 0.2, and 0.1 percent. The addition of 1 to obtain $(c + 1)$ tends to bias the data initially, until a sufficient quantity of items is tested to produce the first real failure which is plotted at $(c + 1) = (1 + 1) = 2$, after about 1750 units.

Comment 1: For the next 2000 units tested, the failure rate is approximately that of the dashed line, *A*, which is nearly parallel to the 0.2 percent radial. During this period of very active procurement, which lasted about a year, the process which produced these parts would be judged as quite stable. However, since that period the product appears to show improvement. The improvement is deduced from the succession of points at $(c + 1) = 4$ which has crossed the 0.1 percent radial in a left-to-right direction.

Comment 2: This plot exemplifies three important points in testing. First, the portion of the plot along $(c + 1) = 1$ tells us that we really do not know very much. This is largely because we have not observed sufficient test results to have real information. Second, the portion of the plot typified by the dashed line, *A*, is quite typical of a heavy production phase. Materials, methods, and procedures tend to be maintained in a status quo configuration, particularly if there are no customer complaints forthcoming, and, in this case, there were no customer complaints. Third, the latter portion of the plot is indicative of the pattern which characterizes at least two important situations. A heavy production period can develop a lot of worthwhile experience and expertise which is often implemented in a subsequent period when activity eases off. This kind of pattern can also occur from the emergence of new technology, particularly in materials and processes. In the case illustrated, both of the preceding kinds of situations actually occurred.

Comment 3: Since the tests developing this data were of 1000-hour duration, the observed failure rate on the binomial plot can also be stated as 0.1%/1000 hours at 90 percent confidence. If the appropriate derating factors for this part in a specific use condition are known, then the observed test failure rate can be converted to a use failure rate simply by dividing the observed test failure rate by the established derating factor.

Starting a New Plot
after Test Experience Is Developed

There are times when the accumulated test experience results in a large amount of data such that a plot then exceeds the dimensions of the paper which is used for plotting. In such a situation, it becomes necessary to start a plot on a new sheet of plotting paper. Obviously, one could start from scratch and initiate a totally new plot. This would practically ignore the accumulated results up to that point. The accumulated results can be used advantageously to initiate such a new plot. When the plot merely "runs off" the paper, there is no need to wait for some initial period until a "real" failure occurs as was shown in the first part of the plot of Fig. 22-3. Instead, one can use the achieved test level to initiate a new plot which utilizes the accumulated test results up to the point where the plot runs off the paper. A new plot is derived from an old plot by using the currently demonstrated failure rate under conditions which are equivalent to assuming that one failure has occurred. This is easily done by using the values represented by the intercept of the demonstrated failure rate line and the line $(c + 1) = 2$.

Example 22-2
Given: The data of Table 22-2 for the results of 1000-hour life tests on film dielectric capacitors. At Lot 22, the plot exceeds the limits of the dimensions of the plotting paper.

Table 22-2. Results of Life Tests on Film Dielectric Capacitors Operated at 85°C and 150% Rated Voltage; 100-Hour Testing to Lot 29; 250 Hours Subsequently

Lot No.	No. Tested	Cum. No. Tested	No. Failed (c)	Cum. (c+1)
1	10	10	0	1
2	10	20	0	1
3	75	95	0	1
4	70	165	0	1
5	35	200	0	1
6	35	235	1	2
7	50	285	0	2
8	35	320	0	2
9	10	330	0	2
10	35	365	0	2
11	35	400	0	2
12	10	410	0	2
13	35	445	2	4
14	35	480	1	5
15	35	515	0	5
16	10	525	0	5
17	270	795	2	7
18	10	805	0	7
19	10	815	0	7

Table 22-2 (Continued).

Lot No.	No. Tested	Cum. No. Tested	No. Failed (c)	Cum. (c+1)
20	32	847	0	7
21	8	855	0	7
22	270	1125	1	8
Restart:		330	2	2
23	270	600	1	3
24	32	632	0	3
25	32	664	0	3
26	32	696	0	3
27	8	704	0	3
28	32	736	1	4
29	32	768	0	4
Start:		330	2	2
30	32	362	1	3
31	32	394	0	3
32	8	402	0	3
33	32	434	0	3
34	32	466	0	3
35	32	498	0	3
36	32	530	0	3
37	32	562	0	3
38	8	570	0	3
39	32	602	0	3
40	32	634	1	4
41	8	642	0	4
42	32	674	0	4
43	50	724	0	4
44	270	994	0	4
45	50	1044	0	4
46	32	1076	0	4
47	32	1108	0	4
48	32	1140	0	4
49	50	1190	0	4
50	270	1460	0	4
51	32	1492	0	4
52	32	1524	0	4
53	50	1574	1	5
54	32	1606	0	5
55	32	1638	0	5
56	32	1670	0	5
57	32	1702	2	7
58	32	1734	0	7
59	32	1766	0	7
60	32	1798	0	7
61	270	2068	0	7
62	50	2118	0	7
63	50	2168	0	7
64	32	2200	0	7
65	50	2250	0	7

Required: Restart the plot, using the accumulated results at this point.

Procedure:

Step 1. Plot the results up to Lot 21 where the plot runs off the paper, Fig. 22-4.

Step 2. At Lot 21, the plot approaches the 1.0 percent radial, at A. Use this radial as an approximation of the achieved failure rate.

Step 3. Follow the 1.0 percent radial backwards to the point where it crosses the line $(c + 1) = 2$. This has the coordinates of $n = 330$ and $(c + 1) = 2$. Therefore, start the new plot at 330, 2, point B.

Step 4. The data for Lot 22 and subsequent lots must be added cumulatively to the values obtained in Step 3. For convenience, it is desirable to make these values the first two entries in the cumulative $(c + 1)$ and n columns of the data table. This entry is shown in Table 22-2. Subsequent data are now cumulated from the coordinate values of 330, 2.

Step 5. The continuation of the data and the 90 percent radials are now plotted in Fig. 22-5.

Starting a New Plot When Test Conditions Are Changed

Another reason which can lead to the need to restart a plot is when the conditions under which certain tests are being conducted are changed for some reason. If the test conditions are changed, one expects apparently better results if the test conditions are made less stringent and worse results if test conditions are made more stringent. In either case, it is advantageous to restart the plot from the currently achieved level and to observe the direction of change which occurs under the new test conditions. The restart of a plot, if test conditions change, is made in the same way as when a plot runs off the grid.

Example 22-3
Given: The data of Table 22-2. At Lot 30, the duration of the life test is reduced to 250 hours.
Required: Restart the plot of Fig. 22-5 and plot the 250-hour life test results.
Procedure: Steps 1 through 5 as in Example 22-2 except by starting with the results of Lot 30. Results are plotted in Fig. 22-6, starting with point C which is derived from Fig. 22-5, similarly to B in Fig. 22-4.

Comment: The data for the 250-hour life test approach and cross the 0.5 percent failure rate line

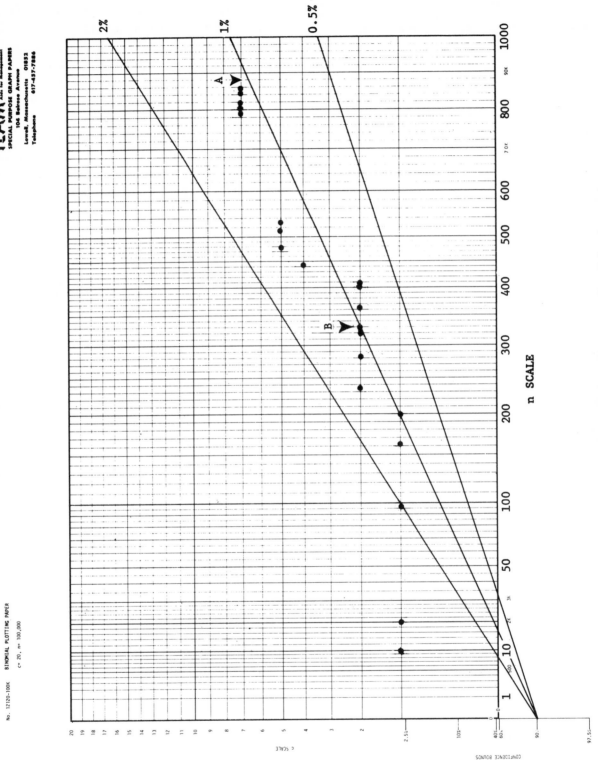

Fig. 22-4.   Cumulative results of 1000-hour life tests on film dielectric capacitors.

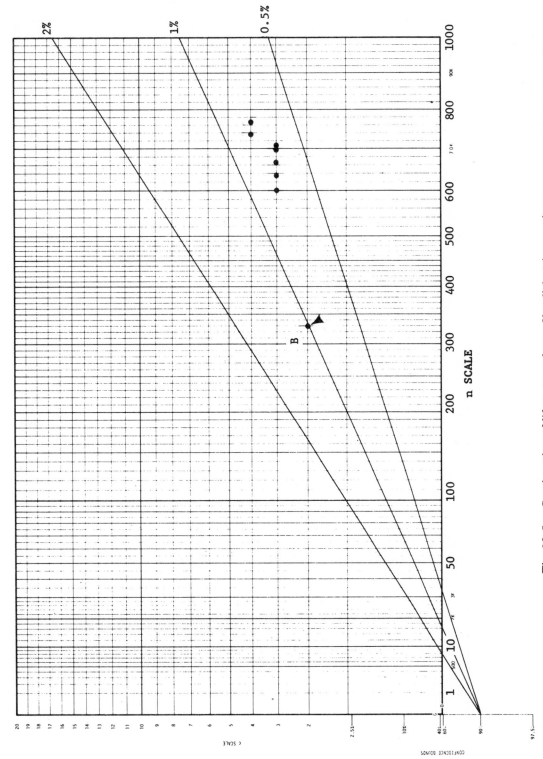

Fig. 22-5.   Continuation of life-test results on film dielectric capacitors.

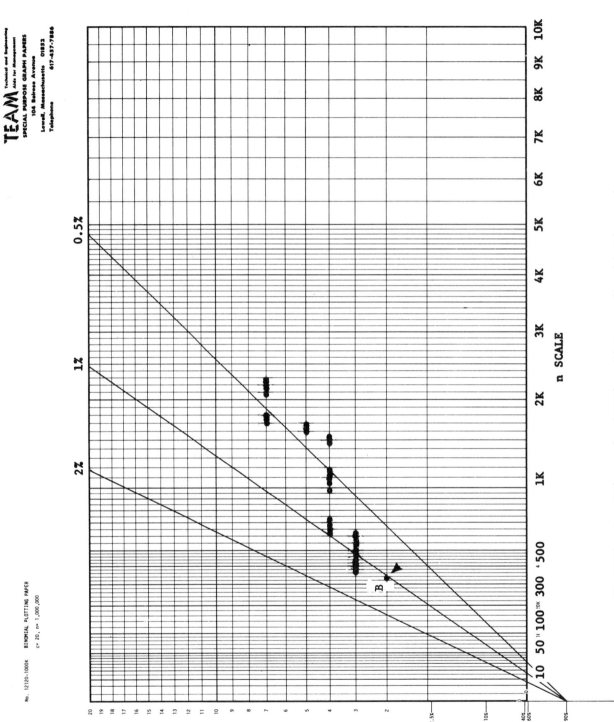

Fig. 22-6.   Cumulative results of 250-hour life tests on film dielectric capacitors.

so that there is some evidence of a reduction of the *test* failure rate. The failure rate of the parts does not change. The test time duration was reduced by a factor of 4 and the test failure rate has apparently been reduced by about a factor 2. It has been observed that test failure rates of high-reliability electronic components tend to increase in approximate proportion to the square root of the time exposure. Therefore, with the time decreased to 1/4 of the initial test time, then the test failure rate should decrease by about $\sqrt{1/4}$, or 1/2, which is just about what happened in this example.

This generalization permits comparison of test results with varying durations.

Modification of an Existing Plot
Based on Test Experience

From time to time, things just do not go as planned and subsequent results are drastically worse than anticipated. Unexpected bad results lead to crash programs of redesign, redefinition of processes, modified operating criteria, and/or specific corrective actions. Then the problem arises in answering the question, "Did the crash program work?"

Example 22-4
Given: The data of Table 22-3 for the results of life tests on a miniature tantalum capacitor. The fourth

Table 22-3. Results of Life Tests on Miniature Tantalum Capacitors Operated at 85°C and Rated Voltage

Lot No.	No. Tested	Cum. No. Tested	No. Failed (c)	Cum. ($c+1$)	Adjusted No. Failed	Cum. ($c+1$)
1	225	225	1	2	...	...
2	225	450	1	3	...	...
3	300	750	0	3	...	...
4	300	1050	29	32	1	4
5	150	1200	1	33	1	5
6	225	1425	0	33	0	5
7	150	1575	1	34	1	6
8	300	1875	0	34	0	6
9	200	2075	0	34	0	6
10	200	2275	1	35	1	7
11	125	2400	0	35	0	7
12	315	2715	0	35	0	7
13	300	3015	1	36	1	8
14	315	3330	0	36	0	8
15	315	3645	0	36	0	8
16	315	3960	0	36	0	8
17	315	4275	0	36	0	8
Restart (0.3%) 1400				2		
18	200	1600	0	2	...	...
19	300	1900	0	2	...	...
20	315	2215	0	2	...	...
21	200	2415	0	2	...	...
22	315	2730	0	2	...	...
23	300	3030	0	2	...	...
24	315	3345	0	2	...	...
25	200	3545	0	2	...	...
26	315	3860	0	2	...	...
27	315	4175	2	4	...	...
28	200	4375	0	4	...	...
29	315	4690	0	4	...	...
30	300	4990	0	4	...	...
31	200	5190	0	4	...	...
32	315	5505	1	5	...	...

lot tested was a virtual disaster; 29 failures occurred in a sample of 300 when only 1 failure was normally allowed. This result led to several specific corrective actions which were to be evaluated by subsequent testing.

Required: Analysis of the effects of the corrective actions.

Procedure:

Step 1. Table 22-3 shows the cumulation of samples and the number of failures occurring through Lot 17.

Step 2. The data of Table 22-3 are shown plotted in Fig. 22-7. The results of Lot 4 cause a large shift in the level of the observed test failure rate.

Comment 1: Results from Lot 5 forward, become almost flat and show the left-to-right traversal which is indicative of improvement. One useful criterion for determining if real improvement has occurred is to observe the results of at least ten additional lots. If there is no recurrence of serious failure, then there is about 95 percent confidence that the problem which caused the results of Lot 4 has been corrected.

Comment 2: After deciding that real improvement has occurred, the data may be adjusted in order to reflect the actual state of affairs more closely. In the present example, the data are adjusted by treating Lot 4 as though it had only *one* failure. This is to recognize that failure has occurred in Lot 4 but that the cause(s) of gross discrepancies have been corrected.

Step 3. After assigning one failure to Lot 4, the subsequent results are recomputed and replotted. The computations are shown in Table 22-3 and the replot in Fig. 22-7, as crosses.

Step 4. The demonstrated failure rate on this adjusted basis is now found to be about 0.3 percent instead of 1.0 percent.

Step 5. At Lot 18, the duration of life tests for this part was reduced to 250 hours from 1000 hours, so that it is necessary to restart the plot. Following the procedure of Example 22-3, the starting points are obtained from the 0.3 percent line and the $c = 2$ line as $c = 2$ and $n = 1400$, point *A*, Fig. 22-7. The subsequent cumulation of data is shown in Table 22-3.

Step 6. The 250-hour life test data are plotted in Fig. 22-8.

Comment 3: These data show a decrease of failure rate to between 0.1 percent and 0.2 percent which is again about half of the previously demonstrated test failure rate level.

Comment 4: This example shows a method of analyzing the effects of corrective action(s). In this case, the corrective actions which were taken were demonstrably effective. In addition, the effect of changes in test conditions was further demonstrated.

Corrective Actions Are Not Always Favorable

The following example illustrates the case that not all so-called corrective actions are improvements:

Example 22-5

Given: The data of Table 22-4 for results of an immersion and moisture resistance test which was

Table 22-4. Result of Immersion and Moisture Resistance Tests Followed by 250-Hour Life Test on Ceramic Capacitor Operated at Rated Condition

Lot No.	No. Tested	Cum. No. Tested	No. Failed (c)	Cum. (c+1)
1	150	150	0	1
2	500	650	1	2
3	150	800	1	3
4	150	950	0	3
5	500	1450	0	3
6	300	1750	2	5
7	300	2050	0	5
8	200	2250	2	7
9	300	2550	0	7
10	300	2850	0	7
11	300	3150	0	7
12	300	3450	1	8
13	300	3750	0	8
14	200	3950	0	8
15	300	4250	0	8
16	150	4400	0	8
17	300	4700	2	10
18	300	5000	3	13
19	500	5500	1	14
20	200	5700	0	14
21	150	5850	0	14
22	150	6000	3	17
23	150	6150	2	19
24	100	6250	1	20
25	150	6400	11	31
26	100	6500	5	36
27	150	6650	7	43

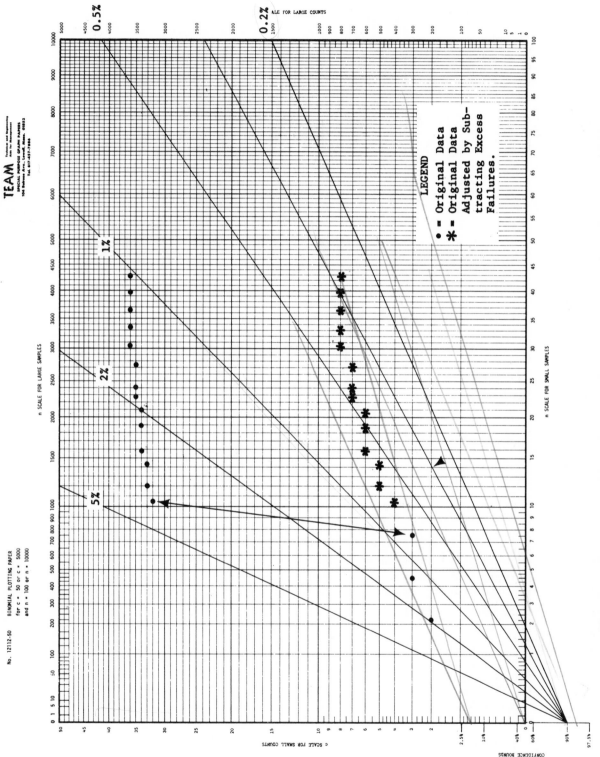

Fig. 22-7.   Cumulative results of 1000-hour life tests on miniature solid tantalum capacitors.

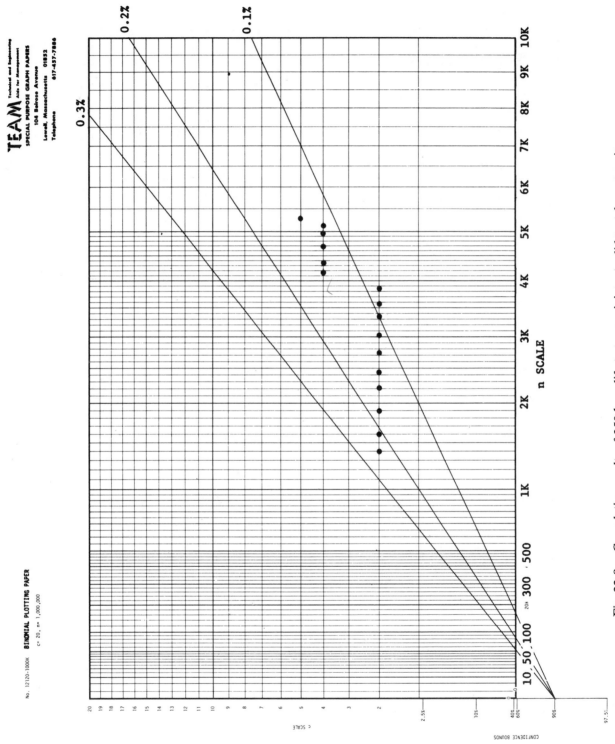

Fig. 22-8.   Cumulative results of 250-hour life tests on miniature solid tantalum capacitors.

followed by a short life test on a family of ceramic capacitors.

Required: Plot and interpret the results.

Procedure:

Steps 1 and 2 as for Example 22-1. Results are plotted in Fig. 22-9.

Step 3. This plot crosses the radials from left to right which is taken to indicate improvement with time. Results accumulate until the 0.3 percent line is crossed. After this point, the plot becomes increasingly steeper and recrosses increasingly higher radials up to nearly 0.6 percent failure. There is reason to believe that this process has become worse for some reason.

Comment 1: Investigation of these results disclosed that the manufacturer of these parts introduced a new ceramic formulation, beginning with Lot 18, point *A*. The new formulation was intended as a corrective action for problems which had purportedly been identified through detailed failure analysis of parts which had failed to meet test requirements in earlier tests. The plot of Fig. 22-9 demonstrates quite dramatically that the corrective action was not effective.

Comment 2: To make matters worse, the manufacturer then introduced a "new improved formulation" at Lot 25. The apparent increase in failure rate was accelerated by the additional change.

An Application of Binomial Plotting to Sports Data

The preceding examples of applications of binomial plotting have all been derived from a very narrow area which is the testing of high-reliability electronic capacitors. The examples presented were chosen for two reasons:

1. The examples illustrated important industrial types of applications.

2. The author was acquainted with the important peripheral details.

However, lest the reader be misled into thinking that one must have test data to develop interesting and informative applications of binomial plotting, we return to sports data to illustrate the great generality of binomial plotting in the analysis of dynamic processes.

Within the period of any given sports season, there are reasons to expect stochastic behavior of sports performance. There is an underlying continuity within the duration of any given season. The performance of teams and individual players depends on both the present and the cumulative effect of many random variables. These variables include weather conditions, time of day, playing conditions, officials, coaching, and lineups from an overall team standpoint; and health, immediately prior activities, personal talent, motivation, and attitude from a player standpoint. On the basis of such assumptions, there are strong grounds to consider the potential of stochastic methods of evaluation of the record of sports results. Some interesting sports examples were presented in Chapter 20. To further emphasize the point, some additional and interrelated examples of one individual's performance are presented below.

Example 22-6

Given: Carl Yastrzemski's batting record for the 1968 baseball season. At-bats and base hits for each game as well as the cumulative totals for the batting data are given by game in Table 22-5.

Required: Plot and interpret the results.

Procedure:

Step 1. The data of Table 22-5 are plotted in Fig. 22-10.

Note: Scales are modified to accommodate the range of the data more conveniently. The vertical scale is multiplied by 10 and the horizontal scale is divided by 100.

Step 2. Yastrzemski's season's batting average of 0.301 is drawn through the data.

Step 3. The confidence bounds are adjusted by dividing the distance from 0 to the 2.5 percent and 97.5 percent point by $\sqrt{10}$. The adjusted points are indicated by *A* and *A'*. This adjusts the 95 percent confidence interval to the modified vertical scale. The 95 percent confidence interval is shown as a dashed line.

Interpretation: On an overall cumulative basis, Yastrzemski batted all through the season in a way which was consistent with his final batting average of 0.301 with 95 percent confidence. However,

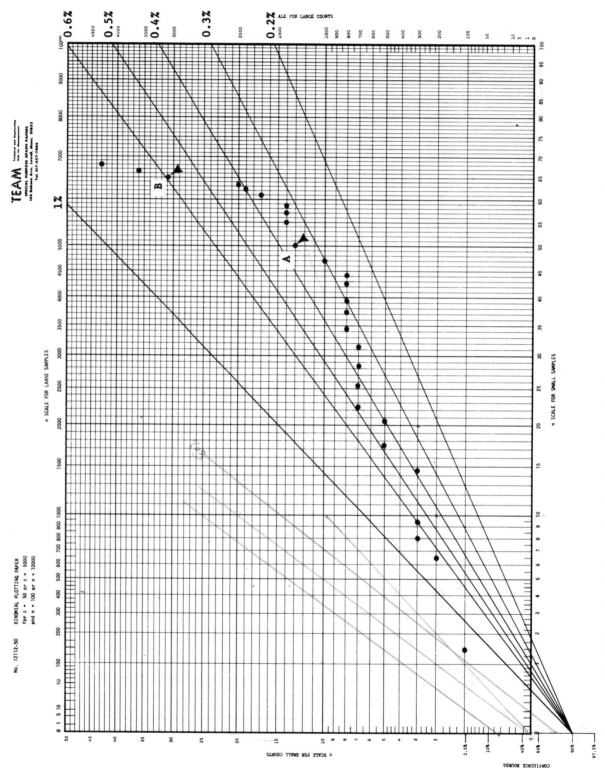

Fig. 22-9.   Cumulative results of an immersion and moisture resistance test followed by a 100-hour life test.

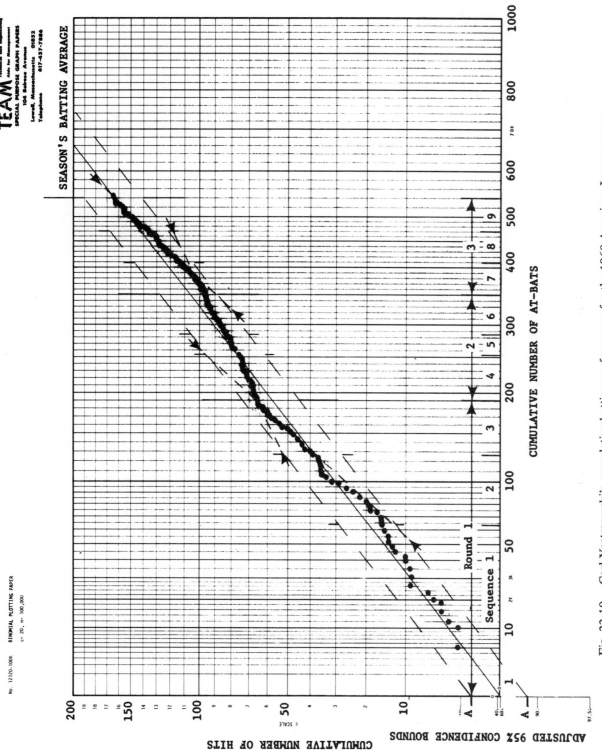

Fig. 22-10.   Carl Yastrzemski's cumulative batting performance for the 1968 American League season.

Table 22-5. Yastrzemski's Batting Record for the 1968 American League Season.*

Game No.	AB	Cum. AB	H	Cum. H	TB	Game No.	AB	Cum. AB	H	Cum. H	TB	Game No.	AB	Cum. AB	H	Cum. H	TB
1	5	–	2	–	8	55	2	191	0	64	0	109	4	344	0	95	0
2	5	10	0	2	0	56	3	194	1	65	1	110	2	346	1	96	4
3	2	12	1	3	4	57	5	199	3	68	6	111	4	350	1	97	2
4	3	15	1	4	1	58	3	202	0	68	0	112	4	354	0	97	0
5	4	19	0	4	0	59	2	204	0	68	0	113	3	357	1	98	2
6	1	20	1	5	4	60	1	205	0	68	0	114	2	359	1	99	1
7	3	23	1	6	1	61	4	209	0	68	0	115	7	366	0	99	0
8	4	27	3	9	5	62	2	211	0	68	0	116	3	369	1	100	1
9	4	31	0	9	0	63	2	213	1	69	3	117	2	371	0	100	0
10	4	35	0	9	0	64	5	218	1	70	2	118	4	375	1	101	1
11	5	40	1	10	1	65	0	218	0	70	0	119	4	379	2	103	3
12	2	42	0	10	0	66	3	221	1	71	1	120	4	383	1	104	1
13	4	46	2	12	3	67	3	224	0	71	0	121	3	386	1	105	1
14	3	49	1	13	1	68	4	228	0	71	0	122	4	390	1	106	1
15	3	52	1	14	1	69	3	231	2	73	2	123	6	396	1	107	1
16	4	56	0	14	0	70	3	234	0	73	0	124	4	400	3	110	3
17	4	60	1	15	1	71	3	237	0	73	0	125	4	404	2	112	3
18	4	64	1	16	1	72	4	241	0	73	0	126	4	408	0	112	0
19	4	68	0	16	0	73	1	242	0	73	0	127	2	410	1	113	1
20	2	70	0	16	0	74	2	244	0	73	0	128	3	413	2	115	2
21	3	73	1	17	1	75	5	249	1	74	1	129	4	417	2	117	2
22	3	76	2	19	2	76	2	251	1	75	1	130	4	421	3	120	4
23	3	79	0	19	0	77	3	254	1	76	2	131	7	428	2	122	5
24	4	83	1	20	1	78	4	258	1	77	1	132	3	431	1	123	2
25	3	86	2	22	2	79	4	262	1	78	4	133	5	436	2	125	2
26	4	90	2	24	2	80	3	265	2	80	5	134	3	439	1	126	4
27	4	94	3	27	4	81	4	269	0	80	0	135	3	442	2	128	2
28	4	98	2	29	3	82	4	273	0	80	0	136	3	445	0	128	0
29	3	101	3	32	4	83	3	276	0	80	0	137	4	449	0	128	0
30	3	104	1	33	1	84	4	280	1	81	2	138	3	452	2	130	5
31	3	107	1	34	2	85	2	282	0	81	0	139	4	456	0	130	0
32	4	111	1	35	1	86	–	——	–	——	–	140	0	456	0	130	0
33	2	113	0	35	0	87	–	——	–	——	–	141	5	461	4	134	7
34	3	116	0	35	0	88	–	——	–	——	–	142	1	462	0	134	0
35	5	121	1	36	1	89	–	——	–	——	–	143	4	466	2	136	6
36	3	124	0	36	0	90	3	285	0	81	0	144	4	470	0	136	0
37	4	128	3	39	4	91	3	288	1	82	1	145	5	475	2	138	2
38	6	134	3	42	6	92	4	292	1	83	2	146	4	479	3	141	3
39	4	138	1	43	1	93	3	295	0	83	0	147	5	484	4	145	6
40	4	142	1	44	1	94	0	295	0	83	0	148	4	488	1	146	1
41	4	146	2	46	5	95	–	——	–	——	–	149	2	490	1	147	4
42	4	150	3	49	5	96	4	299	1	84	1	150	4	494	1	148	1
43	3	153	1	50	2	97	4	303	1	85	1	151	2	496	1	149	1
44	4	157	2	52	3	98	3	306	0	85	0	152	4	500	2	151	4
45	3	160	1	53	4	99	3	309	3	88	6	153	3	503	1	152	1
46	5	165	4	57	4	100	2	311	2	90	2	154	4	507	3	155	6
47	3	168	2	59	5	101	5	316	1	91	2	155	4	511	1	156	1
48	3	171	1	60	1	102	4	320	0	91	0	156	4	515	0	156	0
49	3	174	0	60	0	103	4	324	1	92	1	157	7	522	1	157	1
50	3	177	1	61	1	104	3	327	1	93	1	158	4	526	2	159	5
51	3	180	0	61	0	105	3	330	0	93	0	159	3	529	1	160	1
52	4	184	2	63	5	106	3	333	1	94	1	160	4	533	2	162	6
53	2	186	1	64	4	107	2	335	0	94	0	161	1	534	0	162	0
54	3	189	0	64	0	108	5	340	1	95	1	162	5	539	0	162	0

* *Note:* AB — Times at Bat; H — No. of Hits; TB — Total Bases.

there were two periods during which the plotted points obviously had slopes steeper than the line for the season's average. These are indicated by short dashed lines. The steeper slopes represent periods of a batting performance better than the season's average. These periods covered sequences

2–3 and 8–9. There was another period which had an obvious slope less steep than the season's average which indicated poorer batting performance than the season's average. This poorer period is also shown in Fig. 22-10 as a dashed line through sequences 4–6.

Comment: Subsequent investigation of the periods of different slope led to the definition of a *round*. In the present 10-team league, each team plays each other team 18 times on an almost round-robin basis. There is a complete cycle of home-and-home exchanges every 54 games, more or less, which we will call a round. It is of interest to note that each period of better or poorer batting performance was within one 54-game round. There-

fore, it should be informative to look at batting performance within each round as an independent set of data. This is done in the following example using the data in Table 22-5.

Example 22-7
Given: Yastrzemski's batting record in Table 22-5. This table is presented in three parts, each representing 54-game rounds.
Required: Plot and interpret the results of each 54-game round.

Procedure:
Step 1. The data from each column of Table 22-5 are plotted independently, using $(c + 1)$ for hits, as in Fig. 22-11, *A*, *B*, and *C*.

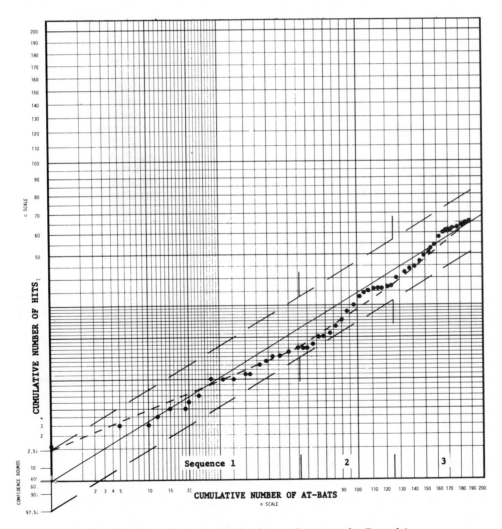

Fig. 22-11A. Yastrzemski's batting performance for Round 1.

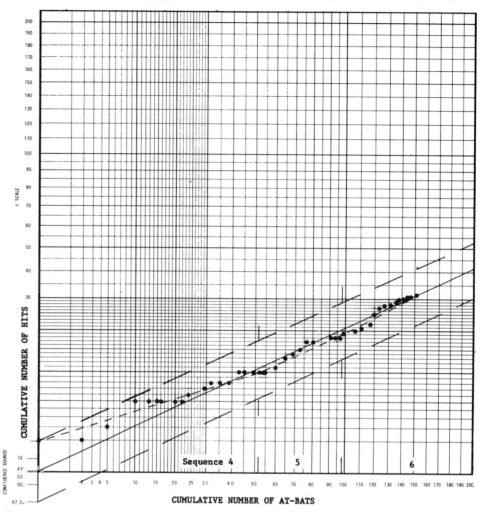

Fig. 22-11B.   Yastrzemski's batting performance for Round 2.

Step 2. The batting average for each round is drawn in simply by connecting the origin and the last point plotted.

Step 3. The 95 percent confidence interval is drawn in.

Interpretation: On a cumulative basis, the batting performance within each round is consistent at the 95 percent confidence interval. Each plot for a round shows positive curvature up to the right which implies that the batting performance is showing a more or less continuous improvement from start to end of a round on a nonrandom basis.

Comment: The similar patterns of behavior in each of the three rounds were a provocative sug-

gestion that some further subgrouping might yield other interesting results. Examination of the baseball season schedule showed groupings of 16–20 games duration with an average grouping of 18 games. Such a grouping was called a *sequence.* This is also a rational subgrouping of a 54-game round in that 18 games is exactly one-third of a round. Further, each sequence of each round represented a similar, although not identical, set of games with the same opposing teams. An additional tier of analysis was performed using 18-game sequences. Each of these sequences showed great consistency of batting performance within any one sequence. This is demonstrated in Fig. 22-11, *A, B,* and *C* by means of intermediate dashed lines drawn between the first and last points in a sequence.

A summary of results for each sequence is shown in Table 22-6. The ratio of hits to at-bats is given as well as the batting average, in parentheses, for each sequence. Also shown, in the margins and under each column, are the averages for each round and for the same sequences of each round. Numerically, the results for the different sequences spread over a range of 0.173 to 0.431, or 0.258 points. This is a large range compared to a batting average of 0.301, and, in baseball terms, very significant. The averages for rounds vary from 0.204 to 0.338. The averages for sequences go from 0.223 to 0.349. Such variation

Table 22-6. Summary of Results for Nine Sequences

Round	Sequence (1–18)	(19–36)	(37–54)	Average
1–54	16/64 (0.250)	20/60 (0.333)	28/65 (0.431)	(0.338)
55–108	9/52 (0.173)	8/43 (0.186)	14/55 (0.254)	(0.204)
109–162	17/69 (0.246)	24/62 (0.387)	26/72 (0.361)	(0.331)
Average	0.223	0.301	0.349	

appears to be too large to be random. In order to attempt to determine if significant nonrandom influences are present, the data of Table 22-6 can be further evaluated in a manner similar to

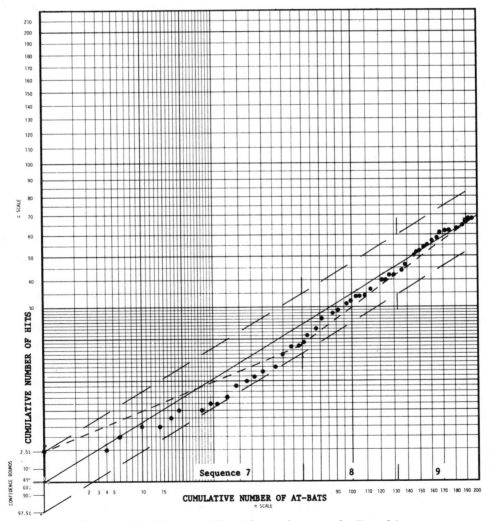

Fig. 22-11C.   Yastrzemski's batting performance for Round 3.

Example 20-1, using paired counts of the hits/at-bat data as demonstrated in the next example.

Example 22-8

Given: Data on 9 batting sequences in Table 22-6.
Required: Do all of the sequences agree with the season's average?

Procedure:

Step 1. Convert the hits/at-bat ratios to paired counts.

Step 2. Plot the paired counts as in Fig. 22-12.

Step 3. Draw in the 95 percent confidence interval.

Interpretation: The point for sequence 3 is above the 95 percent confidence interval and the points for sequences 4 and 5 are below. 3 out of 9 points are outside the 95 percent confidence interval for a 0.301 overall batting average. These are simply too many points to be due to chance alone. Some additional factors need to be considered. Actually, a simple-minded review of the playing schedule quickly revealed the following almost improbable situation:

1. The first sequence in each round was played against teams which ultimately finished higher in the final standings than did Yastrzemski's team, the Boston Red Sox.

2. In the second sequence, the teams played were those which finished in the middle of the standings as did the Red Sox.

3. In the third sequence, the teams which were played were those teams which finished at the bottom of the standings.

Comment 1: The apparent correlation between the standings of teams to their playing sequence in the 1968 season cannot be construed as having any significant purpose. Since league schedules are made up well in advance of any given season, there is no reason to try to relate the required sequence of play between any one team and another.

However, it is greatly instructive in this case to consider just how clearly the sequences, as subgroups of play within any round and over the entire season, emerge as significant elements in the performance of a single player. For those familiar with

control-chart theory, we have discovered an assignable cause of variation. There are three essentially complete patterns of sequences within the three rounds which constitute the entire season. It is equally demonstrable that in many industrial, economic, and financial processes, there are also significant kinds of repetition within definable patterns. Related examples are machine/operator combinations within work shifts; work-group to work-group between shifts, often due to supervisory differences; or, plant-to-plant differences in measurable areas of performance within a single company.

Comment 2: In the examples of analysis of Yastrzemski's batting performance for an entire season, we find the following key points:

1. On an overall basis, treating Yastrzemski's performance for the season as a stochastic (continuous) process, we find that his batting average computed from *cumulative performance* is consistent at the 95 percent confidence level. In other words, he averages out over the season.

2. If one considers the rounds of the playing schedule as a substructure within the season, one discovers three presumably independent but graphically similar patterns, as in Fig. 22-11.

3. Yastrzemski's performance within each round is not consistent, as evidenced by the positive curvature of cumulative performance within each round in spite of the fact that performance between rounds is relatively similar.

4. Performance within any sequence is remarkably consistent. This is the kind of pattern one looks for to discover homogeneous process conditions. However, the level of performance varies from sequence to sequence and is significantly different in three out of nine sequences.

5. There was also a significant difference between the results of the first and third rounds compared to the second round. On the whole, the second round was lower at the 99 percent confidence level. This indicates that, although factors such as sequence of

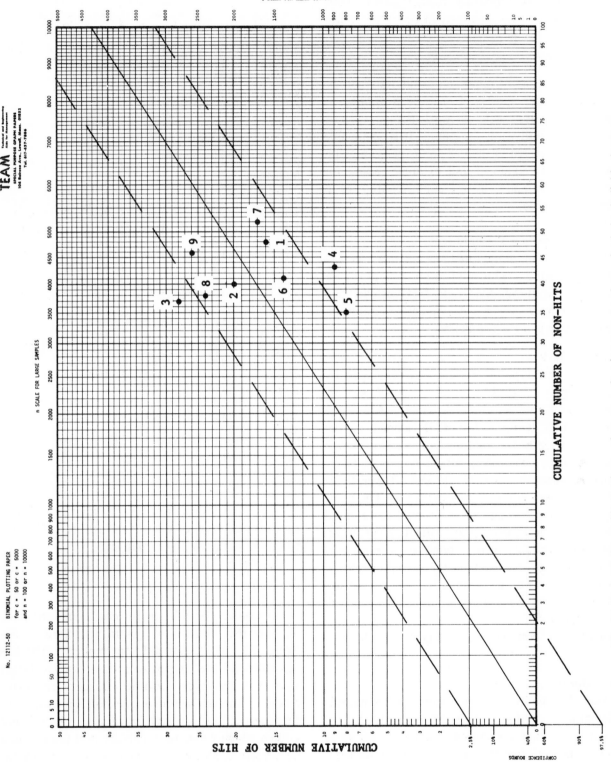

Fig. 22-12. Yastrzemski's batting performance showing averages for each of nine individual sequences.

play can account for part of Yastrzemski's batting performance, further factors must ultimately be identified in order to understand his personal results in batting performance.

The same general approach in analysis can be applied to other sports. It has been applied to football statistics such as yards-per-carry; pass completions; and yards-per-punt. It is applicable to basketball statistics such as points-per-game and percentage of rebounds; and to horse racing for jockey performance, using lengths-behind as a working variable.

A Sales Forecasting Example

Cumulative binomial functions are also useful in sales forecasting. This application was also suggested to the author by Dr. P. S. Olmstead in a private communication. A sequence of forecasting examples is presented below.

Example 22-9

Given: A new type of product was developed by a company. There was a wide range of possible options available with this product. After due consideration, two models were developed: Model A was a wide-range, multipurpose version which was relatively expensive; Model G had a lesser range of capability and would serve fewer functional purposes but was less expensive. The combination of the two models reasonably represented the extremes of the price/range/function spectrum. The new products were offered to a randomly selected group of customers for a trial period of 18 months. The sales results for this period are given in Table 22-7, Part A, by month and by cumulative total.

Required: A comparative evaluation of the two models.

Procedure:

Step 1. The cumulative results for 18 months sales of each product are plotted in Fig. 22-13.

Note: These data are plotted in units of 100 items sold. The addition of 1 to obtain $c + 1$ for such data is trivial and, therefore, omitted since it would have a scale value of only 0.01 units.

Table 22-7. Sales Data. Cumulative Sales Volume, in 100's

Month	Part A Model A	Part A Model G	Part C Month	Part C All Models
July	1.0	4.0	Jan.	3.0
Aug.		5.0	Feb.	7.2
Sept.			March	13.9
Oct.			April	21.8
Nov.		5.2	May	42.8
Dec.	2.2	5.3	June	49.1
Jan.	2.5	5.7	July	59.9
Feb.	2.6	7.1	Aug.	69.9
March	2.7	8.3	Sept.	77.3
April			Oct.	85.9
May	2.9	8.5	Nov.	92.3
June		10.9	Dec.	98.4
July		11.4	Jan.	110.0
Aug.	3.0	12.6	Feb.	120.7
Sept.	3.1	12.9	March	125.2
Oct.	3.7	15.6	April	128.4
Nov.	4.2	21.2	May	138.2
Part B			June	148.1
Jan.	2.6	10.6	July	163.8
Feb.	4.0	15.0	Aug.	172.4
March	6.8	20.8	Sept.	185.1
April	9.7	28.4	Oct.	199.3
May	12.1	37.6	Nov.	207.0
June	13.2	41.9	Dec.	215.9
July	15.5	51.7		
Aug.	18.0	55.5		
Sept.	19.3	60.3		
Oct.	21.6	66.2		
Nov.	21.8	68.6		
Dec.				

Step 2. A line is drawn from the origin through the achieved level of sales at the end of 18 months to establish the average sales level.

Step 3. The 95 percent confidence intervals are drawn for each set of data.

Comment: The 95 percent confidence intervals indicate that there is a significant difference between sales of the two different models. The less versatile and less expensive model enjoyed larger sales than the more versatile but more expensive model. This answered a question for which no sure answer had existed previously. It was not known which range of capability and price would be preferred although opinion was originally inclined to expect greater sales of the more versatile model. The results of the trial sales period were

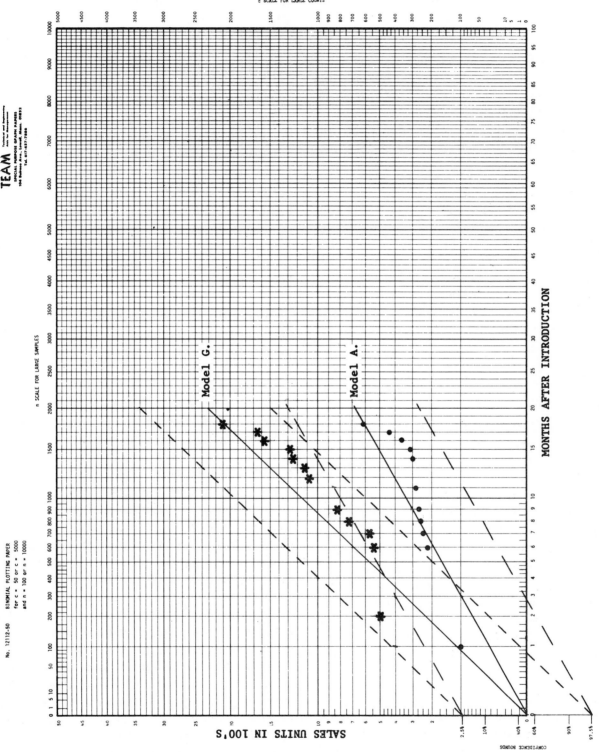

Fig. 22-13.   Results of introductory sales phase for two different models.

considered satisfactory, so the products were released on a national basis. The results of national sales are analyzed in the next example.

Example 22-10
Given: Models A and G were marketed on a national basis for twelve months. The data for this sales period are given in Table 22-7, Part B, by month and by cumulative total.
Required: A comparative evaluation of the two models against the random sample results obtained in the trial period.

Procedure:
Step 1. The random sample used in the trial sales period was approximately 25 percent of the established customer list. Therefore, on a national basis, about a four times increase in sales is anticipated. Thus, the achieved sales level in Table 22-7, Part A, is multiplied by four to obtain preliminary estimates of expected sales volume. The preliminary estimates are used to draw in an average line and the 95 percent confidence interval for each model in Fig. 22-14.

Step 2. Plot the cumulative data for each model from Table 22-7, Part B.

Comment 1: The results for Model A stay within the 95 percent limits but are running on the high side. The results for Model G exceed the limits after 5 months.
Comment 2: During the trial period, Model G sold 3.37 times more than Model A. During the first year of national sales, Model G was 3.15 times higher than Model A. The trial period was successful in estimating the probable sales split.
Comment 3: The ratio of relative sales between the two models raised a question regarding the desirability of producing additional models to cover the price and function spectrum more completely. Customer inquiries also indicated that this would be desirable.

Example 22-11
Given: At the end of the first six months of the national sales period, the sales level was sufficiently large to allow the introduction of additional models to the market. As a result, eight additional models

were designed and offered for sale. The combined sales data for all models are given in Table 22-7, Part C.
Required: A comparison of sales results with the full line of models to sales results achieved with the first two models.

Procedure:
Step 1. From Table 22-7, Part B, we obtain the total sales for Models A and G for twelve months; this is 90.4 100s. Use this total as a preliminary estimate of the total market.

Step 2. Using the estimate of 90.4, draw in a line to represent average sales and the 95 percent confidence limits.

Step 3. Plot the cumulative data for sales of all models from Table 22-7, Part C. This is shown in Fig. 22-15.

Comment 1: The plot starts out below limits for three months and then runs on the high side of the average for the next 17 months, and then exceeds the upper 95 percent limit.
Comment 2: The choice of Models A and G to bracket the market was quite successful. In addition, the sales forecast from these two models was also valid for a complete line of models.

A Stock Market Example
For many people, the perennially fascinating process of modern times is the behavior of the stock market. In the following examples, we intend to illustrate that the stock market may be represented as a series of binomial processes of varying time duration. The length of duration and the direction of change are true random variables. The level of market activity reflects the cumulative effect of the judgments of many people and the price responds to the reasons for activity or lack of activity in a particular stock. These are the basic characteristics of processes which are called *nonstationary time series*. Such processes are also called *fluctuating, variable,* or *erratic.* Although the fluctuations are not truly predictable, they are detectable, and investment decisions can be made with some simple rules which will be demonstrated here.

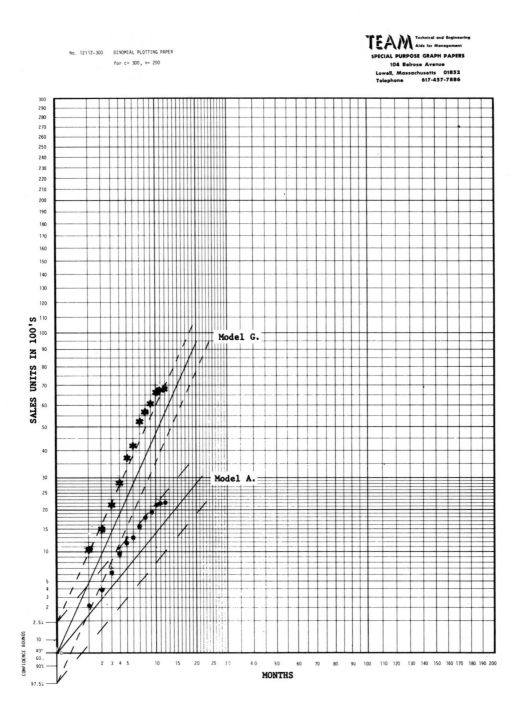

Fig. 22-14.   Results of first 12 months of national sales.

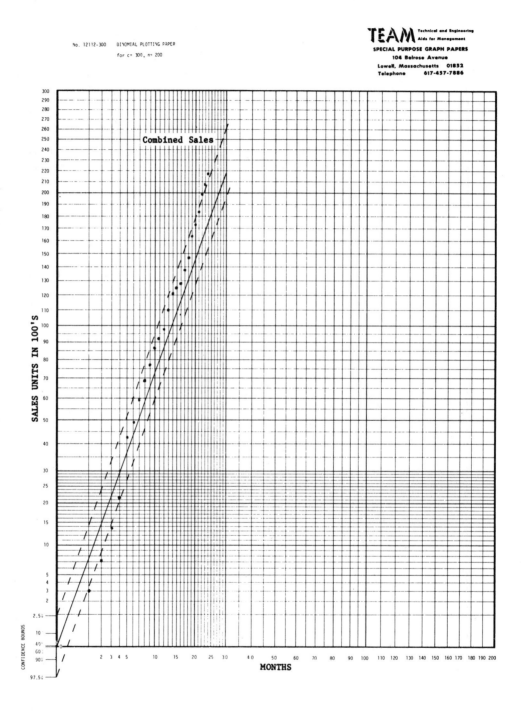

Fig. 22-15.   Results of sales for a 10-model line.

Many conventional methods of technical analysis of the stock market try to assume that the market for any given stock has a "normal" level for some fairly long period and that the observed short-term changes are merely random variations about the normal level. In reality, the stock market is a dynamic process which is forever changing due to the expectations of individual company performance, relative company performance against other companies, general and particular economic and political events, the cost of money, tax law revisions, and moods of the investing public. The conditions of real life suggest that the stock market should be ideal for methods of stochastic evaluation. What is needed is:

1. A method of detecting that a change has taken place.
2. A decision logic to establish a course of action based on the detection of a change.

Such requirements are developed in the following examples:

Example 22-12
Given: The data of Table 22-8, giving weekly volume of trading activity in Avco Corporation stock for the second half of 1961.
Required: An analysis of trading volume activity for this period.

Procedure:
Step 1. Plot the cumulative results as shown in Fig. 22-16.

Note: Units represent 10,000 shares traded.

Step 2. Draw a line from the origin through the last plotted point to represent the average weekly volume traded.

Step 3. Draw in the 95 percent confidence interval.

Interpretation: The results during this period are definitely not stable with respect to the average volume traded. The bulge above the upper 95 percent limit at *A* is even wider than the entire confidence interval. This indicates that there is no compromise value for this period which would result in an apparent typical level and a 95 percent interval which would satisfy this collection of points.

Comment: The plotting units used are 10,000 shares traded which also represents 100 blocks of 100. The average weekly volume is about 15 10,000-share units, or 1500 blocks. Although institutional trading may be in large blocks of stock, many individual trades are made in 100 share units. Therefore, it may be assumed that the trading of a total of 1500 blocks of stock represents a large sample size of investment opinion, probably in excess of 1000 individual judgments.

Since individual points can be argued to be significantly large sample sizes of investor opinion in and of themselves, let us examine the trading performance on a week-by-week basis.

Example 22-13
Given: The data of Table 22-8.

Table 22-8. Weekly Volume of Trading Activity in Avco Corporation Common Stock for the Second Half of 1961

Week	3rd Quarter					4th Quarter				
	Volume, 10,000's	Cumulative Volume	Cumulative, by Weeks from Change Point			Volume, 10,000's	Cumulative Volume	Cumulative, by Weeks from Change Point		
1	19.70	19.70	19.70	...	...	18.43	301.30	...	...	39.72
2	27.63	47.33	47.33	...	...	9.59	310.89	...	...	49.31
3	30.95	88.28	88.28	30.95	...	4.93	315.82	...	...	54.24
4	15.24	103.52	...	46.19	...	6.00	321.82	...	...	60.24
5	26.85	130.07	...	73.04	26.85	6.65	328.47	...	...	66.89
6	43.88	173.95	43.88	...	70.73	13.88	342.35	...	...	80.77
7	20.50	192.45	64.38	20.50	...	12.39	354.74	...	...	93.16
8	20.02	212.47	...	40.52	...	6.24	360.98	...	...	99.40
9	19.17	231.64	...	59.69	...	8.97	369.95	...	...	108.37
10	10.32	241.96	...	70.01	...	12.44	382.39	...	...	120.81
11	17.32	259.28	...	87.33	...	5.51	387.90	5.51	...	126.32
12	11.67	270.95	...	99.00	11.67	4.46	392.36	9.97	...	...
13	9.62	180.57	...	...	21.29	3.81	396.17	13.78	...	...

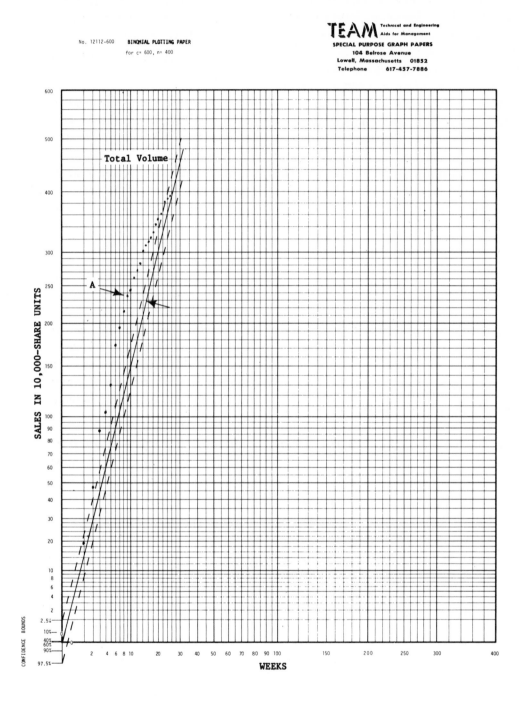

Fig. 22-16.   Cumulative trading volume, by weeks, in the stock of Avco Corporation for the second half of 1961.

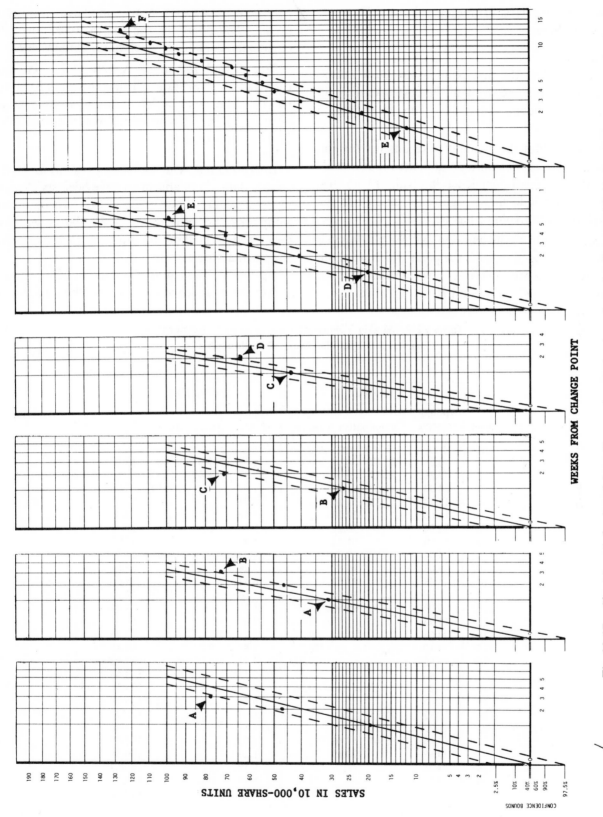

Fig. 22-17.   Short term behavior of Avco Corporation stock sales volume for the second half of 1961.

Required: Analysis of trading volume on a week-by-week basis.

Procedure:

Step 1. Use the first point to establish an expected average and draw in the corresponding 95 percent confidence interval. This is shown in Fig. 22-17 as point *A*.

Step 2. Plot the cumulative results for the following weeks. The third point plotted falls outside of the 95 percent confidence interval. From this, we can conclude that a significant change in the level of trading volume has occurred.

Step 3. On the assumption that the trading volume has changed in level, the point which went out of the confidence interval is now used to start the next plot, Fig. 22-17, point *B*.

Step 4. Data are now cumulated from this point. The point for the fourth week now falls outside the confidence interval on the low side.

Step 5 and forward. A new plot is initiated each time a point falls outside the confidence interval. The point which falls out is used as an estimate of the change which has occurred, Fig. 22-17, points *C* to *F*.

Interpretation: On the basis of analysis of the weekly data, there appear to have been six changes in trend within a span of 26 weeks. Using the assumptions and procedures given above, we have developed a method of indicating change using simple and orderly rules.

Comment: The count of sequences which remain within the confidence interval and the direction of

Table 22-9. Weekly Volume of Trading in Avco Corporation Common Stock for the Years 1962 through 1964

| | 1962 | | | | | | | |
| | First Half | | | | Second Half | | | |
Week	Volume, 10,000's	Cumulative Volume			Volume, 10,000's	Cumulative Volume		
...	...	13.78 (from 1961)			...	...	...	...
1	6.63	20.41	...	...	6.62	6.62	...	82.65
2	9.51	29.92	...	...	27.87	34.49	27.87	...
3	14.30	44.22	...	...	7.99	...	35.86	7.99
4	13.10	57.32	13.10	...	4.35	...	...	12.34
5	14.10	...	27.20	...	9.56	...	...	21.90
6	22.96	...	50.16	...	5.51	...	...	27.41
7	11.69	...	61.85	...	15.57	...	...	42.98
8	7.94	...	69.79	...	9.38	...	...	52.36
9	7.08	...	76.87	...	5.28	...	...	57.64
10	6.68	...	83.55	...	6.42	...	...	64.06
11	7.19	...	90.74	...	6.10	...	...	70.16
12	5.09	...	95.83	5.09	8.28	...	...	78.44
13	3.93	...	...	9.02	9.89	...	...	88.33
14	0.65	...	...	9.67	7.22	...	...	95.55
15	9.10	...	...	18.77	3.88	...	...	99.43
16	4.85	...	...	23.62	7.72	...	...	107.15
17	5.48	...	...	29.10	15.33	...	...	122.48
18	11.26	...	...	40.36	6.88	...	...	129.36
19	8.65	...	...	49.01	6.64	...	...	136.00
20	15.73	15.73	...	64.74	11.05	...	...	147.05
21	18.25	33.98	...	...	5.81	...	...	152.86
22	52.46	86.44	52.46	...	16.03	...	...	168.89
23	20.69	...	73.15	20.69	11.26	...	...	180.15
24	19.25	...	...	39.94	6.48	...	...	186.63
25	15.04	...	...	54.98	5.70	...	...	192.33
26	21.05	...	...	76.03	4.83	...	...	197.16

Table 22-9 (Continued). Weekly Volume of Trading in Avco Corporation
Common Stock for the Years 1962 through 1964

	1963					
	First Half			Second Half		
Week	Volume, 10,000's	Cumulative Volume		Volume, 10,000's	Cumulative Volume	
...	...	... 197.16 (from 1962)		...	... ...	...
1	7.22	... 204.38	...	4.50	... 399.31	...
2	6.38	... 210.76	...	5.14	... 404.45	...
3	6.05	... 216.81	...	6.59	... 411.04	...
4	9.03	... 225.84	...	6.12	... 417.16	...
5	5.02	... 230.86	...	3.56	... 420.72	...
6	6.41	... 237.27	...	3.42	... 424.14	...
7	6.69	... 243.96	...	7.03	... 431.17	...
8	4.43	... 248.39	...	6.51	... 437.68	...
9	5.24	... 253.63	...	5.75	... 443.43	...
10	4.33	... 257.96	...	8.28	... 451.71	...
11	2.57	... 260.53	...	6.60	... 458.31	...
12	5.48	... 266.01	...	7.76	... 466.07	...
13	6.07	... 272.08	...	13.63	... 479.70	...
14	5.85	... 277.93	...	5.41	... 485.11	...
15	8.52	... 286.45	...	16.44	... 501.55	...
16	12.66	... 299.11	...	6.10	... 507.65	...
17	7.55	... 306.66	...	6.48	... 514.13	...
18	13.06	... 319.72	...	7.37	... 521.50	...
19	8.51	... 328.23	...	4.60	... 526.10	...
20	9.17	... 337.40	...	3.93	... 530.03	...
21	5.43	... 342.83	...	4.95	... 534.98	...
22	4.68	... 347.51	...	5.13	... 540.11	...
23	15.43	... 362.94	...	4.97	... 545.08	...
24	15.84	... 378.78	...	6.06	... 551.14	...
25	6.91	... 385.69	...	5.15	... 556.29	...
26	9.12	... 394.81	...	3.90	... 560.19	...

change was 2+, 2−, 1+, 1−, 5−, and 12−. The quick changes in the early part of this period could be interpreted as an indecisive investment situation. The last three sequences, which account for half of the total period, all show successive decreases in the trend of trading volume. This can be interpreted to mean that after a period of indecision the market volume turned downwards.

Example 22-14
Given: The data of Table 22-8 and Table 22-9 showing the weekly trading volume for Avco Corporation during the years 1961 through 1964.
Required: Analysis of the trading volume on a week-by-week basis.

Procedure: Same as for Example 22-12; see Fig. 22-17 and 22-18.

Interpretation: During the three-and-a-half-year period, there are 20 changes in trend of trading volume. The frequency of changes from 1962 through 1964 is only about half of that observed during the last six months of 1961. This is confirmation of the stochastic nature of the stock market. In particular, it appears that the trading volume is highly dependent on the conditions occurring around the time of the observed trading volume.

Comment: The sequences and direction of change for these data are 2+, 2−, 1+, 1−, 5−, 12−, 6+, 7−, 8+, 2+, 1−, 4−, 1+, 1−, 76−, 2+, 2−, 7−, 2+, and 28−. The duration of change trends varies from one week to eighteen months. Note that of the total of 20 trend changes indicated in Figs. 22-17 and 22-18, there were three (3) trends lasting from one to six quarters.

Table 22-9 (Concluded). Weekly Volume of Trading in Avco Corporation
Common Stock for the Years 1962 through 1964

	1964							
	First Half				Second Half			
Week	Volume, 10,000's	Cumulative Volume			Volume, 10,000's	Cumulative Volume		
...	...	...	560.19 (from 1963)		...	...	...	...
1	5.90	...	566.09	...	3.43	60.69	...	...
2	6.45	...	572.54	6.45	4.44	65.13	...	...
3	12.03	...	...	18.48	2.86	67.99	...	...
4	14.05	14.05	...	32.53	3.12	71.11	...	...
5	5.02	19.07	...	...	3.17	74.28	...	...
6	6.65	25.72	6.65	...	5.06	79.34	...	...
7	4.06	...	10.71	...	3.44	82.78	...	...
8	4.78	...	15.49	...	4.88	87.66	...	...
9	4.29	...	19.78	...	7.12	94.78	...	...
10	3.51	...	23.29	...	3.51	98.29	...	...
11	5.96	...	29.25	...	3.41	101.70	...	...
12	4.12	...	33.37	...	3.12	104.82	...	...
13	2.25	...	35.62	2.25	3.59	108.41	...	...
14	5.18	...	...	7.43	4.45	112.86	...	...
15	5.07	5.07	...	12.50	2.55	115.41	...	...
16	5.25	10.32	...	...	4.68	120.09	...	...
17	6.87	17.19	...	...	2.52	122.61	2.52	...
18	9.06	26.25	...	...	2.97	...	5.49	...
19	4.42	30.67	...	...	2.25	...	7.74	...
20	5.25	35.92	...	...	4.54	...	12.28	...
21	3.21	39.13	...	...	4.28	...	16.56	...
22	4.41	43.54	...	...	2.97	...	19.53	...
23	3.96	47.50	...	...	3.15	...	22.68	...
24	3.02	50.52	...	...	3.50	...	26.18	...
25	4.53	55.05	...	...	4.37	...	30.55	...
26	2.21	57.26	...	...	6.72	...	37.27	...

These were 12-, 76-, and 28-week sequences which covered 9 of the 14 quarters covered by the data. This is not really surprising, since the financial situation of companies is officially announced in quarterly reports. Favorable or unfavorable situations which persist would be expected to result in trends which are multiples of thirteen weeks.

The price behavior of stocks is usually taken as the most important factor in the stock market. However, it can be argued that the price is the result of a number of investment decisions made by a fairly large number of people. This is why the volume behavior was considered first. The examination of price behavior at the time of volume trend changes for a number of stocks over a long period of time showed that, on the average, there is

a very simple logic for making investment decisions, which is shown in Table 22-10.

The gist of Table 22-10 is that when price and volume trends are in the same direction, buying is indicated, and that when price and volume disagree as to trend, it is time to sell. This may be rationalized by considering that when price and volume are increasing, there is potential for profit; when

Table 22-10. Logic Table for Investment Decisions

Price Trend	Volume Trend	
	Increasing	Decreasing
Increasing	Buy	Sell
Decreasing	Sell	Buy

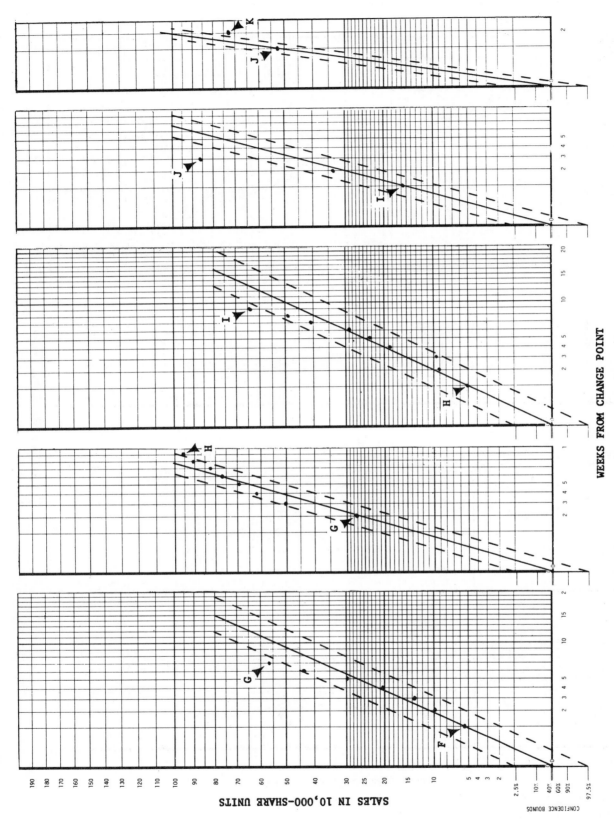

Fig. 22-18A.   Short-term behavior of Avco Corporation stock sales volume for the years 1962, 1963, and 1964.

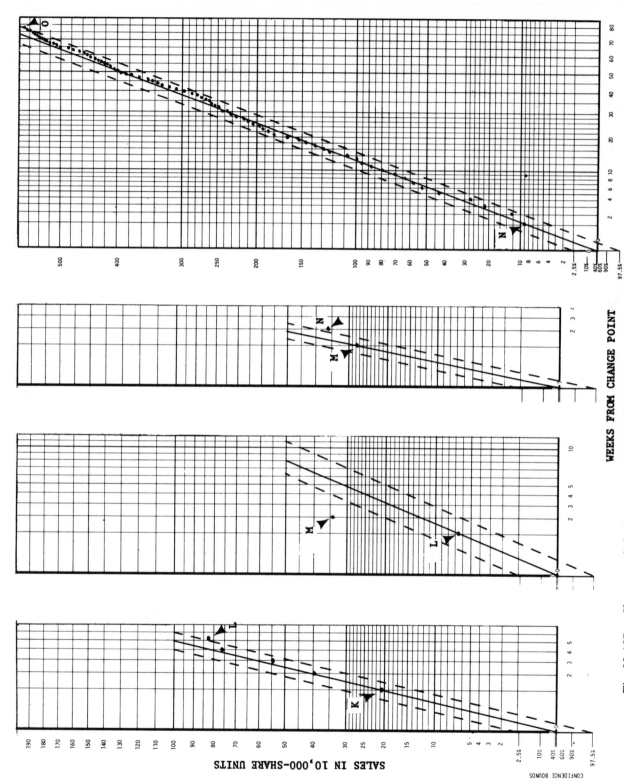

Fig. 22-18B.   Short-term behavior of Avco Corporation stock sales volume for the years 1962, 1963, and 1964.

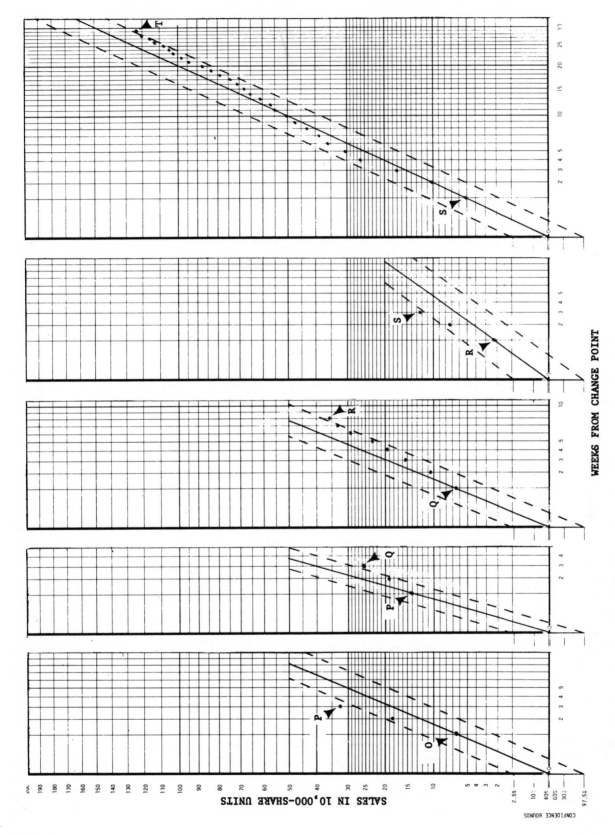

Fig. 22-18C.   Short-term behavior of Avco Corporation stock sales volume for the years 1962, 1963, and 1964.

Table 22-11. Record of Investment Decisions and Results

Symbol	Volume Trend	Price Trend	Indicated Decision	Buy	Sell	Profit per 100 Shares
A	+	+	Buy	23 3/4		$ 150.00
B	−	+	Sell		25 1/4	
C	+	+	Buy	26 1/8		− 37.50
D	−	+	Sell		25 3/4	
E	−	−	Buy	23 1/2		112.50
F	−	+	Sell		24 5/8	
G	+	+	Buy	26		112.50
H	−	+	Sell		27 1/8	
I	+	−	Sell		23 1/2	275.00
J	+	−	Sell		21 1/2	75.00
K	−	−	Buy	20 3/4		
L	−	−	Buy	20 7/8		250.00
M	+	+	Buy	22 3/4		− 37.50
N	−	+	Sell		22 3/8	
O	−	−	Buy	21 7/8		−125.00
P	+	−	Sell		20 5/8	
Q	−	−	Buy	22 5/8		100.00
R	−	+	Sell		23 5/8	
S	+	−	Sell		22 3/4	37.50
T	−	−	Buy	22 3/8		

Total Trading Profit. $1025.00

Average Profit for 11 Transactions Excluding Brokerage $ 93.18

price and volume are both decreasing, the stock is usually low priced but there is little interest in that price and so it represents a potential bargain; when volume is increasing and price is decreasing, there are a lot of people losing interest in that stock so that prices are likely to decline; and, when volume is decreasing and price is increasing, there is little real interest in the stock.

The weekly closing price and the price trend for the Avco Corporation stock for the years 1961–64 are shown in Fig. 22-19. The points at which volume changes are indicated and are keyed to the change points indicated by the letters *A–T* in Figs. 22-17 and 22-18.

Example 22-15
Given: The volume and price behavior of Avco Corporation stock for the years 1961–64.
Required: To determine the results of using the decision logic of Table 22-10 to determine investment decisions.

Procedure:
Step 1. Determine the direction of volume and price trend at the same point in time. Use +s for increasing trends and −s for decreasing trends. This is shown in Table 22-11.

Step 2. When the signs agree, make a Buy decision, and when they disagree, make a Sell decision.

Note: For simplicity, if more than one Buy decision has been made when a Sell decision is indicated, sell everything. If more than one Sell decision has been made when a Buy is indicated, buy enough to cover all of the short sales. For the purposes of this example, we are ignoring the cost of broker's fees.

Interpretation: The record of decisions over the 1961–64 period is also given in Table 22-11. If we consider that a transaction which results in a profit is successful and a transaction which results in a loss is a failure, then there were eight successful and

An EXEC-U-CHART by

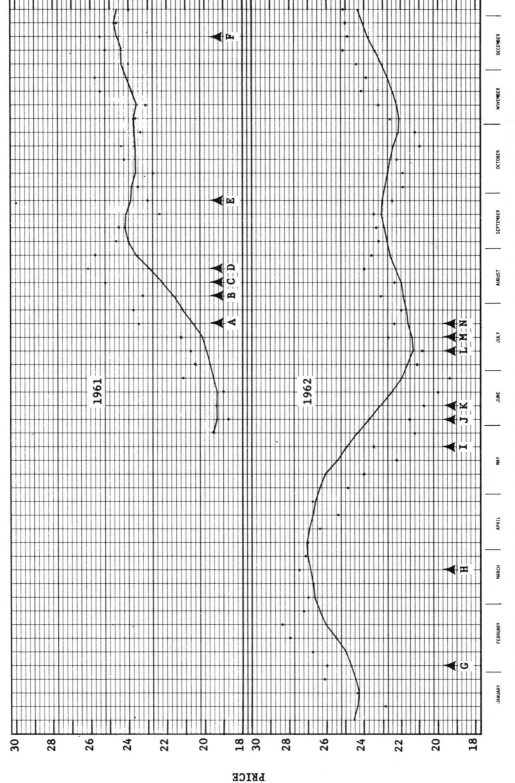

Fig. 22-19A.   Weekly closing price and price trend for Avco Corporation stock for the years 1961 and 1962.

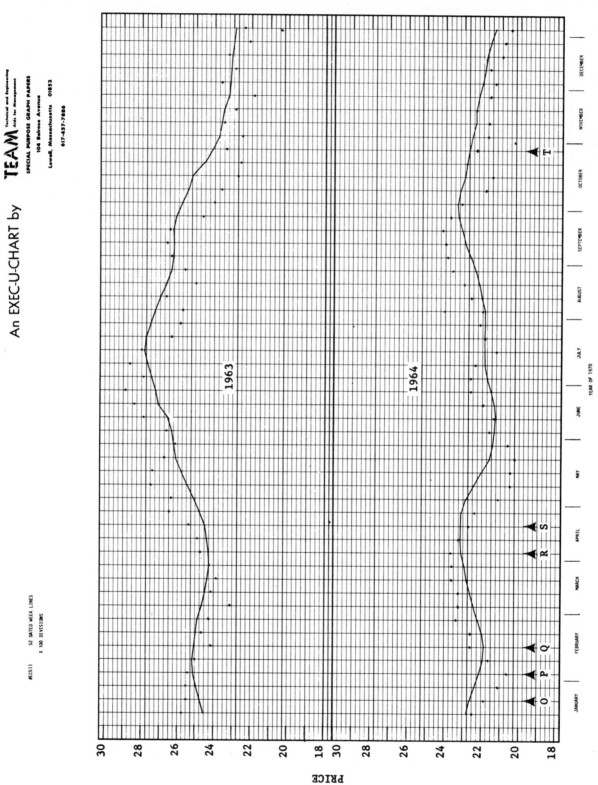

Fig. 22-19B.   Weekly closing price and price trend for Avco Corporation stock for the years 1963 and 1964.

three unsuccessful transactions. This is about 73 percent successful transactions. Other similar experiments have resulted in up to 90 percent success.

Comment 1: This example is *not* presented as a recommended investment method. It is presented primarily as a provocative example of the power of stochastic evaluation in an extremely complex area. Furthermore, it serves to illustrate that by the use of apparently unconventional assumptions, simple analytical methods lead to remarkable results.

Comment 2: This example has certain features in common with the example of Yastrzemski's batting performance examples. One is that long-term performance in a complex dynamic environment consists of many smaller periods of consistent performance. Each period of consistent performance may be quite different from the period immediately preceding it or the period immediately succeeding it.

If we were able to discover the reasons for the significant changes in trends, there would nearly always be some assignable cause to explain the change. However, we are rarely in the position to determine any or all possible causes for changes. The methods and procedures presented above show that we are usually quite well off just to know that significant changes have occurred when we have a companion logic to lead to decisions at such key points.

Comment 3: The sensitivity of the methods given above for stock market analysis are dependent on the period of observation. If daily trading data were used, more trading opportunities would be indicated and more frequent changes would be required in investment decisions. This leads to a practice called *churning,* or excessive turnover, which is highly frowned on by the Securities and Exchange Commission.

CHAPTER 23

Summary and Conclusions

Mathematics, Processes, and Statistics

In earlier chapters, we have used the approach of developing one distribution after another through the application of prescribed mathematical operations on random variables. This approach was used because:

1. The concepts of mathematical operations are taught more widely and are therefore better known than statistical operations.

2. The generation of random variables by means of coin tossing and dice throwing is directly observable to the student. Simple experiments based on coins and dice lead to a combined experiential and intuitive sense of how random data actually occur.

3. Mathematical expressions developed from combinations of mathematical operations can be used to represent the way that things happen in real life. Such expressions are referred to as *mathematical models*. The way that things actually happen is called a *process*.

The connotation of a process is many things to many people. Some of the wide variety of interpretations of a process may be seen by a series of examples. For example, birth is the terminal phase of a complex biological process and birth itself is a complex substep thereof. Alternatively, the growth in the number of bacteria under specific nutrient and temperature conditions is another biological process which is more amenable to description by a mathematical model. The act of driving to work is a physical process with many subtle complexities, while the filling of cans with motor oil can be described by a series of relatively simple mathematical models. Digestion of one's food is a complex chemical process, while the dissociation of water into hydrogen and oxygen by electrolysis can be defined by a detailed mathematical description. The national economy is a complex economic process, but the level of department store sales is often related to the percentage of disposable income by a fairly simple model. Here, disposable income is considered to be that fraction of income left after fixed obligations — such as the costs of taxes, food, clothing, shelter, debt repayment, insurance, and savings — are met.

There is an important inner structure of the development of the several statistical distributions which we have developed in the earlier chapters. This inner structure interrelates the areas of mathematical operations, process description through models, and the associated resultant statistics. Understanding the interrelationships between mathematics, processes, and statistics can contribute to large improvements in the definition of problems, to improved problem-solving logic and to more rational conclusions and decisions.

Table 23-1 tabulates the more significant relationships between mathematical models, process descriptions, and the typical resultant statistical distributions. There is an increasing order of complexity in the statements defining the mathematical models. The several categories of models correspond to general categories of processes. Note that there are also categories of statistical distributions which are in correspondence with the mathematical models and processes. The statistics are held to be *resultants* of mathematical operations on random input variables associated with the phenomena of processes.

The value of such categorization is that we do not pursue statistics in a blind way. Statistics can now be used as a check on the expected results of a given kind of mathematical model or process

Table 23-1. Relationships between Mathematical Models, Process Description, and Resultant Statistical Distribution

Mathematical Operation	Mathematical Model	Process Description	Example	Resultant Statistical Distribution
Counting	$p = \dfrac{c}{n}$	Enumeration or Classification	Inspection Sorting	Binomial
Addition	$f(y) = \sum\limits_{i}^{n} (x_i)$	Linear Additive	Addition or subtraction of materials; i.e., cutting, weighing, etc., also mechanical assembly.	Normal
Multiplication	$f(y) = \prod\limits_{i}^{n} (x_i)$	Rate-Dependent Proportional Response	Simple chemical processes, i.e., etching, corrosion, gaseous diffusion. Simple biological processes; i.e., growth rate. Simple economic processes; i.e., distribution of income.	Log-Normal
Simple Exponentiation *or* Addition of Transcendental Terms	$f(y) = ax_0 + bx_1 + cx_2^2$ *or* $f(y) = e^{x_0} + e^{x_1} + e^{x_2}$	Algebraic Polynomial Solutions of Linear Differential Equations with Constant Coefficients.	Complex processes involving the combined effects of a number of independent causes each with a different operational form; i.e., breaking strengths, meteorological and geophysical phenomena, electronic and chemical measurements, financial data.	Extreme Value
Counting of Time Duration to an Event	$f(x; n, \lambda) =$ $\dfrac{\lambda^n}{\Gamma(n)} x^{(n-1)} e^{-\lambda x}$	Waiting Time	Time required for an event(s) to occur or to obtain some service.	Gamma
Addition of Squared Normalized Vectors	$f(y) = \sum\limits_{l}^{n} \left(\dfrac{x_i}{\sigma_l}\right)^2$	Vector Sums	Resultant value in a system of n-fold vector spaces from physics, space-time, and probability applications.	Chi-Square
Multiplication of Transcendental Terms	$f(y) = e^{(x_0 \cdot x_1 \cdot x_3 \cdots)}$ $f(y) = e^{(x_1/x_2)(x_3/x_4)}$	Solutions of General Differential Equations Particle Sizing	Complex exponential processes involving the interdependent effects of independent causes; i.e., breakage of particulate materials, solid state diffusion, chemical kinetics.	Log-Extreme Value
Sums, Products, and Powers of Exponents of Transcendental Terms	$f(y) = e^{\left(\frac{\omega-x}{\omega-\mu}\right)^\beta}$	Solutions of Differential Equations with Boundary Conditions "Upper-Limit" Distributions	Processes involving limits and maxima-minima; i.e., life/failure distributions, bounded particle size distributions, and general potential, gradient, and field problems.	Weibull

behavior. Alternatively, given a sound basis of knowledge of the appropriate mathematical model or generic process description, one can examine the statistics to determine, at least qualitatively, that the right kind of result has occurred so that the appropriate analysis can be applied.

Another way of looking at this is that we can relate theory (mathematical model); practice (a process described/applied/assumed as in engineering, economics, or biology); and results (measurements and statistics). When theory and practice are correct, the statistical results should be predictable. If the gross predicted results (statistical distributions) are not obtained, then specific questions are raised:

1. Are the theory and practice correctly defined?
2. Are there any questionable assumptions involved?
3. Are the measurements of the results correct?

If the predicted results are grossly correct, then we can check to see if the actual results agree in detail with the predictions of the mathematical model. If the results and model do not agree, then the following questions occur:

4. How precisely are values known for any coefficients used in the model?
5. Is there any possibility that unexpected causes of variation occurred?
6. How carefully were the methods represented by the model applied in operating the process?
7. What is the effect of equipment sensitivity on the values of measurements obtained?
8. Can variations or errors occur in recording measurements of results?

In an investigative situation where little is assumed to be known of the underlying theory or of proper practice, the observed statistical results can provide useful clues to more plausible assumptions regarding the category of process which may be operating. This, in turn, leads to more efficient estimation of the type of mathematical model which will describe the process. The increase in efficiency occurs because the presence of certain statistical distribution forms eliminates certain possibilities immediately and this reduces the remaining number of possibilities which must be considered.

To the degree that we can eliminate causes of uncertainty, we contribute to an increased probability of a correct conclusion or decision. It has been the experience of the author that the wrong decision, which is defined as either an incorrect or highly inefficient decision, in the absence of an adequate decision logic, occurs as frequently as 80 percent of the time. This means that only 20 percent of

the decisions made under such conditions are worthwhile. There is a highly significant psychological reason for such a state of affairs. In the absence of a sound logic (the use of reason), conclusions are derived and decisions are made on the basis of feeling or emotion (lack of reason).

Consider that decisions made by tossing a coin will average out at about 50 percent correct. So there is something wrong with a hit-or-miss approach to decision making.

In a recent large-scale test program conducted to improve the reliability of electronic components for an important military weapon system, a test and evaluation plan was specified. The objective of the test and evaluation plan was to test adequate quantities of parts against prespecified criteria in order to determine if the purposeful changes introduced to improve one or more characteristics of the components was, in fact, an improvement. A number of significant improvements were achieved, but there were a noticeable number of errors, as well. A detailed hindsight analysis of all of the program results revealed that about 32 percent of the changes introduced were incorrect. All of the incorrect conclusions and decisions were traced to *faulty use of test equipment* which resulted in *incorrect data*. Most of the incorrect data would have been detected by simple routine application of probability plots.

The use of a nominal logic, as simple as the comparisons used in Table 23-1, coupled with the routine use of probability plots to screen for pathological data, can result in improved decision making. There is no reason to settle for less than 90 percent good decision.

Statistical Continuity

As further evidence of a continuum of relationships, Table 23-2 shows the probability distribution function and the normalized unit variable for the five major categories of distributions developed in this book. Each expression illustrates the sequence of increasing complexity of mathematical operations more clearly than does Table 23-1. Further, the relationships of the terms in the normalized unit variables are convenient clues to the kinds of mathematical models which are appropriate to a

Table 23-2. Probability Density Functions and Normalized Unit Variables

Distribution	Probability Density Function	Normalized Unit Variable
Normal	$f(x) = \dfrac{1}{(2\pi)^{1/2}} e^{-1/2\, z^2}$	$z = \dfrac{x - \mu}{\sigma}$
Log-Normal	$p(x) = \dfrac{1}{(2\pi)^{1/2}} e^{-1/2\, [f(u)]^2}$	$f(u) = \dfrac{\log x - \mu_l}{\sigma_l}$
Extreme Value	$\phi(x) = \alpha e^{-y - e^{-y}}$	$y = \alpha(x - \mu_0)$
Log-Extreme Value	$\pi(x) = -k(\mu_0/x)^{k-1} \exp\, -(\mu_0/x)^k$	$y' = k(\log \mu_0 - \log x)$
Weibull	$f(x) = \dfrac{\beta}{\alpha}(x - \gamma)^{\beta-1} \exp\left(\dfrac{(x-\gamma)^\beta}{\alpha}\right)$	$y'' = k \log\left(\dfrac{\omega - x}{\omega - \mu_0}\right)$

given situation, such as addition, multiplication, exponentiation, etc.

Graphical Comparison of Distributions

Figure 23-1 displays the approximate appearance of each major probability distribution when plotted on the several kinds of probability paper. Here we see that, in general, the distribution plots which are made on a probability paper of a lower mathematical complexity than the distribution of interest are concave, while the more complex distributions are convex. The plots shown in Fig. 23-1 represent ideal results for each distribution type. Two kinds of plots are given for the Weibull distribution. The upper plot is made with the probability scale horizontal, to maintain correspondence with the scale arrangements of the other probability distributions. The lower plot is made showing the appearance of the data when plotted on Weibull paper with its own conventional scale arrangements.

For certain combinations of parameter relationships, it is difficult to distinguish between one or more of the distributions. Therefore, it is particularly valuable to have additional information such as Table 23-1 to referee the choice of which distribution to assume for plotting and analytical purposes. From earlier discussion, it is important to note that the choice of paper for plotting will influence the values of parameter estimates which

are obtained, the mathematical form of estimating equations, and the conclusions derived from extrapolation of observed data.

Special Consideration of Life Phenomena

Table 23-3 lists the expected life distribution which will occur from observed initial distributions of values of a variable of interest. The key assumption here is that the kinds of processes which lead to the distribution of values of a particular variable also define, at least to a first order of approximation, the kinds of processes by which wear-out or degradation failures will occur. Normally distributed variables wearing or degrading by additional linear additive factors result in log-normal distributions of times to failure. Log-normally distributed characteristics which wear or degrade through further rate-dependent processes also result in log-normal distributions of times to failure. Observe that the failure estimating equations in each case arrive at a multiplicative form which is the kind of mathematical operation which leads naturally to the log-normal distribution.

Also, observe how the life-estimating equations for the extreme value and the logarithmic extreme value distributions lead into the form of the Weibull distribution under the assumption that the kinds of processes which cause the extreme value behavior in the first case continue on into life.

CHOICE OF PROBABILITY PAPER

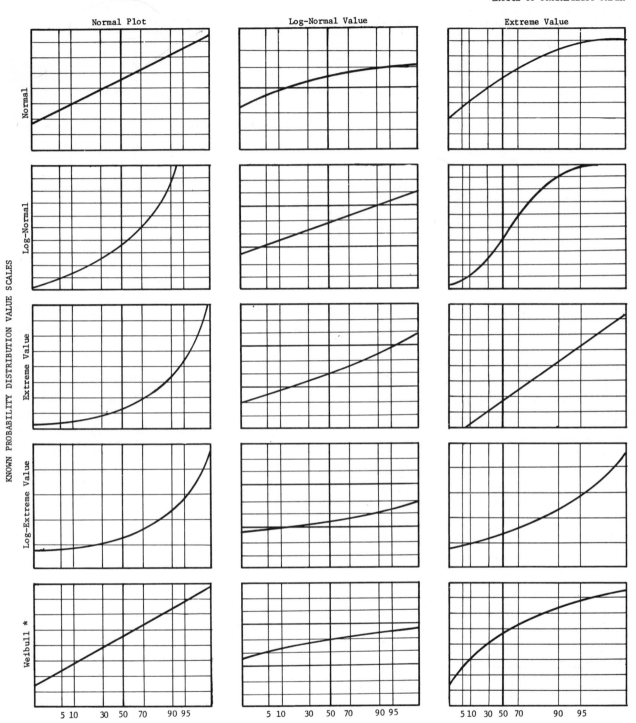

* Weibull plot using same orientation of axes as other distributions.
** Weibull plot against conventional Weibull paper layout.

Fig. 23-1.   Comparative probability plots of the five major

FOR PLOTTING (Cumulative Percentages)

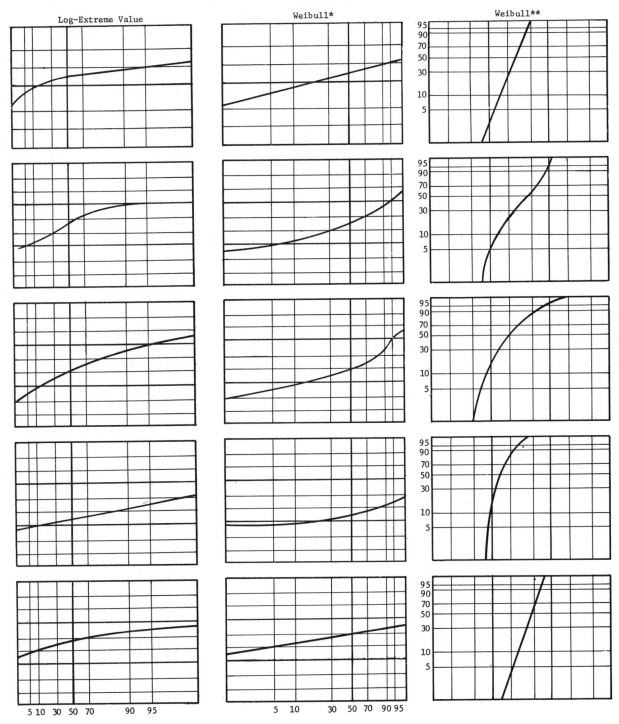

probability distributions on different types of probability papers.

Table 23-3. Probability of Failure Formulas for Characteristics Having a Stated Initial Distribution and Stated Wearout Behavior

Normal Distribution with Linear Wearout.

$$k = \frac{(\text{Limit} - \overline{X_o})}{\sigma_0} \cdot \frac{(1 - \rho t)}{\sqrt{1 + \eta t}} \qquad (10\text{-}3)$$

Log-Normal Distribution with Rate-Dependent Wearout.

$$k = \frac{\text{Limit}}{\tilde{x} \log g} \cdot \frac{(1 - \rho t)}{\sqrt{1 + \eta t}} \qquad (10\text{-}6b)$$

Extreme Value Distribution with Exponential Wearout.

$$y = \beta \log \left(\frac{1}{\mu_0 - \text{Limit}} \right) \cdot \frac{(1 - \rho t)}{\sqrt{1 + \eta t}} \qquad \begin{array}{l}(14\text{-}6 \text{ modified} \\ \text{by } 15\text{-}1)\end{array}$$

Logarithmic Extreme Value Distribution with Exponential Wearout.

$$y = \frac{\beta}{\log g'} \log \left(\frac{1}{\mu_0 - \text{Limit}} \right) \cdot \frac{(1 - \rho t)}{\sqrt{1 + \eta t}} \qquad \begin{array}{l}(13\text{-}5 \text{ modified} \\ \text{by } 15\text{-}1)\end{array}$$

From the foregoing relationships, we conclude that there are only two, significant, underlying life distributions, the log-normal and the Weibull. The log-normal represents a termination of purely arithmetical processes and the Weibull represents the termination of exponential processes.

Appendix

Item Rank in Sample	Sample Size																		
	15	16	17	18	19	20	21	22	23	24	25	26	27	28	29	30	31	32	33
1	.062	.059	.056	.053	.050	.048	.045	.043	.042	.040	.038	.037	.036	.035	.033	.032	.031	.030	.029
2	.125	.118	.111	.105	.100	.095	.091	.087	.083	.080	.077	.074	.071	.069	.067	.065	.062	.061	.059
3	.188	.176	.167	.158	.150	.143	.136	.130	.125	.120	.115	.111	.107	.103	.100	.097	.094	.091	.088
4	.250	.235	.222	.211	.200	.190	.182	.174	.167	.160	.154	.148	.143	.138	.133	.129	.125	.121	.118
5	.312	.294	.278	.263	.250	.238	.227	.217	.208	.200	.192	.185	.179	.172	.167	.161	.156	.152	.147
6	.375	.353	.333	.316	.300	.286	.273	.261	.250	.240	.231	.222	.214	.207	.200	.194	.188	.182	.176
7	.438	.412	.389	.368	.350	.333	.318	.304	.292	.280	.269	.259	.250	.241	.233	.226	.219	.212	.206
8	.500	.471	.444	.421	.400	.381	.364	.348	.333	.320	.308	.296	.286	.276	.267	.258	.250	.242	.235
9	.562	.529	.500	.474	.450	.429	.409	.391	.375	.360	.346	.333	.321	.310	.300	.290	.281	.273	.265
10	.625	.588	.556	.526	.500	.476	.455	.435	.417	.400	.385	.370	.357	.345	.333	.323	.312	.303	.294
11	.688	.647	.611	.579	.550	.524	.500	.478	.458	.440	.423	.407	.393	.379	.367	.355	.344	.333	.324
12	.750	.706	.667	.632	.600	.571	.545	.522	.500	.480	.462	.444	.429	.414	.400	.387	.375	.364	.353
13	.812	.765	.722	.684	.650	.619	.591	.565	.542	.520	.500	.481	.464	.448	.433	.419	.406	.394	.382
14	.875	.824	.778	.737	.700	.667	.636	.609	.583	.560	.538	.519	.500	.483	.467	.452	.438	.424	.412
15	.938	.882	.833	.789	.750	.714	.682	.652	.625	.600	.577	.556	.536	.517	.500	.484	.469	.455	.441
16		.941	.889	.842	.800	.762	.727	.696	.667	.640	.615	.593	.571	.552	.533	.516	.500	.485	.471
17			.944	.895	.850	.810	.773	.739	.708	.680	.654	.630	.607	.586	.567	.548	.531	.515	.500
18				.947	.900	.857	.818	.783	.750	.720	.692	.667	.643	.621	.600	.581	.562	.545	.529
19					.950	.905	.864	.826	.792	.760	.731	.704	.679	.655	.633	.613	.594	.576	.559
20						.952	.909	.870	.833	.800	.769	.741	.714	.690	.667	.645	.625	.606	.588
21							.954	.913	.875	.840	.808	.778	.750	.724	.700	.677	.656	.636	.618
22								.957	.917	.880	.846	.815	.786	.759	.733	.710	.688	.667	.647
23									.958	.920	.885	.852	.821	.793	.767	.742	.719	.697	.676
24										.960	.923	.889	.857	.828	.800	.774	.750	.727	.706
25											.962	.926	.893	.862	.833	.806	.781	.758	.735
26												.963	.929	.897	.867	.839	.812	.788	.765
27													.964	.931	.900	.871	.844	.818	.794
28														.966	.933	.903	.875	.848	.824
29															.967	.935	.906	.879	.853
30																.968	.938	.909	.882
31																	.969	.939	.912
32																		.970	.941
33																			.971

Table A-1. Cumulative Probability

Item Rank in Sample	Sample Size																
	34	35	36	37	38	39	40	41	42	43	44	45	46	47	48	49	50
1	.029	.028	.027	.026	.026	.025	.024	.024	.023	.023	.022	.022	.021	.021	.020	.020	.020
2	.057	.056	.054	.053	.051	.050	.049	.048	.047	.045	.044	.043	.043	.042	.041	.040	.039
3	.086	.083	.081	.079	.077	.075	.073	.071	.070	.068	.067	.065	.064	.062	.061	.060	.059
4	.114	.111	.108	.105	.103	.100	.098	.095	.093	.091	.089	.087	.085	.083	.082	.080	.078
5	.143	.139	.135	.132	.128	.125	.122	.119	.116	.114	.111	.109	.106	.104	.102	.100	.098
6	.171	.167	.162	.158	.154	.150	.146	.143	.140	.136	.133	.130	.128	.125	.122	.120	.118
7	.200	.194	.189	.184	.179	.175	.171	.167	.163	.159	.156	.152	.149	.146	.143	.140	.137
8	.229	.222	.216	.211	.205	.200	.195	.190	.186	.182	.178	.174	.170	.167	.163	.160	.157
9	.257	.250	.243	.237	.231	.225	.220	.214	.209	.205	.200	.196	.191	.187	.184	.180	.176
10	.286	.278	.270	.263	.256	.250	.244	.238	.233	.227	.222	.217	.213	.208	.204	.200	.196
11	.314	.306	.297	.289	.282	.275	.268	.262	.256	.250	.244	.239	.234	.229	.224	.220	.216
12	.343	.333	.324	.316	.308	.300	.293	.286	.279	.273	.267	.261	.255	.250	.245	.240	.235
13	.371	.361	.351	.342	.333	.325	.317	.310	.302	.295	.289	.283	.277	.271	.265	.260	.255
14	.400	.389	.378	.368	.359	.350	.341	.333	.326	.318	.311	.304	.298	.292	.286	.280	.275
15	.429	.417	.405	.395	.385	.375	.366	.357	.349	.341	.333	.326	.319	.312	.306	.300	.294
16	.457	.444	.432	.421	.410	.400	.390	.381	.372	.364	.356	.348	.340	.333	.327	.320	.314
17	.486	.472	.459	.447	.436	.425	.415	.405	.395	.386	.378	.370	.362	.354	.347	.340	.333
18	.514	.500	.486	.474	.462	.450	.439	.429	.419	.409	.400	.391	.383	.375	.367	.360	.353
19	.543	.528	.514	.500	.487	.475	.463	.452	.442	.432	.422	.413	.404	.396	.388	.380	.373
20	.571	.556	.541	.526	.513	.500	.488	.476	.465	.455	.444	.435	.426	.417	.408	.400	.392
21	.600	.583	.568	.553	.538	.525	.512	.500	.488	.477	.467	.457	.447	.437	.429	.420	.412
22	.629	.611	.595	.579	.564	.550	.537	.524	.512	.500	.489	.478	.468	.458	.449	.440	.431
23	.657	.639	.622	.605	.590	.575	.561	.548	.535	.523	.511	.500	.489	.479	.469	.460	.451
24	.686	.667	.649	.632	.615	.600	.585	.571	.558	.545	.533	.522	.511	.500	.490	.480	.471
25	.714	.694	.676	.658	.641	.625	.610	.595	.581	.568	.556	.543	.532	.521	.510	.500	.490

Plotting Points by Samples and Item Rank.

Item Rank in Sample	Sample Size																
	34	35	36	37	38	39	40	41	42	43	44	45	46	47	48	49	50
26	.743	.722	.703	.684	.667	.650	.634	.619	.605	.591	.578	.565	.553	.542	.531	.520	.510
27	.771	.750	.730	.711	.692	.675	.659	.643	.628	.614	.600	.587	.574	.562	.551	.540	.529
28	.800	.778	.757	.737	.718	.700	.683	.667	.651	.636	.622	.609	.596	.583	.571	.560	.549
29	.829	.806	.784	.763	.744	.725	.707	.690	.674	.659	.644	.630	.617	.604	.592	.580	.569
30	.857	.833	.811	.789	.769	.750	.732	.714	.698	.682	.667	.652	.638	.625	.612	.600	.588
31	.886	.861	.838	.816	.795	.775	.756	.738	.721	.705	.689	.674	.660	.646	.633	.620	.608
32	.914	.889	.865	.842	.821	.800	.780	.762	.744	.727	.711	.696	.681	.667	.653	.640	.627
33	.943	.917	.892	.868	.846	.825	.805	.786	.767	.750	.733	.717	.702	.687	.673	.660	.647
34	.971	.944	.919	.895	.872	.850	.829	.810	.791	.773	.756	.739	.723	.708	.694	.680	.667
35		.972	.946	.921	.897	.875	.854	.833	.814	.795	.778	.761	.745	.729	.714	.700	.686
36			.973	.947	.923	.900	.878	.857	.837	.818	.800	.783	.766	.750	.735	.720	.706
37				.974	.949	.925	.902	.881	.860	.841	.822	.804	.787	.771	.755	.740	.725
38					.974	.950	.927	.905	.884	.864	.844	.826	.809	.792	.776	.760	.745
39						.975	.951	.929	.907	.886	.867	.848	.830	.812	.796	.780	.765
40							.976	.952	.930	.909	.889	.870	.851	.833	.816	.800	.784
41								.976	.953	.932	.911	.891	.872	.854	.837	.820	.804
42									.977	.955	.933	.913	.894	.875	.857	.840	.824
43										.977	.956	.935	.915	.896	.878	.860	.843
44											.978	.957	.936	.917	.898	.880	.863
45												.978	.957	.937	.918	.900	.882
46													.979	.958	.939	.920	.902
47														.979	.959	.940	.922
48															.980	.960	.941
49																.980	.961
50																	.980

Table A-1 (*Cont.*). Cumulative Probability Plotting Points by Samples and Item Rank.

Table A-2. Values of k_1 for Selected Sample
Sizes

n	k_1	n	k_1
5	2.57	19	2.09
6	2.45	20	2.085
7	2.36	21	2.08
8	2.31	22	2.075
9	2.26	23	2.07
10	2.23	24	2.065
11	2.20	25	2.06
12	2.18	30	2.04
13	2.16	40	2.02
14	2.14	50	2.01
15	2.13	60	2.00
16	2.12	90	1.99
17	2.11	120	1.98
18	2.10	> 120	1.96

Table A-3. Selected Percentiles with k and k^2

Percentile	k	k^2
50	0.000	0.000
30–70	0.524	0.2746
10–90	1.282	1.6435
5–95	1.645	2.7060
1–99	2.326	5.4103
0.1–99.9	3.090	9.5481
0.01–99.9	3.719	13.8310

Table A-4. Factors for Confidence Intervals

Sample Size	Solutions to $k_1 \sqrt{\dfrac{1}{n} + \dfrac{k^2}{n-1}}$ for selected percentiles						
	Percentiles						
n	50	30–70	10–90	5–95	1–99	0.1–99.9	0.01–99.99
5	1.149	1.332	2.009	2.406	3.203	4.134	4.915
6	1.000	1.152	1.724	2.061	2.738	3.530	4.196
7	0.892	1.025	1.524	1.819	2.412	3.108	3.692
8	0.817	0.936	1.386	1.652	2.189	2.819	3.348
9	0.753	0.862	1.277	1.515	2.005	2.582	3.066
10	0.705	0.806	1.185	1.412	1.867	2.403	2.851
11	0.663	0.757	1.112	1.321	1.749	2.250	2.671
12	0.629	0.717	1.052	1.251	1.653	2.124	2.522
13	0.599	0.682	0.999	1.188	1.569	2.016	2.393
14	0.572	0.650	0.952	1.132	1.480	1.921	2.280
15	0.550	0.625	0.914	1.086	1.434	1.843	2.188
16	0.530	0.602	0.879	1.045	1.379	1.772	2.104
17	0.511	0.581	0.848	1.007	1.329	1.708	2.027
18	0.495	0.562	0.819	0.973	1.284	1.650	1.958
19	0.479	0.543	0.793	0.941	1.242	1.596	1.893
20	0.466	0.529	0.771	0.915	1.206	1.550	1.840
21	0.454	0.514	0.749	0.889	1.173	1.507	1.788
22	0.442	0.501	0.730	0.866	1.142	1.467	1.741
23	0.432	0.489	0.712	0.845	1.114	1.430	1.697
24	0.422	0.478	0.694	0.824	1.087	1.396	1.655
25	0.412	0.467	0.678	0.805	1.061	1.363	1.617
30	0.372	0.422	0.612	0.725	0.957	1.228	1.457
40	0.319	0.361	0.523	0.621	0.818	1.049	1.244
50	0.284	0.322	0.465	0.551	0.726	0.929	1.105
60	0.259	0.292	0.422	0.500	0.688	0.845	1.002
90	0.210	0.237	0.342	0.405	0.534	0.685	0.812
120	0.180	0.204	0.294	0.349	0.459	0.589	0.699
150	0.160	0.180	0.261	0.309	0.406	0.522	0.618
200	0.139	0.157	0.226	0.267	0.352	0.451	0.535
250	0.124	0.140	0.202	0.239	0.314	0.403	0.478
300	0.113	0.128	0.184	0.218	0.287	0.363	0.436
350	0.105	0.118	0.170	0.202	0.266	0.340	0.404
400	0.098	0.111	0.159	0.189	0.348	0.319	0.378
500	0.088	0.099	0.143	0.169	0.222	0.285	0.338
600	0.080	0.090	0.130	0.154	0.203	0.260	0.308
700	0.074	0.084	0.120	0.143	0.188	0.241	0.286
800	0.069	0.078	0.113	0.132	0.176	0.225	0.267
900	0.065	0.074	0.106	0.124	0.165	0.212	0.252
1000	0.062	0.070	0.101	0.120	0.157	0.201	0.239
2000	0.044	0.050	0.071	0.084	0.111	0.142	0.169
3000	0.036	0.040	0.058	0.071	0.091	0.116	0.138
4000	0.031	0.035	0.050	0.060	0.078	0.101	0.119
5000	0.028	0.031	0.045	0.053	0.070	0.090	0.107
6000	0.025	0.028	0.041	0.049	0.064	0.082	0.097
7000	0.023	0.026	0.038	0.045	0.059	0.076	0.090
8000	0.022	0.024	0.036	0.042	0.055	0.071	0.084
9000	0.021	0.023	0.034	0.040	0.052	0.067	0.080
10000	0.020	0.022	0.032	0.038	0.050	0.064	0.075

Table A-5. Expected Means and Standard Deviations by Sample Size

Sample Size N	Expected Mean $y(N)$	Expected Standard Deviation $\sigma(N)$	Sample Size N	Expected Mean $y(N)$	Expected Standard Deviation $\sigma(N)$
15	0.5128	1.0206	50	0.5485	1.1607
16	0.5153	1.0301	51	0.5489	1.1623
17	0.5174	1.0384	52	0.5493	1.1638
18	0.5196	1.0471	53	0.5497	1.1658
19	0.5217	1.0558	54	0.5501	1.1667
			55	0.5504	1.1681
20	0.5236	1.0628	56	0.5508	1.1696
21	0.5252	1.0696	57	0.5511	1.1708
22	0.5268	1.0754	58	0.5515	1.1721
23	0.5283	1.0811	59	0.5518	1.1734
24	0.5296	1.0864			
25	0.5309	1.0915	60	0.5521	1.1747
26	0.5320	1.0961	61	0.5524	1.1759
27	0.5332	1.1004	62	0.5527	1.1770
28	0.5343	1.1047	63	0.5530	1.1782
29	0.5353	1.1086	64	0.5533	1.1793
			65	0.5535	1.1803
30	0.5362	1.1124	66	0.5538	1.1814
31	0.5371	1.1159	67	0.5540	1.1824
32	0.5380	1.1193	68	0.5543	1.1834
33	0.5388	1.1226	69	0.5545	1.1844
34	0.5396	1.1255			
35	0.5403	1.1285	70	0.5548	1.1854
36	0.5410	1.1313	71	0.5550	1.1863
37	0.5418	1.1339	72	0.5552	1.1873
38	0.5424	1.1363	73	0.5555	1.1881
39	0.5430	1.1388	74	0.5557	1.1890
			75	0.5559	1.1898
40	0.5436	1.1413	76	0.5561	1.1906
41	0.5442	1.1436	77	0.5563	1.1915
42	0.5448	1.1458	78	0.5565	1.1923
43	0.5453	1.1480	79	0.5567	1.1930
44	0.5458	1.1499			
45	0.5463	1.1519	80	0.5569	1.1938
46	0.5468	1.1538	90	0.5586	1.2007
47	0.5473	1.1557	100	0.5600	1.20649
48	0.5477	1.1574	150	0.5646	1.22534
49	0.5481	1.1590	200	0.5672	1.23598
			∞	0.5772	1.28255

Table A-6. Factors for Obtaining Extreme Value
Confidence Intervals

Cumulative Percentage Plotting Positions	Use	Constant Factors		
15%	$\|1/\alpha\| \div \sqrt{n}$	×	2.51	= Vertical
30		×	2.54	Offset
50		×	2.89	
70		×	3.67	
85		×	5.17	
2nd Largest Value	$\|1/\alpha\|$	×	1.51	
Largest Value		×	2.28	

Table A-7. 95% Confidence Intervals for the Weibull Distribution.
Lower Limit (L) and Upper Limit (U) Expressed as Percentages at
Pre-Selected Percentile Points for Several Sample Sizes

Sample Size (n)	Pre-Selected Percentiles																	
	1		5		10		30		50		70		90		95		99	
	L	U	L	U	L	U	L	U	L	U	L	U	L	U	L	U	L	U
10	...	...	0.005	24	0.3	34	7.5	60	21	79	40	92.5	66	99.7	76	99.995	...	...
20	...	...	0.1	18	1.2	26	12.6	51	29	71	49	87.4	74	98.8	82	99.9	...	...
30	...	...	0.4	15	2.2	24	15	50	32	68	50	85	76	97.8	85	99.6	...	...
40	0.006	9	0.7	15	3.3	22	17	46	35	65	54	83	78	96.7	85	99.3	91	99.9994
50	0.006	8	0.8	14	3.7	21	19	45	36	64	55	81	79	96.3	86	99.2	93	99.9994
100	0.003	4	1.8	6	5.5	18	22	40	40	60	60	78	82	95.5	94	98.2	96	99.9997

Table A-8. Hazard Values 100/K for K = 1 to 200

K	100/K	K	100/K	K	100/K	K	100/K
1	100.00	51	1.96	101	.99	151	.66
2	50.00	52	1.92	102	.98	152	.66
3	33.33	53	1.89	103	.97	153	.65
4	25.00	54	1.85	104	.96	154	.65
5	20.00	55	1.82	105	.95	155	.65
6	16.67	56	1.79	106	.94	156	.64
7	14.29	57	1.75	107	.93	157	.64
8	12.50	58	1.72	108	.93	158	.63
9	11.11	59	1.69	109	.92	159	.63
10	10.00	60	1.67	110	.91	160	.62
11	9.09	61	1.64	111	.90	161	.62
12	8.33	62	1.61	112	.89	162	.62
13	7.69	63	1.59	113	.88	163	.61
14	7.14	64	1.56	114	.88	164	.61
15	6.67	65	1.54	115	.87	165	.61
16	6.25	66	1.52	116	.86	166	.60
17	5.88	67	1.49	117	.85	167	.60
18	5.56	68	1.47	118	.85	168	.60
19	5.26	69	1.45	119	.84	169	.59
20	5.00	70	1.43	120	.83	170	.59
21	4.76	71	1.41	121	.83	171	.58
22	4.55	72	1.39	122	.82	172	.58
23	4.35	73	1.37	123	.81	173	.58
24	4.17	74	1.35	124	.81	174	.57
25	4.00	75	1.33	125	.80	175	.57
26	3.85	76	1.32	126	.79	176	.57
27	3.70	77	1.30	127	.79	177	.56
28	3.57	78	1.28	128	.78	178	.56
29	3.45	79	1.27	129	.78	179	.56
30	3.33	80	1.25	130	.77	180	.56
31	3.23	81	1.23	131	.76	181	.55
32	3.12	82	1.22	132	.76	182	.55
33	3.03	83	1.20	133	.75	183	.55
34	2.94	84	1.19	134	.75	184	.54
35	2.86	85	1.18	135	.74	185	.54
36	2.78	86	1.16	136	.74	186	.54
37	2.70	87	1.15	137	.73	187	.53
38	2.63	88	1.14	138	.72	188	.53
39	2.56	89	1.12	139	.72	189	.53
40	2.50	90	1.11	140	.71	190	.53
41	2.44	91	1.10	141	.71	191	.52
42	2.38	92	1.09	142	.70	192	.52
43	2.33	93	1.08	143	.70	193	.52
44	2.27	94	1.06	144	.69	194	.52
45	2.22	95	1.05	145	.69	195	.51
46	2.17	96	1.04	146	.68	196	.51
47	2.13	97	1.03	147	.68	197	.51
48	2.08	98	1.02	148	.68	198	.51
49	2.04	99	1.01	149	.67	199	.50
50	2.00	100	1.00	150	.67	200	.50

Bibliography

1. Abbott, W. H. *Probability Charts*. Private publition, 1960.
2. Aitchison, J., and Brown, J. A. C. *The Lognormal Distribution,* New York, N.Y.: Cambridge University Press, 1963.
3. Bennett, J. G. 1936. "Broken Coal." *Journal of the Fuel Institute 10,* 22.
4. Berretoni, J. N. 1962. "Practical Applications of the Weibull Distribution." *ASQC National Convention Transactions.*
5. Botts, R. R. "Extreme Value Methods Simplified." *Agricultural Economic Research 9* (3). July, 1957.
6. Burr, I. W. "A New Method for Approving a Machine or Process Setting." *Industrial Quality Control.* Part I: vol. V, no. 4; Part II: vol. VI, no. 2; and Part III: vol. VI, no. 3. 1949.
7. ———. "Some Theoretical and Practical Aspects of Tolerances for Mating Parts." *Industrial Quality Control* vol. XV, no. 3. 1958.
8. ———. 1965. *Specifying the Desired Distribution Rather Than Maximum and Minimum Limits.* ASQC National Technical Conference.
9. Darnell, Paul S., and Committee. May, 1960. *Parts Specification Management for Reliability* vols. I and II. Office of the Director of Defense Research and Engineering, Washington, D.C.
10. Diviney, T. E., and David, N. A. "A Graphical Method for Transforming Non-Normal Distributions." *Industrial Quality Control* vol. XIX, no. 6. December, 1962.
11. Dixon, W. J., and Massey, F. J. *Introduction to Statistical Analysis.* 2nd ed. New York, N.Y.: McGraw-Hill Book Company, 1957.
12. Enrick, Norbert L. *Quality Control and Reliability.* 5th ed. New York, N.Y.: Industrial Press Inc., 1965.
13. ———. *Meaningful Charts and Graphs.* Printed series no. 7. Bureau of Economic and Business Research, Kent State University, Kent, Ohio, 1968.
14. Ezekiel, M. *Methods of Correlation Analysis.* 2nd ed. New York, N.Y.: John Wiley and Sons, Inc., 1941.
15. Feller, W. *An Introduction to Probability Theory and Its Applications* vol. I. New York, N.Y., John Wiley and Sons, Inc., 1957.
16. Ferrell, E. B. "Probability Paper for Plotting Experimental Data." *Industrial Quality Control* vol. XV, no. 1. 1958.
17. Freund, J. E. *Modern Elementary Statistics.* 2nd ed. New York, N.Y.: Prentice-Hall, 1960.
18. Goldthwaite, L. R. 1961. "Failure Rate Study for the Lognormal Lifetime Model." *Proceedings of the Seventh Symposium on Reliability and Quality Control.*
19. Grant, E. L. Statistical Quality Control, 3rd ed. New York, N.Y.: McGraw-Hill Book Company, 1966.
20. Gumbel, E. J. *Probability Tables for the Analysis of Extreme-Value Data.* NBS, AMS 32, 1954, available from the Government Printing Office.
21. Gumbel, E. J. *Statistical Theory of Extreme Values.* NBS, AMS 33, 1954.
22. Hahn, G. J., and Shapiro, S. S. *Statistical Models in Engineering.* New York, N.Y.: John Wiley and Sons, 1967.
23. Hald, A. *Statistical Theory with Engineering Applications.* New York, N.Y.: John Wiley and Sons, 1952.
24. Haviland, R. P. *Engineering Reliability and Long Life Design.* Princeton, N.J.: D. Van Nostrand Co., Inc., 1964.
25. Herd, G. R. 1960. "Estimation of Reliability from Incomplete Data." *Proceedings of the Sixth Symposium on Reliability and Quality Control.*
26. Hicks, C. R. "Have You Tried BIPP?" *Industrial Quality Control* vol. XIII, no. 5. 1956.
27. Johnson, L. G. "What the Test Engineer Needs in the Way of Statistics." *Industrial Mathematics,* 1958.
28. Kao, J. H. K. April, 1957. "A New Life Measure of Electron Tubes." *IRE Transactions on Reliability and Quality Control.* PGRQC-7.
29. ———. "Graphical Estimation of Mixed Weibull Parameters in Life Testing of Electron Tubes." *Technometrics,* vol. 1, no. 3. November, 1959.

30. ———. 1960. "A Summary of Some New Techniques of Failure Analysis." *Proceedings of the Sixth Symposium on Reliability and Quality Control.*

31. ———. 1965. "Statistical Models in Mechanical Reliability." *Proceedings of the Eleventh National Symposium on Reliability and Quality Control.*

32. King, J. R. 1964. "The Underlying Mechanics of Weibull Distribution Behaviour." *Transactions of the 18th Annual Convention, ASQC.*

33. ———. "Graphical Data Analysis with Probability Papers." *Technical and Engineering Aids for Management,* 1965.

34. Lapple, C. E. "Particle-Size Analysis and Analyzers." *Chemical Engineering,* May 20, 1968.

35. Mills, F. C. *Statistical Methods.* New York, N.Y.: Henry Holt and Company, 1938.

36. Monroney, M. J. *Facts from Figures.* Pelican Book, 3rd ed. Baltimore, Md.: Penguin Books, Inc. 1956.

37. Mosteller, F., and Tukey, J. W. "The Uses and Usefulness of Binomial Probability Paper." *Journal of the American Statistical Association* vol. 44 (June, 1949): 174–212.

38. Mugeles, R. A., and Evans, H. D. "Droplet Size Distribution in Sprays." *Industrial and Engineering Chemistry* vol. 43, no. 6. June, 1951.

39. Myers, B. L., and Enrick, N. L. *Derivation of Statistical Functions by Elementary Mathematics.* Kent, Ohio: Kent State University, 1969.

40. Nelson, W. "Hazard Plotting for Incomplete Failure Data." *Journal of Quality Technology* vol. 1, no. 1. January, 1969.

41. ———. "Hazard Plot Analysis of Incomplete Failure Data." *Proceedings of 1969 Symposium on Reliability.*

42. Olmstead, P. S. 1964. "Stochastic Evaluation of Reliability." *Proceedings of the Tenth Annual Symposium on Reliability and Quality Control.*

43. Plait, A. "The Weibull Distribution." *Industrial Quality Control,* vol. XIX, no. 5. November, 1962.

43. Rosin, P., and Rammler, E. 1933. "The Laws Governing the Fineness of Powdered Coal." *Journal of the Fuel Institute* 7, 29.

45. Satterthwaite, F. E. "Comparison of Two Fractions Defective." *Industrial Quality Control* vol. XIII, no. 5. November, 1956.

46. Scott, G. S. December, 1943. *Application of the Rosin-Rammler Law to the "Missing Sizes" in Screened Coal.* Washington, D.C.: R. I. 3732, Bureau of Mines, U. S. Department of the Interior.

47. Shooman, M. L. 1965. "Mathematical Models for Drift Failure Analysis." *Proceedings of the Eleventh National Symposium on Reliability and Quality Control.*

48. Tukey, J. W. "Discussion of Random Balance Papers." *Technometrics* vol. 1, no. 2, 1959.

50. ———. "The Technical Tools of Statistics." *The American Statistician* vol. 19, no. 2, 1965.

51. Wallis, W. A., and Roberts, H. V. "Statistics, A New Approach," Free Press of Glencoe, 1956.

52. Weaver, L., and Scarlett, T. 1965. "Reliability and Failure Distributions of Inertial Sensors." *Proceedings of the Eleventh National Symposium on Reliability and Quality Control.*

53. Webb, J. W. 1962. "Prediction of Failure Rates by the Weibull Method." *ASQC 16th Annual Convention Transactions.*

54. Weibull, W. 1951. "A Statistical Function of Wide Applicability." *Journal of Applied Mechanics* vol. 18.

Index